500 WAYS TO
EAT LIKE A LOCAL

A TRAVEL GUIDE TO THE
REGIONAL FOODS OF THE U.S.

JON DOUGLAS

Good Dog Publishing
Seattle, WA

Table of Contents

List of Map Illustrations

REGIONS OF THE U.S. IN THIS BOOK

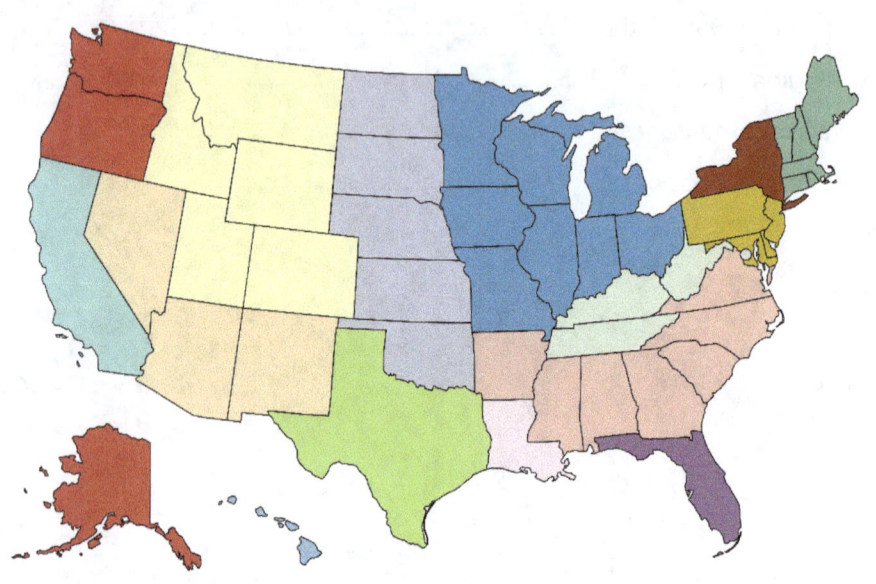

The Pacific Northwest and Alaska

Hawaii

California

The Mountain West

The Southwest

The Heartland

Texas

The Midwest

Louisiana

Appalachia

The South

New England

New York

The Mid-Atlantic

Florida

INTRODUCTION

WHY YOU SHOULD CHOOSE REGIONAL FOOD

Every time you pull into a drive-through restaurant or order a meal from a nationwide chain, you're making a series of choices – about where you're spending your dining budget, about which companies you're supporting economically, and above all, about what food items you're going to put into your mouth. But with a little effort, it's possible to make better decisions that are not only more financially sound and more ethical, but also much more delicious.

This book is a traveler's guide to the regional foods of the United States. Regional food is defined as dishes that are only found in certain parts of the country or are connected to a particular locale through their history. I'll have much more to say about what's included in my classification – and what isn't – in the sections below.

Just about every major city in the U.S., and most states, have at least one unique food item that's worth tasting while you're in town. It's likely that you already have an innate curiosity about what makes your destination different from everywhere else you've been. But if not, there are at least two good reasons to seek out local dishes whenever you can. First, it'll help remind you that despite the growing homogenization of American cuisine, there are still pockets of individuality that can make your travel experience far more interesting than if you stuck to familiar foods. And second, you'll be supporting local businesses that often struggle to compete against corporate behemoths, and are at risk of being steamrolled by these giant brands. While many examples of regional food have become permanent fixtures of American cuisine, others are in danger of extinction. Choosing to eat regional food can help preserve history and protect against every place you visit starting to feel the same.

WHERE REGIONAL FOOD COMES FROM

The American culinary landscape includes hundreds of examples of regional food, each with its own history of how it became associated with a particular geographic area. In some cases, a dish developed organically from the available natural resources. New England clam chowder, for example, makes use of the region's abundant bivalves as well as locally grown potatoes and onions, and milk or cream from its dairy cows. Other dishes are the result of patterns of immigration that brought settlers from different countries to specific parts of the U.S. North Dakota, for instance, is one of the only places where you'll find knoephla, a dumpling soup popular among the Germans of Russian descent who settled in the upper Midwest beginning in the 1870s. Some specialties were simply created anew by innovative cooks, like the hot brown invented by a hotel chef that's now become the signature sandwich of Louisville. And some were shameless attempts by companies to sell more of their products, like the Frito pie that was likely created by the Frito-Lay marketing department for a 1950s corporate cookbook.

These stories raise a host of interesting questions about how certain dishes came to be identified with individual places, and how they achieved their current popularity. To take another example, there's nothing particularly Southern about red velvet cake (except that it sometimes uses buttermilk as an ingredient), but it's now part of the dessert canon of that region, and has become part of Juneteenth celebrations in the Black community. And pimento cheese was popular throughout the country before becoming a Southern icon only in the past few decades. There are no obvious answers for how the South developed its culinary identity, but this book aims to trace the history of these dishes and explain their place in the region's culture.

Determining how, and when, a food became popular in a particular area is also challenging to sort out. It's well-established who created the Philly cheesesteak, but the journey that made it an icon of the city is less clear. Sometimes it's as simple as a successful concept being copied by a competitor, and then others joining in once they saw how good it was for business. But often similar ideas arose in more than one place at a time, making it impossible to determine exactly, for example, who invented the Coney Island hot dog that's popular in both Detroit and Cincinnati.

Many stories told about the origin of certain foods are likely apocryphal, having been passed down through the generations without challenge. Though Nashville's hot chicken is said to been invented as a punishment for a philandering lover, there isn't any hard evidence to support that claim. Whenever possible, I've used journalistic acumen and a critical eye to sort out the various legends around regional dishes, some of which provide colorful context but aren't necessarily true.

With only a few exceptions, like the Harlem chopped cheese that originated in the 1990s, regional foods tend to have long histories, with some dating to the earliest settlers in a particular place, and others being the product of entrepreneurship during the first half of the 20th century. This suggests that despite the continual evolution of American culture, and its ever-changing population that incorporates new waves of immigrants every year, the foods invented today tend to have less staying power than those created decades – or centuries – ago.

At the same time, the steady flow of people bringing ideas from their hometowns to other places means that you're now more likely to find regional specialties outside of their original locations, such as the Detroit-style pizza that's trendy in many large cities today. As more Americans migrated from one part of the U.S. to another, especially in recent decades, many transplanted the distinctive foods of their former homes. This had the effect of providing more access to regional foods in far-flung corners of the country, but at the same time weakening the connections to where these dishes originally came from.

Fortunately, only the regional specialties that are truly iconic, like the fajitas that were invented in Texas, have almost completely lost their geographic identities – although the chances are good that you'll find the country's best versions in the places where they were first created. By eating a food in its original location, you'll have a richer experience of the destination you're visiting. And hopefully, you'll gain a deeper understanding of its history that will strengthen your connection to that locale and make you want to come back for a return visit.

WHAT COUNTS AS REGIONAL FOOD

The dishes included in this book are those commonly connected to a particular destination, either an individual city, one or more states, or an entire region. Sometimes the geographic affiliation is because the specialty is mainly eaten there, like Colorado's green chile stew. But in other cases, it's because the food was invented there, like New York City's vichyssoise or Chicago's gyros. And as is discussed in more detail below, there's a lot of overlap between geographies, and you'll often find foods that cross boundaries and pop up in surprising places. But each dish covered below is associated with the locale where it's most prevalent, with cross-references pointing to its primary domain if it's prominent in more than one region of the country.

Because this is a traveler's guide, I've left out foods, like South Carolina's pine bark stew or Connecticut's election cake, that you'd be hard-pressed to find outside of a home setting today. I'm also focusing on preparations rather than individual ingredients. Oregon's marionberries are a unique type of blackberry grown only in that state, but I'm assuming that, should you desire to, you'll be able to track down the fruit in season in any local grocery store. Instead, I've directed you to where you can find a pie made with these tasty berries. And this book mostly covers foods, not drinks, except for a few iconic examples like New York's egg cream and Kentucky's mint julep.

There are a million restaurants with excellent cuisine, but to be included in this book, an eatery has to serve something that's a distinctive local specialty. Also, I've excluded foods, with rare exceptions, that can only be found in a single establishment. Old Town Tap in Truckee, California, may be known for its soft-serve ice cream topped with olive oil and sea salt, but this wouldn't qualify as a regional dish unless other local restaurants started serving a similar item – or if it developed into such a local institution that it became a signature of the city, like Baltimore's Berger cookies have become. I've generally chosen to leave out branded products, like Philadelphia's Tastykakes and Tennessee's Goo Goo Clusters, in favor of homemade specialties. And when I'm recommending places to eat, I tend to favor individually owned restaurants rather than fast-food chains, although I'll include the latter when they're an iconic part of local history, like Pittsburgh's Primanti Bros.

Also left out are some dishes that may have once been prominent in a location's cuisine but are now relics of history. A good example is New England's Marlborough pie, a custard apple pie heretofore a common dessert on Thanksgiving tables but now found only in vintage recipes. Another is Mississippi pear salad, in which the fruit is mixed with cherries and Cheddar cheese. It's just one of many such mid-century dishes that mix together surprising combinations of ingredients – often in a mayonnaise dressing – that many would find odd today.

The question of which ethnic specialties to include in this book was a tricky one, as nearly every city has restaurants that feature the cuisine of cultures from around the world. To count as an example of American regional food, a dish has to not only be associated with a specific place, but also has to have been transformed in some way or evolved into a new American creation. For example, egg foo yung is a Cantonese omelet eaten in lots of old-school Chinese restaurants across the country. But when cooks in St. Louis put it between two slices of white bread, with toppings of lettuce, tomatoes, pickles and mayonnaise, it became a regional specialty now known as the

St. Paul sandwich. Similarly, although the pizzas created by the earliest Italian immigrants resembled the Neapolitan pies they were familiar with in their homeland, their use of coal-fired stoves resulted in something that's become known as apizza, or New Haven-style pizza, with local clams providing a unique and characteristic topping.

But even when ethnic foods don't count as regional dishes, there are plenty of places to sample international flavors in the U.S. For example, I've left out the signature foods of Solvang, California, and Leavenworth, Washington, which have styled their architecture and their local cuisine to appeal to tourists seeking Danish and German culture, respectively. But these are interesting places to visit if you want to try some ethnic specialties (despite being only slightly more authentic than the bag of Thai-flavored potato chips I once received on an airplane when I accidentally ordered an Asian vegetarian meal).

Other pockets of America where you can encounter cultures that may be unfamiliar to you include the Jamaican eateries of Cape Cod, Massachusetts; the roadside dhabas in Texas, Pennsylvania and other places where South Asian curries are frequently on the menu; and the Somali restaurants of Minneapolis – just one example of the ethnic neighborhoods that exist in just about any large U.S. city. They're not instances of regional food per se, but they're part of the international fabric that makes American cuisine endlessly fascinating.

And finally, there are a handful of dishes that seem like perfect candidates for inclusion in a book about regional food, except for their stubborn resistance to being found on any restaurant menus. One good example here is Maryland's smothered chicken, fried chicken that's said to be served in a white cream gravy. Despite tons of recipes online, and many references to this being a characteristic food of the Old Line State, I've yet to locate anywhere you can try it outside of someone's home – so I've had to leave it out of this book. If you find it anywhere in a restaurant setting, please do let me know.

WHERE YOU CAN FIND REGIONAL FOOD

When you'd like to start exploring the regional food of a particular place, your best bet is to start with locally owned restaurants. Many of these establishments have long histories, and continue to serve the specialty that helped develop its reputation as a good place to eat. I'd recommend reading the section about the destination you're planning to visit to learn about its characteristic foods, and check my recommendations on a map to see if any are nearby where you're going to be staying.

Another approach is to look for places where you can partake of a favorite food, or one you're especially curious about (check the index for a complete listing). Many of the specialties discussed in this book, like jambalaya and the Whoopie pie, have individual festivals devoted to them where you can try several different versions of a particular dish. And a minor league baseball stadium isn't just a great place to enjoy a game on a warm summer evening – it's where you'll sometimes find examples of unusual regional food, like the garbage plate that's considered a delicacy in Rochester, New York.

Even if you can't travel to a particular place, it's still often possible to sample its regional food. Many businesses sell their most famous dishes online, so you can still try Maryland's Smith Island cake even if you can't get to that remote location (or the nearby communities on shore where the confection is also sold). And many specialties are available on Goldbelly, where you'll pay a premium for New York-style bagels or Kansas City burnt ends, but from which you can have carefully packaged, often frozen, versions shipped to your doorstep in just a few days.

THE MESSINESS OF REGIONAL FOOD

For each of the items covered in this book, I've provided the relevant historical background as well as suggestions on where you can sample the food. Each region also has a handful of specialties for which not much is known about their origin (or there isn't very much to say about it), so I've included those within each section in a separate sidebar of additional dishes to seek out.

I've divided the U.S. into 15 regions (see the map illustration opposite page 1), with some comprised of a just a single state that has a well-defined cuisine, like California and Texas, while others, like the Midwest and South, made up of a handful of states that share many common foods. Some states could easily represent more than one region – such as North Carolina, the western portion of which has much in common with neighboring Tennessee, part of Appalachia – but to simplify the organization of this book, each is featured in only one chapter.

The geographical complexity of a nationwide survey is only heightened because the boundaries between regions themselves are blurry, and foods don't adhere to strict borders and easily cross state lines. It's not unusual, for example, to find a dish that I've discussed in one place, like banana pudding, also prominent in another adjoining locale. But as much as possible, I've tried to showcase a dish in the place where it's most prevalent, referencing other spots nearby where you might also find it, especially if they're more likely to be your travel destination. Springfield-style cashew chicken, for instance, isn't just available there, but also in other Missouri cities like St. Louis and Kansas City. But of course, different places might have slightly different versions of the same dish – which only means that you'll never quite be finished exploring the world of regional food.

In general, this book follows a west-to-east and north-to-south trajectory, with each chapter covering its major metropolitan areas first, before moving on to foods that are characteristic of an entire state, or of multiple states within a region. (Dishes that belong to more than one place are included in the "Other foods" sections of each chapter.) Because the map of the U.S. isn't a simple grid, there isn't a perfect way to organize its geography, but I'm hopeful that my choices are intuitive and easy to follow. Only a handful of states – Arkansas, Delaware, Nevada, New Hampshire and Wyoming – either don't have any unique regional dishes or only ones that they share with another state. Wherever possible, I've included examples of local foods you might want to eat in case you find yourself in one of those places. But I haven't written anything about the cuisine of U.S. territories like Puerto Rico, Guam or the Virgin Islands, which is better left for a different book.

My advice about where to eat comes from a wealth of personal experience, and multiple trips to just about every state in the country. But I haven't been everywhere, and despite my best efforts over a lifetime of exploration, I haven't eaten everything. So I've had to incorporate the suggestions of countless other travelers who have rated and reviewed restaurants all over the U.S. I've also relied on research to make my recommendations as accurate as possible (names of restaurants and other places to eat that remain open appear in bold). But establishments shut down and move to new locations all the time, and you may find that somewhere I've suggested is no longer a good option. It's worth checking online or calling a restaurant before you go to make sure it's still open, especially if you're traveling out of the way to visit it. And if you find something in this book that's inaccurate, please let me know so I can keep it as up-to-date as possible in future editions.

One final note: I apologize in advance for what you're about to read. Much as a chef might aim to surprise and delight you with an unusual combination of flavors, my hope is that the pop-culture references, ridiculous jokes and terrible puns you'll find sprinkled throughout the text will season your experience of consuming this book. And my aim is that it leaves you hungry to explore the incredible range of American regional food, making just about anywhere you travel in the U.S. a more delectable place to visit.

Cedar planked salmon

THE PACIFIC NORTHWEST AND ALASKA

To fully understand the food and drink of the Pacific Northwest, you'll need to look past the readily available stereotypes of salmon and coffee. Sure, there are plenty of both in the culinary mix, but other influences are more prominent – namely, the abundance of fresh produce and other types of seafood, the diversity of the population, which lends a wide range of influences to the cuisine found in the region, and the lasting impact of Oregon native James Beard, who helped shape Northwest sensibilities around the pleasures of local food.

The region's frequent rainfall and fertile soils make it one of the nation's best places to enjoy fresh fruits and vegetables. As a food-loving tourist, your first stop will likely be **Pike Place Market** in downtown Seattle, where you should walk right past the vendors throwing fish to sample the juiciest red raspberries around (over 60 percent of the nation's crop is grown in Washington State) or one of the 30 types of apples that collectively make it the country's leading producer. You'll also see numerous types of local mushrooms at the market, including the Pacific golden chanterelle, morel and chicken-of-the-woods, which might inspire you to make a trip out to the Olympic Peninsula to forage for them yourself. And in the summer, you'll also find produce you can't get anywhere else, like the Rainier cherry and the Shuksan strawberry, both of which were cultivated by Washington State University scientists.

While Alaska can lay claim to 95 percent of the wild salmon consumed by Americans, Washington is the biggest producer of oysters on the Pacific Coast, so a few slurps should be in order during your trip to the Northwest. Other iconic seafood to try include Alaskan red king crab, especially during the short fall season when crabs are caught off the Alaska coast; Dungeness crab, which can be found throughout Pacific Coast waters but is abundant on the Washington coast; the giant saltwater clam known as geoduck (pronounced "gooey-duck"), which comes from the inland waters of Puget Sound; and halibut, which is especially prominent on the Kenai Peninsula in Southeast Alaska.

The ethnic makeup of the region, while overwhelmingly white, is a mélange of people from all over the world who have been drawn to the Northwest for its moderate climate, wealth of outdoor recreation, generally tolerant character, and economic opportunities with large companies like Microsoft, Amazon, Starbucks and Nike. The region includes a substantial Asian population (about 10 percent in Washington, and 5 percent in Oregon) that has flavored its cuisine with influences from China, Japan, Vietnam, Korea, India and other nationalities.

But these cultures represent only a few of the strands that have helped weave the tapestry of Northwest gastronomy. Huge numbers of Scandinavian immigrants settled in the Pacific Northwest in the late 19th century, and that heritage is still an important part of the region's DNA, especially in the bakeries that produce iconic Swedish and Danish baked goods, like **Larsen's** and **Byen Bakeri,** both in Seattle. You'll find plenty of Mexican and soul food as well, although some continue to (wrongly) insist that you can't find good plate of BBQ or a decent taco in the Northwest. And the indigenous people who made the region home before it was settled by Europeans have also left an imprint on local cuisine. You can sample some of these flavors at the **Off the Rez Cafe** at the Burke Museum of Natural History and Culture at the University of Washington, or on the room service menu at the Alaska Native Medical Center in Anchorage.

Perhaps no single culinary personality has been more influential to food in the Pacific Northwest than Portland-born James Beard (1903-1985). Beard, a chef and cookbook author who hosted the nation's first televised network cooking show, was one of the first proponents of using local ingredients and preparing them simply. His approach was a forerunner of the food philosophy that remains a hallmark of the region – to care deeply about where your ingredients come from and how they're used (an ideology that was satirized brilliantly in the "Colin the Chicken" sketch on the show Portlandia).

When you're traveling in the Pacific Northwest and Alaska, you have a myriad of choices for experiencing the region's gastronomic pleasures. You can go high end, and try out the culinary creations by well-regarded chefs like Ethan Stowell, Renee Erickson, Gabriel Rucker and Naomi Pomeroy. Or visit one of the literally hundreds of food trucks and carts, especially in downtown Portland, which represent one of the best ways to travel around the world while eating lunch. Be sure to sample a few of the brews that have made the region a mecca for both coffee- and beer-lovers. Enjoy a bowl of pho, a Dungeness crab roll, a pint of fresh blackberries or some Cheddar from **Tillamook Creamery** on the Oregon coast. And for a souvenir to take home, pick up a box of Almond Roca, a chocolate-covered toffee with an almond coating that's made in Tacoma, Washington. Or skip all that and just try one of these unique food items that you'll rarely find anywhere else.

WASHINGTON

SEATTLE

Seattle-style teriyaki

What first comes to mind when you think about the cuisine of the Emerald City? You're probably conjuring up a plate of salmon or a cup of coffee. But the most iconic food in Seattle is actually teriyaki chicken. You'll find this filling, usually inexpensive meal in just about every neighborhood across the city, as well as in strip malls in the outlying suburbs.

Seattle-style teriyaki is meat (usually chicken, but it can also be beef) that's marinated in a sweet soy sauce (often made with ginger and garlic), sliced and grilled. In the best versions, the protein is slightly charred on the outside and tender and juicy within. It's usually served alongside white rice, a simple salad of cabbage or iceberg lettuce with slivers of carrot, and extra teriyaki sauce.

A Japanese immigrant named Toshi Kasahara opened Seattle's first teriyaki spot, Toshi's Teriyaki, in 1976 in Uptown, a few years after coming to the Northwest to study at Portland State University. In the following decades, numerous restaurants called Toshi's, some opened by Kasahara himself, some that licensed his brand, and some that were copycats, all capitalized on the popularity of the original.

Although the city boasted a third fewer teriyaki restaurants by 2016 than it did a decade prior, you can still find this dish at dozens of establishments across Seattle. **Grillbird** in West Seattle makes the best version I've had, but another good option is **Toshi's Teriyaki Grill** in Mill Creek, where Kasahara continues to own and operate a small restaurant. It's a solid choice if you're in the 'burbs, and a great way to experience nirvana while trying one of Seattle's greatest hits.

Seattle-style hot dog

Whether you're hitting up Capitol Hill for a bar crawl or a music show, or taking in a game at Lumen Field or T-Mobile Park, it'll be hard to miss the carts selling another one of Jet City's most iconic foods: the Seattle-style hot dog that's usually just called a Seattle dog.

A Seattle dog is a hot dog (or Polish sausage) that's grilled, served in a hot dog bun or hoagie roll, and topped with cream cheese and sautéed onions. Adding other condiments as well as jalapeños and sauerkraut is left to the diner's choice.

The origins of the Seattle dog are murky but, surprisingly, seem to be more closely connected to bagels than they are to hot dogs. In one version of the story, a bagel vendor in the late 1980s named Hadley Longe sold hot dogs in Pioneer Square on bagel-like rolls called bialy sticks. But another bagel seller, Otmane Bezzaz, also claims to have invented the Seattle dog in the early 1990s, after he added a hot dog to a bagel with cream cheese. As grunge exploded in popularity during the '90s, so too did the Seattle-style hot dog, and both became trademarks of the city.

When you're needing to satisfy a late-night craving for a Seattle dog, two popular choices are **Monster Dogs** and **Hawk Dogs**, both in Capitol Hill. For a daytime option in the vicinity of Pike Place Market, try **Deez Dogz** downtown. And if you're looking for a vegan version, head on over to **Cycle Dogs** in Ballard, where the Seattle dogs are prepared with Field Roast frankfurters and non-dairy cream cheese. (The restaurant's owner announced its closure just before publication of this book, but said he hopes the business will continue under new ownership.) For a great view of the Olympics on a sunny day, head on over to Golden Gardens Park, overlooking Puget Sound. That's a good place to eat your lunch while watching Seattle dogs – the canine versions – run around the off-leash area.

Cedar planked salmon

It's hard to think of a more quintessentially Northwest dish than cedar planked salmon. Based upon on a Native American cooking technique, this simple dish consists of wild salmon that's grilled (or baked) over strips of cedar. The wood infuses the fish with a smoky flavor that's redolent of the forests of the Olympic Peninsula.

Cooking over cedar planks is a delicate way to treat your salmon, as the wood provides a barrier that insulates the fish from the direct heat source. Before grilling, be sure to soak the cedar planks in water (or a different liquid, if you wish to provide the fish with another subtle flavor) for an hour or two. A little salt and pepper is all the seasoning you'll need, along with a squeeze of lemon once the fish comes off the grill.

You'll find cedar (or alder) planked salmon in Seattle at popular seafood restaurants like **Ivar's Salmon House** on Lake Union, **Six Seven** at the Edgewater Hotel on the waterfront and **Chinook's** on Salmon Bay. You can also easily cook this dish at home, even if you're not a Northwest local: just pick up some fish from **Pike Place Market**, famous for the vendors who throw salmon over crowds of tourists and can pack your seafood in dry ice for easy transport. Then once you arrive in your own town, get a few cedar planks from a nearby lumber store (make sure the wood is untreated) and fire up your backyard grill. No matter where you are in the country, you'll quickly be transported right back to the Pacific Northwest. Especially if while you cook, a light, misty rain is falling.

Salmon candy

What could be sweeter than salmon candy? This Seattle specialty is made with wild salmon that's been marinated in a brown sugar brine and cold smoked for several days. It's usually prepared with either King salmon (also known as Chinook) or sockeye. After being cooked, the fish has the texture of jerky and is sweet, smoky and savory all in the same bite.

Salmon candy is sold at fish markets and upscale grocery stores all around the Pacific Northwest, including **Wild Salmon Seafood Market** in Interbay, and **B&E Meats and Seafood**, with locations in Queen Anne, Newcastle, Burien and Des Moines. Or if you're making a stop at **Pike Place Market**, you'll find salmon candy at vendors such as **Jack's Fish Spot** and **City Fish**, both of which sell their wares online as well. The market is also good place to pick up a package of another Northwest specialty: chocolate-covered Chukar cherries – should you want some locally produced candy that doesn't taste even a little bit fishy.

Seafood chowder

With the abundance of seafood that's available all along the Washington coast, as well as in Seattle and environs, it's no wonder that there are as many versions of seafood chowder as there are fish in the sea.

Taking their cue from the classic New England style of clam chowder, the best seafood chowders in Washington start with a cream-based broth. They're loaded with hunks of local fish as well as chunks of potato, morsels of bacon and fresh herbs.

A few of the best soups in the Seattle area include the seafood chowder at **White Swan Public House** on Lake Union, with a varying selection of fish and shellfish; the "North by Northwest" chowder at the **Duke's Seafood** chain, which includes Alaskan salmon, halibut and cod; and the smoked salmon chowder at **Pike Place Chowder** in Post Alley, which is prepared with Northwest salmon and capers. At the latter option – super-convenient for visiting tourists, though it's only open for lunch – you can also purchase quarts of frozen chowder to go. Choose among smoked salmon, scallop or clam chowder, or, if you're feeling blasphemous, a seafood bisque that's made with a tomato-based broth.

Crab Louie

See San Francisco

Although the Louie salad is more typically associated with San Francisco than with Washington State, some claim that it was invented by Louis Davenport, who ran an eponymous hotel in Spokane, Washington, that opened in 1914, or that it was originally served at Seattle's Olympic Club a decade earlier.

If the song "Louie, Louie," most famously recorded by the Portland, Oregon, band The Kingsmen, whets your appetite to try a Louie while you're in the Pacific Northwest, you'll find a version with salmon and shrimp at the waterfront restaurant **Palisade**, overlooking Elliott Bay in Seattle.

Dutch baby pancake

A Dutch baby pancake is a dish that must have picked up someone else's passport, because it's more closely related to Germany than the Netherlands.

This puffy pancake was invented in Seattle in the early 1900s at a restaurant called Manca's Cafe. A daughter of the owner, Victor Manca, is said to have mispronounced the word "deutsche," meaning German, and called the plate of three small German popovers that the restaurant served Dutch babies instead.

More typically, the Dutch baby is a single large pancake made with eggs, sugar, flour and milk that's baked in the oven and served immediately, because it deflates quickly. It's often served with freshly squeezed lemon and powdered sugar, but can also be accompanied by other fruits or vegetables.

A good place to try a Dutch baby in Seattle is **Tilikum Place Cafe** in Belltown, whose brunch menu features a classic variety with lemon and maple syrup as well as a sweet carrot cake-inspired version, and a savory one with asparagus and pancetta. You'll also find a Dutch baby in SeaTac at a restaurant near the airport called **The Pancake Chef,** where the dish – perhaps having straightened out its paperwork – is rightfully called a German pancake.

OREGON

Totchos

A potato dish that originated in Oregon is a fortuitous combination of two other food items: tots (as in tater tots), and nachos. Totchos, as you might have already guessed, are tater tots that are covered with melted cheese and served with nacho toppings like salsa, sour cream, olives and jalapeños.

Tater tots can be found in every grocery store's frozen food aisle now, but you may not know that they're also the product of Northwest ingenuity, a creation of the Ore-Ida food processing company in 1954.

A couple of years earlier, a pair of Idaho farming brothers named F. Nephi and Golden Grigg had purchased a factory on the Oregon border, hoping to capitalize on American housewives' insatiable demand for frozen corn and French fries. As their sales grew, they realized that the machines that sliced the potatoes into fries were creating a lot of wasted slivers. Initially they turned those pieces into cattle feed. But they eventually realized they could be seasoned, formed into barrels, fried and flash-frozen, and a new potato product was born. Within a few years, Ore-Ida had gained a substantial chunk of the frozen-potato market, and after Grigg sold the company to H.J. Heinz in 1965, Tater Tots became even more firmly entrenched in the freezers of America.

Totchos didn't become part of the story until 2006, when Jim Parker, the owner of a bar in Southeast Portland, **Oaks Bottom Public House**, put them on his menu. Parker's business partner and cook were skeptical that the dish would be anything more than "stoner food," he once said, but the dish became a bestseller and was widely imitated in other Portland bars. And in subsequent years, it spread to dive bars and upscale restaurants across the country.

Parker may not have been the first to think of putting nacho toppings on potatoes – a fast-food franchise called Taco John's sold a Mexican-inspired side called "Super Potato Olé" as early as 2001, and the Northwest chain Taco Time offered seasoned tater tots as a side dish to burritos and tacos a few decades before that – but the name totchos wasn't used until Parker's bartender, Jonathan Carmean, suggested it. That's much better than the moniker Parker had originally come up with: nacho tots.

Chocolate-covered hazelnuts

Oregon produces nearly all of the country's hazelnuts, which became the official nut of the Beaver State in 1989. But some people still call them filberts. That's the name that early French settlers to Oregon gave them, possibly in honor of the seventh-century abbot St. Philibert, whose feast day in August is when the nut tends to start ripening. In the 19th century, though, English settlers to Oregon started using the term hazelnut to describe the fruit of the hazel tree, and as commercial production grew in the state, the Oregon Filbert Commission adopted the term beginning in 1981.

Whatever you call them, when you eat them mixed with honey or black pepper, according to first-century Greek physician Dioscorides, they can help cure the common cold or your chronic cough. And if you burn their shells, mash them in suet, and smear them on your head, he says, you can cure baldness.

Another technique for preparing hazelnuts that many people – even those without hair up there – might find more appealing is to cover them in chocolate. You can buy the nuts in a variety of flavors, including dark chocolate, milk chocolate, cherry and mint, from **Pacific Hazelnut Farms**, which also sells raw and roasted nuts as well as toffee and other hazelnut products. And just down the road in Aurora, Oregon, about a half-hour from Portland, you'll also find **Filberts Farmhouse Kitchen**, a restaurant with a handful of dishes on their menu that feature hazelnuts, though perhaps the owners just preferred the alliteration.

My favorite place to pick up hazelnuts, whether roasted or chocolate-covered, is at the **Portland State University** farmers' market that's open in downtown Portland on Saturday mornings year-round. It's a lot easier to buy a bag there there than to head for the city's NW Filbert Street and hope you can shake some off a neighborhood tree.

Marionberry pie

No, marionberries aren't named after the two-time former mayor of Washington, D.C. Actually, they're a variety of medium-size blackberry that's only grown in Oregon. They're sometimes referred to as the cabernet sauvignon of the berry world because of their sweet, earthy flavor.

Researchers at Oregon State University first cultivated the marionberry in the 1940s and released it commercially in 1956. Today, marionberries are the dominant type of blackberries produced in Oregon, with most of the crop being produced in Marion County, from which it got its name, as well as the Willamette Valley.

Another Oregon dish to sample:

- **Ocean roll**, a pastry baked with croissant dough and flavored with cardamom and vanilla that's made by **The Sparrow Bakery** in Bend, Oregon, and sold at bakeries, cafés, and grocery stores all over town. You'll also find a branch of Sparrow in the St. John's neighborhood in Portland.

You'll find fresh marionberries at farmers' markets and grocery stores during July and August, and frozen berries are used to make jams, shakes and baked goods like tarts and pies year-round. If you want to try this uniquely Oregon creation, a good option is to order from **Willamette Valley Pie Company** in Salem. They sell turnovers, cobblers, and pies (as well as jam and syrup) during every season, and distribute in many Whole Foods Markets and other grocery stores around the country. But sadly, not in Washington, D.C., where the late politician was truly one of a kind.

ALASKA

Alaska-style hot dog

You might shudder at the idea of eating Santa's little helper. But an Alaska-style hot dog is typically made with reindeer – or more accurately, its North American cousin, caribou – which has been an important part of the diet of indigenous people in Alaska for centuries.

In downtown Anchorage, where this type of sausage has become popular over the past two decades, it's sometimes just called a reindeer dog. It's not 100% Rudolph, though. Caribou is a lean, mild-tasting meat so it's mixed with beef and sometimes pork during processing. The hot dog is usually grilled and served on a steamed bun with mustard as well as onions that have been sautéed in Coke.

You can order reindeer sausages online or pick one up at **International House of Hotdogs** during your next trip to Anchorage. If you go during the colder months, it's best to bundle up, or you'll be the one left with a red nose.

Akutaq

Unless you're a patient or guest at the Alaska Native Medical Center in Anchorage, or traveling among rural villages in Western Alaska, you're unlikely to find the traditional native dessert known as akutaq. Based on a Yup'ik word meaning "mix them together," akutaq (pronounced "ah-goo-duck") is traditionally made from whipped reindeer or moose fat, seal oil and native berries, and sometimes ground fish or meat, all combined with fresh snow to make an ice cream-like substance. It was typically prepared for marriages, funerals and other community festivals, and was often brought along on hunting expeditions.

Modern versions of akutaq can be produced with commercially available vegetable shortening as well as sugar, which indigenous people did not have. The dish is sometimes called Eskimo ice cream. However, the term Eskimo is considered offensive by many Yup'ik, Inuit and other native peoples, although this idea is based on a disputed etymology, and some organizations continue to use the word.

Regardless of what you choose to call it, akutaq doesn't share any heritage with the chocolate-covered vanilla ice cream bar that was created in 1920 at a candy store in Iowa. For the next century, that frozen treat was known as Eskimo Pie. But in early 2021, Dreyer's Grand Ice Cream, the company that now makes it, changed its name to Edy's Pie, in the wake of a nationwide reckoning with product names that many considered inappropriate. Good news: Whether you're in Alaska or not, Edy's Pie is much easier to find than akutaq – and adding to its appeal, you can be pretty sure that your ice cream bar won't contain any ground fish.

OTHER FOODS OF THE PACIFIC NORTHWEST AND ALASKA

JoJos

In many parts of the country, try ordering some JoJos and you're likely to be met with a blank stare. But in the Northwest, you'll be served a plate of breaded, seasoned and pressure-fried potato wedges, crispy on the outside and light and fluffy on the inside. They're usually cooked in the same oil that's used to make fried chicken, so they can take on a slightly meaty flavor.

Why are they called JoJos? That's the name that a Vancouver, Washington-based salesman named Nick Nicewonger spontaneously gave them while demonstrating the Flavor-Crisp pressure fryer at a restaurant trade show in 1958. As the story goes, his booth was stationed next to some potato sellers from Idaho, and he used wedges of potato to help keep the oil in his fryer clean. Nicewonger went on to distribute pressure fryers throughout the Portland area and across Oregon and the Northwest, as well as in Northeastern Ohio and other parts of the country, and JoJos caught on as a popular way to use these high-tech machines.

But Oregon isn't the only state with a claim to JoJos. Another Flavor-Crisp salesman is said to have created them in 1961 at a Chicago trade show. The former president of a Nebraska-based company that sold the fryers, Ron Echtenkamp, says the sales pitch was that you could cook a small roast chicken and a potato – as he called it, "a complete fried meal" – at the same time. People started making JoJos anywhere that pressure fryers were sold, in the Midwest as well as upstate New York, but the name stuck only in the Northwest and in Ohio, especially around Akron. (You may also encounter the term in unexpected places, as I was once surprised to in Butte, Montana.)

Today, you'll find JoJos throughout the Pacific Northwest at truck stops and roadhouses that serve fast-food staples like fried chicken and burgers. **Quick Pack Food Mart**, a convenience store in Seattle's Central District, has some of the best fried chicken in town (wait for a fresh batch and eat it piping hot in your car), and their JoJos are top-notch as well. Another good place to sample them is at Portland's **Jojo**, a restaurant in the Pearl District and food truck in Southeast Portland, both serving fried chicken as well as JoJos in both classic as well as vegan varieties. The only reason you'd get a blank stare there is if you decide not to order any with your meal.

Walla Walla onion rings

The delightfully double-named Walla Walla, known today as one of the Northwest's premier wine regions, is also home to Washington's official state vegetable: the Walla Walla sweet onion. The crop started around 1900 when a French soldier named Peter Pieri brought an onion seed from the island of Corsica to the area. Many of the farmers in Walla Walla around that time were Italian immigrants, and they and Pieri realized that the onion crop was hardy enough to survive the long, rainy Northwest winters. Over the years, they cultivated onions that were distinctively large, sweet and round, and Walla Wallas became prized for their mild flavor and juicy texture.

Today, farmers grow these alliums over about 400 acres in Southeastern Washington and Northeastern Oregon. Seeds are typically planted in September for harvest during just a few weeks the following summer, between mid-June and the end of July.

Walla Walla onions have a well-oiled marketing machine, and you'll find a few dozen recipes on their website for cooking them in tarts, salads, casseroles, and even as onion steaks. But perhaps the best way to try this seasonal delicacy is at the fast-food chain **Burgerville**, with nearly 40 locations around Portland, Oregon, and Vancouver, Washington. During the heart of the Northwest summer, you can sink your teeth into a Walla Walla Wonder Burger, a burger topped with caramelized onions, Cheddar and barbecue sauce. Or just order a side of thickly sliced, deep-fried Walla Walla onion rings and dip them into chipotle mayo, garlic aioli or the chain's signature Burgerville spread. Tasty tasty!

Maple bar

In other parts of the country, you might know these rectangular yeasted donuts as Long Johns. But in the Northwest, as well as California, when they're covered with a maple-flavored glaze, they're called maple bars, and people go wild for them. (There's even a Facebook group for maple bar aficionados.) The classic version is unfilled, but it can also be filled with custard or cream, and it's sometimes also topped with bacon, a version that Portland's **Voodoo Doughnut** helped popularize in the early 2000s.

A few years later, in one of the most notorious incidents in Northwest donut history, Bellevue, Washington, police issued Seattle Seahawks rookie wide receiver Golden Tate a warning for trespassing in a Top Pot donut shop at 3 a.m. one Saturday in 2010. Tate lived in the same building as the Top Pot and entered it through a back door that had been left open. He explained the offense by describing the maple bars as "irresistible," a notion that head coach Pete Carroll seconded. "I do understand the allure of the maple bars," Carroll said.

You'll find alluring versions of the maple bar all over Seattle, including at any of the 15 or so locations of **Top Pot**. This is the archetypal Seattle donut stop – not the best in town, but where you'll always get a fresh, warm donut that's above-average in size (with a proportionately higher cost) and a thick covering of maple goodness. I've eaten maple bars all over town, and I'd also recommend the pillowy-soft maple bars at **Chuck's Donuts** in Renton, Washington; the fluffy version at **Family Donut Shop** in North Seattle; and the gooey ones at **Good Day Donuts** in White Center, south of the city. And in Portland, the best maple bars can be found at **Sesame Donuts** and **Coco Donuts**, both with multiple locations around town.

Loco moco

HAWAII

It's at least 2,500 miles between Hawaii and the closest airport on the mainland, so it shouldn't surprise you that the Aloha State has developed a unique food culture that's unlike anything in the continental U.S. And if you're going to invest the time and money to fly all the way to the islands for sunshine and sand, there's no reason to settle for room service fare or cooking in your condo. Instead, it's worth leaving your resort or rental property to explore all of the delights that Hawaiian cuisine has to offer.

A good place to start is by sampling products grown in Hawaii that make their way into many of its iconic dishes. Although Hawaii is no longer the pineapple or macadamia nut capital of the world, you can still visit the Maui Gold pineapple plantation or the Mauna Loa Macadamia Nut Plantation and pick up goodies to take home with you. On the four islands that tourists typically visit – Oahu, Maui, Kauai and the Big Island – farmers' markets are good places to buy locally grown mangos, papayas, lilikoi (passionfruit) and other tropical fruits that you can enjoy in Hawaii while they're fresh and juicy. And roadside stands all over the islands offer fresh coconuts, warm banana bread and of course, bold coffee roasts from Kona and other regions that's worth pulling over for.

Whenever you see these ingredients on a restaurant menu, there's a pretty good chance that the chefs are cooking with local produce. But don't limit yourself to name-brand establishments – although there are certainly plenty of those, with celebrity chefs like Roy Yamaguchi, Sheldon Simeon and Lee Anne Wong infusing island influences into their Asian-inspired menus, as well as fancy places like **Mama's Fish House** and **Hali'imaile General Store** that provide consistently high-quality, if expensive, dining.

Step off the beaten path, though, and you'll soon begin to understand all the ways in which modern eating in Hawaii has been shaped by native cuisine. Sure, you can encounter many of these dishes – such as kālua pork, laulau and haupia – at your hotel's beachfront lu'au. But a neighborhood eatery that's been in business for decades will give you a much better sense of what, and how, locals eat. Be sure to order a Hawaiian plate lunch, an excellent way to sample a variety of native specialties in a single meal, pick up a pound or two of poke at your nearest grocery store or fish market, and finish your day at the beach with a trip to the nearest shave ice stand.

You'll also quickly realize how much of Hawaii's regional food has adapted to the diversity of cultures that makes up its modern demographics. Over a third of the current population is of Asian descent, with substantial numbers of Chinese, Japanese and Korean immigrants each having left their stamp on local cuisine. And laborers from these places as well as Portugal, Puerto Rico, the Philippines and other parts of Asia and the Pacific who came to work in the islands' plantations contributed culinary traditions from their own cultures, leading to dishes such as saimin and malasadas.

The result is a fascinating blend of traditional Hawaiian food, new dishes inspired by the immigrant populations, and modern cooks who have taken local ingredients and mixed them in new ways. A group of a dozen local chefs first labelled this concept Hawaiian Regional Cuisine in 1991, helping to elevate the state's reputation on the international culinary map. But the idea is still shaping contemporary dining and attracting mainland tourists to visit the islands for reasons that have little to do with sun and surf.

HAWAII

Poke

More than any other food that originated in Hawaii, poke (pronounced "poh-kay") is available in just about every city in the U.S. But it's prepared differently on the islands and is fresher and tastier, too. If you want to eat like a local in Hawaii, there's no better way than with a container of chilled poke.

Poke is cubed, raw fish that's marinated with soy sauce and sesame oil and mixed with sea salt and green or white onions. There are dozens of varieties that use salmon (lomi), octopus (tako) or other kinds of seafood, but tuna (ahi) is the most common type. The fish can also be combined with ginger or spicy mayo, and there's also a traditional Hawaiian version that mixes ahi with sea salt, roasted candlenuts (inamona) and seaweed (limu kohu).

Poke, a Hawaiian word meaning slice or chunk, likely originated with tuna fishermen preparing the less desirable portions of their catch. Its current form started to become popular in Hawaii in the 1970s, but it exploded in popularity all across the U.S. in the early 2010s.

On the mainland, you'll often find poke served in a bowl with rice or salad with toppings like corn, cucumber and pickled ginger that aren't mixed with the fish. Sometimes poke gets even more trendy and is served in a burrito (the poke-rito) or over nachos. In Hawaii, though, it's customary to eat poke by itself with warm rice on the side.

You'll find poke at plenty of high-end restaurants, but a better way to explore a few different varieties is to purchase it by the half-pound or pound at grocery stores or fish markets. Two of my favorite places to buy poke are the fish counter at **Tamura's Fine Wine and Liquors** (with multiple locations on Oahu and

Maui) and **Foodland** (which you'll also find all over the Big Island, Oahu, Maui and Kauai). I've also enjoyed particularly fresh poke from **Fish Market** in Lahaina on Maui, and at **Ishihara Market** in Waimea on Kauai.

Plate lunch

It probably won't shock you to learn that Hawaii is expensive – and I'm not even talking about the cost of plane tickets to get there or what you'll pay for your resort hotel or rental property. Instead of shelling out additional cash to dine in a fancy restaurant, a good way to get a filling meal that won't break the bank is to order a carb-heavy plate lunch.

Plate lunch usually consists of a meat entrée with two scoops of white rice and a scoop of mac salad (in this context, it's short for macaroni, not macadamia), all served on the same plate. The meat can be a Hawaiian dish like kālua pork, huli huli chicken or loco moco, but dishes with Asian heritage like chicken katsu, kalbi beef or char siu pork can also be the star (and two or more meats makes your order a mixed plate). In the Hawaiian version of a plate lunch, you might also get a side of poke or poi (mashed taro) and a square of haupia (coconut milk pudding) alongside the meat and rice.

The plate lunch dates back to the 1880s when laborers came from around the world to work in the islands' fruit and sugar plantations. They would typically eat the leftover meat from the previous night's dinner with rice in takeaway containers similar to a bento box. Mac salad was a later addition to the plate lunch, but you'll rarely find one today without it.

You can order a plate lunch at any casual, local restaurant on the islands that serves Hawaiian food. A few well-regarded places are **Papa Ole's** in Hauula on Oahu, known for its huge portions, and **Kawaihae Kitchen** in the town of that name on the Big Island, praised for its Korean fried chicken. On my last trip to Maui, I particularly enjoyed a plate lunch at **All Kine Maui**

Grindz, a food truck in Haiku that freshens up the traditional menu by offering a variety of proteins including ahi katsu and lemongrass chicken, as well as a choice of mac or green salad. The hearty portions were reasonably priced and were plenty for a second lunch the next day, helping me stretch my food budget even further.

Huli-huli chicken

There's nothing like trying to get a restful night's sleep on your first night on vacation in Hawaii – only to be woken up at 4 a.m. by the incessant crowing of the neighborhood roosters. When that happened to me, I wasn't displeased to learn that some of the islands' poultry get turned into one of its most delicious dishes, huli-huli chicken.

Huli-huli chicken is meat that's been glazed with a sweet sauce and grilled on a barbecue or rotisserie. The sauce usually contains pineapple juice, brown sugar and ketchup, as well as soy sauce, ginger and garlic, although many chefs put their own spin on the recipe. The chicken is usually cooked over mesquite to lend it a smoky flavor. The word huli means turn, referring to the practice of flipping the bird over so that it cooks evenly on all sides.

A Portuguese-American businessman, Ernest Morgado, who owned the Pacific Poultry Company on Oahu, first developed the dish in 1955 for a gathering of farmers. As it became popular, he began selling it at fundraisers in Hawaii, a practice that spread widely across the state over the next several decades. Morgado never released the recipe for his huli-huli sauce, which he based on his mother's recipe for teriyaki, although he trademarked the term huli-huli and later sold bottles of it in stores.

You can order huli-huli chicken at many local restaurants that serve plate lunch, as well as at roadside BBQ joints. A perfectly named spot that's also highly regarded is **Huli Huli Chicken**, located on Koki Beach in Hana on Maui. One of the most memorable lunches I enjoyed in Kauai was the huli-huli chicken from Keo's in Anahola, a roadside stand (sadly, now closed) serving up tender and juicy charbroiled half-birds alongside rice and green salad with a tangy papaya dressing. The chicken was so tasty I almost forgot about its cousins having woken me up so early that morning.

Kālua pork

No, kālua pork isn't pig that's been basted with the coffee liqueur that comes from Mexico. Actually, kālua refers to a method of cooking meat (usually pork, but also chicken or turkey) in an underground oven called an imu that's often showcased at traditional lu'au celebrations. The mesquite hardwood called kiawe that's used to build the fire, as well as the ti leaves that cover the pig, give kālua pork its distinctive smoky flavor. After the pig cooks for a few hours, the meat is shredded and served with rice or as part of a plate lunch with other Hawaiian specialties.

At some Hawaiian restaurants, kālua pork is cooked together with cabbage, producing a savory stew. It's also used as an ingredient in fancier dishes like the kālua pork quesadilla with sweet chili mango sauce that's served as an appetizer at **Merriman's** (which has locations on Oahu, Maui, Kauai and the Big Island).

You won't have any trouble tracking down kālua pork, as it's one of the most common dishes in Hawaii. **Foodland** and other grocery stores sell premade versions of it, and your favorite plate lunch joint or sandwich spot will almost always have it on hand. If you're in Oahu, check out **Yama's Fish Market** in Honolulu, which despite its name also sells both kālua pig and chicken, with or without cabbage. One of the best versions I've eaten came from the **Aloha Aina BBQ** truck in Haiku on Maui, which served the meat with accompaniments of cilantro coconut sticky rice and pohole fern salad. And I didn't detect even a hint of coffee flavoring.

Laulau

Don't you hate it when you're invited to a wedding and you need to decide months in advance whether you'll want to eat meat or fish? Well, if you're lucky enough to be served the Hawaiian dish called laulau, you won't have to make that choice.

Laulau consists of salted butterfish (the Hawaiian term for black cod) and fatty pork that are wrapped together in taro leaves and steamed. Beef or chicken can stand in for the pork, and sweet potatoes are sometimes used for diners who don't eat meat. In a traditional preparation, the fish and meat are wrapped in edible taro leaves, and then the whole package is encased in ti leaves.

Laulau can be steamed for several hours on the stove, or in an underground pit oven called an imu that uses a wood fire to cook food that's covered with heated stones and banana leaves. If you've ever been to a traditional Hawaiian lu'au, you've likely seen this method used to roast a whole pig for kālua pork. Laulau is typically served hot, accompanied by rice and poi.

A few popular places to try laulau are **Helena's Hawaiian Food** in Honolulu on Oahu, and **Da Kitchen** in Kihei on Maui. Or just wait to be invited to a Hawaiian wedding, hopefully one that doesn't make you choose your entrée ahead of time.

Loco moco

When you're craving comfort food on the mainland, you might tuck into a big bowl of mac-and-cheese or a steaming crock of chicken soup. But in Hawaii, the dish that'll really hit the spot is loco moco.

Loco moco is white rice that's topped with a hamburger patty and a fried egg, all smothered in brown gravy. Although there can be many variations, and some chefs have taken it upscale, it's about as down home as diner food can get. The hamburger is typically made with ground beef that's mixed with breadcrumbs and seasoned with soy sauce; the egg is fried sunny-side up, leaving the yolk runny; and the brown gravy is made from beef stock, sometimes with the addition of mushrooms and onions.

The dish is believed to have been invented in 1949 at the Lincoln Grill in Hilo on the Big Island. The owners, Richard and Nancy Inouye, wanted to create something that would satisfy a group of local teenagers who were looking for a filling but quick and inexpensive meal. One of the boys who tried it had the nickname "loco," meaning crazy, and Richard Inouye suggested using the word moco in the name of the dish just because it rhymed.

Here's another tidbit about this dish that's a little loco: In 2014, Chef Hideaki Miyoshi of **Tokkuri Tei** restaurant in Honolulu led a group of volunteers in creating an 1,126-pound version that used over 600 pounds of rice, 200 pounds of ground beef, 300 eggs and 200 pounds of gravy to set a Guinness World Record for the heaviest loco moco ever made. (The dish was then donated to feed the homeless.)

If you're looking for a portion that's a bit smaller, some highly regarded spots include **Rainbow Drive-In**, which operates multiple locations on Oahu and serves loco moco as part of a plate lunch or by itself; **Zippy's**, a chain on Oahu, Maui and the Big Island where you can order a classic loco moco or a version with chili instead of brown gravy; and **Cafe 100** in Hilo on the Big Island, which calls itself "Home of the Loco Moco." You'll feel comforted there with over 30 varieties to choose from, including loco moco with bacon, Portuguese sausage or even Spam. Pretty loco!

Spam musubi

If you're able to put your phone away while you're on vacation, you won't have to worry about getting any unwanted robocalls or emails. The only spam you should be thinking about on the islands is the processed meat that's part of one of Hawaii's most iconic foods.

Spam musubi is a handheld snack consisting of a piece of Spam on top of a block of rice, with a strip of nori wrapped around both that holds them together. The Spam is usually lightly fried or grilled, basted with a glaze containing soy sauce and sugar. The rice is molded into a block (musubi means rice ball) that sometimes forms a sandwich with the Spam, often with a sprinkling of furikake, a dry Japanese condiment, on top. There are also endless variations with egg, avocado and other ingredients.

Spam, a processed blend of pork shoulder and ham, was introduced by Hormel Foods in 1937. It spread throughout the U.S., Europe and Asia during and after World War II, especially as part of military rations, and later became widely adopted as part of the Hawaiian diet. (Its ubiquity was famously spoofed in a 1970 Monty Python sketch set in a café that served "egg and Spam, egg bacon and Spam, Spam egg sausage and Spam, Spam egg Spam Spam bacon and Spam.") The exact origins of Spam musubi are unknown, but by the 1980s, a woman named Mitsuko Kaneshiro was selling as many as 500 handmade Spam musubi per day from her store in Honolulu.

While Spam isn't a huge part of food culture on the mainland today, it remains extremely popular in Hawaii, where residents have the country's highest consumption rate per capita. **McDonald's** includes Spam on its special Hawaii menu, and there's even an annual springtime festival in Waikiki on Oahu called Spam Jam, during which local restaurants showcase Spam in their dishes.

You'll find this snack at supermarkets, convenience stores and casual restaurants all over the islands. Two good places to explore the variety of options for Spam musubi are **Foodland** supermarkets and **7-Eleven** convenience stores. Just be careful if you sign up for their mailing lists, or your inbox might start filling up with spam.

Squid lū'au

Despite the name of this dish, the squid are sometimes spared when it's being prepared. Squid lū'au is just as commonly made with octopus (tako), beef or chicken.

Squid lū'au is a savory stew consisting of taro leaves that are cooked with water and salt and sometimes other ingredients including butter, onions and coconut milk. The seafood or meat is browned before being added to the pot to be braised. Depending on how substantial the stew is, it can be eaten either as a main or a side dish. It's usually accompanied by rice or poi as well as other traditional Hawaiian specialties, and is often featured at the festival that gives the recipe its name.

A good place to taste squid lū'au, if you're not attending a lū'au where it's being served, is at a restaurant that serves Hawaiian cuisine. One popular option if you're on Oahu is **Haili's Hawaiian Foods** in Honolulu, where they're not playing games with the squid lū'au – the stew is chock-full of tender tentacles.

Saimin

There's nothing simple about saimin. This hearty noodle soup dish is made with a dashi-based broth, wheat egg noodles and toppings that include surimi (the processed fish cake called kamaboko in Japanese), char siu pork, green onions and sliced egg.

The origins of the dish are murky but date back to the ethnic groups who shared communal meals during Hawaii's plantation era. With its similarities to both ramen and wonton noodles, it contains elements of both Japanese and Chinese cuisine – but it's a uniquely Hawaiian comfort food. As its popularity grew, it was sold in local restaurants and schools as well as at concession stands during sporting events.

Today you'll find saimin all over the islands at old-time shops that have been in business for decades, including **Palace Saimin** in Kalihi and **Shige's Saimin Stand** in Wahiawa, both on Oahu. You can also order it at both extremes of the dining spectrum: at upscale restaurants like **Monkeypod Kitchen** in Wailea on Maui, where the dish is gussied-up with toppings like pork and broccoli, and at **McDonald's**, where saimin – the first local food to be sold in any of its franchises – is one of the most popular menu items today.

A dish that's similar to saimin but doesn't have any broth is called fried saimin, in which the noodles are boiled, stir-fried and topped with similar ingredients as traditional saimin. Another variation of saimin worth trying is dry noodles, also known as dry mein. This dish consists of seasoned, boiled egg noodles that are garnished with char siu, green onions and bean sprouts, with a cup of dashi broth served on the side. I've enjoyed it at **Sam Sato's**, an institution in Wailuku on Maui that's been open since 1933, and if you're following my recommendations in this chapter, just consider this paragraph another round of Saimin Says.

Malasada

If you're fortunate enough to travel to Hawaii for a winter vacation, and you've arrived before Ash Wednesday, consider yourself doubly lucky – you'll be able to celebrate Malasada Day and Mardi Gras all at once.

Malasada Day, coinciding with Fat Tuesday, is the most popular day to eat malasadas, which are enriched yeasted donuts without a hole that are dusted with sugar after frying. They can be unfilled doughy pillows, or filled with custard or pineapple, coconut, guava or other tropical flavors. They're similar to the Polish pastries known as pączki that are also commonly eaten during the week before Lent begins, in Midwestern cities such as Chicago, Detroit and Pittsburgh.

Malasadas came to Hawaii via the Portuguese laborers who arrived in the islands beginning in 1878, mostly from Madeira and the Azores, to work on the sugarcane plantations. These immigrants were mainly Catholic, and they made malasadas (the word means "poorly cooked") in the days leading up to Lent in order to use up their supplies of butter and sugar.

You'll find malasadas in bakeries all over the major islands. One of the most popular places to get them is **Leonard's Bakery** in Honolulu on Oahu, which claims to have popularized the practice of eating malasadas on Fat Tuesday, and also operates several mobile locations. If you're on Maui, wake up early and head over to **T. Komoda Store and Bakery** in Makawao, which also bakes malasadas year-round but often sells out by mid-morning. I make a point of visiting every time I'm on Maui, especially for their guava-filled malasadas that are best when eaten warm. But keep in mind that it's a decent drive from where most tourists stay and is closed on Wednesdays and Sundays. So another good choice on the island is **Home Maid Bakery** in Wailuku – where every day is Malasada Day.

Chantilly cake

One of my favorite food facts is that German chocolate cake has nothing to do with Germany. It was actually named after a type of chocolate created in the 1850s by an American baker named Samuel German. A century later, the Dallas Morning News published a recipe using "Baker's German's sweet chocolate" with a coconut-pecan filling. This dessert became popular and later became known as German chocolate cake, without the apostrophe.

Well, if you imagine a German chocolate cake, and remove the nuts from the frosting, you'll have a good approximation of the Hawaiian confection known as chantilly cake. (There's also a Southern cake of the same name, but that one has berries and a sweet frosting with mascarpone cheese and whipped heavy cream, also known as crème Chantilly.)

The frosting of a Hawaiian chantilly cake is usually spread on top of and between layers of a light chiffon-like chocolate cake and has a butterscotch-like flavor. Sometimes macadamias or coconut flakes are sprinkled on top, making the dessert quite similar to a German chocolate cake.

The most popular place for chantilly cake in Hawaii is **Liliha Bakery**, which opened in 1950 and now has multiple locations in Honolulu on Oahu. Liliha is also famous for its "Coco Puff," filled cream puffs that are topped with chantilly frosting. You'll also find chantilly cake on the menu at **Standard Bakery** in Kealakekua on the Big Island. They don't offer the famous American chocolate cake, but if you want a dessert that did actually originate in Germany, try the peach or strawberry Bavarian.

Happy Cake

One of the unique pleasures of a visit to Hawaii is touring farms where you can taste distinctive island products like macadamia nuts on the Big Island, coconuts on Maui or pineapples on Oahu. But a great way to enjoy all of those flavors at once is with a Hawaiian Happy Cake.

Happy Cake is a dense, sweet fruit cake that comes in two flavors: pineapple macadamia nut and chocolate mac nut fudge brownie. The dessert was created by Dick Rodby in 1967 at Kemo'o Farm in Oahu, and was a favorite of U.S. President

Ronald Reagan and his wife, Nancy, as well as Hollywood royalty like Frank Sinatra and Lana Turner.

Although the ownership of the company changed hands in 2002, today you can still buy Happy Cakes online, order them for pickup or delivery in Waikiki, or purchase them at **KCC Farmers' Market** in Honolulu on Saturday mornings. Regardless of where you get one, it won't take more than a few bites for you to understand why the cake has such a joyful name.

Haupia

Why send a postcard when you can mail a coconut? Through the "Post-a-Nut" program on the island of Molokai, you can pick up a free coconut at the post office and send it – unpackaged – through the U.S. mail, usually for a cost of between $12 and $20. (You can mail coconuts from other islands as well, though you'll have to buy them yourself from a vendor.)

But there's an easier way to sample the fruit from Hawaii's legendary life-giving tree, and you won't even have to wait in line for stamps. The dish known as haupia is a chilled coconut milk pudding with a firm, jiggly texture that's often served in rectangular pieces as a dessert at lu'aus or with plate lunches. It consists of just four ingredients: coconut milk, sugar, water and cornstarch.

Haupia is often used as a flavoring for other desserts like pies, cakes and ice cream. In one common variety of haupia pie, the bottom layer contains purple sweet potatoes, with haupia on top. Another popular version is chocolate haupia pie, with a layer of chocolate mousse underneath the haupia. Two good places to try these pies are **Ted's Bakery** in Haleiwa on the North Shore of Oahu, and **Leoda's Kitchen and Pie Shop** in Lahaina on Maui. Then be sure to tell everyone you meet which place is your favorite, using Hawaii's famed word-of-mouth communication system, the coconut wireless.

Kulolo

As a visitor to Hawaii, your first encounter with taro might very well have been your last. Poi, the mashed root of the starchy taro plant, is often served as an accompaniment at lu'aus, and was once described in a national newspaper as being "mainly for decoration" because it "looks something like wallpaper paste."

Poi is traditionally eaten with your hands, so it's typically classified as being either "one-finger," "two-finger," or "three-finger," depending on how thick its texture is (that is, how many fingers you need to scoop up a mouthful). Whether you eat it fresh, or after a few days, when it starts to ferment and becomes slightly sour, it may be an acquired taste.

But if you want to give taro a second try, a good way to sample it is in the form of kulolo, a sweet, pudding-like dessert. Kulolo is made from a mixture of taro, coconut milk and sugar that's wrapped in ti leaves and steamed. It's rich and dense and is sometimes likened to the Japanese rice cake called mochi.

Kulolo is easiest to find on Kauai, which produces approximately 80 percent of the state's taro. **Kapa'a Poi Factory**, the oldest commercial kulolo factory in the state, makes a fresh batch every Thursday, and distributes it to **Foodland** and other grocery stores on the island as well as at farmers' markets. If you're on the lookout for kulolo on Oahu, you should stop by **Waiahole Poi Factory** in Kaneohe on the island's eastern shore. Its menu includes a dessert called Sweet Lady of Waiahole, haupia ice cream that's topped with warm kulolo. You'll probably decide to eat it with a spoon, though I wouldn't blame you if you decided it was worthy of four fingers.

Other Hawaii dishes and a drink to sample:

- **Lomi salmon**, a chilled salad that contains salted salmon, tomatoes and onions. One place to try it is at **Ono Seafood** in Honolulu.
- **Chicken long rice**, a brothy noodle dish consisting of vermicelli noodles, chicken, ginger and green onions. You can sample it at **Fort Ruger Market** in Honolulu.
- **Pipikaula**, a snack similar to jerky (the word means "beef rope") that's made from salted, dried beef. One place to try it, in either a wet or dry version, is **Highway Inn Restaurant** in Waipahu on Oahu.
- **Hawaiian rolls**, a sweet bread brought to the islands by Portuguese immigrants and eventually mass-produced by a bakery that was founded in Hilo and later became King's Hawaiian Bakery. You'll find the packaged version in grocery stores across the country, and freshly made ones at local establishments such as **Liliha Bakery** in Honolulu.
- **Butter mochi**, a Japanese-inspired confection made with glutinous rice flour and coconut milk that's also made in flavors like chocolate and lilikoi (passionfruit). You can order them for pickup from **The Girls Who Bake Next Door** in Honolulu.
- **Mai Tai**, a rum-based cocktail with pineapple juice that's believed to have been invented in Oakland, California, but became a staple at Hawaiian bars beginning in the 1950s. One of the most famous places to try one is the **Mai Tai Bar** at the Royal Hawaiian resort in Honolulu.

Shave ice

Hawaiian locals won't even need to look at your sunburned skin to tell you're not from the islands. As soon as you order "shaved ice" they'll know you're just visiting (unless, of course, you've read this book and learned the lingo).

No, it's not shaved ice, it's shave ice – except on the Big Island, where it's sometimes inexplicably called ice shave. This frozen treat consists of just two ingredients – ice that's been finely grated until it has the texture of powdery snow, and sweet syrup, often made from fruit, that coats the ice. If you want to get fancy, top your shave ice with mochi, haupia cream, or a snowcap of sweetened, condensed milk, or order a scoop of ice cream for the syrupy ice to melt into underneath.

Shave ice was brought to Hawaii in the mid-1800s by Japanese immigrants who came to work in its sugar plantations, mainly on the Big Island. They created a dessert similar to the frozen treat known as kakigori that they were familiar with at home.

You'll find shave ice just about anywhere you travel in Hawaii. A few of the most well-known spots include **Matsumoto's** in Haleiwa on the North Shore of Oahu, which offers over 40 flavors of shave ice including a rainbow combination with strawberry, lemon and pineapple; **Original Big Island Shave Ice Co.** in Waikoloa on the Big Island, where customers line up to choose from a dazzling array of flavors and toppings; and **Ululani's Hawaiian Shave Ice**, which has seven locations all over Maui and boasts particularly fine ice and syrups made with pure cane sugar. My favorite spot is **JoJo's Shave Ice** in Waimea on Kauai (with other branches in Kapa'a and Hanalei), where you can choose from dozens of flavors and get your shave ice atop either vanilla or mac nut ice cream.

Hawaiian pizza

You might be tempted to visit the Aloha State and sample its namesake creation, Hawaiian pizza. There are two good reasons why you shouldn't do that. First, because it was actually invented in Canada, and second, because pineapple on pizza is, well, an abomination.

Let's dispense with the supposed Hawaiian origins first. In 1962, a Greek-born Canadian named Sam Panopoulos was experimenting with mixing sweet and savory flavors on pizza, which at the time wasn't widely available in that country. He topped it with ham as well as canned pineapple and used the Hawaiian brand of the packaged fruit, from which his creation got its name.

In the ensuing decades, Hawaiian pizza eventually became the most popular variety in Australia, and was once named the number-one most influential pizza of all time. (Influential, of course, is not a synonym for good.) Then, in 2017, Iceland's president, Guðni Th. Jóhannesson, kicked off an international dispute when he answered a high schooler's question by saying he was "fundamentally opposed" to pineapple on pizza and would ban it if he could. After Canada's Prime Minister Justin Trudeau tweeted that he stood behind this "delicious Southwestern Ontario creation," Jóhannesson backed down, clarifying that although he preferred seafood, he didn't have the power to decide whether pineapple should be allowed on pizza.

If you decide that warm, sweet fruit is the perfect complement to tomato sauce and mozzarella, you might be in the majority – only about a quarter of Americans listed pineapple as one of their least favorite pizza toppings in a recent survey. So, I guess, go ahead and call in an order for "Hawaiian" pizza while you're on the islands, perhaps at **Big Kahuna's Pizza** in Honolulu or **Pizza Madness Maui** in Kihei. But if I ever get elected president of Iceland, you can probably guess what my first executive order will be.

REGIONAL PIZZAS OF THE U.S.

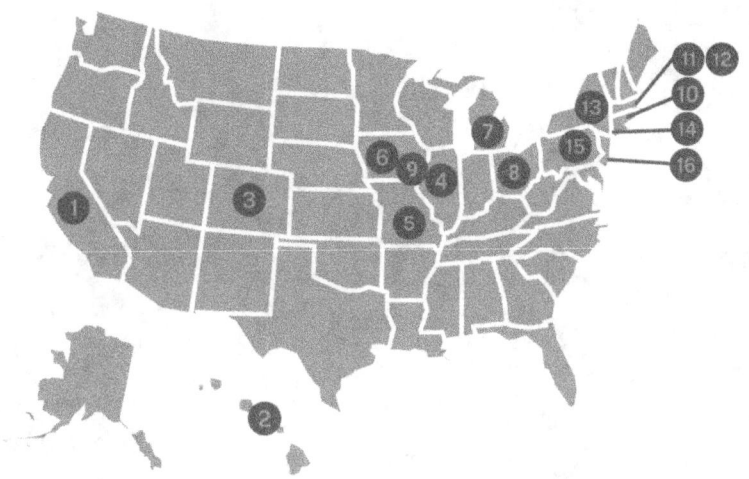

1. California-style pizza
2. Hawaiian pizza
3. Colorado Mountain Pie
4. Chicago-style pizza
5. St. Louis-style pizza
6. Taco pizza
7. Detroit-style pizza
8. Ohio Valley-style pizza
9. Quad City-style pizza
10. New Haven-style pizza
11. Red strips
12. Grilled pizza
13. New York-style pizza
14. Grandma pizza
15. Altoona-style pizza
16. Tomato pie

Cobb salad

CALIFORNIA

When James W. Marshall struck gold at Sutter's Mill in 1848, two years before California was granted statehood, hundreds of thousands of people began migrating west to seek their fortunes. Many soon discovered the abundance of produce that could be grown in the state's warm, sunny climate, as well as the bounty of seafood available in the nearby Pacific waters. A few dishes created by early prospectors remain staples of its cuisine, like sourdough bread and cioppino. But others are a product of a few major influences that have shaped food in California during the subsequent 175 years. These include the state's strong Latino and Hispanic roots, the rich history of Asian immigration to the West Coast, the importance of Hollywood and celebrity culture in codifying a few classic preparations, and the rise of California cuisine, a chef-driven trend that uses seasonal ingredients to create often-healthy dishes that highlight what can be grown, fished or foraged locally.

In the centuries before it became a state, California was first colonized by Spain, which set up missions and pueblos that developed into some of its major cities. But after gaining independence from Spain in 1821, Mexico ruled the area for the next several decades. Both of these strands have contributed to the wide diversity of Latino and Hispanic food available in the state more than 200 years later. Taquerias in Southern California as well as enclaves in major metropolitan areas, like San Francisco's Mission District, are where to head for some of the country's best tacos, burritos and tortas, as well as less ubiquitous regional Mexican specialties. And in communities with large concentrations of people from El Salvador, Guatemala, Honduras, Puerto Rico and other Latino and Hispanic cultures, you'll find a variety of fried pupusas, seafood stews and more.

According to the 2020 census, a little over 15 percent of California's population is of Asian ancestry. And these cultures –

Filipino, Chinese, Vietnamese, Indian, Korean, Japanese and more – have all left a lasting imprint on the state's cuisine, both in large, diverse cities like Los Angeles and San Francisco, as well as in towns surrounding tech industry centers in Silicon Valley, and elsewhere in California. Look for adobo, lumpia and more in Filipino neighborhoods in Orange County and the Inland Empire; Sichuan, Cantonese and other regional Chinese dishes in San Francisco, San Jose and the San Gabriel Valley; and pho and banh mi in Vietnamese communities in San Jose and Orange County. And especially in Los Angeles, it'll be hard to miss the prominence of Koreatown and Little Tokyo, both home to a wealth of excellent eating options.

Despite all of the change that growth and immigration have brought to California in recent decades, the state's food culture is also rooted in the Golden Age of Hollywood and the wealth that movie and television studios produced for many in the entertainment industry, especially around Los Angeles. Some of California's most iconic dishes, like the Cobb salad and the chili burger, came into prominence after their reputation spread among Hollywood celebrities. And the entertainment elite still dine at upscale restaurants in Hollywood and Beverly Hills, where celebrity-spotting remains a favorite pastime. Up the coast, restaurants at fancy hotels like the Palace in San Francisco created dishes in honor of celebrities staying at the property, and popularized others that have become part of the California canon. The city remains a hotspot for high-end dining that caters to both old-school tastes and more innovative palates.

Over the past 50 years or so, no trend has shaped what's eaten in the Golden State like the rise of California cuisine. This movement originated at Alice Waters's restaurant **Chez Panisse**, in Berkeley, in the 1970s, and spread in the following decade as Wolfgang Puck, Mark Peel and other chefs innovated with its concepts. California cuisine is characterized by the use of fresh ingredients, grown locally, harvested at their peak season and cooked simply to highlight their natural flavors. Puck was one of the first to incorporate influences from other cultures, especially

Asian, in his restaurants, and this sort of fusion cooking has also become a hallmark of California cuisine. In more recent decades, the trend has evolved to include an emphasis on healthful eating, and on sustainable, organic farming.

Perhaps the pinnacle of American fine dining is the multi-course tasting menu served in Yountville at **The French Laundry**, which Thomas Keller has been operating since 1994. The restaurant serves dishes that feature exacting French technique, but the influence of California cuisine is present in the prominent use of fruits and vegetables that are grown in the nearby gardens. It's a worthy landing spot if your trip to Northern California includes a detour to the wineries in Napa Valley – another great way for you to strike gold as you sample all of the culinary treasure the state has to offer.

CALIFORNIA

Los Angeles

Chili burger

You'll probably want to get familiar with the local lingo before your trip to L.A. So here are a few terms you should know. The 101 is a traffic-choked highway that runs through town, surfers describe difficult waves as being gnarly, and a burger topped with chili is known as chili size or just size.

Although putting chili on a burger doesn't seem like it would be worthy of a trip to the patent office, the chili burger is reputed to have been the invention of a local restaurateur, Tommy DeForest, in the 1920s. At his eponymous establishment called Ptomaine Tommy's, DeForest's chili was popular among Hollywood royalty. As the story goes, DeForest had two ladles he'd use to dish it out, a larger one for bowl-sized servings, and a smaller one for spooning chili onto a burger, which he called hamburger size. Later, he came up with the idea of serving an open-faced sandwich with the larger amount of chili topped with Cheddar cheese and onions, and that became known as chili size. Sometimes customers would just order the chili as a bowl of size, and both names were eventually used to describe the chili burger itself.

Ptomaine Tommy's closed in 1958, but you can easily find chili burgers all around the Los Angeles area. At **Bob's Big Boy**, a once-ubiquitous fast-food chain that only has a handful of restaurants left, including a landmark location in Burbank, the chili burger is still known as a chili size. Nearby, at **Chili John's of CA**, the chili burger is topped with American cheese, onions and Fritos. And at **Original Tommy's**, with 30 locations around Southern California, you can get single, double or triple cheeseburgers, all smothered in chili. There, whatever your appetite happens to be, you'll find an appropriate chili size.

Los Angeles-style hot dog

Tinseltown isn't renowned for its walkability, but it's worth getting out of your car to discover one of the city's signature street foods, the Los Angeles-style hot dog known as a danger dog.

A danger dog is a grilled hot dog wrapped in bacon and topped with grilled onions, jalapeño and bell peppers, ketchup, mustard and mayonnaise. This style of hot dog is derived from the Sonoran dog that was first popular in Mexico before it came to the U.S. It was originally sold by illegal street vendors in Los Angeles (which is presumably where it got its pejorative nickname), although in 2010 the bacon-wrapped frank became adopted as the city's official hot dog.

You'll still find vendors selling these dogs on street corners in Hollywood and downtown, as well as outside sporting events and nightclubs. Another option is to visit an iconic hot dog stand like **Pink's** in Hollywood, a decades-old institution that serves 9-inch "LA Street Dogs" alongside dozens of other choices, including some named for Rosie O'Donnell, Martha Stewart and other celebrities. A second good choice is **Dirt Dog**, which has four locations in the greater Los Angeles area. There you can order the "House Dog," a gussied-up version of a classic danger dog, as well as versions of bacon-wrapped dogs topped with chili, pastrami or BBQ.

Dodger Dog

For a traveler visiting Southern California, there's no more quintessential L.A. experience than sitting in traffic on the way to a baseball game, then snacking on a hot dog while watching the local nine play at **Dodger Stadium**.

But this isn't just any ordinary ballpark frank – it's the most famous hot dog in baseball, the Dodger Dog, introduced in 1962 when the team opened its new stadium in Chavez Ravine. The

55

dog was originally going to be called a footlong, an homage to Coney Island, located in Brooklyn, the New York City borough that the Dodgers had moved to from California a few years earlier. But because the frank was only 10 inches long, the Dodgers opted to give it the alliterative moniker instead.

The Dodger Dog is an all-pork wiener served in a steamed bun and topped with standard hot dog condiments like ketchup, mustard, relish and onions. (There's also an all-beef "Super Dodger Dog," as well as a vegan version.) In 2021, to the howls of loyal fans, the Dodgers introduced a new hot dog supplier, Papa Cantella's, after more than a half-century of the dogs being made under the Farmer John brand.

The popularity of Dodger Dogs has led to some surprising offshoots, including a Dodger Dog statue outside the ballpark and even a Dodger Dog bobblehead. But to be frank, if you're visiting in the offseason, you don't have to miss out on this classic local delicacy: you can still order a Dodger Dog, as well as other stadium food, on Postmates. You'll also find them in SoCal grocery stores such as **Vons** and **Albertsons**.

French dip

There's no need to put on your beret or read Voltaire before you go in search of Los Angeles's most iconic sandwich. The French dip has very little connection to Paris, and although there's no consensus on exactly who invented the dish, its original form may surprise you.

A French dip is a hot sandwich in which thinly sliced meat is piled onto a baguette or roll, with a cup of broth left over from the cooking process (jus) served on the side. The diner typically dunks the sandwich into the meat juice while eating it. Most often, a French dip is made from beef, usually prime rib, but other meats including pastrami, turkey, lamb or ham are common variations.

Two Los Angeles restaurants both claim to have created the French dip in the early 20th century. **Philippe the Original** opened in 1908, and a decade later, its founder, a Parisian named Philippe Mathieu – as the story goes – accidentally dropped a sliced French roll into a roasting pan that had come straight from the oven. The patron, a policeman, said he would take the sandwich anyway, and came back the next day with some of his friends to eat it again. However, Cole's Pacific Electric Buffet (now called **Cole's French Dip**), founded the same year as Philippe's, also boasts inventing the sandwich. According to their version, a chef at Cole's, Jack Garlinghouse, once dipped some hard French bread into the jus for a customer who had recently had dental work done, and other customers requested their order prepared the same way. Regardless of which account you believe, the name of the sandwich likely comes from the type of bread used, and perhaps also from Mathieu's French heritage.

What doesn't seem to be in dispute is that the original sandwich, despite its modern iconic form, was actually made from a pork roast. And it may have even been topped with pickles, onions and olives – none of which are classic French dip accompaniments today.

Both Philippe's and Cole's are still open, a little over a mile from each other in downtown L.A., so it's worth comparing to see which version you prefer. At Philippe's, you can choose to have your roll served "wet," with it already having been dipped in the jus, or to have one or both halves of the sandwich dipped. And at Cole's, the broth is typically served on the side. But there is some common ground between the two: Both establishments offer a choice of cheese, as well as an accompaniment of spicy mustard. And if you'd rather try a more modern version of the sandwich, you'll find dozens of other spins on the French dip across town, like the well-regarded one at **Z's Place**. Some of them – should you be interested in a taste of Paris after all – are even served with a side of French fries.

Cobb salad

If you want to invent an eponymous dish that'll remain popular for nearly a century, it's a good idea to have a well-stocked refrigerator with lots of leftovers. That was the case for Robert Cobb, the owner of the Brown Derby restaurant in Hollywood. As the story goes, Cobb and his friend, theater owner Sidney Grauman, were hungry one night in 1937 or 1938, so Cobb prepared a salad from the ingredients he had on hand, including chicken, bacon, avocado, Roquefort cheese, hard-boiled eggs, tomatoes and salad greens. Because Grauman had recently had dental work done and couldn't chew easily, Cobb chopped everything finely for his friend. (Maybe he should have made a French dip instead?)

The Cobb salad soon became popular among Hollywood celebrities and was even featured in an episode of I Love Lucy set at the Brown Derby, which is also the restaurant where the drink named after child actress Shirley Temple was invented.

The dish is traditionally made using four kinds of salad greens: iceberg and romaine lettuce, watercress and endive, and is tossed with a red wine vinaigrette. It's typically prepared so that each ingredient is arranged in a separate row atop the greens before the whole salad is mixed together at the table. Its appeal comes from its variety of textures and flavors, as well as the potential for endless variation, including additional proteins like turkey, steak or even lobster substituting for the chicken.

You'll find fresh, artfully presented Cobb salads at restaurants and cafés all over the Los Angeles metropolitan area (and likely in your city as well). A few well-regarded Cobbs include the versions at **Green Street Restaurant** in Pasadena, **Reggie's Deli and Cafe** in Echo Park, **Tender Greens** in Culver City (and other locations) and **FoodLab** in West Hollywood. Just be sure to ask for your salad finely chopped if you've recently been to the dentist.

Shandong beef rolls

Los Angeles is one of the most diverse cities in the country, with scores of languages spoken and dozens of ethnic neighborhoods with concentrations of immigrants from Korea, Bangladesh, Armenia, Ethiopia and many other places. But if you'd like to sample the unique Chinese-American creation known as the Shandong beef roll, you'll need to head east of downtown, to restaurants frequented by Chinese customers in the San Gabriel Valley.

The Shandong beef roll is a fried green onion pancake that's smeared with soybean paste and topped with sliced beef, scallions, cilantro and often cucumbers. It's then rolled up like a burrito and sliced into rounds before serving. Although the dish was likely first created in California, it's reminiscent of a specialty of the Eastern Chinese province of Shandong called jianbing juan, a thin savory pancake containing similar flavors but using egg instead of beef.

The late L.A. food critic Jonathan Gold heralded the Shandong-style beef rolls at **101 Noodle Express**, which now has locations in Arcadia, Alhambra and Irvine. But there are other versions worth trying, including the ones at **Mandarin Noodle House** in Monterey Park and the similarly named **New Mandarin Noodle Deli** in Temple City, where the "Chinese burritos" on the menu can be stuffed with chicken, pork, shrimp and of course, beef. That one multicultural dish is emblematic of the fusion cuisine you'll find all across the Los Angeles area.

Other Los Angeles dishes to sample:

- **Patty melt**, a sandwich containing a hamburger with melted Swiss cheese and caramelized onions between slices of grilled rye bread. It's believed to have been invented in the late 1940s or early 1950s at Tiny Naylor's, a restaurant in Los Angeles. You can try a well-regarded patty melt at **Cassell's Hamburgers**, with locations downtown and in Koreatown.
- **Tuna tartare**, an appetizer consisting of chopped raw tuna mixed with egg yolks, capers, mustard, lemon juice and other spices and seasonings, and usually served with crackers or toast. The dish was invented in 1984 by Shigefumi Tachibe at Chaya Brasserie in Los Angeles, as an alternative for a guest who didn't want to eat steak tartare, and quickly became a staple of California cuisine. One place you'll find it today is **Koi**, with locations in Los Angeles, New York and Las Vegas.
- **California roll**, an inside-out sushi roll containing cucumber, crab and avocado. It may have been invented by one of several sushi chefs in Los Angeles in the late 1970s, although other accounts say that it was created there a decade earlier, or attribute its invention to a chef in Vancouver, Canada, around that time. Regardless, the California roll helped introduce sushi to the American palate and contributed to its growing popularity from the 1980s until the present. You'll find a California roll at most sushi restaurants, but a favorite spot in Los Angeles is **Kura Revolving Sushi Bar** in Little Tokyo.

- **Chiffon cake**, a light but moist pastry that's baked in a tube pan and often flavored with citrus or chocolate. It was created in the late 1920s by a Los Angeles-based insurance salesman named Harry Baker, who may have been inspired by the chiffon pie, which was invented in Los Angeles by Monroe Boston Strause in 1926 and contained an airy filling made with beaten egg whites. Two decades later, Baker sold his secret recipe, which used vegetable oil instead of shortening to lighten the cake's texture, to General Mills. The company marketed the cake widely in the late 1940s and 1950s, promoting 14 different variations of the dessert it called "the first really new cake in 100 years." Today you'll find it at bakeries including **Angel Maid Bakery** in Los Angeles, which sells lemon, mocha, guava and passion fruit-flavored chiffon cakes.

SAN FRANCISCO

Sourdough bread

You might already associate foods like Rice-A-Roni ("The San Francisco Treat") and Ghirardelli chocolate with the City by the Bay. But its signature product is one you probably have in your own neighborhood, so you might not realize it was actually invented in San Francisco: sourdough bread.

In 1849, when prospectors came to California as part of the Gold Rush, bakers in San Francisco noticed that their loaves had a distinctive sour taste. They eventually realized that the yeast they were using thrived in the city's foggy climate. Although the specific strain of bacteria that gave the bread its tangy flavor was later found elsewhere, it became named after the city and was known as lactobacillus sanfranciscensis. Sourdough became so ingrained in the city's culture that the local football team, the 49ers, eventually called their mascot Sourdough Sam.

If you want to taste sourdough from a business that traces its history back to the original Gold Rush settlers, there's no better spot than **Boudin Bakery**, with one location at Fisherman's Wharf where you can watch their bakers through an observation window, and other branches across the city and metropolitan area. It's also a great place to try a dish you'll often see on the menu in other San Francisco restaurants, especially those that cater to tourists: a sourdough bread bowl filled with New England-style clam chowder.

In the past few decades, the artisan bread movement has taken firm hold across the city, and it's now chock full of bakeries with their own renowned sourdough loaves (many of which are scored with a checkerboard pattern or other designs). Customers line up daily outside **Tartine Bakery** in the Mission District for their sourdough as well as croissants and other pastries. At **Acme Bread Company** in the Ferry Building (with another location in Berkeley), you can pick up sourdough baguettes, rounds or loaves, as well as other sweet and savory breads. Or sample the sourdough from **Manresa Bread**, sister to the three-Michelin-star, now-closed restaurant Manresa in Los Gatos. Of course, you can always try making your own sourdough loaves at home – but without the unique flavors inherent to San Francisco yeast, it probably won't taste as good.

Mission burrito

Your local Mexican chain might very well satisfy your burrito cravings while you're at home. But when you're visiting San Francisco, bring a healthy appetite and head to the Mission District, the epicenter of the influential burrito named after the neighborhood that, despite rapid gentrification, remains inhabited by many immigrants from Mexico and Latin America.

A Mission burrito is a large flour tortilla filled with meat, beans, salsa and often rice, rolled tightly and wrapped in aluminum foil. The ingredients typically include carne asada, chicken or pork carnitas as the meat, whole pinto beans, and pico de gallo as the salsa. Most taquerias also offer a "super" version of their burrito that adds cheese, sour cream, guacamole or avocado, and sometimes lettuce, as additional fillings.

Two neighborhood restaurants claim to have created the Mission burrito in the 1960s: **El Faro** in 1961, which built burritos using two smaller tortillas (instead of one large one) for a group of firefighters, and **Taqueria La Cumbre**, in 1969. But the dish gained popularity in the following decades as other taquerias imitated the style and competed for neighborhood business.

Both of the original establishments are good choices if you want to trace the burrito's history. But my favorite spot is the nearby **La Taqueria**, known for its hefty burritos that don't use rice as a filling and were once named America's best. Another well-regarded option in the district is **El Farolito**, with three locations serving enormous Mission-style burritos until the wee hours of the morning. Or, if tasting a local burrito isn't enough of a reason for you to head to the Mission, there are eight locations of **Chipotle** in San Francisco. But you'll only get a pale imitation of a Mission-style burrito – and none of the branches stays open past 10.

Cioppino

When immigrants from Northern Italy settled in San Francisco, first as part of the Gold Rush and then in increasing numbers in the late 19th and early 20th century, many were fishermen who sought their daily catch at Meiggs Wharf in the North Beach neighborhood. They would often prepare a stew from the shellfish and other seafood they had reeled in that was similar to the familiar Ligurian dish called ciuppin, a word meaning chopped.

In the 1930s, a version of this stew began to be served at a seafood restaurant on Fisherman's Wharf, Alioto's. By then the stew was already known by its current name, cioppino. One colorful, but likely apocryphal, retelling of its origin says that fishermen who returned from the bay empty-handed would walk around the docks and ask for contributions from their colleagues who'd had a plentiful catch. In broken English, they would call out to others, "Chip in, chip in."

Regardless of which origin story you believe, modern preparations of cioppino also contain a variety of Pacific seafood, based on whatever happens to be in season and fresh that day. Typically, it includes Dungeness crab, mussels, clams, shrimp and cod or other white fish, all cooked in a rich broth with tomatoes, white wine, garlic and herbs. (Other, less traditional versions of the soup add flavorings such as fennel and orange or saffron.) It's usually served with the crab and other seafood still in its shell, and with sourdough bread on the side to soak up some of the liquid from the bowl.

Alioto's closed just a few years ago, but nearby on Fisherman's Wharf, the restaurant called **Cioppino's** adds snapper and calamari to the bounty of seafood in its eponymous stew. Other establishments, though, are less geared toward tourists and may give you a better experience. Head to North Beach for the cioppino at **Sotto Mare**, which some describe as the city's best. Or visit **Anchor Oyster Bar** in the Castro, where the cioppino comes in two sizes, the larger of which may be enough to feed your whole table. It's expensive, though, so don't be surprised if the person picking up the check asks you to chip in.

Oyster loaf

See New Orleans

A 1926 article claimed that a San Francisco tavern called Gobey's invented the oyster loaf, a hollowed-out roll stuffed with fried oysters. While it's more likely that the sandwich originated in

New Orleans, you can still find excellent versions of an oyster po' boy in town, such as the one at **Hog Island Oyster Co.**, in the Ferry Building as well as other locations.

Crab Louie

We'll probably never know which Louis – or Louie – the dish known as the "King of Salads" was named for. Was it Louis Coutard, chef of Bergez-Frank's Old Poodle Dog Restaurant, who is said to have invented Louis dressing? Louis Davenport, who founded the Davenport Hotel in Spokane, Washington, in 1914 and placed the salad on its opening menu? Or even King Louis XIV, attributed to him because of his enormous appetite?

Or perhaps the salad wasn't named for a Louis at all. Some accounts claim that it was being served at Seattle's Olympic Club in 1904, while others credit its invention to the St. Francis Hotel in San Francisco or the restaurant in the same city called Solari's, which had the salad on its menu in 1914. What's known for certain is that in the subsequent decades, the dish became popular in both cities as well as in Portland, where the Bohemian restaurant trumpeted its famous version in radio advertisements.

OK, enough with all the Louie hooey. The dressing is what makes this salad shine. It's a spicy, creamy mayonnaise-based sauce with the addition of chili sauce, onions and lemon juice, although the exact ingredients can vary based on the recipe. Typically, the salad includes iceberg lettuce, tomatoes, asparagus, chopped hard-boiled eggs and Dungeness crab meat, but some versions include avocado or olives as well. And if crab isn't in season, the salad is sometimes made with shrimp instead, in which case the dish is, naturally, called Shrimp Louie.

Crab Louie is a bit of an old-fashioned salad, so you'll no longer find it on the menus of fancy San Francisco hotels where it was once popular, like the St. Francis, now a Westin, or the Palace Hotel, also part of the Marriott family. But if you're stopping in at **The Rotunda** at Neiman Marcus for high tea, you'll still find a combination salad with both crab and shrimp on the menu. Another good place to try Crab Louie is at **Swan Oyster Depot**, a cash-only seafood counter that's open during the day in the Nob Hill neighborhood. There'll likely be a long line, so while you wait, you can pass the time with a couple verses of "Louie, Louie."

Green Goddess dressing

Another seafood salad that became popular at the Palace Hotel in the early 20th century was simply known as the Palace Hotel salad. It consisted of crabmeat or shrimp, artichokes, iceberg lettuce, tomatoes and hard-boiled eggs, all topped with a creamy, herbaceous dressing. And that dressing is now a supermarket staple that's used for salads as well as dips – Green Goddess dressing.

Green Goddess dressing was invented in the early 1920s by Chef Philip Roemer in honor of a guest staying at the hotel, George Arliss, who was the lead actor in a play called The Green Goddess. The original recipe contained mayonnaise, parsley, tarragon, green onions and anchovies, but today it's sometimes also made with other green herbs like basil, as well as avocado for creaminess.

Although the name of the dressing obviously refers to its green color, the theatrical Green Goddess was actually a racist caricature of an Indian deity. But those origins have been forgotten at the Palace Hotel, which serves its signature crab salad, accompanied by Green Goddess dressing, in the richly decorated **Garden Court** restaurant. Another option for tasting the dressing is to pick up a bottle at your local grocery store – and focus your attention on the green part of its name.

Joe's Special

There are at least a half-dozen restaurants called Joe's in San Francisco. There's Original Joe's, Little Original Joe's, Joe's Coffee Shop, Big Joe's, Little Joe's Pizza and Joe's Ice Cream. And at several of them, you'll find an egg scramble on the menu called Joe's Special – which seems to have originated in the 1920s at yet another Joe's that's no longer in business: New Joe's.

Joe's Special is a mixture of scrambled eggs, spinach, onions and ground beef, sometimes with the addition of mushrooms. There are various stories about its invention, but one frequently repeated is that it was created for some jazz musicians late one night after the dance halls had closed for the evening. The chef was preparing them a spinach omelet but the diners asked if it could contain something more substantial, so he threw in some ground beef he had left over from that night's dinner service.

The restaurant that's most associated with Joe's Special today is **Original Joe's**, with locations in North Beach and Westlake. During World War II, a plate of Joe's Special cost just 75 cents, but today it will set you back more than $20, with mushrooms available for an extra two bucks. You'll find it for about half the price at **Joe's Coffee Shop** in Richmond, and even at diners without Joe in their name, like **New Taraval Cafe** in Parkside. Both places are good spots to start your day with a hearty breakfast – especially accompanied by a steaming cup of joe.

Other San Francisco dishes and a drink to sample:

- **Oysters Kirkpatrick**, a dish of oysters topped with bacon and seasoned with Worcestershire sauce or ketchup and other flavorings such as cheese and parsley before being broiled. It was likely invented in the early 20th century by a chef at the Palace Hotel who named it for John C. Kirkpatrick, the hotel's manager. You can find it on the menu at oyster shacks like **The Marshall Store** in Marshall, California, about 50 miles up the coast from San Francisco. Interestingly, a similar dish in Australia is called Oysters Kilpatrick.
- **Tetrazzini**, another dish invented at the Palace Hotel in the early 20th century, named after the Italian opera star Luisa Tetrazzini. It consists of diced turkey or chicken with mushrooms in a sauce with cream and wine, topped with cheese and served over pasta. You'll likely have to travel down the coast to find a version of this dish, which is still on the menu at **Di Roma Cucina** in Torrance.
- **Garlic noodles**, a dish consisting of thin noodles, garlic, butter and oyster sauce, often topped with roasted crab or other seafood or meat. It was invented at a Vietnamese restaurant called **Thanh Long** in the 1970s, and can still be found there, at other Vietnamese spots in San Francisco, and across the bay at **Noodle Belly** in Oakland.
- **Dutch crunch**, a type of soft sandwich bread with a crispy top that likely originated in the Netherlands and came to San Francisco in the mid-20th century. One well-regarded spot where you can find sandwiches made on Dutch crunch is **Roxie Food Center** in Balboa Park.
- **Irish coffee**, a drink made with coffee, Irish whiskey and cream. It was invented in Ireland but became popular in San Francisco in 1952 when a travel writer for the local newspaper, Stanton Delaplane, introduced it to **The Buena Vista Cafe** near Ghiradelli Square, where the drink is still served today.

OTHER FOODS OF CALIFORNIA

California-style pizza

If you enjoy BBQ chicken pizza or pies with toppings like goat cheese and figs, your tastes have likely been shaped by the innovations that California chefs brought to pizza in the 1980s.

California-style pizza is characteristically a single-serving pie that's cooked in a wood-burning oven. Its thin crust is a mashup of New York and Neapolitan styles, but the unusual toppings are what makes this pizza distinctive. In about 1980, chefs at two restaurants in the Bay Area began experimenting with putting unconventional ingredients on their pies. At Alice Waters's **Chez Panisse** in Berkeley, chefs used goat cheese and duck sausage in the pizzas they served in their highly acclaimed café addition, while across the bay, Ed LaDou, a pizza chef at San Francisco's Prego, was known to try out new combinations of flavors on his pies. On one occasion, a pizza he made with mustard, ricotta, pâté and red peppers as toppings so impressed the diner, Chef Wolfgang Puck, that Puck hired LaDou to be the pizza chef at his new restaurant called **Spago** that he opened in West Hollywood in 1982.

Puck and LaDou invented hundreds of pizza concepts at Spago that used seasonal California ingredients as inspiration, and the restaurant – and its signature pies such as one with smoked salmon as a topping – became immensely popular among Hollywood celebrities and local diners. A few years later, LaDou joined with two partners to create the restaurant brand California Pizza Kitchen, using many of Spago's recipes. With hundreds of locations around the world and inventory in supermarket freezer aisles, the chain eventually became known to a mass audience for its BBQ chicken and Thai chicken pizzas, among others.

California-style pizza is now so widespread that its influence on your local pizzeria might not be immediately apparent. But if you're traveling in California, it's worth looking for restaurants that are innovating with the fresh, seasonal ingredients that California is known for. A few of the pizza places I've enjoyed during my travels in the state are **Beretta** in San Francisco, where pizzas can be topped with traditional Italian ingredients but also with arugula and artichokes, and **Pizzeria Mozza** in Los Angeles, where you'll find pies with brussels sprouts as well as pea tendrils and green garlic. Other well-regarded places to check out include **Pizzeria Delfina** in San Francisco and **Gjelina** in Venice. But there are so many chefs experimenting with pizza that you'll probably find a good choice almost anywhere you go in California – or even in your own hometown.

California-style burger

If you've lived in only one half of the country, you might not know that there's a difference between East Coast and West Coast butter. While East Coast sticks are long and skinny, West Coast butter comes in short, fat blocks that are sometimes called stubbies.

This digression into the shape of butter illustrates just one of the differences between food in the eastern and western parts of the country. Another is the definition of what constitutes a California-style burger. On many burger menus in the West, a California burger is simply one with guacamole or avocado (and perhaps bacon) added, owing to the avocado being one of the Golden State's primary agricultural exports. But in the East, a California burger just means one that's topped with lettuce, tomatoes and raw onions – possibly due to the association between vegetables and California being a place for healthy eating.

It's also likely that the latter definition spread due to the popularity of the cheeseburgers at the chain **In-N-Out**, which was founded in California in 1948. Its hallmark was using fresh, not frozen, ingredients and serving its burgers with lettuce, tomatoes and onions, two traits that likely solidified the definition of the California burger for at least the part of the country where the chain was known by reputation alone. (Today it has several hundred locations across seven states, and is probably most famous for the secret menu that includes "double-double, animal style," which means a double cheeseburger with mustard-grilled patties, sautéed onions, pickles and extra sauce.)

A competing fast-food chain founded in 2011, **CaliBurger**, also associates California with freshness, serving its cheeseburgers with lettuce and tomato (but no onions). It has locations in California, Washington, Florida and Washington, D.C., as well as in 11 international countries. The chain is also known for employing, at some locations, a robot named Flippy who grills burgers and cooks French fries. No word on whether it takes requests for adding avocado and bacon to your California-style burger.

Santa Maria-style BBQ

If you find yourself in the Santa Maria Valley on California's central coast, between the cities of Santa Barbara and San Luis Obispo, you won't find a more local food tradition than Santa Maria-style BBQ. It consists of beef, usually tri-tip, that's dry-rubbed with salt, pepper and garlic, and grilled on iron grates over red oak wood that produces a distinctive smoky flavor. It's usually served with salsa, small local beans called pinquitos, green salad and French bread dipped in melted butter.

This style of barbecuing meat originated in the mid-19th century when local ranchers would host feasts for their vaqueros, or cowboys, after cattle roundups. Originally, top sirloin was the favored cut of beef for Santa Maria-style BBQ. But in the 1950s, a local butcher named Bob Schutz began championing the tri-tip, a small steak from the bottom of the sirloin that previously had only been used for ground beef or stew.

Today you'll find tri-tip sandwiches all over the Central Coast, including at **Woody's Butcher Block** in Santa Maria. For a taste of the full Santa Maria-style BBQ experience, plan your trip to coincide with the Santa Maria BBQ Festival (usually held in April or May), or visit a local steakhouse that offers a wide range of cuts, such as **Shaw's** in Santa Maria, **Jocko's** in Nipomo or **Hitching Post** in Casmalia. The region is also known for its wine, so a glass of local pinot noir could be a perfect accompaniment to your Santa Maria-style steak.

Carne asada fries

San Diego has many attributes that make it a worthy vacation destination: endless sunshine, spectacular beaches, a world-class zoo and amazing craft beer. But hungry travelers will find a culinary feature that lends it additional appeal: Mexican restaurants all over town that offer what's become one of the city's signature dishes, carne asada fries.

Carne asada fries are thinly cut potatoes that are smothered with carne asada (grilled skirt or flank steak), guacamole, sour cream and cotija cheese. The dish is believed to have been first created in the late 1990s at **Lolita's Mexican Food**, now with three locations in the San Diego area. But the idea of adding French fries to Mexican food appears to have started a decade earlier, with the invention of the California burrito at one of the many taco stands in the city called **Roberto's**.

Unlike Mission-style burritos, the California burrito doesn't include rice or beans. But it does contain similar ingredients as carne asada fries: steak and French fries, as well as guacamole and cheese, along with pico de gallo and sometimes sour cream as well, all wrapped up in a flour tortilla. (Sometimes you'll see a carne asada burrito on the menu at your local taco shop. But these aren't as large as California burritos, and the flour tortillla usually just includes steak, guacamole and pico de gallo.)

When you're finished with a day of surfing or visiting adorable pandas – and especially after hoisting a pint or two – you'll find well-regarded versions of carne asada fries at **Taco Centro** and **La Puerta** in the Gaslamp Quarter, **Humberto's Taco Shop** in Golden Hill and **The Taco Stand**, with locations downtown as well as in La Jolla and Encinitas. It's an inexpensive, filling meal, perfect for those whose budgets, like the potatoes in carne asada fries, are shoestring.

Hangtown fry

On a classic episode of The Simpsons, when Homer and Marge are dining with Moe and his girlfriend at the Gilded Truffle, Moe asks the waiter for "the finest food you got, stuffed with the second finest." "Excellent, sir," the waiter replies. "Lobster stuffed with tacos."

A similar concept is employed in the omelet that's known as the hangtown fry, invented during the Gold Rush in Placerville, California, about 40 miles east of Sacramento. As the story goes, a gold prospector celebrated his day's discoveries by going to the Cary House Hotel and asking the kitchen to cook the most expensive dish it could. The chef took eggs, which were delicate and had to be carefully shipped into town; bacon, a luxurious ingredient not readily available in the state; and oysters, which had to be transported on ice from San Francisco, and created the hangtown fry. (Placerville was known as Hangtown because of the harsh justice often delivered there in the form of hanging.)

Another tale told about the hangtown fry is that it was the last meal of an imprisoned man sentenced to death, who wanted to postpone his execution as long as possible by requesting ingredients that would take time to reach town.

If you find yourself in Placerville, you can sample this decadent dish at **Buttercup Pantry Restaurant**, where the menu warns that you should "eat this at your own risk." Or try it in San

Francisco's Financial District at **Tadich Grill**, which claims to be the oldest continuously run restaurant in California. It doesn't serve taco-stuffed lobster, but if you're feeling like you've struck it rich and the hangtown fry doesn't hit the spot, you could order the most expensive food item on its menu: a dozen oysters on the half-shell. Hold the eggs and bacon.

Fortune cookie

The rivalry between the Dodgers and Giants is one of baseball's most heated. It dates back over a century, even before the two teams moved to California after the 1957 season, from their decades as fierce crosstown competitors in New York City. But sports isn't the only arena in which Los Angeles and San Francisco are arch-nemeses. The two cities have also battled head-to-head over a surprisingly complicated question: which one can take credit for inventing fortune cookies in America.

The fortune cookie is a staple of Americanized Chinese food, with cellophane-wrapped, vanilla-flavored cookies that contain short aphorisms or lucky numbers on small slips of paper. They're usually delivered with the bill at a restaurant or included along with chopsticks and napkins in a takeout order.

But the fortune cookie actually has stronger roots in Japan than with China. Makoto Hagiwara, an immigrant from Japan who was the caretaker of the Japanese Tea Gardens in San Francisco, is said to have initially served fortune cookies there in the first decade of the 20th century. They were similar to Japanese rice wafers, with embedded messages, and were made by a local bakery, Benkyodo.

That's not the end of the story, though. Around the same time, a Japanese-American named Seiichi Kito, founder of the Fugetsu-do bakery in Los Angeles's Little Tokyo neighborhood, also claimed to have invented the fortune cookie. He's said to have been inspired by the practice of delivering messages on small slips of paper at temples or shrines in Japan, and he sold his cookies to local Chinese restaurants, where they started to become popular.

A third origin tale is that a Chinese immigrant living in Los Angeles, David Jung, invented the fortune cookie in about 1918 after founding the Hong Kong Noodle Company a couple of years earlier. This version of the story says that Jung baked cookies to hand out to the homeless, and enclosed passages from Scripture inside the cookies.

The issue of which city could take credit for the fortune cookie came to a head in 1983 when the San Francisco Court of Historical Review held a mock trial to debate between Hagiwara and Jung's claims. (Perhaps in an attempt to influence the judge's decision, someone delivered him a fortune cookie containing the message, "S.F. judge who rules for L.A. not very smart cookie.") The court eventually ruled that San Francisco had the strongest case and could claim the invention.

So why, despite its invention by a Japanese immigrant, did the fortune cookie become associated with Chinese restaurants, and not Japanese? It's likely because the restrictions placed on Japanese-Americans during World War II forced the bakeries that made these confections to close, and allowed Chinese businesses to take over their manufacture instead. One such business is **Golden Gate Fortune Cookie Factory** in San Francisco's Chinatown. Open since 1962, it still offers tours to the public, and sells custom-made fortune cookies to both Giants and Dodgers fans alike.

Maple bar

See Other foods of the Pacific Northwest and Alaska

The yeasted donut with a maple glaze that's commonly called a maple bar in the Pacific Northwest is also prevalent in California, where you'll find it at old-school diners and bakeries. A few popular spots include **California Donuts** in Los Angeles, **Bob's**

Donut & Pastry Shop in San Francisco and **Marie's Donuts** in Sacramento.

Frozen banana

As fans of the TV series Arrested Development know, there's always money in the banana stand. The Bluth family business in question is fictional, but similar frozen banana stands exist in real life on Balboa Island, part of Newport Beach in Orange County.

In this popular local dessert, frozen bananas are dipped in chocolate or peanut butter and topped with sprinkles, nuts, candies or other flavorings. The original frozen banana stand was opened in 1940 by Don Phillips on the nearby Balboa Peninsula. But it was a second banana stand that opened across the street in 1963 after the original had closed – the Original Banana Rolla Rama, operated by Bob Teller – that made the treat popular and inspired the fictional banana stand in Arrested Development. Teller is also responsible for a second dessert that's famous on the island: the Balboa Bar, originally called a Beach Bar, a vanilla ice cream bar that's dipped in chocolate and rolled in nuts.

Today you'll find both frozen bananas and Balboa Bars all over Balboa Island, including at two competing businesses: **Sugar 'n Spice**, which it says originated the frozen banana in 1945, and **Dad's Donut Shop & Bakery**, which boasts the original Balboa Bar. Better save up some cash before your trip to Newport Beach, so that both of these establishments can soon claim to have your money in the banana stand.

Date shake

Every night is date night in the Coachella Valley near Palm Springs. The most distinctive flora in this desert region is the date palm, a crop of trees that were brought from the Middle East and North Africa in the late 1800s and thrived in its hot, dry climate. And in the arid heat, a popular way to eat the sweet, sticky fruit that they produce is in the form of a date milkshake.

Beginning in the 1920s, gardens that cultivated dates began to open in Thermal, Indio, Westmoreland and other towns in the valley, and they became attractive destinations for tourists from Los Angeles and other California locales who would visit the area. (Starting in 1947, the annual Arabian-themed National Date Festival was a popular draw in February, and it, along with the springtime Coachella music festival, continues to bring visitors to the region, though both events were cancelled for several years during the pandemic.)

A date shake is typically made with ice cream and milk, along with date crystals, a sweetened form of dates invented at **Shields Date Garden** in Indio in 1936. Some establishments use fresh dates or date paste instead of crystals, and there are also vegan versions, like my favorite date shake, the one made by **Lappert's** using coconut ice cream and nondairy milk.

In addition to Lappert's and Shields, good places to try date shakes when you're in the Coachella Valley are **Great Shakes** in Palm Springs, where the thick, creamy shakes are served, gratuitously, with a mini donut around the straw, and **Oasis Date Gardens** in Thermal. Unfortunately, the latter spot was closed on the day I stopped by, so you might want to call ahead and talk to someone before you travel there. That way, they'll know about your visit in advance and can be sure to save the date.

Other California dishes to sample:

- **California-style chili**, a type of chili also known as white chili that's made with ground turkey or chicken instead of beef, and white beans rather than kidney beans. It's often prepared with Anaheim chili peppers and topped with Monterey Jack cheese, two ingredients named after California cities that may contribute to its being seen as a regional chili style. One spot that offers both a chicken- and a turkey-based chili is **Chili John's of CA** in Burbank.
- **Monte Cristo**, a grilled cheese sandwich containing ham or turkey, similar to the French croque monsieur, that's dipped in eggs and fried in butter. It's believed to have been first served in Southern California in the late 1950s or early 1960s. It later became popular after Disneyland featured it, starting in 1967, on the menu of its **Blue Bayou** restaurant, where the sandwich is made with both turkey and ham, topped with a dusting of powdered sugar, and served with berry purée.
- **Fish tacos**, a San Diego staple made with either fresh or beer-battered and fried mahi mahi, pollock or other seafood, served on a flour or corn tortilla with toppings of cabbage slaw and crema. It's likely that indigenous fishermen off the Baja coast were the first to eat fish tacos, but their invention is often credited to Japanese fishermen in Ensenada in the 1920s. Fish tacos were popularized in the Golden State by the local chain **Rubio's Coastal Grill**, which operates numerous locations in Southern California (and a few up north). But there are dozens of other spots with worthy offerings, including **Pacific Beach Fish Shop**, **Oscars Mexican Seafood** and **Roxy's Tacos**.

- **Taquitos**, a dish prepared with a meat or cheese filling that's rolled into corn tortillas and fried, and served with salsa and guacamole. Taquitos were likely invented in Mexico, where they're called flautas or tacos dorado, but they became popular in Southern California during the first half of the 20th century. Two spots that were among the first to sell taquitos and have been in operation for more than 80 years are **Cielito Lindo** in Los Angeles and **El Indio Mexican Restaurant** in San Diego. I'd also recommend **Señor Taquero** in San Diego's Gaslamp Quarter, where I sampled some tasty taquitos during a recent visit.
- **Ranch dressing**, made from buttermilk, mayonnaise, herbs and spices, and invented in the 1950s by Steven Henson, owner of Hidden Valley Ranch near Santa Barbara. You'll find the original recipe in bottles in any grocery store, and at most restaurants as a salad dressing or a dip for fried appetizers. When you're in Santa Barbara (as well as Corona, Laguna Beach and Anaheim Hills), you can try the condiment at **Reunion Kitchen + Drink**, which serves its buttermilk ranch as an accompaniment to crispy asparagus spears.

Denver omelet

THE MOUNTAIN WEST

Travelers fortunate enough to be spending time in the Mountain West, perhaps on a city excursion to Denver or a national parks road trip through Utah or Montana, will encounter a wealth of regional dishes that draw upon the area's diverse heritage and rich natural resources. The food of this region has been heavily influenced by its development as a center for cattle farming and mining in the U.S., as settlers moved west and town centers grew up around the new transcontinental railroad lines. But it's also been shaped by the ranchers who made good use of local fish and game, the Mormon pioneers who established the Church of Latter-Day Saints in the Territory of Utah and adapted Native American farming and foraging techniques, and the modern chefs, especially in Denver, who have forged a regional cuisine incorporating locally available food products as well as influences from Latino and Hispanic cultures.

Cattle ranching in the Mountain West began to boom in the mid-19th century, when Texas cowboys relocated some of their livestock to feast on the region's abundant grasses. In the 1860s, many ranchers as well as Irish immigrants moved into Montana, drawn by the territory's status as a mining boomtown for metals like gold, silver and copper. Meanwhile, the construction of the first transcontinental railroad during the same decade brought thousands of laborers to the area, especially from China. The influence on the region's cuisine from both of these developments can be seen in dishes like the Denver omelet and the Butte pasty.

Cooking on the frontier made heavy use of beef and bison, and you'll still find both of these meats served as steaks and burgers in Western-themed restaurants throughout the region. (And don't miss your chance to try Rocky Mountain oysters, which you'll quickly learn are not seafood.) The abundance of freshwater fish in the region's many lakes and rivers provided another option for the Western pioneers, and today's travelers should keep an eye out, too, for freshly broiled or grilled trout, especially in Wyoming (one of a small handful of states in this book that aren't represented by a unique regional dish). Meanwhile, hunters added game meats like elk, venison and quail to the settlers' diet, and you'll also see these animals represented on restaurant menus in or near national parks, like **Old Faithful Inn** at Yellowstone or **King's Landing Bistro** in Springdale, Utah, near Zion.

Perhaps the most distinctive regional food in the Mountain West comes from the dishes that are part of Mormon foodways. The pioneers who settled in the area that later became the state of Utah, drawing from the experience and knowledge of indigenous tribes, became experts at foraging vegetable, herbs and wild berries, hunting game, and preserving goods to help survive long winters of deprivation. Maintaining a cellar stocked with homemade food is a concept that many Mormon households still adhere to, and the influence of Native American cultures can also be seen today in the Mormon scones that are similar to fry bread. After World War II, however, these families, like many American housewives, began to make use of processed food like canned soups and boxed cake mixes. Some of the unique dishes you'll find today in Mormon enclaves in Utah and Idaho, like fry sauce and funeral potatoes, grew out of this tradition of using common ingredients that were available in most American kitchens.

The most upscale cooking you'll encounter in a region that's largely rural, with a few small- to medium-size cities like Salt Lake City, Boise and Billings dotting the landscape, is in Denver and the surrounding metropolitan area. There, well-regarded chefs like James Beard Award-winners Alex Seidel, Jennifer Jasinski and Alon Shaya are attracting diners with farm-to-table concepts that highlight the state's agricultural resources (including the renowned Palisade peaches, a summer staple), and menus that feature a range of ethnic influences including Mediterranean and Mexican. Neighborhoods with a wealth of culinary options in the Mile High City include LoDo (Lower

Downtown), which contains the city's landmark Larimer Square, RiNo (River North), a nightlife hotspot that's home to many of the city's well-regarded breweries, and Central Park in nearby Aurora, where Stanley Marketplace is a worthwhile dining stop.

Meanwhile, some of the most local food you'll find in Colorado draws from the state's significant Latino and Hispanic populations (about 22 percent, according to the 2020 U.S. census). Be sure to try a Mexican hamburger – not just a burger with Mexican toppings – or a Pueblo Slopper, especially if you're visiting the southern part of the state. And if you're traveling through Boise, be sure to sample some Basque dishes and drinks, a cuisine that's derived from the traditional foods eaten by the European sheep farmers who settled in Idaho in the mid-1800s, at restaurants such as **Bar Gernika** and **The Basque Market**.

As you wander through the Mountain West, don't miss sampling some of the foods that highlight singular products that grow in the region – like huckleberry pie and green chile stew – as well as the unique dishes you'll find only there, like Utah's pastrami burger or Idaho's finger steaks. And be sure to leave enough room for an unusual dessert, whether it's the sweet pasta dish called frogeye salad or the sundae that looks like a spud, Boise's ice cream potato.

COLORADO

DENVER

Denver omelet

Venture to California Street in downtown Denver and you'll find a surprising plaque. It's unusual for highlighting one of the city's namesake food items and for including a recipe on how to make it. But what's even odder is the explanation it gives for how the Denver omelet came into being – leaving out the critical fact that the dish likely originated as a sandwich.

A Denver omelet, sometimes called a Western omelet, is prepared by combining scrambled eggs with ham, onions and diced green peppers. The official plaque commemorating it says that you can substitute bacon for ham, but makes no mention of cheese, which is also sometimes included in its list of ingredients. And its account of the dish's origins, that it was developed "to mask the stale flavor of eggs shipped by wagon freight," is equally curious. More likely is that it was created in the late 19th or early 20th century by Chinese laborers working on the transcontinental railroad who adapted the Cantonese omelet called egg foo yung using locally available ingredients. It was typically served between slices of bread, making the meal more portable, and was called a Denver or a Western sandwich.

If you're in the Mile High City and want to try its eponymous dish, head to **Sam's No. 3**, a diner with locations downtown as well as in Aurora and Glendale. On my last trip to Colorado, I tucked into a hearty Denver omelet at **Goody's Eatery** in Westminster, which topped it with cheese and served it with hash browns and toast. Had I known the dish's history then, I might have constructed a sandwich and taken it to go.

Mexican hamburger

Don't be fooled when you see a Mexican hamburger on the menu at a restaurant in Denver. It won't resemble the dish you're probably imagining in your head: a spicy beef patty on a bun, maybe with some pico de gallo or guacamole as a topping. No, the Mexican hamburger here is something completely different. It's more like a smothered burrito: a beef patty covered with refried beans and wrapped in a flour tortilla. It's then topped with green chile (like many other dishes in this region) and melted cheese and is served with lettuce and tomato on the side.

The Mexican hamburger, often described as a Den-Mex hybrid, is believed to have been invented at a now-closed restaurant called Joe's Buffet in the 1960s. Today you'll find it at the fast-food joint **The Original Chubby's** in Northwest Denver, as well at Mexican restaurants all over town like **Los Amigos Kitchen** in Twin Lakes and **Guadalajara** in Westminster – a couple of places where you can also enjoy traditional Mexican specialties with sides of salsa and guacamole.

Fool's Gold Loaf

If you associate any American city with Elvis Presley, it's probably Memphis, where he made his home at Graceland. Or maybe Las Vegas, where the King gave over 600 performances during his career. It's almost certainly not Denver. But the Mile High City stars in one of the oddest chapters of Elvis's gluttonous culinary history.

As the story goes, Elvis was eating at a restaurant called the Colorado Mine Company one night in 1976, and asked the teenage cook, Nick Andurlakis, what he recommended from the menu. Andurlakis suggested the Fool's Gold Loaf, a hollowed-out loaf of sourdough bread stuffed with a jar of peanut butter, a jar of blueberry jam and a pound of bacon. Elvis liked it so much that later that year, after entertaining a couple of members of Colorado law enforcement at Graceland, he decided that they should take his private jet to Denver that very night so he could eat it again. The owners of the restaurant met him at the airport hangar with 22 sandwiches as well as bottles of Perrier sparkling water and Champagne. After the group enjoyed their late-night feast, Elvis returned to Memphis without having ever left the airport.

You might be all shook up by this next bit of info, but if you want to try a Fool's Gold Loaf, you're going to have to put on your blue suede shoes and make your own version. The one place that served it, Nick's Cafe in Golden, run by – you guessed it – Nick Andurlakis, closed in March 2022 after three decades in business. It's a good reminder that when it comes to novelty sandwiches, it's now or never.

Other foods of Colorado

Green chile stew

If you're fortunate enough to find yourself in Southern Colorado in September, don't miss the Chile & Frijoles Festival in Pueblo, home to the food that the local NPR affiliate in 2019 named the state's most iconic dish.

Green chile stew, also known as chili verde, is a savory dish made with pork as well as diced green chiles. (A related dish that employs red chiles, usually prepared with beef, is known as chili Colorado.) The Pueblo chile that's often used in the stew is typically hotter than its better-known cousin from New Mexico, the Hatch chile, which is used in that state to make a similar stew. And according to Colorado's governor, Jared Polis, the Pueblo chile tastes better, too. The two states have a, well, heated rivalry over which one makes the best chiles, and Polis once blamed the local baseball team's poor play on the Hatch chile-and-cheese bratwurst that was being served at the Rockies' home, Coors Field.

If you agree with the governor that you'd prefer Colorado green chile stew over New Mexico's version, you'll find it on the menu at Mexican eateries as well as other restaurants all across the state. Try a bowl of the stew by itself, topped with sour cream or cheese, or use it to smother burritos or hamburgers. One well-regarded place to try green chile stew in Pueblo is **Tortilleria Delicias**. And in Northeast Denver, check out **Sullivan Scrap Kitchen**, where on my last trip to the Mile High City I enjoyed a hearty burger covered in green chile – and where I learned firsthand just how hot Colorado chiles really are.

Other Colorado dishes to sample:

- **Toro Pot**, a creation of a now-closed restaurant that's served at a handful of old-school diners across Denver, including **Swift's Breakfast House**: ground beef and crispy hash browns (the "Pot" in the dish's name stands for potato), smothered in either tomato-based chili or chili verde, and wrapped inside a tortilla.
- **Colorado Mountain Pie**, a style of pizza served at the **Beau Jo's** chain of restaurants across the state. It features a huge amount of toppings that are contained by a thick, braided crust that's made with honey. The pizzas are sold in either one, two, three or five-pound sizes, and are served with a side of honey for dipping the crust into.

Pueblo Slopper

A version of a green chile burger that's available in taverns across one city in Southern Colorado has been given an unappetizing moniker that sounds more like it should belong to a local serial killer: the Pueblo Slopper. This dish consists of a pair of open-face cheeseburgers served in a bowl, covered with green chile, and then topped with additional cheese, raw white onions, and sometimes fries as well.

You'll find the Pueblo Slopper on menus at several restaurants in Pueblo, including **The Senate Bar & Grill**. But the best place to eat one is at either of the two establishments in its namesake city that claim its invention (either in the 1950s or 1970s, depending on which account you believe): **Gray's Coors Tavern** and **Star Bar**. At Gray's, you can order your Slopper with anywhere from one to six patties, and with or without fries, and at Star Bar, you can add an extra patty to your Slopper for just 50 cents. But whichever version you choose, you're going to want to eat it with a fork, knife and spoon, and with a pile of napkins nearby. It's a real slopper of a meal.

IDAHO

Finger steaks

Idaho locals are known to boast proudly that the Gem State has more cattle than people. So it's only natural that the state's most iconic dish makes good use of all the beef it produces.

Finger steaks are strips of beef that are battered or breaded and then deep-fried until they're golden and crispy. Similar to chicken fingers, they're often served in bars and casual restaurants with cocktail or barbecue sauce to dip them into and a side of French fries.

It's believed that finger steaks were first served at the now-closed Milo's Torch Lounge in Boise in 1957, when the chef needed to make use of leftover scraps of tenderloin. Today you'll find this dish at restaurants in Boise such as **Lindy's Steak House**, where the finger steaks are made with top sirloin and are breaded with seasoned tempura-like flour; the two locations of the '50s-era **Westside Drive In**, which some believe has the city's best version of finger steaks; and **Big Jud's** (also with Idaho locations in Archer and Meridian), where the restaurant's signature one-pound cheeseburger makes ordering a finger steak basket seem like a healthy choice.

Ice cream potato

It's only fitting that there's an attraction in the town of Blackfoot called the Idaho Potato Museum, as the state produces over 13 million pounds of spuds per year. (If you're visiting from outside Idaho, you'll be able to export one yourself, as the museum offers "free taters for out of staters.") And at its Potato Station Cafe, you can order a baked potato, potato salad, potato bread and even ice cream made with potato flakes added into the mix.

But suppose you prefer your frozen treat to look like a potato but not have any actual vegetable content. Well, Idaho has you covered, with its bizarre optical illusion of a dish called the ice cream potato. First created at the **Westside Drive In** in the late 1980s, and still available there as well as at state fairs and festivals, the ice cream potato is a scoop of vanilla ice cream that's coated with cocoa powder to mimic a baked potato's brown skin, with a pool of chocolate syrup underneath to stand in for the dirt it's grown in. The ice cream potato is then topped with whipped cream, chocolate shavings or crushed Oreos and peanuts. (Some versions use yellow frosting to simulate butter or green sprinkles to mimic chives.) It's a fun way to honor Idaho's main agricultural product while eating a sweet potato that's actually just a frozen dessert. And while it wasn't the only potato I consumed during my recent visit to Boise, it was certainly the sweetest.

MONTANA

If you find yourself passing through Butte, perhaps on the way to Yellowstone National Park, it's worth stopping for one of the state's signature food items: the Butte pasty. (It rhymes with nasty, not tasty, although you'll surely decide the latter word is a more accurate descriptor.)

The Butte pasty, often called an Irish Butte pasty, is a baked meat pie in which inexpensive cuts of beef are mixed with diced potatoes and onions and encased in a flaky crust. It dates back to the late 19th century when Butte was a center of the Western mining industry, particularly for copper, and thousands of laborers emigrated from Ireland to the U.S. to work in what was described as the richest hill on Earth. Although pasties are sometimes smothered in gravy, the miners ate them as handheld pies and often considered them a letter from home. Today about a quarter of Butte's population is of Irish descent, and, surprisingly, it has the largest population of Irish-Americans per capita of any city in the U.S.

A few of the cafés that specialized in the town's namesake pasties have closed in the past several years, but you'll still find them in a handful of casual restaurants and bakeries. Well-regarded spots include **Joe's Pasty Shop,** where I enjoyed a pasty made with a mixture of steak and ground beef; the cash-only **Town Talk Bakery**, which serves up both standard dinner pasties and breakfast ones with sausage and egg (and makes perhaps the most ethereal maple bar I've ever eaten); and **Truzzolino Tamales**, which offers both beef and pork "party pasties" as well as beef dinner pasties. And since they only cost a few dollars each, you won't have to spend too much of your hard-earned copper for an inexpensive meal.

Pork chop sandwich

Another reason to visit Butte is to pay homage to the stunt performer Evel Knievel, who grew up in Butte and was buried there after his death in 2007. Knievel helped popularize the pork chop sandwich at **Freeway Tavern**, which is filled with Knievel memorabilia and where the sandwich is still called by an offensive rhyming nickname that was given to it by the restaurant's late Italian-American owner, Muzz Faroni. (During a recent visit, it was shocking to hear the bartender use that term when I ordered my sandwich by its proper name.)

The pork chop sandwich is a breaded and fried boneless pork steak that's served on a soft bun with pickles, onions and mustard. The dish dates back to the 1920s, when John Burklund, who was known as Pork Chop John, sold sandwiches from the back of a wagon in Butte. Burklund opened a restaurant called **Pork Chop John's** uptown in 1932, and that location, along with another one in downtown Butte, is still serving up single or double pork chop sandwiches. This was my first of the two pork chop sandwiches I ate within a few hours, so I went with the single. But if you're feeling like a daredevil yourself, order a double and get it deluxe, with the addition of lettuce, tomatoes and mayonnaise.

Huckleberry pie

Though the huckleberry was named Idaho's official state fruit in 2000, the small, purple-colored berry is more closely associated with Montana. It's used there to flavor food items like ice cream, pancakes, jam and candy. But the best way to enjoy this wild berry that looks like a blueberry but is a little less sweet is in the form of pie.

You'll find huckleberry pie at bakeries throughout the state, especially during the short season between mid-August and mid-September when the berries are foraged in the state's mountainous regions. The best bakeries make their huckleberry pie using fresh berries and a buttery, flaky crust. But because fresh huckleberries are expensive, some establishments combine them with blueberries, blackberries or other fruits in their pie filling.

If you're planning a trip to Glacier National Park, a good place to eat huckleberry pie – where the filling isn't combined with other berries – is at **Glacier Highland**, only open from May through October, and located near the park's entrance in West Glacier. Other well-regarded places to try it include **Two Sisters Cafe** in Babb, also open only during the summer months; **Loula's Cafe** in Whitefish; and **Lake Baked** in Bigfork. These bakeries prove that an iconic dish doesn't need to be an official state food to still be worth making a stop for. Take that, Idaho!

UTAH

Pastrami burger

You might not expect a state that's sometimes thought of as a culinary desert to have a signature food item inspired by multiple cultures. But the pastrami burger defies any such preconceptions.

This local delicacy, sometimes called a Crown Burger after the chain that first popularized it, is a char-grilled patty that's topped with cheese and a thick layer of thinly sliced pastrami, along with a pinkish condiment called fry sauce as well as crisp lettuce, sliced tomatoes and raw onions. It was created in the 1960s by James Katsanevas, a Greek-American working in Los Angeles who learned it from a Turkish colleague. Katsanevas first brought the pastrami burger to a restaurant he opened in the early 1970s in Anaheim, California, but the dish took off later that decade when several of his family members opened the first Crown Burgers in Salt Lake City in 1978 and put his pastrami burger on the menu.

Today you'll find the pastrami burger at any of **Crown Burgers'** eight Utah locations (including the one I visited blocks from Temple Square), as well as at other casual restaurants in the Salt Lake City area, many of them Greek-owned. Two fast-food alternatives where you can order a pastrami burger as well as a gyro sandwich are **Apollo Burger** and **Astro Burgers**. Or try an upscale version like the one at **Lucky 13** in Salt Lake City, where the burger is topped with smoked pastrami and Swiss cheese. With the addition of sauerkraut, you might find yourself transported to a classic Jewish deli in New York City, and completely forget you're in the desert.

Fry sauce

When Heinz introduced its new condiment mayochup in the U.S. in 2018, the company may have thought it was breaking new culinary ground. But a similar sauce created in Utah dates back some 70 years before that, and remains popular throughout the state today.

At its heart, fry sauce, like its corporate cousin, is just a mixture of mayonnaise and ketchup – but the secret recipe also includes garlic and a handful of other spices and seasonings. A chef named Don Carlos Edwards created the blend in the 1940s while he was operating a barbecue restaurant in Salt Lake City, which he converted the following decade into a fast-food joint called **Arctic Circle**. Today the chain has a few dozen locations, mostly in Utah, with a few in a handful of other Western states, and goes through about 50,000 gallons of fry sauce annually. It's used as a condiment for sandwiches and burgers as well as, naturally, for dipping one's French fries into.

You'll find countless other versions of fry sauce at burger spots like **Crown Burgers** and fast-food chains all across the state, some of which include pickle juice in their list of ingredients (but which Arctic Circle disavows). And, surprisingly, you'll also find similar sauces in far-flung countries such as Argentina, where salsa golf was apparently invented a few decades before Edwards' creation, at a golf resort; Colombia, where salsa rosada (pink sauce) is sometimes employed as a salad dressing; England, where Marie Rose sauce was popularized as an accompaniment for seafood in the 1960s by the television chef Fanny Cradock; Germany, where a mixture of mayonnaise and ketchup is sometimes used as the sauce served with currywurst and fries; and Puerto Rico, where mayoketchup has been described as the island's quintessential condiment. But Utahns will tell you that you'll be hard-pressed to find real fry sauce anywhere else but the Beehive State.

Utah scone

The ancient capital of Scotland, the town of Scone, is the original home of the Stone of Scone, an oblong block of sandstone that's been used for centuries during the coronation of U.K. monarchs (including Queen Elizabeth II in 1953 and Charles III in 2023). Linguists aren't certain about the derivation of the word scone, but traditionally the pastry was baked on griddles in that town as early as the 16th century and was triangular in shape.

Don't be looking for three sides when you come to Utah in search of a scone, however. What you'll find there is a far cry from the traditional British version that often contains fruit and is topped with icing. Instead, Utah scones (also known as Mormon scones, after the 19th century settlers who likely first created them) have been likened to Navajo fry bread or Southwestern sopaipillas. It's puffy, deep-fried bread made from a sweet, yeasted dough, often covered with powdered sugar, and served with butter and honey.

In a paper presented to the Deseret Language and Linguistic Society Symposium in 1993, scholars at BYU investigated why such a different food had been given the name scone (as well as how to properly pronounce the word, rhyming with either bone or don). Their leading theory was that the early Latter-Day Saints, many of whom had English ancestry, adopted the term because it was a generic word that described a biscuit. But despite the short-o pronunciation being common among Anglophiles in the U.S., almost everyone pronounced the Mormon version with a long o.

Although the Utah chain that specialized in scones, Sconecutter, shut down in 2021, an equally punny food truck, **Sconey Island**, serves up these fried treats in the Draper area south of South Lake City. (Check their website for location details.) Another well-regarded place to try Utah scones is at **Sill's Cafe** in Layton on the north side of town. Its menu also offers a few British specialties, including fried fish and "English chips." But don't let that concern you: the scones here are the real Utah deal, and served, as I found during a recent visit, with more honey butter than any human should probably eat.

OTHER FOODS OF THE MOUNTAIN WEST

Rocky Mountain oysters

They're sometimes called cowboy caviar. Or calf fries. Or even Montana tendergroins. But whether you label them by any of those names or by the most common designation, Rocky Mountain oysters, there's no escaping this reality: what you're really talking about is testicles – usually from a bull, but sometimes from other animals like sheep, pigs or bison.

Rocky Mountain oysters are typically skinned, pounded flat, coated in flour, salt and pepper, and deep-fried. They're usually eaten as an appetizer and served with (ahem) cocktail sauce. Some describe them as having a gamey taste, while others liken them to calamari.

Early ranchers in the West who would typically castrate their young cattle to reduce sexual aggression began eating these organs in a desire to not let any part of the animal be wasted. They found that the testicles were rich in protein and other nutrients, and some considered them to be an aphrodisiac.

Today you'll find Rocky Mountain oysters throughout the region as a novelty food item in Western-themed restaurants like **The Fort** in Morrison, Colorado, as well at other spots including **Molly B's** in Estes Park, Colorado, and **Legends Rock Bar** in Colorado Springs. You'll also see them at town festivals such as the one held every July in Eagle, Idaho (but no longer at the famous annual Testy Festy in Clinton, Montana, which ended after 35 years following a fatal accident in 2017). Rockies fans can also pick up an order at the (ahem) ballpark in Denver, **Coors Field**. But don't be confused when you see the name of the stand just a few sections down. There's only one place in the stadium to get your Rocky Mountain oysters, and it's not at Simply Nuts.

Frogeye salad

If you're lucky enough to be invited to a Mormon Thanksgiving dinner, you'll undoubtedly encounter frogeye salad (also known as frog's eye salad) on the buffet table. This dish, which the New York Times reported in 2014 was the most commonly searched Thanksgiving-related term in Utah, Idaho, Colorado and Wyoming, is an ambrosia-like dessert salad that's often served at large gatherings in the Mountain West.

Frogeye salad consists of cooked small, round pasta, typically acini di pepe (Italian for peppercorns), that's mixed with a citrus-flavored custard and whipped cream, along with canned mandarin oranges and pineapples, marshmallows and sometimes coconut. Its name comes from the pasta, which looks like frog eyes – but it doesn't contain any actual amphibian.

This dish likely dates back to the late 1960s, when a recipe for the salad appeared on the box for Creamette pasta. You're more likely to encounter it at someone's home than at a restaurant, but I've seen it on the menu at **Chuck-A-Rama**, a chain of buffet restaurants with 11 locations in Idaho and Utah. Pile your plate with a scoop or two of lime jello (which is so popular in Utah that the 2002 Olympics in Salt Lake City sold a souvenir pin commemorating it as the official state snack) and some frogeye, and you can say you're eating salad when it's really just dessert.

Funeral potatoes

Another comfort food with Mormon origins, typically eaten at gatherings in Utah and Idaho, is such a part of the region's cultural identity that it was also commemorated with an Olympic pin: the macabre-sounding casserole known as funeral potatoes.

Funeral potatoes typically consists of frozen hash browns or tater tots that are mixed with onions, cream of chicken soup and sour cream, topped with shredded cheese and corn flakes or potato chips, and baked until it's gooey and melty. The name of the dish comes from the practice of bringing a casserole to a post-funeral meal to comfort the family members of the deceased. It may have been first created in the early 1900s by members of the Mormon female auxiliary organization known as the Relief Society, who would bring it to funerals as well as other life events and social gatherings attended by churchgoers.

If you want to try this dish while visiting the Mountain West (and you're not inclined to crash a Mormon funeral), good places to go in Salt Lake City include **Garage on Beck**, where the funeral potatoes come with a side of ranch dressing and are "baptized in hot oil," and **Tradition**, a restaurant where an order of funeral potatoes includes a topping of bacon jam. You may have thought the dish already sounded comforting, but that addition makes it really to die for.

Another Mountain West dish to sample:

- **Hawaiian haystack**, a dish usually eaten at Mormon homes or church potlucks in Utah and Idaho. It consists of white rice topped with cooked chicken, vegetables such as diced celery, carrots and tomatoes, fruits including canned pineapple and maraschino cherries, and toppings like shredded coconut, gravy, Chinese noodles and grated Cheddar cheese. The ingredients are typically laid out buffet-style, and each diner creates their own stack. The dish is likely associated with Hawaii because it uses tropical ingredients such as coconut and pineapple. Although its origin is unknown, it may have been influenced by the strong presence of the Church of Latter-Day Saints in Hawaii, which was established there in 1851. One place where you'll occasionally see this dish served as a weekly takeout special is **Dinnertime Meals** in Draper, Utah.

Chimichanga

THE SOUTHWEST

As you drive around the Southwestern U.S., perhaps in search of sunshine on the golf courses in Phoenix, desert landscapes on the outskirts of Tucson, sculpture in the fine art galleries of Santa Fe, or hot air balloons at the annual festival in Albuquerque, it'll be hard to miss the influence of the various cultures that have done more to shape the cuisine of this region than any other. The Southwest is a mecca for Mexican food, with corn, beans and chiles showing up in many familiar, classic preparations like tacos, tamales and enchiladas. But you'll also find unique dishes, especially in New Mexico, that have evolved from the traditions of both the Spanish colonists who arrived in the 16th century and the Native American tribes who began living off the land hundreds of years before that. This region also includes Nevada, a state whose food culture ranks as among the most peculiar in the country, lacking much of a unique culinary identity but absorbing strands from people of many cultures who came to the desert seeking fame and fortune.

Beginning in around 1910, tens of thousands of Mexicans crossed the border to the Southwest, hoping to escape the violence of the Mexican Revolution and drawn to the U.S. by the promise of agricultural work. Naturally, the traditional dishes that these immigrants brought to the U.S. began to gain a foothold in the region, aided by the wide availability of corn for making tortillas and tamales. But it wasn't until the second half of the 20th century that a version of Mexican food known as Tex-Mex began to become part of mainstream U.S. cuisine. The mass production of ingredients like packaged tortillas, bottled salsa and canned chili helped familiarize Americans with Mexican flavors, and restaurants serving staples like tacos, enchiladas and burritos increasingly became part of the culinary landscape. New regional specialties like the chimichanga, in Arizona, and Frito pie, in New Mexico, emerged from a mixture of Mexican flavors and American cooking techniques, and dishes like the Sonoran hot dog crossed the border to become popular in the U.S.

In New Mexico, a food culture unlike anything else in the U.S. has grown out of locally available ingredients, especially the green chile (which is used in many dishes, including the state's signature green chile cheeseburger), as well as the influence of both Spanish and Native American cultures. The Spanish colonists who came to the New World in the 16th century brought new ingredients and flavors, and some of the dishes that evolved under their rule include posole, a stew made with pork and dried corn, and biscochitos, anise- and cinnamon-flavored cookies. Meanwhile, indigenous tribes contributed preparations such as blue corn tortillas, now frequently used for making the stacked casserole known as enchiladas montadas, and fry bread, which forms the basis of Navajo tacos.

Although you'll easily find plenty of Mexican food in Nevada, as you will in almost every corner of the U.S., the Silver State is one of just a few places in the country that doesn't have much to offer in the way of unique regional dishes. In Las Vegas, the destination for a majority of visitors to the state, you'll encounter plenty of prime rib specials as well as all-you-can-eat buffets. But you're just as likely to find upscale establishments helmed by celebrity chefs like Jose Andres, Gordon Ramsay and Wolfgang Puck, featuring a wide range of European cuisines. You'll eat just as well if you venture off Strip to try some of the well-regarded Asian restaurants in the area, including **Lotus of Siam** for Northern Thai, **Aburiya Raku** for grilled Japanese meats and **Joyful House** for Cantonese specialties. If you're staying at one of the many resorts on the Strip, you might celebrate a lucky roll of the dice with some giant shrimp cocktail or an expensive cut of steak – but neither of these indulgences really qualifies as an iconic state dish.

One exception that's out of the way for most travelers is the Basque country of Northern Nevada. The Basque, who came to the U.S. from the region straddling France and Spain, arrived in

Nevada (as well as Idaho) in the 1860s, following the discovery of silver in 1859. Many of those who settled in the state became shepherds, and the traditional dishes you can enjoy today in places like Reno and Carson City include lamb stew, as well as a brandy cocktail known as Picon.

While the Southwest has plenty of familiar food items, it's still full of culinary surprises. Even if you're a connoisseur of breakfast burritos, you probably didn't realize that they originated in this part of the country. And though you might have eaten sopaipillas after a Mexican meal, you probably haven't had them stuffed with meat and covered in chile and cheese, as they're eaten in New Mexico. Whether you're on your way to the Grand Canyon or to Carlsbad Caverns, don't waste your time with national chain restaurants or fast-food fare. These regional specialties will provide you a much better sense of the local culinary scene.

ARIZONA

Sonoran hot dog

A dish with roots in the Northern Mexican state of Sonora but eaten all over Arizona is the hot dog called by the same name as the state's major desert. A Sonoran hot dog is one that's wrapped in bacon and grilled, and served on a baguette-like roll called a bolillo. It's then topped with a variety of ingredients including pinto beans, tomatoes and onions, as well as mustard, mayonnaise and jalapeño sauce.

The Sonoran hot dog likely originated in the late 1980s in Hermosillo, Mexico, where it was sold at street carts by vendors called dogueros, but it made its way across the border to Tucson shortly after that. Over the past few decades these dogs have become so popular in Arizona that it was estimated in 2009 that over 200 carts sold them in Tucson alone.

If you're traveling in the southern part of the state, your first taste of a Sonoran hot dog should be at one of the three branches of that city's **El Güero Canelo**, which received a James Beard Award for America's Classics in 2018. Another good choice in Tucson is **BK Tacos**, with locations on both the north and south sides of the city.

In Phoenix, one of the most popular spots for a Sonoran hot dog is a late-night food cart called **Nogales Hot Dogs** (a second location across town is open all day and serves additional Mexican specialties). If you're in Scottsdale, try **Simon's Hot Dogs**, a small restaurant serving Sonoran dogs as well as Colombian (with pineapple and crushed potato chips), German (brown mustard and sauerkraut), and "cowboy" (chili and cheese) styles. But only the Sonoran version includes bacon – making it the one I'd want to try first – as well as plenty of sauce to ensure this dog isn't as dry as its namesake desert.

Chimichanga

Like the Quesarito or the Crunchwrap Supreme, the chimichanga sounds like it might have been created for the menu at Taco Bell. But while it's probably not a traditional Mexican dish either, it is one with roots in Arizona that's now widely available in restaurants all across the country serving Tex-Mex and Southwestern cuisine.

A chimichanga is essentially a deep-fried burrito. Like a burrito, it starts with a flour tortilla, which can be filled with a variety of ingredients that may include meat (chicken or beef are common fillings) or vegetables, as well as rice, beans and cheese. It's typically served on a plate with accompaniments of salsa, guacamole and sour cream.

Although Mexican immigrants may have first brought the chimichanga across the border to the U.S., more colorful accounts ascribe its invention to one of two Arizona restaurants. One version says that in 1922, Monica Flin, the owner of **El Charro Café** in Tucson, accidentally dropped a burrito in the deep fryer, and began to utter a profanity in Spanish that instead came out as the word chimichanga, a nonsense word roughly meaning thingamajig. Another story is that a chef named Woody Johnson had a similar mishap in 1946 (some accounts say it was an intentional experiment). The fried burritos became popular at the restaurant he owned at that time, and at **Macayo's Mexican Food** after he founded the chain in 1952.

In addition to El Charro in Tucson and the six locations of Macayo's in the Phoenix area, other well-regarded spots for chimichangas today include **Taqueria El Pueblito** in Tucson, where the chimis can be ordered with carne asada, carnitas, chicken or green chile pork, among other fillings, and **Anaya's Fresh Mexican Restaurant** in Glendale, where you can choose between traditional, veggie or seafood styles. Just don't go to Taco Bell looking for your chimi fix. In 2017, the company tested out a close cousin in the Midwest, a new menu item called Crispy Dipping Burritos – but they never made it to national release.

Cheese crisp

There are some dishes, like a mother-in-law or a garbage plate, whose names are so mysterious that you just have to sample them to know what's in them. And then there's the cheese crisp, an Arizona specialty that's exactly what it sounds like.

A cheese crisp is a large flour tortilla that's buttered, covered with cheese, and broiled in a round pizza pan until it's crisp and melty. The cheese is often queso fresco, Cheddar or Monterey Jack, and roasted green chiles are sometimes added on top. The dish is similar to a quesadilla, but rather than being folded over, a cheese crisp is open-faced, and is usually cut into wedges before serving. It's prepared with tortillas native to Sonora, Mexico, which are thinner than typical flour tortillas.

The origin of the cheese crisp is unknown, but it was popularized by **El Charro Café** in Tucson. You'll find them on the appetizer menu there as well as at other Mexican restaurants like **Mi Nidito** in Tucson, and **Maria's Frybread & Mexican Food** and **Cien Agaves Tacos & Tequila**, both in the Phoenix area – with the latter serving more dishes than its straightforward name suggests it might.

Another Arizona dish to sample:

- **Tamales**, a Mexican specialty made with masa dough as well as meat, cheese and green chile or other vegetables, all wrapped in a corn husk or banana leaf and steamed. They're a staple of Arizona and are often sold by immigrant vendors on the street as well as at restaurants including **The Tamale Store** in Phoenix.

King cake

See New Orleans

The rosca de reyes, or king's wreath, is an Arizona sweet bread similar to a New Orleans king cake that often has candied fruit on top as well as a plastic baby figurine hidden inside. You'll find it at Mexican bakeries such as **La Purisima Bakery** in Glendale.

NEW MEXICO

Green chile cheeseburger

How important is the green chile cheeseburger to the food culture of New Mexico? The state tourism board created a green chile cheeseburger trail to highlight restaurants that serve them, and even McDonald's has a green chile cheeseburger on its menu. So if you're traveling in the Land of Enchantment, you shouldn't pass up the opportunity to try the state's most iconic dish.

A green chile cheeseburger is made with whole or chopped New Mexico-grown green chiles and American cheese, along with other toppings such as lettuce, tomatoes and onions. There are numerous varieties of green chiles, with different heat levels, but ones grown in the Hatch Valley are among the most famous. Green chiles are typically harvested between July and October, and are often frozen after roasting for use year-round. When chiles are allowed to grow until they ripen, they turn red and develop an earthier flavor; unlike green chiles, though, they're typically dried and blended into a purée. While dining in New Mexico, you'll often be asked the official state question, "red or green?," and if you want both on whatever you're eating, the correct answer is "Christmas style."

If you plan to travel the cheeseburger trail, you'll find plenty of places all over the state to get your chile fix. One good itinerary would take you from Santa Fe southwest to Albuquerque and then south toward the chile-growing areas near Hatch and Las Cruces. A few burger spots worth checking out along this route include **El Parasol**, with multiple locations, including three in Santa Fe; **Blake's Lotaburger**, a fast-food chain with 20 locations in the Albuquerque area alone; **Sparky's** in Hatch, where your burger comes in its purest form, without any toppings other than chile and cheese; and **Burger Nook** in Las Cruces. And if you happen to be passing through Hatch over

Labor Day weekend, don't miss the town's annual festival devoted to its namesake crop, which includes a chile-eating contest, a chile-tossing contest and of course, an endless supply of green chile cheeseburgers.

Breakfast burrito

Want to continue traveling in search of New Mexico's best bites? The enterprising marketers at the state tourism board created a second foodie trail that highlights another of New Mexico's culinary gems, calling it the breakfast burrito byway.

While the idea of eating a flour tortilla stuffed with breakfast foods like scrambled eggs, bacon and potatoes may seem commonplace today, New Mexico was where this dish was first called a breakfast burrito – in 1975, on the menu of a Santa Fe diner called **Tia Sophia's**. And the Land of Enchantment puts its own spin on the concept, with chile adding a layer of spice to the rest of the ingredients, and two different ways of serving it. You'll not only have to decide whether you want your breakfast burrito red, green or Christmas style, but also whether you want it to be served smothered, with chile sauce covering the burrito, or handheld, with chopped chiles in place of sauce.

There are as many variations of the breakfast burrito as there are omelets, with some versions including Cheddar or Monterey Jack cheese, vegetables such as tomatoes, onions and beans, or other meats like chorizo or ham. You'll find these burritos on the breakfast menus of restaurants and diners all across the state. A few recommended spots are **Katrinah's East Mountain Grill** in Edgewood, east of Albuquerque; **Golden Pride**, with four locations in the Albuquerque area; **Michael's Kitchen** in Taos; and of course, Tia Sophia's. That's a perfect place to stop for breakfast if you know the way to Santa Fe.

Enchiladas montadas

If you get tired of all the flour tortillas on your travels in the Southwest, a good alternative is a blue corn tortilla. (I suppose you could eat something other than tortillas, but why would you want to do that in this part of the country?) Blue corn was originally developed by several Native American tribes including the Hopi in Arizona and the Pueblo in New Mexico, and tortillas made from blue corn meal have become a staple of New Mexican cuisine.

One of the best ways to try these tortillas is in the dish known as enchiladas montadas. You may already be familiar with enchiladas, which are tortillas that are rolled around combinations of meat, cheese and vegetables, and covered with sauce. By contrast, enchiladas montadas are stacked layers of similar ingredients, with chopped onions, shredded cheese and either red or green chile sauce used to separate the strata. After more sauce is ladled on the whole stack, it's sometimes topped with a fried egg.

Look for enchiladas montadas (sometimes they'll just be called stacked enchiladas) on the menus of New Mexican restaurants like **Monica's El Portal** in Albuquerque; **Sadie's**, with three locations in the Albuquerque area; and **The Shed** in Santa Fe. If you don't finish your meal, you can ask to take the leftovers home – but I'm guessing you'll want to eat the whole enchilada.

Posole

During holidays and special occasions in the 16th century, the Aztec people of Mesoamerica would often celebrate with a rich, meaty stew called pozole. But not everyone got to participate in the festivities. According to Mexican government and university research, the Aztecs were cannibals and would create this dish using maize as well as the flesh of their human prisoners.

Once cannibalism was banned after the Spanish conquered the Aztec Empire, pozole was typically cooked with pork instead of people, and the dish became a staple of Mexican cuisine, usually made with hominy. You'll find it in countless restaurants throughout the Southwest, but New Mexico's version – spelled with an s instead of a z – is a distinct regional specialty.

This variety of the stew uses dried white corn kernels that are also called posole, along with pork shoulder or chicken, red chile, onions, garlic and oregano. Like its antecedent, it's usually eaten during the holiday season and at celebratory events like weddings.

You can enjoy posole year-round at restaurants throughout the state that serve New Mexican specialties. A few recommended spots include **Frontier Restaurant** in Albuquerque; **Casa Chimayo Restaurant** and **Posa's Tamale Factory**, both in Santa Fe; and **Orlando's New Mexican Cafe** in Taos. Fortunately for 21st-century travelers, none of these places cook their posole using traditional Aztec methods.

Green chile stew

See Other foods of Colorado

The green chile stew, or chili verde, that's eaten in New Mexico is frequently prepared with locally grown Hatch chiles. You'll find this dish at just about any restaurant specializing in New Mexican cuisine, but a standout in Albuquerque is **Frontier Restaurant**.

Frito pie

Even if you've never set foot in New Mexico, chances are you've already eaten one of its regional specialties, maybe at the state fair or at a high school football game. In the Midwest and parts of the East, Frito pie is known as a walking taco, or sometimes a

Frito boat or a taco-in-a-bag. But no matter what you call it, the idea is the same – a mixture of chili, cheese and corn chips, with toppings such as salsa, sour cream and jalapeños adding creaminess and heat to the meatiness and crunch. In its more portable form, the dish is sometimes eaten directly from a single-serving bag of Fritos, a style that gives Frito pie its alternative names – although in New Mexico it's usually served as a casserole.

Some people attribute the original version of Frito pie to Texas, where a San Antonio resident named Daisy Doolin – the mother of the inventor of Fritos – is said to have come up with the dish in the 1930s. But others believe that it was first created in the 1960s by a woman named Teresa Hernández, who worked at the Woolworth's lunch counter in Santa Fe and ladled her mother's red chile con carne into a bag of Fritos. While neither story is likely true – Frito pie appears to have been invented by the Frito-Lay marketing department for a 1950s corporate cookbook – many New Mexicans have staunchly defended their state's claim to the dish, particularly after Anthony Bourdain described it as "warm crap in a bag" in a 2013 episode of his CNN series Parts Unknown.

If you'd like to make your own assessment, a good place to go is the snack bar at Santa Fe's **Five & Dime** convenience store, located in the building that formerly housed Woolworth's and where your Frito pie comes in a bag of chips. A somewhat more upscale version can be found just steps away at the downtown location of **Plaza Cafe**, where your Frito pie is served "upside down" in a bowl with your choice of beef, chicken or calabacitas (a vegetable medley containing squash, corn and green chile). Other spots to try this dish include **La Cueva Cafe** in Taos and **Tia Betty Blue's** in Albuquerque, where you have a choice of meat as well as red or green chile. Don't plan on walking around while you eat, though – the Frito pies served in these places might just as well be called sitting tacos.

Sopaipilla

In Tex-Mex cuisine, you'll typically finish a meal with a complimentary dessert: the cinnamon-dusted, honey-coated fried dough that's known as sopaipillas (sometimes spelled sopapillas). But that's not usually how these triangular pastries are eaten in New Mexico, where they're typically served as a side dish instead of bread, and are sometimes flavored with anise syrup instead of honey. And just as commonly, sopaipillas in New Mexico are stuffed with ground beef or chicken, covered in chile and cheese, and eaten as an entrée.

Although the history of the sopaipilla is murky at best, it's believed that the savory version originated in Albuquerque in the early 19th century. The word derives from the Spanish word sopaipa, which itself comes from a medieval Islamic word meaning bread soaked in oil. Sopaipillas are made with a yeasted dough that contains wheat flour and shortening such as lard. When they're deep-fried, they puff up, leaving a pillowy pocket in the center that's perfect for stuffing savory ingredients into.

You'll find sopaipillas at most restaurants in the state that serve New Mexican specialties. At **Garcia's Kitchen**, with seven locations in the Albuquerque area, you can order sopaipillas as either an appetizer, drizzled with honey, or a main dish, stuffed with your choice of meat. Other places to try them include **Tomasita's**, with branches in both Albuquerque and Santa Fe, where sopaipillas come with every New Mexican entrée, and where you can also order them stuffed for either a main course or dessert. And at **Sopaipilla Factory** in Pojoaque, outside of Santa Fe, you could consume an entire meal consisting only of the restaurant's namesake dish. You probably won't get any complimentary sopaipillas there, but fortunately they won't cost you too much dough.

Biscochito

In 1989, New Mexico became the first state to name an official state cookie, the biscochito. But it was a full eight years before another state picked one – Massachusetts, which chose chocolate chip.

New Mexico's proclamation may be surprising if you're not familiar with these crisp biscuits, which are a state specialty that are often served at weddings, quinceañeras and holiday celebrations. Biscochitos, also known as bizcochitos, are essentially sugar cookies made with lard. They're flavored with cinnamon and anise and can be cut into various shapes including rounds, diamonds, stars and half-moons.

Biscochitos were likely brought to New Mexico in the 16th century by Spanish colonists, who enjoyed a similar cookie in their home country called mantecados. Today you'll find them at grocery stores and supermarkets throughout New Mexico, as well as at bakeries including **Celina's Biscochitos** in Albuquerque, **Osito's Biscochitos** in Las Cruces and **Just Peachy Pueblo Biscochitos** in San Felipe Pueblo, where flavor options include traditional, blue corn and green chile – but not chocolate chip.

Other New Mexico dishes to sample:

- **Carne adovada**, a meat dish found in New Mexico that's similar to the Mexican adobada, consisting of pork that's been marinated in red chile, oregano, cumin and either vinegar or lemon or lime juice. The meat is then covered and baked at low heat to keep it moist. A well-regarded place where this dish appears on the menu is **La Choza Restaurant** in Santa Fe.
- **Huevos rancheros**, meaning ranch-style eggs, which are fried eggs served on charred tortillas with accompaniments that may include refried beans, rice, salsa and avocado. The version served in New Mexico tops the eggs with either red or green chile sauce. One recommended spot to try this dish is **Cafe Pasqual's** in Santa Fe.
- **Natillas**, a light custard-like dessert made with milk, egg whites and sugar, and flavored with vanilla, nutmeg and cinnamon. It was likely brought to New Mexico by Spanish colonists and can be found in many Mexican and New Mexican restaurants, including **Abuelita's New Mexican Kitchen** in Albuquerque and Bernalillo.
- **Panocha**, a thick pudding made from the sprouted wheat flour that gives the dish its name, as well as piloncillo (brown cane sugar) and butter. It was brought by the Spanish colonists to New Mexico and Southern Colorado and is traditionally eaten during Lent. You can sample it at **Socorro's Restaurant** in Hernandez.

OTHER FOODS OF THE SOUTHWEST

Navajo taco

In September 2011, residents of Gallup, New Mexico, set a Guinness World Record by constructing a taco that was 10 feet in diameter. But this was no ordinary taco – it was a Navajo taco, made with 150 pieces of fry bread, 65 pounds each of ground beef and beans, 90 pounds of cheese and 30 pounds of green chiles. And as a finishing touch, the mayor of Gallup used a cherry-picker truck to scatter diced tomatoes in the center of the dish.

Navajo tacos, like their Mexican counterparts, contain a variety of fillings and toppings. But instead of using a corn or flour tortilla, the shell is fry bread, a Native American dough made from wheat flour, sugar, salt and oil or shortening, that's fried until crisp. After the fry bread is topped with whatever ingredients you've chosen, you simply roll it up and eat it with your hands.

Fry bread was first created by the Navajo in 1864 during their forced deportation by the U.S. government from Arizona to Eastern New Mexico, a 300-mile migration that's known as the Long Walk. The government provided the Navajo with staples including white flour, processed sugar and lard, which they relied on for sustenance because their typical crops of vegetables and beans couldn't easily be grown on their new land. Those who survived their exile were allowed to return to Arizona in 1868, as part of a treaty that established a permanent reservation for the Navajo.

Navajo tacos, which are also known as Indian tacos (especially in Oklahoma), remain part of the legacy of this shameful history. Today, you'll find them at fairs and festivals throughout the Southwest, but during your travels it's also worth seeking out restaurants that specialize in Native American cuisine. A few spots to check out in New Mexico include **Indian Pueblo Kitchen** at the Indian Pueblo Culture Center in Albuquerque and **Tiwa Kitchen Restaurant** in Taos. And in Arizona, you can try Navajo tacos at **Fry Bread House** in Phoenix and **The Stand** in Scottsdale, located on the Salt River Reservation.

Fried ice cream

The dessert that encases a scoop of ice cream inside a fried pastry shell was probably first served at the 1893 Chicago World's Fair and today, is generally associated with both Chinese and Japanese cuisines. But in the Southwest you'll more commonly find it on the menus of Mexican restaurants. That's because in the 1980s, the Tex-Mex restaurant chain Chi-Chi's made fried ice cream its signature dessert, and other establishments picked up on and popularized the concept.

Another food of the Southwest to sample:

- **Carne seca**, dried beef jerky with a crispy texture that's often used as a meat filling in Mexican dishes in both Arizona and New Mexico. When the dried beef is shredded, it becomes known as machaca, from the Spanish word machacar, meaning smash or crush. You can pick up some carne seca in a variety of flavors, including red chile, green chile and pineapple habañero, at **Sena's Beef Jerky** in Albuquerque.

Fried ice cream is made by freezing a scoop of ice cream, usually vanilla, to a colder-than-normal storage temperature, rolling it in cornflakes or cookie crumbs, and then quickly deep-frying it so that the exterior crisps up before the interior melts. It's sometimes served on a deep-fried tortilla coated with cinnamon and sugar, or just dusted with those ingredients.

If you'd like to cap off a Southwestern meal with this seemingly paradoxical concoction, a few places to try it include **Popo's Fiesta del Sol** in Phoenix, **Garduños** in Albuquerque and **Pecos Trail Cafe** in Santa Fe. Chi-Chi's now exists only outside North America, so unless you have a time-traveling DeLorean, you'll have to fly to Vienna, Austria; Bruges, Belgium; or Luxembourg to try the original Mexican version.

REGIONAL BURGERS OF THE U.S.

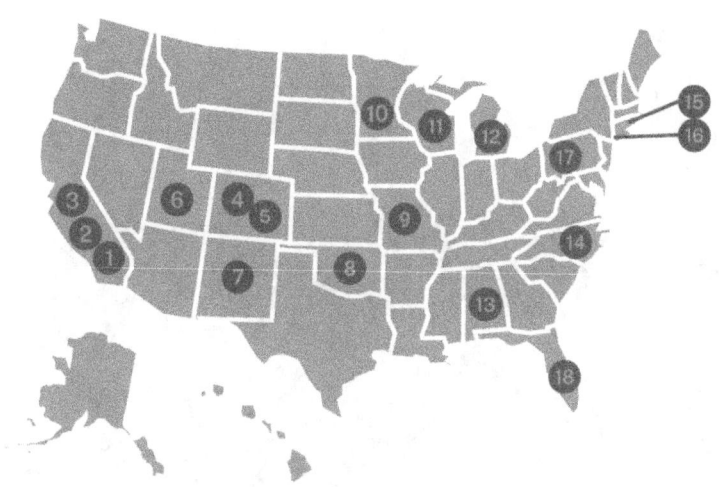

1 Chili burger
2 Patty melt
3 California-style burger
4 Mexican hamburger
5 Pueblo Slopper
6 Pastrami burger

7 Green chile cheeseburger
8 Onion burger
9 Guber burger
10 Juicy Lucy
11 Butter burger
12 Olive burger

13 Slugburger
14 Carolina burger
15 Steamed cheeseburger
16 Chamby burger
17 Pittsburgh-style burger
18 Frita Cubana

Onion burger

THE HEARTLAND

The states that run north-south from North Dakota to Oklahoma are commonly thought of as flyover country. But if you find yourself passing through on a coast-to-coast road trip, visiting Mount Rushmore or the Badlands, or attending a Division I football game in Lincoln or Lawrence, don't miss the chance to try one of the handful of local specialties, most of which you won't find in any other part of the country.

As with other regions in the U.S., the cuisine of the Heartland has been shaped by both the area's agriculture and by the patterns of immigration that resulted in pockets of the population sharing a common ancestry (as well as by the Native Americans who remain an important part of its culture).

Oklahoma is one of the nation's leading producers of both cattle and pork, and its steakhouses and barbecue joints are a meat-lover's paradise. And just like in Texas, chicken-fried steak is a popular dish. But don't miss the chance to try the state's two most distinctive regional food items, both of which were Depression-era measures of frugality, in one case (the Oklahoma onion burger) extending the supply of expensive ground beef by mixing it with onions, and in the other (smoked bologna) treating inexpensive processed meat like tenderloin.

In South Dakota, another iconic dish, chislic, is based on the red meat produced by the state's cattle industry – sometimes beef, but more often lamb or mutton. Another regional dish that makes good use of beef is the Reuben sandwich, whose creation is sometimes credited to Nebraska (but of course, is more commonly associated with New York City). And in both Kansas and Nebraska, a meat pastry called a bierock – or sometimes a runza – is constructed with the ground beef that's produced on its thousands of acres of cattle ranches, as well as the wheat that's grown across its many farms and fields.

You may be surprised to learn that much of the Heartland's local cuisine – including the bierock – stems from a population of Russian immigrants who arrived in the region in the 1870s and 1880s. For the previous century, these farmers, mostly of German descent, had enjoyed the ability to live freely and prosperously in the Volga region, in a policy first enacted by Catherine the Great in 1762. But as political fortunes in Russia shifted, many decided to leave their homeland and seek new opportunities in the U.S. Naturally, they brought with them several distinctive dishes – like knoephla, a dumpling soup, and kuchen, a sweet pastry with a custard or fruit filling – that should definitely be on your list of foods to try if you're visiting the Dakotas.

Other cultural groups have also left a mark on this region's cuisine, although this book more fully tells their stories in other chapters. But even sampling some of the different baked goods you'll find in the Heartland, like lefse, a Norwegian flatbread (which you'll find in North Dakota); kolache, a sweet pastry (available in certain corners of South Dakota); and fry bread, a fried dough whose history reflects a shameful chapter in U.S. history (most prevalent in the Heartland in South Dakota and Oklahoma), will give you a taste of these states' Scandinavian, Czech and Native American heritage. If you try any of these items, or any of the other regional dishes I've mentioned, you'll soon realize that the Heartland isn't just somewhere you should quickly fly over.

NORTH DAKOTA

Knoephla

North Dakota is one of the very few U.S. states I've still never been to. But whenever I get there, the first thing I'll want to eat is a hearty dumpling soup called knoephla. It usually consists of a creamy chicken broth with chunks of potato, and sometimes also contains celery and carrots. The dumplings are made with flour and eggs, and are typically rolled out into little buttons (the German word knöpfle, from which the soup's name is derived, means little knob, or button). You'll sometimes find the dumplings prepared without soup, which was also a common way of eating them in the Old World.

Knoephla was a favorite dish of the Russian Germans who settled in the upper Midwest beginning in the 1870s. By the end of the century, nearly 70,000 immigrants with a German-speaking background had moved to North Dakota, and today about half of the state's population has Russian-German heritage.

Whether you're visiting North Dakota or just passing through on a cross-country road trip, a good place to stop is the town of Dickinson, where a local restaurant called **Jack's** is well-regarded for its knoephla as well as borscht, a beet soup that also has Russian roots. The restaurant closed during the pandemic, but its knoephla is still available in local grocery stores, including **Cash Wise**. Another option is to visit **Kroll's Diner**, a casual restaurant that has locations in Fargo, Bismarck, Mandan and Minot. The knoephla here are served in two ways: in soup and on a plate with sausage and sauerkraut. The chain's been around since 1969 and has a loyal local following. But just so I can vouch for it myself, I may have to start looking into flights to Fargo.

Lefse

See Minnesota

This flatbread and other Norwegian delicacies are celebrated every September at Norsk Høstfest in Minot, an event billed as the largest Scandinavian festival in North America. You can also pick some up year-round at **Freddy's Lefse and Nordic Kitchen** in Fargo.

Another North Dakota dish to sample:

- **Fleischkuekle**, a deep-fried Russian-German meat pastry found in North Dakota that's sometimes served with gravy, or with pickles and ketchup on the side. You can sample it on the dinner menu at **Ye Olde Malt Shoppe** in Garrison.

SOUTH DAKOTA

Chislic

If you're out on a cross-country adventure and happen to be driving west on I-90, you won't be able to miss the billboards advertising the World's Only Corn Palace in the town of Mitchell, South Dakota. But what you probably won't realize is that as soon as you enter the Mount Rushmore State (yes, that's its official nickname), you'll also be heading toward the Chislic Circle, a loose geographical designation where you'll find South Dakota's most iconic regional food.

Chislic is a dish consisting of cubes of skewered red meat that are cooked to either a rare or medium-rare temperature and sprinkled with garlic salt or seasoned salt. It's usually made with lamb or mutton, but can also be prepared with beef or venison, and is typically accompanied by saltine crackers. The meat can be either grilled or deep-fried, and is sometimes marinated or served with a variety of dipping sauces.

You're most likely to encounter chislic in Southeastern South Dakota, particularly in the town of Freeman and nearby cities, including Sioux Falls. Although the dish's exact provenance is unknown, it's believed that a Russian-German businessman named John Hoellwarth brought it with him when he emigrated to South Dakota in the 1870s. The world chislic is probably an Anglicized version of shashlyk, which in Crimea, where Hoellwarth came from, referred to skewered cubes of beef, lamb or pork that were grilled over an open fire.

If you'd like to sample chislic, a good first stop is an entire restaurant devoted to it, Sioux Falls's **Urban Chislic**. There you'll be able to customize your order with a choice of seven different proteins, including lamb, beef, bison and venison, nine different seasonings and over a dozen sauces. A more traditional chislic is served up at another establishment in Sioux Falls, **Ode to**

Food and Drinks, where the chislic basket consists of deep-fried top sirloin. Another option is to head off the beaten track to Freeman, the OG chislic town (it even hosts a festival devoted to it every July), where you'll find chislic served at **Meridian Corner**, with a choice of mutton or lamb. But if you can't resist following the highway signs for the Corn Palace, and you're lucky enough to be traveling in late August, just keep an ear out for the sizzling sound of chislic – it's served at the annual Corn Palace Festival.

Kuchen

If South Dakota had an official desert, it would probably be the Badlands, the national park that's home to stunning geologic formations and rich sedimentary fossil beds. (OK, it's not technically a desert, just a semi-arid region, but stick with me.) But South Dakota does have an official dessert – a German pastry known as kuchen that's become a staple of the state's cuisine.

Kuchen is the German word for cake, but this dessert is more like a pie than a cake. It's made with a sweetened dough that's filled with custard, nuts or fruit such as raisins, prunes or apples. It's often topped with streusel or with cinnamon and sugar.

It's likely that kuchen established roots in South Dakota with German immigrants who arrived in the 1880s. Many settled in the southeastern part of the state, and this is where you're most likely to encounter kuchen today. Two options include **Tyndall Bakery** in Tyndall, which serves rhubarb as well as other fruit flavors of kuchen, and **Pietz's Kuchen Kitchen** in Scotland, which bakes peach, cherry, apricot and a few other kinds of kuchen, and distributes them in nearby grocery stores including **Hy-Vee**.

Other groups of Germans settled in the north-central part of the state, as well as in Southern North Dakota, and it's worth looking for kuchen in places such as **The Junction** in Aberdeen, South Dakota, and **Model Bakery** in Linton and **Grandma's Kuchen** in Ashley, both in North Dakota. Kuchen isn't the Northern state's official dessert, but that doesn't make it a bad land for finding something tasty at the local bakery.

Another South Dakota dish to sample:

- **Fry bread**, a fried flat dough that in 2005 was named the official state bread of South Dakota. It was originally created by the Navajo in 1864 during their forced deportation by the U.S. government from Arizona to New Mexico, but has since become a staple of Native American cuisine. Fry bread is often the base ingredient for Navajo tacos (also called Indian tacos in Oklahoma) but can simply be eaten with honey or sprinkled with confectioner's sugar. One place to sample it is **Dakotah Steakhouse** in Rapid City, where it's served either dusted with sugar and accompanied by homemade blueberry sauce, or as the base of an ice cream sundae.

NEBRASKA

Reuben

See New York City

One account of the invention of the Reuben says that it was created for a poker player named Reuben Kulakofsky at the Blackstone Hotel in Omaha. That city has a surprising number of places to enjoy the sandwich, including **Crescent Moon**, located across the street from the erstwhile site of the Blackstone, now called the Kimpton Cottonwood Hotel.

KANSAS

A couple of Kansas dishes to sample:

- **Peppernuts**, cookies spiced with cardamom, ginger, nutmeg and other flavors that were brought to Kansas by Mennonites who settled there beginning in the 1870s. These confections were called pfeffernüsse in Germany and were often eaten during the holiday season. Today you'll find them year-round at bakeries such as **Helmuth Country Bakery** in Hutchinson and **The Breadbasket** in Newton.
- **Turkey fries**, a food item that may seem a little nuts. At **Six Mile Chop House** in Lawrence, you can order a dish with that euphemistic name – but what you're actually eating is deep-fried turkey testicles.

OKLAHOMA

Onion burger

According to Oklahoma state law, it's illegal to take a bite out of another person's hamburger. But you might be sorely tempted to if you're driving Route 66 and stop for lunch in the town of El Reno, west of Oklahoma City. That's the epicenter of the Sooner State's most iconic dish: the onion burger.

An Oklahoma onion burger is a hamburger cooked with a mound of thinly sliced onions smashed into one side of the patty. After the meat is seared on a blazing-hot, flat-top grill, the burger is flipped over so that the onions caramelize and become slightly crispy, and a slice of American cheese is then melted on top. It's served on a standard, soft hamburger bun, with the onions haphazardly sticking out of the patty.

This style of burger was created during the 1920s by a man named Ross Davis, who operated an establishment called the Hamburger Inn. Because onions were cheap and ground beef was expensive, Davis mixed his patties with half an onion per burger in order to add bulk to the meat, and labeled his creation Depression burgers. Other restaurants in El Reno copied Davis's idea, and today, you can find onion burgers at several old-school eateries in the town along Route 66, including **Sid's Diner**, **Robert's Grill** and **Johnnie's Hamburgers and Coneys**.

But that's not the only place you'll find an onion burger in the Sooner State. In Oklahoma City, try **Tucker's Onion Burgers** for a well-regarded version of this specialty. And while **The Hamburger Inn** in El Reno is no longer in existence, a sister restaurant by the same name that opened in 1938 in the Southern Oklahoma town of Ardmore is a good place to stop if you're driving between Oklahoma City and Dallas. But don't even think about taking a bite of your traveling companion's burger until you cross state lines.

Smoked bologna

The most famous barbecue in Oklahoma might be a certain kind of meat that's served at **Oklahoma Joe's** (though the restaurant chain is perhaps best-known for its gas station location in Kansas, now called **Joe's Kansas City Bar-B-Que**). Unlike neighboring locales like Texas, Kansas City and St. Louis, the Sooner State isn't really recognized for having a unique regional barbecue tradition. That is, unless you count the delicacy sometimes called tube steak or Oklahoma tenderloin – but more accurately described as smoked bologna.

Smoked bologna is exactly what it sounds like: a tube of processed meat, often five or 10 pounds, that's sliced in half, scored and slow-smoked at a low temperature for several hours over hickory wood. It's sliced thickly and served as a sandwich, usually with a yellow mustard-based sauce. In Tennessee, where smoked bologna is also a regional delicacy, especially in Memphis, it's often served on white bread with hot sauce and coleslaw.

The origin of smoked bologna isn't well established, but it may date from the 1930s, the lean decade of the Dust Bowl, when an inexpensive, processed meat like bologna was a staple food. Today you'll find it at trendy barbecue joints like **Leo's** in Oklahoma City, **Knotty Pig BBQ** in Tulsa and **Jamil's Steakhouse**, with locations in both of those cities. It's also on the menu at the Tulsa, Broken Arrow and Catoosa locations of Oklahoma Joe's. But you won't find it at Joe's Kansas City, which is renowned for its pulled pork, ribs and burnt ends. The pitmasters there definitely aren't full of bologna.

Chicken-fried steak

See Texas

Like much of the cuisine of the Lone Star State, the dish of battered, deep-fried beef known as chicken-fried steak has crossed the border to become a specialty of Oklahoma as well. You'll find it all over Oklahoma City, with especially well-regarded versions at **Cheever's Cafe**, **Charleston's Restaurant** and **Sherri's Diner**.

Indian tacos

See Other foods of the Southwest (Navajo taco)

In Oklahoma, the Native American dish – known as Navajo tacos elsewhere – that uses fry bread as the base for a variety of toppings, is often called Indian tacos. A good place to sample them is **FireLake Fry Bread Taco** in Shawnee.

Coney Island hot dog

See Other foods of the Midwest

The Coney Island hot dog, a frankfurter with a tomato-based meat sauce and other toppings, is more closely associated with Michigan than Oklahoma, but you'll find a surprising number of standout coneys in the Sooner State. A few places to try include **Kim's Coney Shop** in Coweta; **Coney I-Lander**, with locations in Tulsa, Broken Arrow, Jenks and Owasso; and **The Original Coney Island** in Tulsa.

OTHER FOODS OF THE HEARTLAND

Bierock (Runza)

In the 1870s, thousands of German families who were living in Russia near the Volga River emigrated to Kansas and Nebraska, leaving the European political pressures of the day behind for the economic opportunities they anticipated in the U.S. Some of these immigrants put down roots in established cities like Topeka and Omaha, while others formed smaller communities in the Great Plains. In both states, you'll still see some place names that hint at their Germanic roots, as well as evidence of the impact these settlers made on Heartland cuisine: a savory pastry called a bierock. But like an ex-convict who's entered the witness-protection program, the bierock sometimes goes by a different name. Especially in Nebraska, this handheld pocket is more likely to be called a runza.

A runza – or bierock – is a meat pie with a yeasted dough that's typically filled with seasoned ground beef, cabbage or sauerkraut and onions. While their shapes can vary, they're more likely to be rounded in Kansas, and rectangular in Nebraska (which is why they are sometimes referred to there as runza sandwiches).

Linguists aren't sure about the origin of the word bierock – it may derive from the Russian word pirog (the root of the dumpling known as pierogi), or possibly from the Turkish word börek, which is also a meat-filled pastry. The genesis of the word runza is clearer – in 1949, siblings Sally Everett and Alex Brening opened a restaurant in Lincoln, Nebraska, called the **Runza Drive Inn**, serving a sandwich by the same name made with seasoned ground beef mixed with cabbage and onions. (The word runza itself derives from one of several different German antecedents, but the Anglicized word was eventually trademarked by the restaurant.)

Today there are more than 80 locations of the Runza chain, mostly in Nebraska, and the menu has expanded to include one sandwich topped with American cheese, and other flavors of runza including mushroom and Swiss, and BBQ bacon. You can also order runzas at Nebraska Cornhusker football games – or if you're a fan of former archrival Kansas, there's also a location of Runza in Lawrence. Other options, should you want to try the rounded, more pastry-like version, is to head to either **M&M Bierock** or the **Want Bierock Company & Coffee House** in Wichita. German bakeries are also good places to find bierocks, including **Augustine's Bakery** in Hays (just off I-70, halfway between Kansas City and Denver), where they're served as a lunch special on Wednesdays, and **The Breadbasket** in Newton, north of Wichita, which offers a German buffet on Friday and Saturday evenings that sometimes includes a bierock as one of the options. Just don't blow its cover by calling it a runza.

Kolache

See Other foods of the Midwest

The usually sweet, round pastries called kolache are a staple of the Czech community in South Dakota, and you can find them at local bakeries including **Pietz's Kuchen Kitchen** in Scotland. And the pastry is saluted each May by the citizens of Prague, Oklahoma, at the annual Kolache Festival, said to be the world's largest. In Prague, Nebraska, kolaches are a centerpiece of the annual Czech Heritage Day in August. This celebration is a little more low-key than the one that residents held in 1987, when they baked a massive cherry-filled kolache that was 15 feet in diameter and weighed over 2,600 pounds – just half the size of the one they prepared five years later. If you drive into Prague from the south, you'll see a road sign on Nebraska Highway 79 commemorating the achievement.

REGIONAL BBQ OF THE U.S.

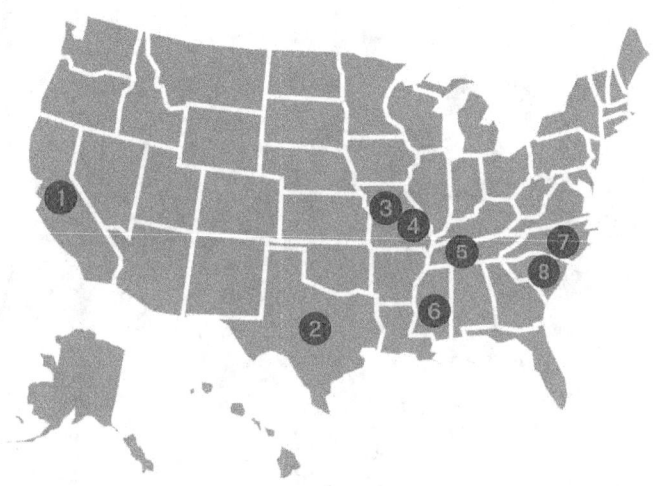

1 Santa Maria-style BBQ

2 Texas-style BBQ

3 Kansas City-style BBQ

4 St. Louis-style BBQ

5 Memphis-style BBQ

6 Alabama-style BBQ

7 North Carolina-style BBQ

8 South Carolina-style BBQ

Nachos

TEXAS

A road trip across the Lone Star State provides the opportunity to see world-class natural, historic and cultural wonders, like Big Bend National Park in West Texas, the Alamo in San Antonio and the Space Center in Houston. But along the way, make sure that you don't discount the appeal of Texas's culinary attractions. In addition to the world-class restaurants in its major cities, especially Dallas, Austin and Houston, the state is renowned for some of the most interesting and diverse food in America. Spend a week here and you'll begin to understand its barbecue traditions, its fusion of Mexican flavors and local ingredients thar forged a Tex-Mex culinary identity, and its strands of multiculturalism that may surprise you if you're expecting Texas to be little more than meat-centric cowboy country.

The story of Texas begins with the Native Americans who first settled there and the early Spanish explorers who arrived in 1519. But it wasn't until after more than a century of Spanish rule, followed by a brief period when Texas was part of Mexico, and then the establishment of the independent Republic of Texas in 1836, that the U.S. annexed Texas and granted it statehood, in 1845. In the subsequent decades, cattle ranching became one of the most important industries in the state, and the American cowboy, which grew out of the traditions of the Mexican cattle drivers called vaqueros, as well as the influence of the English settlers moving westward, helped establish the state's early culinary identity.

Cooking on the frontier made use of simple ingredients cooked over an open fire or in a mobile kitchen known as a chuck wagon. Staples included such dishes as slow-cooked beans, flavored with molasses and water (a far cry from the modern take on cowboy beans, in which pinto beans are simmered with ground beef, bacon and a sweet, tangy sauce that includes ketchup, brown sugar and barbecue sauce); pan de campo, or cowboy bread, cooked in a cast-iron skillet over an open fire with just a few staple ingredients (and today known as the official state bread); and sonofabitch stew, made with the flesh, organs and marrow gut of a freshly killed calf. You'll rarely find these dishes now, even in the most traditional of Texas restaurants. But the influence of cowboy culture is still present in the barbecue of the Hill Country in West Texas, where meat is cooked directly on wood-fired grills, in the dish known as fajitas (which emerged from the practice of Mexican cowboys cooking strips of skirt steak over an open campfire or grill during the 1930s), and, of course, in the steakhouses that serve beef from the many cattle ranches across the state.

Several other familiar dishes reflect the incorporation of food traditions from Northern Mexico, which evolved into a distinctive cuisine called Tex-Mex. The dishes that initially took hold in South Texas along the Rio Grande Valley, and eventually spread to San Antonio and further north, make heavy use of flour tortillas, beef and chili peppers, especially the native chiltepin. Later, Tex-Mex cooking folded in processed American ingredients, including shredded Cheddar or Monterey Jack cheese, canned beans and packaged tortilla shells. As you explore Texas, especially in the southern part of the state, look out for Tex-Mex dishes such as migas, an Austin breakfast staple with scrambled eggs and strips of fried corn tortillas; nachos, a sports-bar stalwart with a surprising history; traditional Texas-style chili, which unlike other regional styles, doesn't include tomatoes or beans; and South Texas barbacoa, a regional variation of barbecue that's often made with cow's head.

When you imagine a plate of Texas barbecue, though, you're more likely thinking of the Central Texas style, with its signature meat being a dry-rubbed, slow-smoked brisket. For this we can thank the German and Czech immigrants who came to Texas shortly after it became part of the U.S.; by 1860, the state's population included about 20,000 Germans, including butchers who developed new methods of smoking meat. These settlers also brought their tradition of breading and pan-frying wiener schnitzel, and extended it to widely available, inexpensive cuts of beef, creating the classic Texas dish known as chicken-fried steak.

Czech immigrants, who began coming to Texas in the 1840s and 1850s, and whose numbers had reached over 60,000 a century later, made additional significant contributions to the Texas food scene. Dishes like the kolache, a sweet, fruit-filled pastry, have become widely available thanks to Czech bakers, and the kolache's savory cousin, klobasnik, often consisting of sausage wrapped inside a yeasted dough, was invented in the town of West in 1953. Today you'll still find pockets of Texas, especially in the central part of the state, where Old World Czech heritage remains an important part of its culture.

Other ethnic traditions have contributed to the vibrancy of Texas's modern culinary landscape. Large communities of Vietnamese immigrants began settling in East Texas in the 1970s, and about half of the roughly 200,000 Vietnamese in the state today reside in Houston, which is home to dozens of storefronts specializing in pho as well as other traditional dishes. But H-Town is also where you'll also find a fusion of these flavors with local ingredients, such as at the James Beard-nominated **Crawfish & Noodles**, which draws upon the city's proximity to the Gulf Coast and Cajun country. In Dallas, you'll find plenty of steakhouses and taquerias, as you might expect, but you should also be on the lookout for the upscale Japanese and Italian restaurants that cater to well-heeled diners. And in Austin, you won't want to miss the well-regarded restaurants that feature Korean, Indian and Ethiopian flavors. You'll even find some places that specialize in vegetables – when it's finally time for a break from eating nothing but brisket and carne asada tacos.

TEXAS

Texas-style BBQ

If there's a single food you should make sure to eat during your trip to Texas, it's barbecue. But calling barbecue a single food is a bit misleading – in Texas, the word covers four distinctly different styles of cooking meat, as well as the sides that accompany each. So you could easily eat nothing but barbecue for a week and never sample the same meal twice.

Perhaps the most well-known style of Texas barbecue comes from the central part of the state, in the area that includes Austin and part of the Texas Hill Country. Barbecue here is characterized by meat – often beef brisket – that's seasoned with little more than a dry rub of salt and pepper. It's smoked for hours at a low temperature, usually over wood such as post oak, mesquite or pecan. The meat is typically served on butcher paper or on a plate (not as a sandwich), and if there's sauce, it's on the side. Pickles, onions and white bread tend to be provided as accompaniments, but the meat is the star of the show. This style of barbecue originated with the German and Czech immigrants who came to Texas during the mid-19th century, who developed techniques of smoking meats as a way of extending their shelf life.

In East Texas, barbecue consists of meat – either beef brisket or pork ribs – that's also slow-smoked over indirect heat, usually hickory wood. It's typically marinated in a sweet, tomato-based sauce. The meat tends to be chopped up and served on a bun with pickles and hot sauce. You're likely to find some traditional Southern sides like potato salad, mac-and-cheese, pinto beans or cornbread, as well as smoked boudin sausage or hot links.

When you're looking for steaks, pork chops or chicken, as well as sausages, head to the Hill Country in West Texas, where the meat is typically grilled directly over hot coals produced by burning mesquite wood. This method of quick cooking is known as the cowboy style of barbecue, and the meat usually develops a characteristic smoky flavor. Standard Texas barbecue sides like pinto beans, potato salad and coleslaw often accompany the main dishes here.

In South Texas, the barbecue tradition is heavily influenced by Mexican cooking. The meat – which traditionally is a cow's head, but can also be beef tongue or a whole goat or lamb – is marinated in a sweet, molasses-based sauce. It's cooked in an in-ground pit using mesquite wood, with a layer of leaves covering the coals. The resulting fall-off-the-bone meat is known as barbacoa, and it's often served in tortillas, with accompaniments of salsa, cilantro and onions.

Ask any Texan nearby and they'll happily tell you about their favorite barbecue joint (as long as you promise not to give away their secret). A few places that frequently rank among the top barbecue spots in Texas include **Franklin Barbecue** in Austin, where pitmaster Aaron Franklin has become nationally recognized for his beef brisket; **Pecan Lodge** in Dallas, which serves up the best brisket I've ever tasted, as well as enormous, one-pound beef ribs; **Gatlin's BBQ** in Houston, known for its East Texas-style sandwiches as well as combination platters; and **The Salt Lick** in Driftwood in the Hill Country (with other locations in Round Rock and at both the Dallas and Austin airports), famous for its brisket, sausage and pork ribs. And if you're interested in South Texas-style barbecue, visit **Vera's Backyard Bar-B-Que** in Brownsville, where traditional barbacoa de cabeza (cow's head) is cooked up every weekend. Looking for something off the beaten track? Wherever you happen to be in the state, follow your nose to the smell of smoked meat and discover your own new favorite spot.

Fajitas

In 2016, the San Francisco Chronicle reported that the restaurant chain Chili's had sold 60 million pounds of fajitas that year, and was responsible for something called "the fajita effect." That's when one diner sees a sizzling platter of fajitas being brought to another's table, and immediately wants to order it for themselves.

But while Chili's may have helped popularize fajitas in mainstream America, the dish dates back nearly a century, and has roots in several Texas towns including Kyle (between Austin and San Antonio), Pharr (on the Mexican border in the Rio Grande Valley), Houston and Austin.

The word fajita is the diminutive of the Spanish word faja, meaning strip or belt. This refers to the little strips of skirt steak that were used in the original form of the dish. Mexican cowboys who were working in the ranches of South and West Texas in the 1930s cooked these trimmings over a campfire or grill and wrapped them in flour tortillas, sometimes calling them tacos al carbon (cooked over coals).

The next milestone in the history of fajitas came in 1969, when a meat market manager from Austin who later became known as the Fajita King, Sonny Falcón, started selling them, to great acclaim, at a taco concession stand in Kyle. That same year, Otilia Garza added them to the menu of the Round-Up Restaurant in Pharr, introducing the idea of presenting fajitas on a sizzling platter with tortillas for making tacos, as well as condiments such as chopped onions, pico de gallo, guacamole and shredded cheese.

A few years later, in 1973, Ninfa Rodriguez opened a Tex-Mex restaurant in Houston called **Ninfa's**, which sold tacos al carbon and further popularized the dish in Texas. **Chili's** first opened its doors in 1975, but it wasn't until nearly a decade later that it first added fajitas to its menu, leading to a crush of people lining up to try the platters of sizzling beef that came alongside grilled peppers and onions. By then, a chef named George Weidmann had opened a restaurant at the Hyatt Regency in Austin, in 1982, and put a dish called sizzling fajitas on its menu, using tender sirloin as the cut of beef. His version became so popular that two years later, Weidmann was selling 13,000 orders of fajitas per month, and many other Hyatt locations also began serving it. As the fajita craze continued during the 1980s, other Tex-Mex restaurants started expanding the definition of fajitas beyond beef, serving similar preparations of chicken, shrimp and vegetables, and the dish's popularity hasn't really waned in the years since.

If you're on a mission to trace the history of fajitas in Texas, you should know that the Round-Up Restaurant is now closed – but in Houston, Ninfa's is still going strong. And nearly four decades after Weidmann's innovation, the **Hyatt Regency** in Austin still serves up fajitas on its dinner menu. As of 2021, there were over 1,200 branches of Chili's in the U.S., including over 200 in Texas – so you won't have any shortage of places where you might fall victim to the fajita effect.

Nachos

A plate of nachos can take many forms, from a gussied-up platter of fancy ingredients to a simple pile of chips with melted cheese and maybe a few jalapeños. But if it weren't for the quick thinking of a restaurant employee named Ignacio Anaya – or the football broadcaster Howard Cosell – we might not have this tasty snack within arm's reach.

The story of nachos begins in 1943, when a group of Army wives crossed the border from Texas into Piedras Negras, Mexico. They went to Club Victoria looking for something to eat, but with the cook nowhere to be found, the maître d', Anaya, went into the kitchen and found some fried corn tortillas. He melted grated Wisconsin Cheddar cheese on top, added some pickled jalapeños and put together a plate for the Americans. When they asked him what it was called, he quickly responded, using his own nickname, "Nachos especiales."

Over the next few decades, the popularity of Nacho's dish started to spread throughout Texas and the Southwest. Then, in 1976, Frank Liberto introduced a version of nachos at Arlington Stadium during Texas Rangers baseball games, using warmed, processed cheese sauce to help reduce the time customers spent waiting in line. The ballpark nachos proved to be such a hit that the Rangers generated over $800,000 in sales during the first season they sold nachos during games. Other sports stadiums began to serve the spicy snack, and two years later, during a Dallas Cowboys game, someone brought Monday Night Football broadcaster Howard Cosell a plate of nachos. He couldn't stop talking about them on air that night as well as over the next several weeks, which cemented their foothold as a staple at both sports bars and stadium concession stands.

One of the places where nachos first became popular in Texas is San Antonio, and that's a good place to explore nachos at both the high and low ends of the spectrum. If you're feeling fancy, **Acenar** on the River Walk features fried oysters on yucca chips with charred pineapple. On the less elevated side, one well-regarded spot is **Chacho's**, a 24-hour Tex-Mex joint. There, you can choose between single-layer or piled-high nachos, with either bean and cheese, chicken or beef, or you can order a combination platter called Monster Kong Nachos that has accompaniments of extra queso, sour cream and guacamole. And if you're visiting the **AT&T Center** for a Spurs game, you could always pick up a plate of stadium nachos. While the players are dunking the ball into the basket, you'll be dunking your chips into a tub of processed cheese.

Texas-style chili

In 1977, chili became the official state dish of Texas. But that's about all that Lone Star chili-lovers can agree on. The two ingredients included in every Texas chili recipe are beef, usually cubed shoulder, and chili peppers, either dried or powdered. Things get contentious when cooks decide to add either tomatoes or beans, vegetables that many chili eaters consider blasphemous. True Texas-style chili, they say, is little more than meat and spices, cooked down until the stew is thickened and takes on a deep hue that gives it the nickname "a bowl of red."

Chili started to become popular in Texas in the mid-19th century when local women began serving up tamales, chili and other dishes cooked over open flames in the plazas of San Antonio. Once railroad service reached the city in 1877 and more people discovered the food of the ladies who became known as the Chili Queens, word started to spread to other cities, many of which soon had their own chili parlors. The Chili Queens lasted in San Antonio until the early 1940s, by which time the dish was popular all over the country, with many places developing their own regional styles of chili con carne, or chili with meat.

Although San Antonio is no longer the center of Texas chili culture, you'll still find a good bowl of red at classic Tex-Mex restaurants there, such as **Mi Tierra Cafe y Panaderia** in Market Square. Elsewhere in the state it's worth checking out the chili at **Texas Chili Parlor** in Austin, which serves classic Texas-style chili as well as white pork chili and venison chili with black beans. In Houston, **Molina's Cantina** has been dishing out its classic chili con carne, topped with melted cheese and chopped onions, since 1941. And in Grapevine, near the Dallas-Fort Worth International Airport, **Tolbert's Restaurant & Chili Parlor** serves chili from a recipe invented by Frank X. Tolbert, founder of the World Championship Chili Cookoff, who opened the restaurant with his son in 1976. But even though Tolbert also wrote a history of chili called A Bowl of Red, his namesake restaurant isn't dogmatic about how it should be eaten. If you prefer, you can order the "north of the border" chili, a style that (gasp!) includes beans.

Frito pie

See New Mexico

Many people erroneously believe that Frito pie was invented in San Antonio by the mother of the inventor of the crunchy corn snack. (It was actually created by the Frito-Lay marketing department.) But if facts don't stand in the way of your desire to try it while you're in Texas, you can find well-regarded versions in Alamo City at **RJ's Snack Shack**, **The Shack** and the delightfully named **Munchies...itsallgood**.

Carne guisada

Carne guisada and carne asada are both made with beef and served on tortillas, but don't confuse these two kinds of taco fillings. While the latter is thinly sliced flank or skirt steak that's been marinated and grilled, the former is a rich, hearty stew made with round steak that's cooked slowly in thickened beef stock, along with tomatoes and chiles as well as other aromatics such as cumin and garlic.

You'll see carne asada nearly everywhere around the country where tacos are sold, but carne guisada is mainly found in South Texas, especially around San Antonio. It's usually served as a filling for flour tortillas, but rarely has any accompaniments except perhaps for some melted cheese or a side of rice and beans.

If you're visiting San Antonio, it's worth seeking out versions of this classic Tex-Mex dish at restaurants such as **Garcia's Mexican Food**, **Henry's Puffy Tacos**, **Little Taco Factory Mexican Restaurant** and **Fidelos Mexican Restaurant**. At this last spot, you can order several different kinds of lunch tacos a la carte, so it's a good place to determine which is your favorite – and ensure that you're not mistaking carne guisada for its similar-sounding cousin.

Puffy taco

If you happen to be visiting San Antonio during baseball season, don't miss seeing the Texas League minor league franchise known as the Missions. It's home to one of the most unusual mascots in all of professional sports: Henry the Puffy Taco, who's known for being chased down and tackled by a child during a mid-inning race around the bases.

Henry is dressed in a brown tortilla coat, a red tomato cap and an overstuffed green and yellow filling of lettuce and cheese. But those elements don't fully encapsulate what makes a puffy taco unique. In contrast to typical hard tacos, which make use of fried corn tortillas, puffy tacos are created with uncooked masa that's deep-fried until it puffs up, giving the shell a crisp exterior and a soft interior. They're served with ground beef, shredded chicken or other fillings, and as Henry's costume suggests, are usually topped with lettuce, tomatoes and Cheddar cheese.

Puffy tacos were the invention of several members of the Lopez family. They started to become famous after 1978, when the youngest sibling, Henry, opened a restaurant in San Antonio called **Henry's Puffy Tacos**. But his brother Ray, who operated a restaurant called **Ray's Drive Inn**, had begun serving a similar dish known as crispy tacos more than a decade earlier. And another brother, Arturo, gave the dish its new name in 1977, when he opened a spot in Southern California called Arturo's Puffy Tacos.

Today you'll find puffy tacos in San Antonio at both Henry's and Ray's, as well as at countless other Mexican restaurants around the city. They're also popular at Tex-Mex joints in nearby Austin such as **Vamonos** and **Vivo Austin**. But don't look for puffy tacos at Nelson Wolff Stadium, home of the Missions. Though the team even changed its uniforms for a few games back in 2020 so they could play as the Puffy Tacos, you'll only encounter standard ballpark food (as well as a few Mexican specialties) at its concession stands. But please, don't try to eat Henry. He has a hard enough time being knocked down during every game.

Migas

When you're staying in Austin, there's no better way to explore the city's cuisine than by eating tacos for every meal. And even if you've been out late into the night listening to music, it's still worth waking up before noon, as many taco spots here specialize in breakfast tacos that feature eggs, meat, cheese and salsa all wrapped up in fresh tortillas. (You'll also find great breakfast tacos in San Antonio as well as border cities such as Laredo, where they're called mariachis.)

In the unlikely event you want to eat something other than a taco, though, another signature Austin breakfast dish you should try is migas – a Spanish word meaning crumbs. Migas is a Tex-Mex dish that features scrambled eggs and crispy strips of fried corn tortillas – the crumbs – that are typically mixed with a tomato-based ranchero salsa. It's endlessly customizable with other ingredients such as onions, chiles, beans and cheese. It's usually eaten as a plated dish, but if you don't want to break your taco-eating streak, it can also be served inside a flour or corn tortilla.

You won't have any trouble finding migas in Austin, but a few recommended spots are **Mi Madre's** in East Austin, which also offers a variety of breakfast tacos; **Veracruz All Natural**, with a half-dozen locations in the Austin area that serve up both a traditional migas taco and one with poblano peppers and black beans; and **Amaya's Taco Village**, an Austin institution with locations in the North Loop and South Austin, where the migas are served plated with refried beans, potatoes and fresh tortillas. Grab a table as soon as they open and you'll still have plenty of time to maximize your taco consumption during the rest of the day.

Chicken-fried steak

If you hear someone talking about CFS in a Texas restaurant, they're probably not discussing chronic fatigue syndrome or misspelling the name of a nationwide drugstore chain. More likely, they're about to order chicken-fried steak, a preparation of beef with a perplexing modifier.

Despite its name, this dish doesn't contain any poultry. Actually, chicken-fried steak is made with inexpensive cuts of beef, such as cube steak or round steak, that are battered and deep-fried, similar to the way you might prepare fried chicken. It's typically served with a cream gravy, as well as sides such as potatoes and Texas toast. (A similar dish, country-fried steak, is usually pan-fried and served with a brown gravy, although the boundary between the two dishes is sometimes blurry.)

It's likely that chicken-fried steak originated with German or Austrian immigrants who came to the Lone Star State during the mid-1800s, though the dish didn't become widespread until the middle of the 20th century. In both countries, wiener schnitzel was a common way of cooking meat such as veal or pork, and with the wide availability of beef in Texas, it was natural that a similar preparation would be used for cheap cuts of steak. The city of Lamesa, west of Dallas, claims to be the place where chicken-fried steak was invented, when, in 1911, a cook was said to have misread a waitress's written order for separate dishes of chicken and fried steak. This story is likely apocryphal (despite Governor Rick Perry's declaration in 2011 that Lamesa was the birthplace of CFS), but still, the city hosts a chicken-fried steak festival annually.

There are numerous restaurants throughout Texas (and Oklahoma) where you can find credible versions of chicken-fried steak. A few recommended spots include **Jake & Dorothy's Cafe** in Stephenville, southwest of Dallas; **Gristmill River Restaurant & Bar** in New Braunfels; and **Mary's Cafe** in Strawn, west of Dallas. If you'd prefer to order something with only one meat in its name, another option at Mary's is the chicken-fried chicken. But keep in mind that almost nobody calls it CFC. You wouldn't want to confuse it with a chemical compound that contributes to global warming.

King Ranch casserole

When you find yourself deep in the heart of South Texas, outside of Corpus Christi, a good way to immerse yourself in the state's culture is with a tour at King Ranch. It's the largest cattle farm in the U.S. and bigger than the state of Rhode Island. And though the ranch isn't exactly known for its poultry, the dish that became known as King Ranch casserole was possibly named for it sometime in the 1950s, though its precise origin isn't known, and the connection to the ranch is loose at best.

King Ranch casserole contains layers of corn tortillas or tortilla chips, shredded chicken, cheese and a sauce made with diced tomatoes, chiles, bell peppers, onions and cream of mushroom as well as cream of chicken soup. The dish became popular enough in the Lone Star State that First Lady Lady Bird Johnson included it in her collection of signature recipes that were served at the President's ranch in Stonewall, Texas, in the early 1970s after her husband Lyndon left office.

King Ranch casserole is more a community cookbook staple than a restaurant-quality dish. But one place you can sample its flavors is at **King Ranch Texas Kitchen** in Houston, a steakhouse that opened in 2020 as a partnership between King Ranch and the Fertitta family. The King Ranch chicken enchilada features smoked chicken in a creamy mushroom sauce, with salsa verde, pico de gallo and pickled red onions. But when I dine at this restaurant, I'll probably order a sirloin, a ribeye or a porterhouse – any of which would have a much closer link to the cattle of King Ranch than its perhaps-namesake chicken casserole.

Texas toast

When it comes to sliced bread, everything's thicker in Texas. And more buttery, too.

Texas toast is white bread that's sliced about twice as thick as a normal sandwich loaf, buttered on both sides, and grilled or broiled until it's a light golden-brown. Sometimes garlic is added to the butter, and cheese may be sprinkled on one side of the bread before it's toasted. It's often served alongside saucy meat dishes like chicken-fried steak or barbecue, but it can also be used for making sandwiches.

This style of toast dates back to 1941, when Royce Hailey, the owner of the Pig Stand drive-in restaurant in Beaumont, requested that his bread supplier slice its loaves thicker than usual for his order. But the slices were too big to fit in the kitchen's toaster, so a cook named Wiley W. W. Cross suggested buttering them and toasting them in the oven. (Another version of the story dates the creation to 1946, at the Denton location of the same chain, which is also said to have invented the onion ring.)

You can find Texas toast at just about any diner or barbecue joint across the state, as well as at the fast-food chain **Whataburger**, with over 700 locations in the Lone Star State alone, where you can enjoy either a patty melt or a chicken strip sandwich served on Texas toast. At over 900 calories for either sandwich, it's a sign that everything is more fattening in Texas, too.

Klobasnik

The cuisine of the Lone Star State isn't just about Tex-Mex and BBQ. You might be surprised to learn that about 200,000 of the state's inhabitants (a little less than one percent of its population) trace their ancestry to the Czech Republic. These

Other Texas dishes to sample:

- **Corn dog**, a hot dog or sausage on a stick that's battered in corn meal and deep-fried. It was likely introduced in the U.S. by German immigrants to Texas in the 1920s, and popularized by Carl and Neil Fletcher, who sold "Corny Dogs" at the State Fair of Texas in the late 1930s or early 1940s. Originally corn dogs were made without sticks, but a patent for preparing fried food on a stick was issued in 1929, and impaling a corn dog on one became a standard way of serving it. Try one at the State Fair of Texas in Dallas if you're visiting the Lone Star State in the fall, or head to **The Corndog Company** in Austin for a taste of this specialty year-round.
- **Picadillo**, a mixture of ground beef, chili peppers, tomatoes, onions and garlic that's usually used as a filling for tacos. You'll have no trouble finding it on Mexican restaurant menus, but a couple of recommended spots include **El Castillo** in San Antonio and **Tacos A Go Go** in Houston.
- **Menudo**, a Tex-Mex soup made with tripe and hominy in a spicy broth. It's typically only served on New Year's Day or on weekends because some believe it helps cure the symptoms of a hangover. A competition for the best menudo in Texas, the Menudo Bowl, is held annually in Laredo. If you're recovering from a Friday or Saturday night of partying too much, try the versions at **Morenita Barbacoa** in San Antonio and **Taqueria Laredo** in Dallas.
- **Borracho beans**, meaning drunken, a South Texas dish of pinto beans cooked in dark beer with bacon, chili peppers, cumin, cilantro, onions and garlic. It's often eaten in tortillas as an accompaniment to carne asada or as a bean dip. One place you can sample it is **Tlahco Mexican Kitchen** in San Antonio.

- **Texas caviar**, also known as cowboy caviar, a mixture of pickled black-eyed peas with chili peppers, onions and bell peppers that's usually presented as a dip for tortilla chips. It was created in 1940 by Helen Corbitt, who first served it on New Year's Eve at the Houston Country Club. You can try it as a side dish to smoked meats at **Roegels Barbecue Co** in Houston.
- **Pecan pie**, made with a pie crust that's typically filled with a combination of pecans, Karo syrup, eggs, sugar, butter and vanilla. Recipes for it first appeared in Texas cookbooks in the 1870s and 1880s, and one that more closely resembles the modern pecan pie was published in a St. Louis cookbook in 1898, submitted by a woman from Texas. The dish became popular starting in the mid-1920s, after the manufacturer of Karo syrup, which was by then widely available, began printing a recipe for pecan pie on its label. (In Arkansas, this confection is sometimes known as Karo nut pie.) Celebrate the Lone Star State's official dessert in its capital city, Austin, at **Tiny Pies** and **Upper Crust Bakery**.
- **Texas sheet cake**, a chocolate cake with a coconut-pecan frosting that's similar to German chocolate cake (which became popular in Texas when the Dallas Morning News published a recipe for it in 1957, referencing a type of chocolate, Baker's German's sweet chocolate, that had been invented a century before by an American baker named Samuel German). Texas sheet cake, sometimes called Texas funeral cake because of the practice of bringing one to a post-funeral meal, is a single-layer cake that's typically big enough to serve a crowd. One place to order it – or grab a slice of German chocolate cake if it's just for you – is **Jen's Place Bakery & Cafe** in Dallas.

Czech Texans have left their stamp on its food culture through a savory pastry known as a klobasnik, sometimes spelled as klobasnek. It uses the dough from the sweet Czech pastry called kolache (*see Other foods of the Midwest*), and wraps it around fillings such as sausage (the iconic klobasnik), ham, cheese and jalapeños.

The klobasnik was invented in the town of West (confusingly located in central Texas) in 1953 at the Village Bakery, which had become known for its fruit-filled kolaches. Although this establishment closed a few years ago, West remains a center of Czech heritage, and you can still find kolaches and klobasniky (sometimes just called savory kolaches) in bakeries all over town. A few well-regarded spots include the **Czech Stop**, **Gerick's** and **Slovacek's**, all of which offer a variety of flavors of kolaches and klobasniky. And if you happen to find yourself in Texas in late September, don't miss the annual Kolache Festival in the town of Hallettsville, halfway between Houston and San Antonio. It's a good place to sample these pastries and czech them off your list of foods to try.

Sopaipilla

See New Mexico

Tex-Mex restaurants sometimes offer complimentary servings of this cinnamon-dusted, honey-coated fried dough, but the dish can also appear on the dessert menu with ice cream or other toppings. A few places where you can try them include **La Calle Doce** in Dallas, **Mi Tierra Cafe y Panaderia** in San Antonio and **La Posada** in Austin.

Fried Coke

In 2006, inventor Abel Gonzales Jr. won the State Fair of Texas competition for most creative deep-fried food with a dish he called fried Coke. Gonzales had won a Big Tex Choice Award the previous year for his creation of a fried peanut butter, jelly and banana sandwich, but fried Coke helped solidify his nickname of Fried Jesus, a reputation he would later cement with his inventions of other fried dishes including deep-fried butter and fried jambalaya.

Fried Coke is a Coke-flavored batter that's deep-fried and then topped with Coke syrup, whipped cream, cinnamon sugar and a cherry. Gonzales sold about 35,000 cups of fried Coke at the 2006 State Fair of Texas, and the dish's popularity led to its rollout at dozens of other state fairs the following year. Today you'll typically find it at state fairs and carnivals throughout the country.

If you're visiting Dallas in late September or October, the State Fair of Texas is the place to go to find this sweet Texas invention. But if you're seeking a new frontier in fried food, other delicacies you can try at the fair include deep-fried pancakes, deep-fried peach cobbler, deep-fried Oreos and even deep-fried shrimp étouffée. All of which would taste great with a cool, refreshing serving of deep-fried Coke.

Chicago-style pizza

THE MIDWEST

When you're visiting the Midwest, maybe to attend a conference in Chicago, to visit your aunt in Des Moines or to watch a Big Ten football game in Columbus, you'll encounter one of the most significant food regions of the entire country. That's not only on account of its substantial size – the region encompasses about 15 percent of the land area of the lower 48 states – but also because of the sheer number and diversity of specialties that have become ingrained as iconic examples of American cuisine.

Before going any further, it's worth taking a moment to discuss what exactly I mean by the Midwest. Regional boundaries are fluid, and there's often substantial disagreement about which states each region should include. In a survey done by the website FiveThirtyEight in 2014, for example, only about 80 percent of respondents thought that Illinois should be in the Midwest (about which there should be little doubt), with lesser consensus about the states nearby.

In this book there are eight states that constitute the Midwest: Illinois, Missouri, Minnesota, Iowa, Wisconsin, Indiana, Michigan and Ohio. While there's often overlap between the foods that represent individual states – such as between Minnesota and Wisconsin, which share a common geography in the upper Midwest – there are many cases of dishes that are prevalent in only one state or city. You'll see that reflected in the organization of this chapter, which discusses state-specific dishes first (with separate sections for the foods of major metropolitan areas), followed by dishes that cross state lines. And when a particular food that's characteristic of the Midwest is treated more fully elsewhere, I've included a reference to that section as well.

So how did this region develop the dishes that we think of today as Midwestern cuisine? There are three major influences that shaped what's eaten in this octet of states, and the story that helps explain the food of the Midwest begins more than 200 years ago.

The first factor is the way in which local settlers, like those in other regions, optimized their use of the natural resources that were available to them. In the final 20 years of the 18th century, when colonists began to migrate west to the area that had long been occupied by Native people, the settlers lived off the land, growing corn, beans and potatoes, fishing in local lakes and rivers and hunting for wild game. In the subsequent decades, as these people established farms and incorporated more products from the region's fields and streams, they developed foods that made use of the local produce, meat and seafood.

Along these lines, two representative dishes that are still eaten today are Minnesota's walleye sandwich and wild rice soup, both of which are staples in the North Star State. In Wisconsin, you'll find cheese curds everywhere, given the significance of the state's dairy farms. And ever-present in the Midwest is corn, either as an ingredient in bread, candy and dozens of other foods, or as a component of barbecue sides and hotdish casseroles.

Second, by the late 19th century, what Midwesterners ate also began to be influenced by the development of the meat processing industry and by the railroad networks that made it possible for livestock and food to be widely transported from place to place. From 1865 until the 1920s, Chicago was the center of U.S. meatpacking production, with its stockyards processing more than 80 percent of all of the beef and pork consumed in the country. Naturally, the Chicago-style hot dog and the Italian beef sandwich, which both made use of meat scraps, later became important building blocks of the city's cuisine during the Depression years.

Although Chicago was once described by the poet Carl Sandburg as Hog Butcher for the World, other cities were also important meat processing centers. These included Cincinnati, which became known as Porkopolis and where German immigrants created the breakfast sausage called goetta; Kansas City, which was the second-most important city for cattle production, inspiring its barbecue tradition that features ribs as well as the fatty pieces of brisket known as burnt ends; and St. Louis, where railroad magnates financed an important stockyard in its eastern suburbs in the 1870s, and where spare ribs and pork steaks later became iconic elements of local cuisine.

And finally, also critical to the formation of Midwestern regional food traditions was the pattern of ethnic and religious immigration by the people who arrived in America, mostly from Europe but also from Asia and Latin America, beginning in the mid-19th century and continuing up until the present day. These settlers created both new American versions of traditional foods, and in some cases completely new dishes.

Among the most significant groups of immigrants were those who came from Italy, who can take credit not only for Chicago's Italian beef and sausage sandwiches but for St. Louis's toasted ravioli and Iowa's steak de Burgo; Poland, who brought foods such as pierogi and pączki to Cleveland, Chicago and other cities and created the dish of skewered pork known as city chicken; Greece and Macedonia, who are responsible for Chicago's Maxwell Street Polish and gyro, Cincinnati-style chili and Detroit's Coney Island hot dog; Germany, who can claim heritage in Wisconsin's beer brats and its tradition of a Friday-night fish fry as well as Ohio's sauerkraut balls and goetta; and Scandinavia, who brought the kringle pastry and the flatbread known as lefse to pockets of Wisconsin and Minnesota, as well as a bitter liquor called malort that's a staple at Chicago watering holes.

Groups of religious settlers also helped shape the cuisine of the region. The Lutherans, for example, are the forebears of hotdish, eaten widely across Minnesota, while the Quakers can take credit for Indiana's sugar cream pie.

And more recently, the influx of Latin Americans and the migration of Blacks from the Mississippi Delta, who worked alongside Mexican farmhands, helped inspire Chicago dishes like the jibarito and the mother-in-law sandwich. Meanwhile, Chinese expats created new culinary traditions like Missouri's St. Paul sandwich and Springfield-style cashew chicken, both of which adapted Asian flavors into dishes that aimed to appeal to local diners.

As you travel across the Midwest, you'll have many options for both high-end and low-end eating. At the top end of the spectrum, the region is known for having some of the country's best places for dining out, like Chicago's **Alinea**, the Midwest's only three-star Michelin restaurant. But other cities, especially Minneapolis, Cincinnati, Detroit and Cleveland, are also known for having a top-notch restaurant scene, with many of its chefs inspired by global flavors. And throughout the region, you'll also find old-school steakhouses and Italian joints worthy of a splurge.

But if you truly want to eat like a Midwesterner, the most efficient way to use your dining dollars is to seek out the foods that each city and state is most famous for. You'd be remiss, for example, in not trying Chicago-style deep-dish pizza and comparing it to the varieties eaten in Detroit and St. Louis. Head to Wisconsin to sink your teeth into a butter burger. Or do as the locals do in Cincinnati and order a five-way bowl of chili over spaghetti. But don't sleep on some of the region's lesser-known dishes that are as fascinating as they are flavorful. Why pass up the chance to eat a tenderloin sandwich in Indiana, a loose meat sandwich in Iowa or some gooey butter cake in Missouri?

You might also be lucky enough to encounter one of the Midwestern dishes that aren't typically eaten in restaurants (and therefore aren't featured in detail in this book). Instead, at community potlucks or church gatherings, you'll find delicacies that aim to feed a crowd, like Watergate salad – a mixture of pistachio instant pudding, canned pineapple and marshmallows

– or sweet potato casserole, made with yams, pecans and usually marshmallows as well. (Both of these dishes are also characteristic of the South.) And be sure to try something you've never heard of before (even if it doesn't contain marshmallows), because it just might become the best thing you've ever eaten in the Midwest – outside, of course, of your Aunt Debbie's cheesy chicken casserole.

ILLINOIS

CHICAGO

Chicago-style pizza

Former Daily Show host Jon Stewart raised the hackles of Chicago pizza lovers in 2013 when he called its hallmark deep-dish style, among other more colorful expressions, "tomato soup in a bread bowl," and famously, a "casserole."

While deep-dish pizza certainly provokes strong reactions, especially from those accustomed to more familiar styles, it's a Chicago specialty worth seeking out while you're in town. But don't overlook the other distinctive styles of pizza that the city has to offer, including stuffed pizza, pan pizza and the thin-cut version known as tavern style.

Deep-dish pizza is cooked in a pan that gives it a high edge, and is usually made with mozzarella cheese, a thick marinara sauce and, under the sauce, other toppings such as Italian sausage or pepperoni. Stuffed pizza is similar to deep dish, but with a second layer of crust that goes between the toppings and sauce. Pan pizza is also made in a deep vessel, but with a more traditional layering of ingredients, with the sauce on top of the crust, and cheese and any additional toppings above that. And tavern style, my favorite, is made with a thin crust and is typically cut in a checkerboard pattern rather than in traditional wedge-shaped slices.

There are several competing claims for the invention of deep-dish pizza, but an oft-repeated story is that it was created at Chicago's **Pizzeria Uno** in 1943, as a wartime method of extending a limited supply of meat and vegetables with ingredients for dough that did not need to be rationed. Other contenders for the originator include a name that may be a familiar one if you've eaten much pizza in Chicago: Adolpho Malnati, an employee at Pizzeria Uno, whose son went on to found one of the main purveyors of deep-dish pizza in Chicago. Another theory says that Alice Mae Redmond, a Black chef who worked at Pizzeria Uno and who went on to work at **Gino's East** for nearly three decades, was the person who perfected the deep-dish style.

If you're the sort who wants to eat their pizza with a knife and fork, either Pizzeria Uno or Gino's East, both in River North, with additional locations elsewhere in the city; **Lou Malnati's**, with about 20 branches throughout the metropolitan area; or **Pizano's Pizza & Pasta**, a chain of five restaurants also founded by the Malnati family, would be suitable options. But it's also worth seeking out the less iconic versions of Chicago-style pizza.

For stuffed pizza, a classic choice is **Giordano's**, which you'll find all across Chicagoland. Or try **Nancy's Pizza**, which, despite Giordano's claims to have created the style, served the city's first stuffed pizzas in the early 1970s, and now has a few dozen locations in the metropolitan area and Southern Illinois, plus branches in Missouri, Georgia and North Carolina.

If you want to sample pan pizza, a highly regarded choice is **Pequod's Pizza**, between Wicker Park and Lincoln Park, known for its caramelized crust (and also, as are Gino's East and Lou Malnati's, available nationwide via Goldbelly).

And for tavern-style pizza, a few good options are **Vito & Nick's Pizzeria** in Ashburn, which is believed to have invented the style; **Marie's Pizza & Liquors** in Albany Park, a combination liquor store and pizzeria that dates to the 1940s; and **Pat's Pizza** in Lincoln Park, my top choice when I lived in Chicago and the thin-crust pizza often voted as Chicago's best. Good news for Jon Stewart: The only casseroles on its menu are pasta dishes like lasagna and eggplant parmigiana.

Pizza puff

On the TV sitcom Parks and Recreation, the character Ben Wyatt, played by Adam Scott, is obsessed with calzones. But his co-worker (and later, wife) Leslie Knope, played by Amy Poehler, says they're "pointless" and just "pizza that's harder to eat." Well, if Ben and Leslie ever decided to road trip from Pawnee, Indiana, to Chicago, they'd do well to try one of the Windy City's hyper-local specialties, the pizza puff. While Ben would enjoy the calzone-like quality of this handheld pocket pastry, Leslie would undoubtedly find it much easier to eat – unless she, as many locals do, burned her mouth while taking her first bite.

A pizza puff isn't exactly a calzone, though. While it's usually filled with the kind of ingredients you'd find in one, like tomato sauce, mozzarella cheese and sausage or pepperoni, a calzone is typically baked, while a pizza puff is deep-fried. And the classic pizza puff, made by **Iltaco Foods**, is made with a wrapper that's more like a tortilla than pizza dough. If you consider the company's name, that makes perfect sense – but your assumption about its origin would be wrong. The "ta" in its name actually stands for tamales, which is what the company primarily sold until it introduced the pizza puff in 1976.

Today you'll find pizza puffs – often frozen ones from Iltaco that are popped in the deep fryer – at hot dog stands and other casual eateries in Chicago, as well at music festivals and sporting events. A spot where you'll find one filled with sausage and mozzarella and served piping hot is **Johnny's Beef & Gyros** in Lincoln Park. They're also on the menu at **Memo's Hot Dogs** in Pilsen, and at **Lulu's Hot Dogs** in the Medical District on the near West Side. Not in Chicagoland? You can order a 24-pack of pizza puffs directly from Iltaco's website. But you'll also see them in the frozen-food sections of groceries and convenience stores across the country, in 15 flavors including spinach and cheese, BBQ pulled pork and Buffalo chicken.

And while it's debatable whether pizza puffs are harder to eat than a pizza, Leslie Knope may be onto something. Because of their oblong shape, it would indeed be accurate for you to call them pointless.

Italian beef

The first season of the acclaimed TV series The Bear, starring Jeremy Allen White as Carmy, a chef who returns to Chicago to take over his family restaurant, The Original Beef of Chicagoland, brought nationwide attention to the Italian beef sandwiches that its overworked kitchen staff slings by the dozens.

Italian beef is a sandwich made from thinly cut roast beef, usually chuck or bottom round, that's cooked in a seasoned broth and served on a soft French roll, often one made by Turano Baking Company. But there's much more to it – the beef is typically topped with either sweet peppers or the spicy vegetable medley known as giardiniera, and the entire sandwich can be dipped in the jus to provide an extra level of beefy flavor.

There's an entire lingo around ordering Italian beef sandwiches: sweet or hot, referring to the peppers; dry, wet or dipped, the amount of jus you want on your sandwich, with dipped referring to the practice of dunking the entire sandwich in the jus, leaving it a dripping, soggy mess; and combo, with the addition of an Italian sausage. Other options include cheesy, with either Provolone or mozzarella, although traditionalists tend to forgo cheese on Italian beef sandwiches; and gravy bread, a dipped roll served without the beef, and with or without peppers.

Italian beef was created in the 1930s by Italian immigrants working in the stockyards who wanted to make use of cheaper cuts of beef. They cooked the meat in broth to tenderize it, and served the sandwiches at large gatherings such as weddings. Although there are competing historical claims, one restaurant that some believe invented the sandwich is **Al's #1 Beef**, which you can still visit in River North (with a second location in Tinley Park).

Other contenders for the title of the best Italian beef in Chicagoland include **Johnnie's Beef** in Elmwood Park and **Tony's Italian Beef** in West Lawn on the South Side. Or make a pilgrimage to **Mr. Beef on Orleans** in River North, the inspiration (and filming location) for the fictional restaurant in The Bear, where sales tripled in the months after the show started airing. You'll likely do better than the customers of the fictitious version of the restaurant, who after a rave review, overwhelmed it with to-go orders that it couldn't fulfill. Though you may have to wait in line for a sandwich, that'll give you plenty of time to think about whether you want yours dry, wet or dipped.

Chicago-style hot dog

"You know what really makes me sick to my stomach?" Clint Eastwood's character, Dirty Harry, asks in the 1983 film Sudden Impact. "Watching you stuff your face with those hot dogs. Nobody, I mean nobody, puts ketchup on a hot dog!"

The Chicago-style hot dog is one of the most iconic regional foods in the entire country. And if there's one cardinal rule about a Chicago dog, it's that you don't put ketchup on it. It's so sacrosanct that Chicago Bears fans at Soldier Field once loudly booed the teenage daughter of sportswriter Joe Posnanski when she dared to ask for ketchup from a hot dog vendor.

Why is ketchup so anathema to hot-dog-loving Chicagoans? It's probably because of the frankfurter's roots in Germany, where dogs were more commonly eaten with spicy mustard.

What does go on a Chicago dog is a variety of specific, colorful vegetables and condiments that explains why this style of hot dog is sometimes described as being "dragged through the garden." The classic Chicago dog includes a dill pickle spear, wedges of tomato, chopped white onions, pickled sport peppers, bright green pickle relish (often made by adding a few drops of blue food coloring), yellow mustard and a dash of celery salt. Its centerpiece is an all-beef frankfurter, often sourced from the local Vienna Beef company, that's either steamed or simmered. (When the hot dog is grilled, you'll usually see it described as a char-dog.) And it's served on a soft, steamed poppy-seed bun, a hallmark of a true Chicago-style dog.

The Chicago dog likely originated during the Great Depression, when Abe Drexler, owner of a hot dog stand called **Fluky's**, began selling a Depression Sandwich, a hot dog with the toppings of the modern Chicago dog, plus French fries, all for just a nickel. The venture was so successful that by the mid-1930s, Drexler was operating four Fluky's stands. Except for a decade following World War II, Fluky's was a fixture of the Chicago food scene for more than 75 years, and besides being famous for its Chicago-style hot dogs, was also known for its "hot dog gum," frankfurter-shaped chewing gum that it would hand out to customers.

Today there's only one remnant of the original Fluky's, a diner inside a Walmart in Niles that, if online reviews are to be believed, does not serve the best hot dogs in the Chicago area. You'll find better options at the nearly 2,000 hot dog stands throughout the city and environs – including **Wrigley Field**, where I make a point of ordering a Chicago dog during every Cubs game I attend. Some classic spots include **Superdawg Drive-In**, which opened in 1948 in Norwood Park (and now has a second location in Wheeling), and is known for substituting a pickled green tomato for a freshly cut one; **Gene & Jude's** in River Grove, another 1940s-era stand, whose trademark is to forgo the pickle and tomato on its dogs and add a pile of greasy French fries on top instead; **Portillo's**, Chicagoland's ubiquitous hot dog chain, which offers a classic Chicago dog as well as a plant-based version; **The Wiener's Circle** in Lincoln Park, dishing out char-dogs and famously rude service until the wee hours of the morning; and **Jimmy's Red Hots** in Humboldt Park, which has banned ketchup ever since it opened in 1954 – even on its French fries, which it serves with a habañero hot sauce.

Think you're going to challenge Chicago orthodoxy by bringing your own bottle of Heinz to one of these spots? Unless you're looking to start a fight, I wouldn't recommend it. The only reaction you're likely to get is, "Go ahead, make my day."

Francheezie

See Other foods of Pennsylvania (Texas Tommy)

Like Pennsylvania's Texas Tommy and the Los Angeles danger dog, the francheezie is a deep-fried, bacon-wrapped hot dog. But the Windy City's version stuffs the frankfurter with cheese (as does the Texas Tommy), and serves it on a poppy-seed bun with the classic toppings of a Chicago dog. One place to find a francheezie is **Mr. Gee's** in Hermosa.

Maxwell Street Polish

Chicago's Maxwell Street on the near West Side is known as the birthplace of several important American traditions. Its longstanding Sunday open-air market, which existed informally as early as the 1870s, officially operated from 1912 to 1994 before moving to a new location several blocks away. Vendors sold discounted goods, much of it from Asia and other overseas markets, to consumers in a shopping environment where immigrants and minorities were welcome. And in the 1940s, Maxwell Street was where Black musicians from the South performed outdoors, and eventually, where they began using amplifiers and electric instruments to be heard over the bustling crowds. These innovations created the musical style that later became known as the Chicago blues.

But Maxwell Street was also home to one of Chicago's signature sandwiches – the Maxwell Street Polish. In 1939, a Macedonian immigrant named Jimmy Stefanovic began working at his aunt's hot dog cart. A few years later, he renamed it **Jim's Original** and started selling seasoned Polish sausages that were made with a mix of spices, served on a white hot dog bun and topped with grilled sweet onions, yellow mustard and spicy green sport peppers. Next door, a second stand, **Express Grill**, which – perhaps misleadingly – called itself the Original Maxwell St. Polish, served up a similar sausage.

While both stands relocated from Maxwell Street during the expansion of the nearby University of Illinois Chicago in the early 2000s, both continue to offer their original menus, which also included a bone-in pork chop sandwich that was served with mustard, onions and sport peppers.

You'll also be able to find Maxwell Street Polishes at other hot dog stands around Chicago, such as **Original Maxwell Street** (but is it really? No one knows) in West Garfield Park, and **Portillo's**, a chain with locations all over the Chicago metropolitan area and the Midwest, with a few additional branches in Florida and the Southwest. If you're not nearby, though, Portillo's will happily ship you a 10-pack of Polish sausages, along with Chicago-style poppy-seed buns and condiments, to enjoy at home. Just put on some Muddy Waters and let the smell of grilled onions waft through your kitchen, and you might be able to picture yourself as a Sunday shopper on Maxwell Street.

Italian sausage

In the pantheon of Chicago foods, the humble sausage sandwich might not be as famous as deep-dish pizza, the Chicago hot dog or Italian beef. But it's just as central to the city's culinary identity. Sausage making has a long history in Chicago, beginning with European butchers who were responsible for some of the most famous brand names in the meat business, including Oscar Mayer, who along with his brother opened a butcher shop in Chicago in 1883, and brothers Samuel Ladany and Emil Reichl, who founded the Vienna Sausage Company a decade later.

The earliest butchers mostly came from Germany (one of whom, Adolph Luetgert, was convicted for murdering his wife in 1897, in a notorious incident that led to rumors – probably untrue – that she had been ground up into sausage), Austria and later, Poland. But Italian sausages are the ones most identified with Chicago cuisine (as well as New England, where they're also a staple, especially in Boston). Markets that specialize in Italian products are dotted throughout the Windy City, and you'll find no shortage of delis to get your sausage fix.

Among the top-rated choices are **Bari Foods** in Noble Square, where you can order your sausage sandwich in 9-inch, 12-inch or 3-foot lengths, and the **Original Nottoli & Son** in Belmont Heights, where you can also satisfy your meatball sub craving. Or if you want to explore the entire world of sausage, head to **Gene's Sausage Shop & Delicatessen** in Ravenswood. There, you can sample a variety of fresh and dried sausages, including bratwurst, kielbasa and even blood sausage, or order a selection of frozen sausages to have shipped home. It's a good place to pretend, as Ferris Bueller once did, that you're Abe Froman, the Sausage King of Chicago.

Gyro

In 1971, the New York Times reported that more than 30 stores selling the Greek sandwich known as the gyro (prounced yee-ro) had opened in Manhattan in the past year, and that they were "selling like hot dogs." But it was the Second City that was apparently first to introduce the gyro to Americans, at the Parkview Restaurant in 1965. And it was Chicago, not New York, that can take credit for the invention that allowed the mass-produced gyro to become a staple menu item at casual Greek restaurants across the country.

The gyro, in its American form, is a sandwich consisting of seasoned meat (usually beef mixed with lamb, but sometimes chicken) that's carved off a vertical rotisserie and served on fluffy pita bread, with toppings that may include tzatziki – a cucumber-yogurt sauce – and slices of tomatoes and raw onions. The gyro is similar to döner kebab, a Turkish sandwich made with shaved, roasted lamb, but in Greece, the meat is usually pork, and the sandwich is sometimes called souvlaki.

Why did Chicago become famous for its gyros? In the 1970s, several Greek entrepreneurs – all of whom claim to be the first to have invented the product – created a method of mass-producing gyro cones of ground, compressed meat that were then flash-frozen and shipped around the country. One of these manufacturers, Kronos Foods, also popularized a vertical broiler that helped it become today's leading producer of gyros in the U.S., selling an estimated 300,000 sandwiches daily.

If you want to sample gyros in the place where they became famous, head to Chicago's Greektown, a 10-square-block neighborhood with some of the most highly regarded gyros in the city. A few recommended spots include **Greek Islands** and **Athena Greek Restaurant**, which both include gyro platters on their extensive menus of Greek specialties. For more casual options, head to **Jimmy's Gyros & Grill** in the Loop, **Central Gyros** near Central and Belmont or **Nick's Drive-In** between Edison Park and Niles. The latter restaurant is known for using homemade ingredients instead of the industrial gyro cone. If you're a champion of these sandwiches, that should be enough to make the owner a personal gyro.

Pepper and egg sandwich

There are around 2.2 million Catholics in the Chicago metropolitan area, nearly a quarter of its total population. And while you might think that at least that many hot dogs, Italian beef sandwiches and Polish sausages are eaten by Chicago Catholics every day, another classic sandwich comes to the forefront during Lent, the period between Ash Wednesday and Easter during which many Catholics don't eat meat on Fridays. (I'm just kidding about their diet, of course. Chicago Catholics eat vegetables, too. Like giardiniera.)

The pepper and egg sandwich, straightforwardly, consists of scrambled eggs and sauteed bell peppers that are served on a soft Italian roll, sometimes with the addition of melted cheese. And while the traditional version doesn't include meat, you'll often have the option to order your sandwich with sausage, bacon or ham.

The origins of this sandwich are unknown, but it's believed that a now-defunct West Town market, Fiore's Delicatessen, which opened in 1970, was the first to serve them. Today you'll find them at breakfast joints like the **Palace Grill** in the West Loop, at Italian delis including **Gio's Cafe and Deli** in Bridgeport on the South Side, and at casual Italian beef spots such as **Johnny's Beef & Gyros** in Lincoln Park. But at the (unrelated) **Johnnie's Beef**, with locations in Elmwood Park and Arlington Heights, you'll be out of luck unless it's Friday, the only day the sandwich is sold. The good news is that you don't have to wait for Lent to come around if you want to try one. Perhaps nodding to an era when Catholics couldn't eat meat on any Fridays, not just during Lent, Johnnie's serves its pepper and egg sandwiches on Fridays year-round. And whether you're a lapsed Catholic, a non-observing Catholic or not Catholic at all, you can still order an Italian beef seven days a week.

Mother-in-law sandwich

Nobody knows where the mother-in-law sandwich got its name, but one Windy City food expert once said that "both types of mother-in-law give you indigestion or heartburn." Whether or not that's true about your own spouse's mom, it's easy to see why this Chicago specialty might give you a stomachache.

The mother-in-law is a bizarre conglomeration. It starts with a processed beef tamale, made by Tom Tom Tamales and distributed without the tamale's characteristic corn husk, which is then plopped onto a poppy-seed bun, smothered with chili and topped with diced raw onions and sliced tomatoes and cucumbers. Add melted cheese and it's called, for no apparent reason, a humdinger. In some establishments, the mother-in-law is dished up without the bun, instead being served on a bed of French fries or in a bowl and called either a tamale boat or tamale sundae.

It's unclear who invented the mother-in-law sandwich, but its first appearance in the culinary lexicon dates to the 1950s. A few decades earlier, the tamale likely came to Chicago during the Great Migration of the early 20th century, when Blacks from the Mississippi Delta, who may have worked alongside Mexican farmhands and adopted one of their traditional foods as their own, made their way north.

The mother-in-law is only served at a handful of establishments on Chicago's South Side, including **Fat Johnnie's Famous Red Hots** in Marquette Park, which calls the humdinger a father-in-law and also serves up a tamale sundae. But at **Joey's Red Hots** in Morgan Park (and a few other Chicagoland locations), the father-in-law is a mother-in-law sandwich with the addition of a hot dog. No matter which combination of ingredients you choose to order, it'll quickly become clear why NPR, explaining the name of the sandwich, quoted one hot dog vendor who described it as having "a fierce bite – just like a mother-in-law."

Jibarito

While you're suffering through a long Chicago winter, the Puerto Rican flavors that are contained in this unusual sandwich might be all that you need to imagine it's about sixty degrees warmer outside.

The classic jibarito consists of thinly sliced steak slathered with garlic-flavored aioli and topped with American cheese, shredded lettuce and sliced tomato. But instead of bread, it's served between two smashed, fried green plantains. The sandwich, whose name means little yokel, was created in 1996 at **Borinquen Restaurant** in Humboldt Park, after its chef read about a similar sandwich at a restaurant in Aguada, Puerto Rico.

More than 25 years later, Borinquen still serves its trademark jibaritos, and offers them with a variety of fillings including steak, pork, chicken, shrimp and vegetables.

In that quarter-century, though, the jibarito has spread throughout Chicagoland to become a staple of its regional cuisine. Now, you can find jibaritos in other Puerto Rican eateries like **La Bomba** in Logan Square and **Papa's Cache Sabroso** in West Town, as well as at restaurants where they're the signature offering on the menu, like **Jibaritos y Más** in Logan Square, **Jibarito Time** in Des Plaines and **The Jibarito Stop** in Pilsen. Even if there's a blizzard raging outside, a few bites of well-seasoned steak and crispy plantains might just have you dreaming of your next trip to the Caribbean.

Chicken Vesuvio

Chicken Vesuvio is a Chicago regional specialty that you'll find on the menus of many of the city's old-school Italian restaurants. It consists of chicken on the bone that's browned until the skin is crispy, alongside potatoes that are sauteed with garlic, oregano, olive oil and white wine. After the dish is baked in the oven to finish cooking, it's usually garnished with green peas.

There are several theories about the origin of Chicken Vesuvio. Some believe that it was first served at a Chicago restaurant called Vesuvio's in the 1930s, but its name may also have been inspired by the volcano-like smoke that's caused by adding wine to hot oil while preparing the dish. Since you'll rarely find it outside Chicago, it's unlikely that it originated anywhere near its namesake mountain.

If you want to sample this classic preparation, try one of Chicago's well-regarded Italian restaurants, like **Il Porcellino** in River North; **La Scarola** in River West, where you can order a similar plate with steak; or **Franco's Ristorante** in Bridgeport, where your protein can either be bone-in chicken or a pork chop. (Some restaurants omit the meat and offer Potatoes Vesuvio as a vegetable.) But if you'd like a side of "Holy Cow" with your order, head to one of the three locations of **Harry Caray's Italian Steakhouse** (or a sister tavern on Navy Pier), whose Chicken Vesuvio the Chicago Tribune once called "best in the city." If the review is to be believed, the combination of flavors is sure to make your taste buds erupt.

Shrimp DeJonghe

Given its heritage as a hub of the meatpacking industry, and its reputation as hog butcher to the world, it's no wonder that Chicago is known more for its steakhouses than its seafood restaurants. When you find yourself sitting down for a porterhouse or a tenderloin, you should still keep an eye out for an appetizer that dates back more than a century, a simple dish known as Shrimp DeJonghe.

Shrimp DeJonghe consists of peeled shrimp that are sauteed with garlic, butter, breadcrumbs and parsley and other spices. It was created at DeJonghe's Hotel and Restaurant, an establishment in the Loop that was open from 1899 to 1923, either by one of its owners, Henri DeJonghe, who managed the hotel with his brothers Pierre and Charles, or by their chef, Emil Zehr. (DeJonghe's is believed to have shut down after the property was raided for violating Prohibition-era alcohol restrictions. Ironically, the dish that represents its legacy is also flavored with white wine or sherry.)

Look out for Shrimp DeJonghe at Chicago steakhouses such as **Bavette's Bar & Boeuf** in River North and **Carson's** in Streeterville. You'll also find it on seafood-heavy menus such as **Joe's Seafood, Prime Steak & Stone Crab** in River North and **Hugo's Frog Bar & Fish House**, also on the North Side. When you order this dish, you may not be eating a product that comes from local waters, but at least you'll be enjoying a preparation that's rooted in Chicago history.

Jigg's Dinner

See Other foods of New England (New England boiled dinner)

As with other cities that have large populations of Irish-Americans, Chicago takes St. Patrick's Day seriously, even dyeing the Chicago River green to mark the occasion. Whether you're visiting then, or at other times of the year, head to one of the city's many Irish pubs, like **Lady Gregory's** in Andersonville and **Mrs. Murphy & Sons** between Lakeview and Lincoln Square, for a traditional boiled dinner of corned beef and cabbage along with root vegetables. Adopting a term more frequently used in Newfoundland, this meal is sometimes known as a Jigg's Dinner.

A Chicago drink to sample:

- **Malort**, a bitter liquor created by Carl Jeppson, a Swedish immigrant to Chicago, in the 1930s, and now a characteristic spirit served in Windy City taverns. One place to try it is **The Beer Temple** in Avondale.

OTHER FOODS OF ILLINOIS

Horseshoe sandwich

A visit to the Land of Lincoln wouldn't be complete without a taste of a dish that's as famous in Springfield as the 16th president's silk top hat. The horseshoe sandwich is a plate consisting of two slices of thick toast, a hamburger patty and a pile of crispy French fries, all smothered in a beer-cheese sauce made with sharp Cheddar that's similar to Welsh rarebit. If that sounds like a lot of food, you can order a pony shoe, made with only a single slice of bread.

In its original incarnation, believed to have been created at Springfield's Leland Hotel by Chef Joe Schweska in 1928 (or possibly by the teenage dishwasher he employed as a cook), the meat was a layer of ham, cut from the bone in the shape of a horseshoe, with potato wedges representing the nails of the shoe. Most restaurants today make their horseshoes with burger patties, but sometimes substitute other meats, and cook a breakfast version of the dish with eggs and bacon or sausage.

When you find yourself in Springfield, perhaps after a visit to the downtown Lincoln Presidential Library and Museum, a good place to sample the horseshoe sandwich is a few blocks away at **Obed & Isaac's Microbrewery**, where you can choose your preferred meat from options that include beef, turkey, lamb or veggie burgers, corned beef, pulled pork or ham. A short drive away is **Charlie Parker's**, where you can also customize your meat (or substitute walleye) and swap out fries for tater tots. Another option is the nearby **D'Arcy's Pint**, which offers a similar range of ingredients with additional toppings such as chili or a vegetable medley of mushrooms, onions and peppers. No matter which option you choose, you can rest easy knowing the plate won't set you back more than a trio of Lincolns.

Burgoo

See Other foods of Kentucky

While this tomato-based stew, containing a variety of meats and vegetables, is most associated with Kentucky, burgoo can also be found at community celebrations in central and Southern Illinois, for example in the town of Arenzville, which proclaims itself to have the world's best burgoo and holds an annual festival in its honor each fall.

MISSOURI

KANSAS CITY

Kansas City-style BBQ

When you're deciding where to go to explore one of the country's tastiest barbecue traditions, you might be singing "Kansas City, Here I Come." Kansas City BBQ is characterized by meat that's seasoned with a dry rub, smoked or grilled, and then accompanied by a thick, tangy tomato-based sauce. You'll find a variety of meats served in the city's BBQ restaurants, including brisket, pulled pork, chicken, ribs and sausage, along with sides like baked beans and coleslaw. Both the seasoning and the sauce tend to be sweeter than those in other regional barbecue traditions, with brown sugar often a component of the dry rub, and molasses used to sweeten the sauce, sometimes as a counterpoint to spicy heat.

KC's barbecue heritage dates to 1908, when Henry Perry began barbecuing meat in an outdoor pit and serving slabs of ribs wrapped in newspaper to workers near the Garment District. As his reputation grew, Perry eventually opened a restaurant in a trolley barn. One of the cooks he trained there was Charlie Bryant, who took over the business after Perry died in 1940. A few years later, Charlie handed over the restaurant to his brother, who changed its name to his own. **Arthur Bryant's Barbecue** became a mainstay of the Kansas City barbecue scene, and exploded in popularity after food writer and humorist Calvin Trillin wrote in 1972 that it was the best restaurant on the planet.

Getting a handle on everything that Kansas City barbecue has to offer will take a few visits. A good place to start is **Joe's Kansas City Barbecue** (formerly known as Oklahoma Joe's). There are three locations, but the original, located in a gas station in the Kansas portion of the city, is the most atmospheric. You won't go wrong with pulled pork or any of the meats that are smoked over Missouri white oak, but the Z-Man sandwich, made with beef brisket, is also a popular choice.

Another favorite Kansas City BBQ restaurant is **Slap's,** also located in Kansas and known for its enormous pork spare ribs as well as smoked turkey, beef and jalapeño Cheddar sausages. Meat lovers also swear by the barbecue at **Q39** in Midtown and Overland Park, known for its hickory-smoked brisket, as well as **Jack Stack Barbecue,** with a half-dozen metropolitan locations that are famous for their crown prime beef short ribs as well as cheesy corn, a side dish made with cream cheese, Cheddar and smoked ham that you'll now find in many barbecue restaurants throughout the region. It's a sign that KC's barbecue traditions aren't stuck in the past – you might even say, as Rodgers and Hammerstein did, that everything's up to date in Kansas City.

Burnt ends

You can't talk about Kansas City barbecue without paying special attention to burnt ends, the crunchy, fatty pieces of a smoked beef brisket that are usually served without sauce. At first, these bits were just discarded trimmings of meat, but customers came to prize the morsels that combined a charred, deeply caramelized bark with a tender, juicy interior, and they became a hallmark of the Kansas City barbecue tradition.

Burnt ends were first served at **Arthur Bryant's Restaurant** as snacks for customers waiting in line. Although the original burnt ends were simply leftovers cut from the point of a brisket, the high demand for burnt ends forced pitmasters to start using cubes of whole briskets, using cooking techniques to mimic the blackened exterior and fatty insides of the trimmings. While some cooks use other meats, especially pork, to make a version of burnt ends, traditionalists say that they can only be prepared with a beef brisket.

Besides Arthur Bryant's, a worthy place to try this specialty is **Gates Bar-B-Q,** a local institution that opened the same year as its rival, and now has five locations around the area that serve burnt ends on a hoagie roll to help soak up their grease. Gates is also known for its peppery house sauce and for its signature, if somewhat banal, greeting, "Hi, May I Help You?" Another highly regarded spot is **Jones Bar-B-Q**, run by sisters Deborah and Mary Jones, nicknamed Shorty and Little, who became nationally recognized after being featured on the show Queer Eye in 2019. Their hot, sweet and tangy, and coconut pineapple sauces are available 24/7 from a vending machine on premises, or via nationwide shipping. Even a barbecue purist would probably forgive you if you decided to sneak some onto your brisket. Why, you might ask? Because the burnt ends justify the means.

Steak soup

Kansas City steak soup is a dish that was made famous at **Plaza III Steakhouse**, a restaurant that operated from 1963 to 2018 at the city's Country Club Plaza, named for that location and for its trio of founders.

By the time the restaurant opened, Kansas City had been a significant center of American cattle farming for nearly a century (its meatpacking industry had become the nation's second-biggest, behind Chicago, and its stockyards once processed as many as 170,000 animals daily). With such a plentiful supply of meat available, it's no wonder that it features in one of the city's signature dishes, a soup made with steak, vegetables and a rich, beefy broth.

While a second incarnation of Plaza III only lasted a couple of years at a new location, the brand was resurrected in 2022 as a mail-order operation, with its former executive chef consulting on its recipes. So you can still try the original version of Kansas City steak soup, made with Angus steak, by ordering a (fairly pricey) gift box containing five 24-ounce frozen servings.

Another option is to head to one of the city's steakhouses to find examples of the dish around town. Two recommended spots are **Majestic Restaurant**, where the steak soup is made with grass-fed prime rib, and **Anton's**, where it's served with cornbread. Or, because the recipe has been frequently reproduced online, you can easily cook your own version at home. Whether you make use of Kansas City strip steak or your own favorite local cut of beef, you might be able to imagine yourself dining out during the heyday of the Plaza.

St. Louis

St. Louis-style pizza

Compared to the regional styles of pizza widely found in New York, Chicago and Detroit, the version that's prevalent in St. Louis is "terrible," late-night talk show host and New York-born Jimmy Kimmel told actor and native son Jon Hamm during an interview in 2013. But Hamm defended the style staunchly, saying that the Gateway City's version is "as tasty as eleven World Series victories."

While it might not be everyone's cup of tea, St. Louis-style pizza has a few unique attributes that make it distinct from what you'll generally find in other cities. While more conventional pizzas are made with a bready dough that produces a tender, chewy base, St. Louis pizza is made without yeast, producing a crisp, cracker-like crust. Rather than traditional slices, it's cut into small squares or rectangles, a method called either tavern cut or party cut. It's often layered with several toppings, because the crust is sturdy enough to hold up under their weight. And the cheese that's typically used is a processed white cheese called Provel, a combination of Provolone, Swiss and Cheddar that melts at low temperatures, making it buttery and gooey. The blend was trademarked in 1950 and is now made in Wisconsin by a subsidiary of Kraft Foods, though it's rarely available outside St. Louis and a handful of Midwestern grocery stores.

The iconic places to try St. Louis-style pizza are **Imo's Pizza**, a chain with more than 100 locations in Missouri and neighboring states, and a competing business, **Cecil Whittaker's**, which has 15 locations spread throughout the metropolitan area. When you're ready to branch out, highly regarded spots for this style of 'za include **Nick & Elena's Pizzeria** in Overland, which some rate as the area's best; **Uncle Leo's Pizza** in South County, known for its plentiful toppings and crispy crust; and **Salvage Yard Bar and Grill** in Princeton Heights, which serves both St. Louis-style and Chicago-style pies. That would be a good place to watch a Cardinals game against the "arch"-rival Cubs and debate which team – and which pizza – has championship stuff.

Toasted ravioli

When you hear someone in St. Louis talking about "t-rav," they're not referring to a Toyota SUV – they're discussing their favorite places for the pillowy pasta pockets that have become one of the city's signature dishes.

Toasted ravioli are breaded, deep-fried squares that are usually stuffed with a meat-based filling and served with a sprinkling of Parmesan cheese on top as well as marinara sauce for dipping. While there are competing stories about their invention, they likely date to the 1940s at one of three restaurants located in the city's Italian-American neighborhood called The Hill.

One account says that an intoxicated chef at Oldani's, now known as **Mama's on The Hill**, once accidentally dropped a plate of ravioli into boiling oil instead of water. He served them at the bar to a few patrons including Mickey Garagiola, the older brother of Cardinals catcher (and later Hall of Fame broadcaster) Joe Garagiola, who loved them. Trying to decide what to call the dish, the owner of the restaurant thought that toasted sounded like a more appealing adjective than fat-fried or greasy-fried, and he put them on his menu with that name.

A second version of how toasted ravioli came to be claims that a German-born cook at an establishment named Angelo's, now called **Charlie Gitto's**, misunderstood a waiter's request and dropped the pasta pockets he had made into the fryer instead of a pot of water. And a third story says that **Lombardo's**, a restaurant that opened in 1934 and now has locations downtown as well as near the airport, had them on their menu as a family recipe that came from Sicily.

While no one will ever know exactly who invented toasted ravioli, any of these eateries would be good places to sample them during your stay in the city. At Mama's, a classic Italian restaurant, the ravioli are small in size but filled with flavorful morsels of either meat or cheese. At Charlie Gitto's, which some believe offers the city's best version, they're served with a rich pomodoro sauce. And at Lombardo's, the oversized ravioli are stuffed with beef, spinach and cheese. At all of these spots, digging into a plate of t-rav will be a good way for you to get baptized in the spirit of St. Louis.

St. Louis-style BBQ

Barbecue in St. Louis generally takes a back seat to the more distinctive styles you'll find in cities like Memphis and Kansas City. But the Gateway to the West is justifiably famous for its spare ribs, the fatty but meaty pork bones that are characteristically cut into a rectangular rack by removing the tips from the section that includes the breastbone. They're usually grilled over an open flame until they're tender, and served with a sweet, tomato-based barbecue sauce.

You wouldn't go wrong by making your first STL food stop a visit to **Pappy's Smokehouse**, with locations in Midtown and St. Peter's that often have long lines of hungry customers. Ribs are a signature menu item here (and were once named as the country's best by the Food Network), but because Pappy's is a Memphis-style BBQ joint, they're slow-smoked rather than grilled. When I visited, that anomaly didn't stop me from ordering a giant combo platter that included a full slab of ribs along with brisket, pulled pork and smoked chicken sandwiches and four sides. You'll find similarly delicious racks at Pappy's sister restaurant **Bogart's Smokehouse**, as well as at **Sugarfire Smoke House**, which serves up well-regarded baby back ribs at nearly a dozen locations around the metropolitan area.

A more traditional spot for St. Louis-style ribs is **Salt + Smoke**, with four locations around town where you can dine in on half or full racks of cherry-smoked ribs, or order frozen, vacuum-sealed slabs online that you can cook at home. Another place to gnaw on some ribs is **Hogtown Smokehouse**, a Dogtown BBQ spot whose racks are often rated as among the city's best. These restaurants make it clear that at least when it comes to one particular meat, St. Louis has a regional barbecue style worthy of its own acclaim.

Pork steak

Meet me in St. Louis when you want to sample the other style of barbecue that the Lou is famous for – pork steak. This cut of meat comes from the part of the pork shoulder known as the butt. When it's butchered with the bone intact, it's known as a pork blade steak.

Most chefs prepare pork shoulder with a low-and-slow cooking technique that breaks down the meat's tough muscle fibers and produces juicy, succulent dishes like pulled pork. But another way to tenderize a pork steak is with high heat over a grill, and this style is a staple of St. Louis backyard cookouts, where the meat is often accompanied by bottled barbecue sauce, especially the brand Maull's.

Though similar cuts had been served elsewhere in the country for decades, pork steak became popular in St. Louis in the 1950s after the owners of a local grocery chain called Schnuck's decided to offer an inexpensive cut of meat for grilling. A few highly regarded places where you can try it today include **Beast**

Butcher & Block in Forest Park Southeast, which also sells raw pork steaks by the pound and offers a live-fire cooking class at which David Sandusky, the restaurant's pitmaster, demonstrates BBQ techniques; **Hwy 61 Roadhouse** in Webster Park, which serves up a menu of Southern specialties along with live music four nights a week; and **Five Aces BBQ**, a food truck and catering operation in the Shaw neighborhood that dishes out pork steaks that are seasoned with a blend of spices and grilled over an open flame. Once you give this cut of pork shoulder a try, you'll never again ask it to butt out of your barbecue rotation.

Gerber sandwich

Thank goodness, a Gerber sandwich isn't one that's made with baby food. But depending upon your appetite for processed cheese, this specialty of River City might be just about as appealing.

A Gerber is essentially a St. Louis version of an open-faced ham-and-cheese sandwich. It starts with a piece of Italian or French bread that's spread with garlic butter, topped with sliced ham, covered with a layer of Provel (or Provolone) and sprinkled with paprika. It's then toasted in the oven until the cheese melts.

This sandwich was first created in 1973 at **Ruma's Deli** by Dick Gerber, a customer and owner of a neighboring business whom the Rumas allowed to cook in their kitchen. They liked the invention so much that they soon put it on their regular menu – and a half-century later, you can still order one at either their original South County location or the one in Imperial.

You'll find a similar sandwich at a few other restaurants around town, but because of trademark issues, it's usually called by other names. At **Kirkwood Deli** in Kirkwood, the Pioneer consists of "toasted garlic bread with a generous portion of ham topped with Provel cheese and a sprinkle of paprika." And at **The Gramophone** in Forest Park Southeast, the Manchester

Melt is "served open faced, ham topped with Provel cheese, paprika on a garlic buttered baguette." They both sound like a Gerber to me – and it's such a simple sandwich that either one would probably be enjoyed by even the most picky of toddlers.

St. Paul sandwich

Don't be fooled by the name of this dish, which sounds like it might have something to do with Minnesota. The St. Paul sandwich is actually a local Chinese-American specialty in St. Louis – albeit one with a cryptic past.

The St. Paul sandwich, in its modern form, consists of slices of soft white bread that surround a layer of the Cantonese omelet called egg foo yung, along with lettuce, tomatoes, pickles and mayonnaise. The egg patty can contain a variety of meats and vegetables, but often includes ham, shrimp and bean sprouts. The sandwich is usually cut in half, and wrapped in wax paper.

Local sandwich aficionados ascribe the origin of the St. Paul sandwich to a Lafayette Square restaurant called **Park Chop Suey**, whose chef, Steven Yuen, hailed from the Minneapolis area and may have created the sandwich in the 1970s to appeal to the Black clientele in his neighborhood. But historical research has uncovered other versions of the St. Paul sandwich, dating to the early decades of the 20th century and found in St. Louis as well as other Midwestern cities, that included chopped ham and scrambled eggs. Some culinary experts believe that the St. Paul sandwich is actually a Denver sandwich – originally made by Chinese chefs cooking for workers on the transcontinental railroad – just called by another name.

Numerous Chinese restaurants around the St. Louis area still serve the St. Paul sandwich, including Park Chop Suey, where you can order one of nine different varieties, including versions made with beef, duck, pork or shrimp. A few other recommended spots include **Mai Lee**, a Vietnamese restaurant in Brentwood that also serves Chinese specialties including egg foo yung and St. Paul sandwiches; **Delmar Lee's**, a Central West End takeaway joint; and **Kim Van Restaurant**, a Fox Park eatery with a giant menu of Chinese dishes as well as St. Pauls made with chicken, beef, ham, pork and shrimp – or a combo containing all of them. That would be a hearty enough sandwich that it could fill you up before a long journey to the Twin Cities.

Gooey butter cake

If you've ever baked a pound cake, you know that modern recipes tend to deviate from the original 18th-century instructions, which called for a pound each of butter, sugar, flour and eggs. (That would make for a very dense cake!) A standard coffee cake today might use nearly twice as much flour as butter, measured by weight. But when a German baker in St. Louis in the 1930s accidentally reversed these proportions, he ended up with a flat, dense confection. Despite the error, the bakery owner decided to sell the gooey cake so that the ingredients weren't wasted, and it eventually became one of the city's favorite sweets.

Gooey butter cake has a firm base and a custardy upper layer. It's typically dusted with powdered sugar, cut into squares like a brownie, and eaten more as a coffee cake than a dessert. While the traditional version made today in St. Louis bakeries tends to mimic the ingredients of the original version, you'll sometimes also see another type of gooey butter cake, made with cream cheese and packaged yellow cake mix. And in national grocery store chains, you'll also find commercial versions, including one that was originally popularized by disgraced Southern chef Paula Deen.

You'll do better, though, seeking out local bakeries that make their gooey butter cake in house. One great spot for gooey butter cake is **Park Avenue Coffee**, which has five branches around town that serve dozens of varieties, including "Mom's traditional," triple chocolate, white chocolate raspberry and red velvet. (They also sell cakes as well as packaged cake mixes online.)

Other recommended spots include **Federhofer's Bakery** in Affton, a German bakery that opened in 1956 and is said to use the original recipe for gooey butter cake; **The Missouri Baking Company** on The Hill, which specializes in Italian pastries like cannoli and tiramisu; and **Gooey Louie**, a Creve Coeur bakery where you can order gooey butter cookies as well as whole cakes in a variety of flavors, as well as individually wrapped pieces with images of the St. Louis skyline. You can even buy gooey butter cake socks and Christmas ornaments, so that even if there isn't a piece of cake nearby, you'll never be able to forget about the kitchen accident that led resourceful bakers to invent a new local specialty.

Another St. Louis dish to sample:

- **Slinger**, a breakfast dish consisting of eggs, hash browns or home fries and a hamburger patty that are all covered in chili and topped with cheese as well as gravy, onions or other toppings. You'll find it at local restaurants including **Chili Mac's Diner** and **Southwest Diner**.

OTHER FOODS OF MISSOURI

Guber burger

When you're traveling between St. Louis and Kansas City, it's worth detouring off I-70 to visit the city of Sedalia. That's where you'll find the Missouri State Fair every August, as well as an annual ragtime festival in honor of Scott Joplin, who made the city his adopted home. And it's the only place where you'll find a burger that only another famous musician – Elvis Presley himself – might have loved.

The guber (or goober) burger is a regular ol' hamburger with toppings of, you guessed it, peanut butter, along with mayonnaise, lettuce and tomato. It was first created at Sedalia's Wheel Inn, probably in the 1940s, and was a staple there as well as at another local drive-in called Eddie's (with both establishments featuring the iconic mascot Mr. Peanut on their doors) until the two businesses both shut down in 2013.

Missouri isn't exactly known for its peanut butter, so the reason this burger took hold is lost to history, but it still appears on the menus of a few restaurants in Sedalia today. **Goody's Steakburgers** is one place that carries on the local tradition, and you'll also find the guber burger at **Kehde's Barbeque**, an eatery located inside an old train dining car. Its menu also includes a slaw- and BBQ sauce-covered patty called the Train Wreck, which if you ask me would be just as suitable a description for the guber burger. Or perhaps, the last few years of Elvis's career.

Snoot

Nose-to-tail cooking describes the philosophy of using all the parts of a butchered animal, not just its most popular cuts. This practice is taken literally in Missouri, where the snout of a pig, minus the nostrils, is either deep-fried or grilled, creating the specialty known as snoot. It's sometimes consumed as a snack, with the crispy pork dipped in barbecue sauce, but snoot sandwiches are also commonly eaten.

Historians believe that snoot was first served in St. Louis by street vendors in the 1940s. But the delicacy gained national attention after Andrew Zimmern, the host of Bizarre Foods, visited a couple of Missouri restaurants during two trips in the mid-2010s. The first, St. Louis's Smoki O's BBQ, was famous for its snoots for nearly 25 years until it closed in 2021. The other, Kansas City's **Tenderloin Grill**, is said to be where local policemen took rookies to eat snoot during their initiation (and they're still described on the menu as a "rite of passage").

If you want to seek out the best snoot around, follow your nose to a few barbecue spots, especially in St. Louis, that still serve this delicacy. A few places to try include **Roper's Ribs** in Jennings, **Big Mama's BBQ Express** in East St. Louis and **Beast Butcher & Block** in Forest Park Southeast, where you can order snoot either by itself or as a combo plate with rib tips. But you'll have to content yourself with eating only the more familiar parts of the pig: as far as I know, there's nothing on the menu made with tail.

Springfield-style cashew chicken

You've probably eaten your fair share of cashew chicken, a standard offering on the menus of Chinese restaurants around the country. But the version created in Springfield, Missouri, became so popular there that the dish eventually spread to menus far beyond the Ozarks, with the city included as a key descriptor in its name.

In 1963, David Leong was planning to launch an eponymous restaurant in Springfield called Leong's Tea House. But shortly before it opened its doors, the building was vandalized, likely due to anti-Asian sentiment. Once Leong repaired the damage, he decided to create a dish that would have broad appeal to the restaurant's patrons, who he believed were more accustomed to eating country fried steak and fried chicken than the Cantonese dishes he tended to prepare. So he invented a version of cashew chicken that blended Chinese and Ozark cooking techniques.

Springfield-style cashew chicken consists of deep-fried, crispy nuggets of chicken that are combined with whole cashews and vegetables, in a gravy made from oyster sauce, soy sauce and chicken stock. The dish became so popular that Leong began sharing his recipe with friends and relatives who started opening other restaurants around town – and today, you can find dozens of establishments that serve their own versions. David Leong died in 2020, but his son, Wing Wah, still runs a family restaurant in a new location, **Leong's Asian Diner**, serving his father's original recipe for cashew chicken. (You can also buy his sauce in bottles online and at local grocery stores.) Other recommended versions of this dish are readily available at Chinese restaurants around town, including **Happy China**, **Chinese Chef** and **Golden Cuisine**.

Sadly, though, the annual Cashew Craze festival that celebrated Springfield's culinary claim to fame with competing versions of cashew chicken no longer exists. You'll either have to make a pilgrimage to the Ozarks to try it – or keep an eye out for Springfield as you peruse menus of Chinese restaurants in St. Louis or Kansas City, or even in far-flung places the dish has been spotted like New York and Hong Kong. If you come across any versions of this Missouri specialty during your travels, make sure to "show me" where you found it.

MINNESOTA

Hotdish

Amy Klobuchar is known for being Minnesota's senior senator, for her 2020 presidential campaign, for once reportedly eating a salad on a plane with a comb – and for her award-winning casserole, the upper Midwest specialty known as hotdish.

Although there is no standard recipe for it, hotdish is served warm, as you might expect from its name, and usually contains a meat, a starch and canned or frozen vegetables, mixed with a creamy sauce that binds the ingredients together. One iconic combination includes ground beef, tater tots, green beans and cream of mushroom soup, which some Minnesotans refer to as the Lutheran binder because the dish is so frequently served at church gatherings. Klobuchar's version, which she served at campaign events known as Hot Dish House Parties (using the alternate spelling), and for which she won the inaugural hotdish competition among Minnesota's Congressional delegation, in 2011, leaves out the vegetables, includes an extra can of cream of chicken soup, and smothers the entire casserole with pepper jack cheese.

The word hotdish was first used in a 1930 Lutheran church cookbook, but the idea of a thrifty one-pan meal likely dates from World War I, when the U.S. government encouraged families to begin conserving food to support the troops fighting abroad. Early versions of hotdish often used pasta to help stretch a limited supply of meat, especially during the Depression years. Wild rice is frequently used for the same purpose today, with potato chips or fried onions occasionally replacing the tater tots as a crispy element. (The tater tots are such an integral part of the dish, though, that it's sometimes just called tater tot casserole.)

When you're traveling in the Land of 10,000 Lakes, keep an eye out for hotdish at casual restaurants and pubs around the state. In St. Paul, the **Bulldog Restaurant & Bar** serves a traditional take on hotdish at its Lowertown location, mixing in peas, carrots and corn as its vegetables. **The Mason Jar** in Eagan offers two varieties: an iconic version with ground beef and corn, and a modern one that uses ground Beyond Meat and dairy-free cream of mushroom soup. And in Minneapolis, Rochester, Duluth and a few smaller cities, you'll find **Crooked Pint Ale House**, which features a Mexican-inspired tortilla hotdish. Or if you're politically connected, you can try and wrangle yourself a taste of Klobuchar's version. But since her recipe is widely available online, you can also make it at home – and eat it with whichever household implement you like.

Juicy Lucy

When you order a cheeseburger in Minneapolis, you might get the impression that the grillmaster forgot your cheese. That's because in the Twin Cities, rather than your standard cheeseburger that has a slice of American or Cheddar melted on top of the meat, it's common to stuff two thin patties with a layer of cheese, causing it to ooze out of the burger when you bite into it. This style of cheeseburger, known as a Juicy Lucy, is famously known to burn diners' mouths with an unexpected burst of molten hot cheese.

Two bars in South Minneapolis each take credit for the Juicy Lucy. At **Matt's Bar**, the burger is misspelled as a "Jucy" Lucy, probably because of a typo in the original sign that was never corrected. As the story goes, a customer in 1954 requested a burger with cheese inside, took a bite and exclaimed, "That's one juicy Lucy!" But a rival bar called **5-8 Club** also claims to have created the Juicy Lucy in the 1950s, and their advertising mocks their competitor, saying "If it's spelled right, it's done right!"

Both restaurants are still serving up this iconic burger, Matt's adhering to its original recipe with American cheese, and 5-8

Club offering a choice of American, blue cheese, Swiss or pepper jack at its four area locations (and online store, in case you want to have one shipped to you). 5-8 Club also sells a version of a Juicy Lucy stuffed with American cheese and "secret sauce," and topped with lettuce, raw onions and Thousand Island dressing that it calls a "Saucy Sally."

Other good options for a Juicy Lucy include the Minneapolis locations of the **Blue Door Pub**, which offers a classic version with American cheese as well as a few different "Blucys" made with blue cheese. Or head out to St. Paul and check out a joint called **The Nook**, which serves up a few different stuffed burgers (including the classic, called the Juicy Nookie), as well as a number of cheeseburgers where you'll find the cheese in its more typical location, on top of the patty. Those sandwiches probably won't make you shout out rhyming exclamations, but they also likely won't burn your tongue.

Wild rice soup

A chilly Minnesota day – and unless you're visiting in the summer, that's most of them – calls for a hearty bowl of wild rice soup, a North Star State specialty that isn't actually made with rice at all.

Wild rice is an indigenous aquatic grain, one species of which grows mainly in shallow lakes in the upper Midwest. Although it's now cultivated commercially for mass production, wild rice was traditionally harvested by Native American tribes such as the Ojibwe using canoes. Being high in protein and containing several vitamins and minerals, the long brown grain, which the Ojibwe called manoomin, has excellent nutritional value.

An intriguing restaurant where you can try wild rice in several different forms is **Owamni by The Sioux Chef** in Minneapolis, which features Native cuisine. There, you can build your own grain bowl with wild rice accompanied by bison, turkey or mushrooms, or try it with currants and root vegetables.

Wild rice is the official grain of Minnesota, where it's commonly eaten as a side dish and as a component of hotdish. The most popular way to enjoy wild rice, though, is in a creamy soup. You can buy containers of a classic version at the upscale grocery chain **Lunds & Byerlys**, which has over a dozen locations around the Twin Cities serving varieties made with either ham or chicken. You'll also find wild rice soup at both casual and fancy restaurants around town, such as the four locations of **Hazelwood Food + Drink**; Minneapolis's **The Loon Cafe**, **Maxwell's American Pub** and **Dave's Downtown**; and the dozens of branches of **Panera Bread**. And when it's too cold to venture outside, you can even get your soup delivered to wherever you are.

Walleye sandwich

Walleye is the official state fish of Minnesota, so it shouldn't be surprising that you'll find a sandwich that features the freshwater swimmer on menus at restaurants and pubs all across the North Star State.

While the fish is sometimes either grilled or blackened, it's most commonly battered and deep-fried. The walleye fillet is typically served on a bun with classic toppings such as lettuce and tomato, as well as tartar sauce, which primarily consists of mayonnaise and pickles.

Your first spot for walleye should be **Tavern on Grand** in St. Paul, which offers an iconic version of the sandwich as well as other preparations of the fish that include walleye cakes, tacos and baskets. Other highly regarded options include **Gluek's**, the oldest restaurant in downtown Minneapolis, which serves either beer-battered or grilled walleye on a hoagie roll with dill-caper tartar sauce; **Buster's on 28th**, a few miles south near Lake Hiawatha, which offers a Reuben-like version that includes Swiss cheese, bacon and apple coleslaw; and **Pickwick Restaurant & Pub** in Duluth, where the walleye can either be sauteed, fried or broiled. The restaurant's located steps from the southern shore of Lake Superior, so you just might be able to spot tomorrow's catch while you're enjoying your lunch.

Lefse

In 1983, residents of the town of Starbuck, Minnesota, set the record for the world's largest lefse. They rolled out nearly 70 pounds of batter and created a nearly 10-foot-by-10-foot example of this Norwegian flatbread, an accomplishment they continue to celebrate at Lefse Dagen (Lefse Days) each spring.

While there are many people with Norwegian heritage in the upper Midwest who are equally proud of their lefse-making skills – there are annual lefse festivals in many communities, including Mankato, Barnesville and Fosston, Minnesota – there's only one Lefse Hall of Fame, an exhibition that Starbuck opened in 2020.

Lefse is made with riced potatoes, flour, butter and milk or cream, and cooked on a large griddle until it resembles a flat pancake or tortilla. It's traditional to eat lefse during the Christmas holidays, when families gather to make it together. It can be consumed in many forms, but is often flavored with butter and sugar or lingonberry jam and rolled up into a tube. It can also be eaten plain, accompanied by the dried whitefish known as lutefisk.

The tradition of making lefse was brought to America by the tens of thousands of Norwegian immigrants who settled in the upper Midwest, many around the Twin Cities, starting in the mid-19th century. Today you'll find many grocery stores and restaurants in both Minnesota and North Dakota that celebrate Scandinavian heritage, where you can find lefse year-round.

A good first stop is **Ingebretsen's Nordic Marketplace** in Minneapolis, which sells packages of fresh lefse as well as all the tools and supplies you'll need to make your own. When you're looking to dine out, visit **Taste of Scandinavia Bakery** in

Bloomington (as well as North Oaks and Little Canada), where you'll find breakfast plates that include lefse as well as sandwiches such as the Norwegian chicken lefse melt. Or stop in at **Finnish Bistro** in St. Paul, where you can order a lefse scramble or a five-pack of lefse. Enjoy them in the restaurant or take them to go, so you can choose to honor the record-breaking lefse makers in the drive-through of a famous nationwide coffee chain.

IOWA

Loose meat sandwich

The Roaring Twenties were an exciting decade of innovation, with the widespread use of new technologies like the automobile and the telephone, as well as a time when artistic creativity blossomed, with the dawn of the Jazz Age and the popularity of new dances like the foxtrot and the Charleston. And in Iowa, the 1920s were also the period when two restaurants created versions of the loose meat sandwich, a dish that's become the most iconic food in the Hawkeye State – except perhaps for corn.

A loose meat sandwich consists of cooked ground beef that's served on a hamburger bun with toppings that may include sauteed onions, pickles, mustard and ketchup. It's not quite a hamburger, since the meat isn't pressed together into a patty, but not quite a sloppy Joe, either, because it doesn't have any sauce.

The sandwich was originally called a tavern burger. That's because it was first sold at a pub in Sioux City in 1924 that later became Ye Olde Tavern. A couple of years later, a restaurant called **Maid-Rite** in Muscatine began serving a similar dish, which it called a loose meat sandwich. Today Iowans will sometimes refer to the specialty as either a tavern sandwich or a Maid-Rite, names that pay homage to the original versions.

While Ye Olde Tavern is long closed, visitors to Sioux City will find well-regarded tavern sandwiches at **Miles Inn** as well as at a drive-in called **Tastee Inn & Out**. And because the original Maid-Rite developed into a popular franchise, you can still find the dish at the dozen or so locations that remain, as well as at other restaurants, sandwich shops and drive-ins around the state. While you eat yours, imagine what our lives would be like today if we didn't have cars, phones or the loose meat sandwich.

Steak de Burgo

Although the name of Iowa's capital, Des Moines, derives from a French word meaning monks, the city has a substantial Italian-American population, with around four percent reporting ancestry from that country. This demographic fact helps explain the popularity of a hyper-local dish that you'll only see on menus in Des Moines, steak de Burgo.

Steak de Burgo is a beef tenderloin that's sauteed to order on the stovetop and accompanied by a rich sauce that contains garlic, Italian herbs such as basil, thyme and oregano, and either butter or cream. While the etymology of the dish has been lost to history, steak de Burgo is believed to have originated in the 1950s at one of two Italian restaurants in Des Moines, Johnny & Kay's or Vic's Tally-Ho.

Today, classic steakhouses and Italian restaurants in Des Moines continue to feature steak de Burgo on their menus. A few recommended spots include **Simon's**, where you can enjoy a similar preparation with beef or pork tenderloin or with chicken; **Johnny's Italian Steakhouse**, located a stone's throw away from the Des Moines airport; and **Christopher's**, an Italian-American mainstay in Des Moines for the past six decades. But there's no requirement in the city to behave like a teetotaling monk when you're dining out – all of these restaurants have extensive menus of wine, beer and cocktails.

Other Iowa dishes to sample:

- **Taco pizza**, a hybrid that first became popular in the Quad Cities in the 1970s after it was invented at **Happy Joe's Pizza** in Bettendorf. This thin-crust pizza is topped with ingredients you'd normally find on a taco, including ground beef, refried beans, Cheddar cheese, lettuce, tomatoes and crushed tortilla chips. In addition to several locations of Happy Joe's across the state, you'll also find taco pizza at a handful of well-regarded spots including **Northern Lights Pizza** in West Des Moines and **Pizza Palace** in Traer.
- **Scotcheroos**, a confection made with a mixture of butterscotch chips, peanut butter and a rice- or corn-based cereal that's typically chilled and cut into bars. One place to sample them is **Mishmash Eats Bake Shoppe** in Indianola.

WISCONSIN

Beer brat

An indelible memory of my first trip to Milwaukee, driving up I-94 from Chicago in the early 1990s, is the strong smell of beer that emanated across the highway from Miller, Pabst and other factories. There's a good reason the city is sometimes known as the Beer Capital of the World. And one way all that beer is put to good use is as a cooking liquid for brats (short for bratwursts), the German sausage that's a mainstay of Wisconsin cookouts.

Brats are mild sausages that can be grilled or fried, but are just as often poached in inexpensive beer as well as butter and onions, a bath that adds flavor before (and sometimes after) cooking. Other ingredients such as cheese or jalapeños are sometimes mixed into the sausage filling, which is usually pork but can also be a blend of other meats such as beef or veal (these are called red and white brats, respectively). Beer brats are usually served on a split hard roll, either as a single sausage, or a double – two brats side-to-side – with toppings that can include sauteed onions and peppers, sauerkraut and mustard (either yellow or brown).

The capital of the beer brat in Wisconsin is Sheboygan, where thousands of German immigrants settled beginning in the late 1840s, and where dozens of butchers made their own brats, mixing salt, pepper and nutmeg into the meat. (The **Johnsonville** factory that was founded in Sheboygan in 1945 is now one of the largest sausage producers in the country, and its Marketplace is a good place to shop for a variety of sausages for your backyard barbecue.) Sheboygan takes its sausages so seriously that its official tourism website highlights a brat-themed oath that includes promises, among others, to "respect the brat ritual" and "denounce overdressing with pickled cabbage and other offensive forms of condimentation."

As you travel around the state, you won't have any trouble finding good places to try a beer brat or pick up sausages you can cook yourself. In Madison, a city that holds a bratwurst festival every Memorial Day weekend, try either **The Old Fashioned** or **State Street Brats**, a University of Wisconsin-themed sports bar. And in Milwaukee, start your shopping at **Usinger's Famous Sausage**, which offers numerous varieties of fresh or cooked brats (as well as many other types of sausage). Across the street (or in Shorewood), at **Milwaukee Brat House**, you can dine on Usinger's brats with your choice of toppings, cheese and condiments.

Another good place for a brat is **American Family Field**, the home of the Milwaukee Brewers, which is one of the only sports stadiums that sells more sausages than hot dogs. Don't miss the sixth-inning live mascot race between the brat and its competitors: Italian, Polish and chorizo sausages, as well as a hot dog. You'd think the brat, by already being steeped in beer, would be at a disadvantage, but it won the first-ever sausage race at the city's old ballpark, Milwaukee County Stadium, in 1993. That's around the time I first visited, and I also remember the stands – like just about everything else in Milwaukee – smelling strongly of beer.

Cheese curds

There's a reason that Wisconsinites (and especially Green Bay Packers fans) are called Cheeseheads. The state produces more cheese per resident than anywhere else in the world, and alone accounts for more than a quarter of all the cheese manufactured in America.

An artifact of the cheesemaking process that has become one of Wisconsin's favorite snacks is cheese curds. These are the irregular pieces that separate from the whey and eventually get pressed into blocks of cheese. But as young curds, they have a mild, slightly salty taste and a springy texture. Due to their hard protein structure that gradually softens over time, fresh curds characteristically squeak when you bite into them. Just as often, though, cheese curds are beer-battered and deep-fried, and are served with ranch dressing, marinara sauce, ketchup or other dips.

You'll be hard-pressed to find too many bars and restaurants in Wisconsin that don't serve cheese curds. But if you're in Milwaukee, it's worth making time for **Clock Shadow Creamery**, a cheese factory that sells fresh yellow and white Cheddar curds in a variety of flavors, and supplies establishments around the city including **Lakefront Brewery** and **Wisconsin Cheese Mart** (which will also ship fresh cheese curds to your door). And if you're lucky enough to be visiting Wisconsin in August, head out to the fairgrounds in West Allis, where you'll find a few dozen different ways to eat cheese curds at the Wisconsin State Fair: fresh, deep-fried, incorporated into tacos and even as a foot-long cheese-curd-on-a-stick. Put on a Cheesehead hat and you could easily be mistaken for a longtime Badger.

Beer cheese

See Other foods of Kentucky

It's only natural that two of Wisconsin's favorite ingredients are combined in beer cheese, a dip often found in pubs and taverns, particularly those that serve German dishes, such as **Von Trier** in Milwaukee. You'll also see these products made into a hearty beer cheese soup that's a specialty of the state, including at **Cheese Counter and Dairy Heritage Center** in Plymouth.

Butter burger

Everything's better with butter, as the saying goes. But Wisconsin takes that to an extreme with the state's favorite style of burger. Imagine all the places where you might stick butter in a burger, and you'd almost certainly have the right idea. A butter burger is simply one that's cooked with butter on the patty, inside the patty or spread on the bun – or sometimes all of the above, until the burger is just dripping with melted butter everywhere.

The butter burger was most likely invented at **Solly's Grille** in Milwaukee in 1936, although the same year, Kroll's Hamburgers in Green Bay also featured a burger cooked with a pat of butter. Both of these restaurants are still serving up butter burgers today and are worthy of a visit (just know that in Green Bay, **Kroll's East** is the original location, but **Kroll's West** near Lambeau Field also cooks up legendary butter burgers).

If you can't get to either of these spots, though, you're probably not far from an outpost of **Culver's**, Wisconsin's favorite fast-food burger (and frozen custard) chain, with nearly 150 locations across the Badger State. Unlike the originators of the style, Culver's adds butter to the bun instead of the patty – but that didn't stop it from trademarking the term "Butterburger" as its own.

In the Milwaukee area, another option is **Kopp's Frozen Custard**, which cooks up well-regarded butter burgers at its three locations. And if you'd like even more dairy to finish up your meal, Kopp's offers more than a dozen regular varieties of its signature dessert, along with daily flavor specials like cherry amaretto cheesecake, turtle sundae and grasshopper fudge. Milwaukee boasts more frozen custard shops per capita than anywhere in the world, and it wouldn't surprise me if its citizens also consumed the most butter burgers, too.

Broasted chicken

Plenty of common English words are examples of portmanteau, the practice of blending two words to make a new one. For example, brunch is a familiar combination of breakfast and lunch. But did you know that Velcro is a mash-up of the French words meaning velours (velvet) and crochet (hook)? Or that gerrymandering is a portmanteau of one-time Massachusetts governor Elbridge Gerry and a salamander?

Well, in Wisconsin, you'll often find chicken described as broasted, which sounds like it's a portmanteau of broiled and roasted. But that's not what broasted chicken means at all. Rather, it's a term for the practice of marinating and breading chicken in a secret blend of spices, then cooking it in a proprietary device called a Broaster that combines pressure-frying and deep-frying.

Broasting was invented by L.A.M. Phelan in 1953 with a device he built to quickly cook fried chicken, and a year later, he founded a Beloit company named for it. You'll find numerous restaurants around the state that use Phelan's trademarked broasting process and serve up crunchy, juicy chicken. (They're vigilant about protecting the brand, so chicken can only be called broasted if it uses their recipe and their equipment.)

A few highly regarded places where you can try this dish include the **Road Dawg** in Beloit, in the shadow of the Broaster Company's headquarters; **Mibb & Viv's** in Lannon, which features broasted chicken every Wednesday and Saturday; **Mary's Family Restaurant** in Appleton; and **Crandall's Restaurant** in Hebron, Illinois, just south of the Wisconsin border, which serves all-you-can-eat broasted chicken dinners daily. Oddly, you may also encounter broasted chicken in distant corners of the world where restaurants have licensed the Broaster, including Saudi Arabia, Pakistan and Colombia – or as I like to call this trio of countries, Saudpakco.

Fish fry

Weekends in Wisconsin start on Fry-day, and a common way to celebrate the end of the workweek is with a fish fry, a meal of deep-fried, battered freshwater fish that's served at traditional restaurants called supper clubs as well as at pubs and taverns around the state.

A fish fry can include various types of fillets that may include perch, walleye or lake trout (although due to concerns about climate change affecting the local seafood supply, additional types of whitefish that are less endangered, such as cod or haddock, are sometimes served instead). Potato pancakes or French fries usually accompany the fish, along with coleslaw, rye bread and tartar sauce or malt vinegar.

The tradition of a Friday-night fish fry began with the German Catholic immigrants who settled in the upper Midwest beginning in the mid-19th century. Their religious practice prohibited them from eating meat on Fridays, and the abundant fish found in the state's lakes and rivers proved to be a suitable alternative.

In some parts of the state, particularly those settled by Scandinavians such as Door County, the fish fry is less common than the fish boil. This Friday meal consists of chunks of whitefish that are cooked in boiling water along with red potatoes and onions, and served with melted butter and lemon.

A few places where the fish fry is still a venerable Friday tradition include **Swingin' Door Exchange** in Milwaukee, where the menu features cod, lake perch and shrimp; **Dexter's Pub** in Madison, where the seafood choices include lake perch, cod and salmon; and **Parnell's Place** in Oshkosh, where you can select your catch among haddock, perch and walleye.

Another option is to look for restaurants with the words supper club or steakhouse in their name, because these places usually serve up a fish fry special on Fridays. While they tend to be in more rural parts of the state, you'll find a few in Wisconsin's bigger cities, like **Toby's Supper Club** in Madison and **Milwaukee Steakhouse** in Milwaukee. There, you can celebrate the weekend with a Friday fish fry of Icelandic cod – or, a day before or after, with the supper club's signature prime rib.

Booyah

Booyah isn't just a ghost's way of responding in the affirmative, and it's not just a catchphrase used by the late ESPN anchor Stuart Scott to underscore an exciting play. Booyah in Wisconsin, and other places in the upper Midwest, is a fall tradition of cooking a communal pot of soup for a community gathering that's also called by the same name. The dish is usually made with chicken (and sometimes beef) as well as vegetables such as potatoes, onions, carrots and peas. The ingredients are all cooked together slowly in broth, often in a giant kettle that's placed over an outdoor fire.

Booyah, sometimes spelled booya, probably originated in Northern Wisconsin among settlers who came from Belgium in the late 19th or early 20th century. The dish's name is likely a bastardization of the French word bouillon, meaning broth.

You're most likely to encounter booyah at church gatherings in Wisconsin as well as in Minnesota and Michigan. But if you want to try it in a restaurant setting, head to Green Bay. **The Booyah Shed** serves its namesake dish by the cup, pint or quart, and you can also order it at **Zesty's Custard**, which has two locations around the area. Another option is to head northeast to the town of Brussels, where you'll find the soup at **Belgian Delight**. There are only a few places that make this dish, so when you find one, don't hesitate to shout out "Booyah!"

Hopple popple

Sometimes dishes have nonsense names for which there's no clear explanation. Hopple popple, a German breakfast casserole that's sometimes spelled hoppel poppel, is a good example. Just from the name alone, you might have guessed that it's a mishmash of ingredients, a hodgepodge of leftover meat and pantry staples.

There's no set recipe for hopple popple, but it generally includes diced potatoes, onions, scrambled eggs and meat such as bacon, ham or salami. Sometimes a deluxe version of the dish also includes melted cheese, or vegetables like green peppers and mushrooms.

It was once a staple in diners across the Midwest as well as in Jewish delis, which typically deployed all-beef salami or kosher hot dogs as the meat. Today you'll mostly find this dish in Wisconsin, at spots including **Benji's Deli** in Milwaukee and Shorewood, and **Blue's Egg** as well as **Tre Rivali** in Milwaukee, where it appears on the two restaurants' brunch menus. These places aren't hoity-toity, but you shouldn't dilly-dally – 2 p.m. is the latest they'll serve up their hopple popple.

Another Wisconsin dish to sample:

- **Cannibal sandwich**, made from seasoned raw beef, sometimes mixed with raw egg, and served on rye bread with raw onions. (In other places in the upper Midwest, this delicacy is known as tiger meat or wildcat.) While the U.S. Department of Agriculture and the Wisconsin Department of Health warn against consuming uncooked meat, which the USDA says sickens hundreds of people each year, butchers around the state sell lean, freshly ground steak that's often used for this purpose, especially during the holiday season. If you want to reduce your risk, head to a high-end restaurant that serves steak tartare, a similar dish that you'll find in Milwaukee on the menus of **Ardent**, **Birch** and **Bavette La Boucherie**.

Kringle

Wisconsin's official pastry isn't made with beer or filled with sausage. A Kringle is actually an oval-shaped confection that's most prevalent in Racine in the southeast corner of the state. It's a Danish pastry consisting of dozens of layers of flaky dough that may be filled with fruit or nuts and is usually topped with icing.

In Scandinavia, the kringle was typically pretzel-shaped, but Danish bakers who settled in Racine beginning in the late 1800s began baking it as an oval, which was quicker to construct and contained its fillings more easily. At traditional bakeries all over town, you'll find kringles in a variety of flavors such as almond or pecan, along with others that make use of Wisconsin fruits like cranberries and Door County Montmorency cherries.

It won't be difficult to find a kringle in Racine. Just follow your nose to one of the town's favorite bakeries, such as **O&H Danish Bakery**, **Bendtsen's Bakery** and **Larsen Bakery**. But even if you're far away, know that several companies will ship their kringles nationwide – so you can crack open a can of Miller, throw some brats on the grill and enjoy the state's official pastry for dessert.

INDIANA

Tenderloin sandwich

The first thing you'll notice when you order Indiana's favorite sandwich is just how large the filling is compared to the bread. In a properly made tenderloin sandwich, a soft hamburger bun surrounds a comically oversized piece of pork, leaving the meat hanging over the edge of your plate.

The method for preparing the tenderloin is similar to a German or Austrian wiener schnitzel. First, the pork is pounded into a thin cutlet, and then it's dipped in flour and an egg wash before being coated in either breadcrumbs or saltine crackers. Finally, the tenderloin is deep-fried until it's crispy and golden. It's served on the bun with some combination of slices of lettuce, tomatoes, pickles and onions, as well as mayonnaise, mustard or ketchup. (You'll sometimes also see a grilled version of the tenderloin sandwich, which leaves off the breading in favor of seasoning or a marinade.)

The tenderloin sandwich originated in 1904 in Northern Indiana in the town of Huntington, when a German-American named Nick Freienstein began serving it out of a downtown cart. A few years later, he opened **Nick's Kitchen**, which is still in operation over a century later. But the dish's popularity led it to promulgate elsewhere, and you'll also find the tenderloin sandwich at tons of other restaurants and bars around the Hoosier State. (The Indiana Foodways Alliance promotes a Tenderloin Trail with dozens of places that serve their own versions. And there's a corresponding trail in Iowa, where a similar sandwich is also popular.)

A few spots to check out when you're ready to spend some tender coin include **Artie's Tenderloin** in Kokomo, **Cappy's Northside Tavern** in Elkhart and **Aristocrat Pub** in Indianapolis.

Don't plan on grabbing a tenderloin to enjoy on the run, though – this is definitely a sandwich that you'll want to eat with a knife and fork.

Beef Manhattan

You're never going to confuse Indianapolis with New York City, but when you're visiting the state's capital, it's worth keeping an eye out for a signature dish whose name pays tribute to the Big Apple.

Beef Manhattan is an open-faced sandwich consisting of sliced roast beef or steak that's piled onto two slices of white bread that are arranged diagonally, with a scoop of mashed potatoes between them, and the entire plate smothered in brown gravy. It's believed to have originated in Indianapolis in the 1940s among naval workers, who enjoyed a version of the dish while training in New York City during World War II, and brought it back to the Hoosier State.

When you're attending a Colts game at Lucas Oil Stadium, a good place to stop nearby is **Shapiro's Deli**, which creates its sandwich with brisket and either brown or Swiss steak gravy. Other options include **MCL Restaurant & Bakery**, a cafeteria-style establishment with multiple locations around the metro area, where the dish rotates on its list of daily specials, and **Sero's Family Restaurant**, where you can substitute turkey, pork tenderloin or meatloaf for the beef – and where you definitely won't be paying New York prices for your meal.

Chicken and noodles

See Other foods of the South (Chicken and dumplings)

Indiana's version of this comfort-food classic, sometimes called Amish noodles, is usually made with chicken, egg noodles and mashed potatoes. You'll find an excellent version at **10 West Restaurant & Bar** in Cicero.

Sugar cream pie

Indiana's favorite dessert goes by a variety of names – desperation pie (because it doesn't contain any eggs), finger pie (because it was traditional for the cook to stir the batter with a finger) and Hoosier pie (because everything in the state has to be called that, even though no one really knows what the word means). But it's most commonly known as sugar cream pie, and since 2009 it's been the official pie of Indiana.

Sugar cream pie has only a few ingredients – flour, butter, sugar and heavy cream, all of which are mixed together and baked in a pie shell, with flavorings that may include vanilla, nutmeg and cinnamon. The dessert probably came to Indiana with the Quakers who settled there during the early 19th century. A similar pie had a strong foothold in Indiana's Amish communities beginning in the 1830s.

The most iconic place to sample sugar cream pie is **Mrs. Wick's Restaurant & Pie Shop** in Winchester, in east-central Indiana (which also sells frozen pies online and distributes them nationally). You'll also find this delicacy at bakeries as well as diners and other casual restaurants in the Crossroads of America, including **My Sugar Pie** in Zionsville (just outside of Indianapolis), **Nick's Kitchen** in Huntington and **Storie's Restaurant** in Greensburg, halfway between Indianapolis and Cincinnati. Any of these spots would be good places to stick your fork into a slice of pie while reminiscing about Indiana's classic 1986 basketball film starring Gene Hackman.

Another Indiana dish to sample:

- **Fried brain sandwich**, a delicacy that used to be widespread across the Midwest (especially in St. Louis), and is still served at one restaurant in Evansville, **Hilltop Inn**. While it was once made with calves' brains, today the sandwich consists of pigs' brains that are breaded and deep-fried. They're served on a bun alongside slices of pickle and onion that help mask a taste that some people find, well, offal.

MICHIGAN

DETROIT

Detroit-style pizza

Until about a decade ago, Detroit's major contribution to the national pizza scene was two ubiquitous chains: Domino's and Little Caesars. But a style of pizza that's native to the Motor City has now made its way to just about every corner of the country.

In 1946, a tavern called Buddy's Rendezvous developed a new pizza recipe based on Sicilian-style pies, which were rectangular pizzas with a deep, focaccia-like crust. Buddy's baked its version in blue steel pans that were used by local automotive companies to hold spare parts. Instead of sprinkling pepperoni on top of the pie, like other pizza makers did, it layered it all the way to the edges of the pizza, which became crispy in the deep-walled pans. And it covered the salty morsels with racing stripes of tomato sauce as well as a thick layer of cheese – Wisconsin brick cheese, which melted to a gooey consistency in the high temperatures of its pizza oven, caramelizing against the edges of the pan and leaving the crust with a buttery sheen.

All of these elements – the shape, the pan, the construction, the crust and the cheese – became hallmarks of Detroit-style pizza, and other pizzerias, many run by chefs who had worked at Buddy's, soon began imitating it.

Buddy's Pizza now has more than 20 locations in the Detroit metropolitan area, including its original spot just off Six Mile Road. After you try the archetype, it's worth checking out the competition, including **Cloverleaf Bar & Restaurant**, which the owners of Buddy's opened in 1953 in Eastpointe; **Loui's Pizza** in Hazel Park, founded by a former pizza chef at Buddy's; and **Jet's**

Pizza, a local chain with locations all over the metro area. Or search your own city for the latest hipster pizza spot, because there's a good chance there's one that makes Detroit-style pies. Even **Domino's** and **Little Caesars** now sell their own versions of the style that a few years ago, Esquire called "one of the hottest food trends across America."

Dinty Moore

The Dinty Moore sandwich isn't one prepared with canned beef stew – it's Detroit's version of a Reuben, a sandwich that typically includes corned beef, Swiss cheese, sauerkraut and Russian dressing. But in the Motor City, the sauerkraut is usually replaced with coleslaw or shredded lettuce and sliced tomato, and the sandwich is often constructed as a triple-decker, on toasted white or wheat bread instead of rye.

Though the sandwich's exact origins are unknown, the Dinty Moore was likely named for the corned beef hash that was a popular canned stew in the 1950s. Corned beef, the cold cut made by salt-curing beef brisket, has roots in both Jewish and Irish cuisines, and both styles of corned beef can be used to make a Dinty Moore. The Detroit area has three main providers of corned beef: Sy Ginsberg, Wigleys and Grobbel's, so depending on where you go, you may get a slightly different sandwich.

Among the most popular places for a Dinty Moore is **Bread Basket Deli**, which has a half-dozen locations including in downtown Detroit, Oak Park and Livonia. Another good option is **Hygrade Deli** in Southwest Detroit, a neighborhood stalwart that opened in 1955 and was sold to new ownership in 2022. And one of the best sandwich stops in the entire state of Michigan is **Zingerman's Delicatessen** in Ann Arbor. There, you can pick up a Dinty Moore, as well as a variety of corned beef and other meats by the pound, just in case you want to make your own stew or hash at home.

Maurice salad

You might think of this dish as just a chef salad. But if you found one that could talk, it would undoubtedly say that "some people call me Maurice."

The Maurice salad consists of greens mixed with julienned ham, cubes of chicken or turkey, Swiss cheese, sweet gherkins, olives and a creamy, mayonnaise-based dressing that contains chopped eggs and herbs. It may have originated in either New York (where a French chef named P.A. Maurice is said to have created it at the Netherland Plaza in the early 20th century), or in Pittsburgh (named for a customer named Maurice at the William Penn Hotel). But the dish became popular at Detroit's J. L. Hudson department store, where bottles of the signature dressing were sold for decades before the building was demolished in 1998.

Today, just down the street from the location of Hudson's, stands **The Hudson Cafe**, a brunch spot where you can get a Maurice made with romaine hearts and all of the classic ingredients. You'll also see the Maurice salad on menus of other restaurants around town, including **7 Greens Detroit Salad Co.** in downtown Detroit, which makes theirs with roasted chicken, Parmesan crisps and bacon, and **Side Street Diner** in Grosse Pointe, which sticks to the traditional components. It's a good place to sit and contemplate exactly what it was that Steve Miller meant by the "pompatus of love."

Other Detroit dishes to sample:

- **Corned beef egg roll**, a snack made from scraps of corned beef, cabbage and mozzarella cheese that are stuffed into an egg-roll wrapper and deep-fried. One place to try it is **Frank's Deli & Grill** in Detroit.
- **Boston cooler**, a combination of ginger ale (usually Vernors, a brand invented in Michigan) and vanilla ice cream. One place to enjoy this cool treat is **MJ's North End Ice Cream Parlor** in Detroit.

OTHER FOODS OF MICHIGAN

Pasty

Cross the Mackinac Bridge into Michigan's Upper Peninsula and you'll find no shortage of places to eat a pasty. No, I didn't leave the letter r out of that last word – the pasty, pronounced so it rhymes with rhinoplasty, is a pocket meat pie that also contains vegetables such as potato and rutabaga. (OK, so it's also a pastry. Fair.)

Like its cousin, the Butte pasty, the Yooper pasty was brought by European miners who came to work in the state's iron and copper deposits beginning in the 1840s, and relied on this dish for an inexpensive, handheld meal. Unlike how Butte pasties are typically consumed today, though, Michigan's are usually eaten plain or with ketchup, instead of being smothered in gravy. And they trace their lineage to Cornwall, England, rather than to Ireland (though the U.P. version was also influenced by Finnish immigrants who typically substituted carrots for rutabagas in their recipes.)

Other Michigan dishes to sample:

- **Cudighi**, a sausage sandwich commonly eaten in the Upper Peninsula, where the ground meat is seasoned with cinnamon, nutmeg, red wine and black pepper, and is served on a sub roll with marinara sauce and mozzarella cheese. You'll find a well-regarded version of a cudighi at **Vango's Pizza** in Marquette, where you can also order the sandwich with toppings of onions, mushrooms and green peppers.
- **Olive burger**, a style of hamburger that tops the patty with a mixture of mayonnaise and pitted green olives. One place to try it is **Olympic Broil** in Lansing, where the dish is believed to have been invented.
- **Zip sauce**, a steak sauce made from melted butter, beef drippings and Worcestershire sauce that you can purchase in bottles online and also find at steakhouses including locations of **Andiamo** across the state.
- **Frankenmuth-style fried chicken**, a specialty of the town of Frankenmuth, famous for its German-style architecture, for celebrating Christmas year-round, and for two competing restaurants that stand across the street from each other, **Bavarian Inn** and **Zehnder's**. Both places serve all-you-can-eat family-style dinners that include egg noodles, mashed potatoes and other sides, as well as ice cream for dessert. While Bavarian Inn leans into its heritage with German baked goods, sausages, schnitzel and other specialties, Zehnder's has more of a colonial American theme – but serves up a few German dishes as well.

- **Michigan salad**, a green salad that includes dried cherries, made from one of the state's primary crops. It may also contain blue cheese, walnuts and pecans, has a vinaigrette dressing and is often found in Detroit as well as other parts of the Great Lakes State. The salad is sometimes named for Traverse City in Northern lower Michigan, which is a major cherry-growing region. Two spots where you can find this dish in Detroit are **Jacoby's** and **Sindbad's Restaurant and Marina**.

At both ends of the bridge that spans the peninsulas, you'll find locations of **Mackinaw Pastie & Cookie Co.** (its spelling of both its location, matching the town of Mackinaw City, and its product are as quirky as their nontraditional shape). But the nexus of the pasty in the U.P., a five-hour drive to the north and west, is Calumet. Located in the heart of Copper Country, the township hosts an annual festival in August and is where you can enjoy pasties at the **Hut Restaurant** (made by **Pasty Central**, which also sells them online) as well as at **Jen's Kitchen** and **Toni's Country Kitchen**. And if you're around Marquette, try **Lawry's Pasty Shop**, which opened its first location in 1946 in nearby Ishpeming and has a second spot in town.

The Detroit area has its fair share of pasties, too, and you'll find worthwhile homages to the Upper Peninsula delicacy at establishments such as **Barb's Pasties & Pizza** in Clawson, **Superior Pasties** in Livonia and **Uncle Peter's Pasties** in Shelby Township (as well as two other locations a bit further out of town). Or if you're attending a baseball game at **Comerica Park**, keep an eye out for its four flavors of pasties that are decidedly non-traditional: brisket with mac-and-cheese, hot dogs with mustard and onions, sausage with pierogi and sauerkraut, and apples and cinnamon. That one, especially, sounds like its name should contain the missing letter r.

OHIO

CINCINNATI

Cincinnati-style chili

The most iconic regional dish in the Queen City is nothing like the chili you'll find in Texas, the Southwest or just about anywhere else in the country. Cincinnati-style chili is a meat sauce spiced with Mediterranean flavors that's most commonly used as a topping for spaghetti and hot dogs. It's typically made with ground beef, tomato paste and spices that may include cinnamon, cumin, cloves, chili powder and sometimes dark chocolate, and is served at chili parlors all around the Cincinnati metropolitan area.

This style of chili was introduced in the early 1920s by two immigrants from Macedonia, Tom and John Kiradjieff. The brothers opened a hot dog stand called **The Empress** in 1922, named after the downtown theater it was adjacent to, and began serving both coneys and spaghetti topped with the meat sauce as well as shredded Cheddar cheese. They also invented the "way" system of ordering a bowl of chili that's still in common use today: a two-way is spaghetti topped with chili; a three-way adds cheese; a four-way includes either chopped white onions or beans; and a five-way contains everything. (Oyster crackers and hot sauce, both typical accompaniments, don't count as "ways.") A similar system is used for hot dogs, with chili, cheese and onions being the most popular toppings for a coney.

In the subsequent decades, cooks who had worked at The Empress opened their own franchises, but today, only one remains, a branch in the nearby suburb of Alexandria, Kentucky, that serves The Empress's original recipe on spaghetti, coneys or pizza. The mantle of the leading chili parlor in Cincinnati has since been taken up by a pair of competing chains: **Skyline Chili**, founded in 1949 by a Greek immigrant, Nicholas Lambrinides, who had worked at The Empress, and **Gold Star Chili**, launched in 1965 by a quartet of brothers from Jordan named Daoud, who took over a hamburger stand but then saw how well the chili was selling and made it their primary focus.

Either of these chains, with dozens of locations around the metro area, would be a good first foray into the Cincinnati chili experience. But there are other worthy options, such as **Camp Washington Chili** and **Blue Ash Chili** (in the Ohio suburb of the same name), that are equally well-regarded.

Just don't make the mistake of ordering a bowl of Cincinnati chili by itself, as you might for another regional style. While many parlors will let you do so, you'd essentially be ordering a serving of deliciously flavored pasta sauce. As residents of the Queen City sometimes say, that's not really chili.

Goetta

You'd better goetta trip to Cincinnati on the calendar if you want to try this German breakfast sausage, as you'll rarely find it anywhere else in the country.

Goetta consists of ground meat, usually pork but sometimes a combination of pork and beef, that's mixed with steel-cut oats, aromatics and spices including rosemary, thyme, marjoram and bay leaves. It's prepared in loaf pans, chilled and then sliced into patties, and is typically fried in butter before serving. It's eaten as a breakfast staple but is sometimes also used for sandwiches or as a pizza topping.

German immigrants brought the dish to the Ohio Valley during the first half of the 19th century, around the time that Cincinnati was developing into the country's largest pork processor. As in similar sausage products, the addition of oats was intended to stretch the supply of meat, which originally made use of pork or beef scraps. A century later, Cincinnati began producing goetta commercially, with Glier's and Queen City Sausage being the primary manufacturers.

You'll find goetta in just about any local supermarket or local butcher, as well as at breakfast spots like **Maplewood Kitchen and Bar** and **Sleepy Bee Cafe**, both downtown, and **Eckerlin Meats** at Findlay Market. But if you happen to be visiting Porkopolis during the summer, Glier's hosts an annual Goettafest along the riverfront in Newport, Kentucky, with a menu that includes such creative dishes as goetta brownies, goetta crab cakes and goetta corn dogs. It's a great place to listen to live music, admire the Cincinnati skyline and of course, goetta bite to eat.

CLEVELAND

Polish Boy

You might be surprised to learn that the signature food of Cleveland wasn't invented by someone in the city's sizable Polish-American community. Instead, a Polish Boy takes its name from the Polish sausage, a kielbasa, that's at the heart of this dish. Sometimes the kielbasa is itself known as a Polish Boy, but the term also refers to one that's grilled, topped with coleslaw, French fries and barbecue sauce and served in a hot dog bun.

The Polish Boy was likely created in the 1940s by Virgil Whitmore, the Black owner of a barbecue establishment in the Mount Pleasant neighborhood who made use of the ingredients he happened to have on hand when constructing a new sandwich. Other barbecue spots – most of which have now closed – took up the torch and served their own versions of the Polish Boy, and today, you'll also find them in restaurants, butchers and bars around the Cleveland area.

One oft-lauded place to get one is **Seti's Polish Boys**, a food truck that's been in operation for over 20 years and is typically parked midday in Ohio City. You'll also see Polish Boys on the menu at **Mt. Pleasant Bar-B-Q**, now run by Whitmore's grandson; **Mabel's BBQ** downtown (as well as in Woodmere), owned by celebrity chef Michael Symon, who serves a "Polish Girl" that includes the standard toppings with the addition of pulled pork; and **Banter**, a bottle shop in the Detroit-Shoreway neighborhood (and in Shaker Heights) that elevates the Polish Boy with frites and a house-made sauce. This isn't just any old hot dog, though – they make the sandwich so grown-up that you might even choose to call it a Polish Man.

Corned beef

New Yorkers may beg to differ, but some of the country's best corned beef comes from a place that has a collection of less than world-famous nicknames – including Forest City, America's North Coast and the Cleve.

Corned beef is salt-cured beef brisket that's a staple of both Jewish and Irish cuisines, with the latter being particularly important in C-Town. The first Irish settlers came to the city around 1820, and thousands more joined them in the subsequent decades, especially spurred on by the potato famine in Ireland, with about 10 percent of Cleveland's population having Irish heritage by 1870. (Today there are hundreds of thousands of Irish-Americans in Cleveland, constituting only a slightly lower percentage.)

Corned beef and cabbage is a staple of St. Patrick's Day – the city boasts one of the country's oldest St. Patrick's Day parades, with the first having stepped off in 1867 – but Clevelanders also celebrate the meat in sandwich form year-round. At **Slyman's Deli**, founded in 1964, the sandwiches are nearly three-quarter-pound behemoths, typically served on rye with an accompanying pickle spear. It's the most famous place for corned beef in Cleveland, having hosted former U.S. President

George W. Bush and celebrities including Rachael Ray and Barenaked Ladies, who once celebrated the restaurant's fare in song. (A sister establishment, **Slyman's Tavern**, opened in Independence in 2015.)

Less than a mile away from Slyman's is another well-regarded spot for corned beef, **Danny's Deli** (which also has a location in Columbus). You could also try **Karl's Inn of the Barristers**, downtown as well, whose corned beef is frequently rated as among the city's best. And in the suburb of Lakewood, it's worth visiting **Joe's Deli & Restaurant**, which boasts sandwiches that rival Slyman's in height. Even a skeptical New Yorker visiting the 216 would quickly realize that corned beef is really what's hot in Cleveland – even if the city's nicknames aren't so much.

Pierogi

Cleveland's famous for many things: It's the birthplace of rock and roll, the home of baseball and football teams with long championship droughts, the city where the Cuyahoga River once caught on fire – and the place where pierogi are as much of a fixture in the local culinary scene as anywhere else in the country.

Pierogi are dumplings made from a pasta-like dough that contain either a savory or sweet filling and are either boiled or pan-fried. A common variety of pierogi is filled with mashed potatoes and cheese and served with butter and sauteed onions, and perhaps a side of sour cream. But you'll also find them stuffed with meat, or with fruit fillings such as cherry or apple.

Pierogi became popular in Cleveland – and other cities in the Midwest and mid-Atlantic, particularly Pittsburgh – in the late 19th and early 20th centuries. That's the period when waves of immigrants from Eastern Europe, especially Poland but also Ukraine, Hungary and Slovakia, settled in the city.

Vestiges of this heritage are still visible around town, at places that highlight pierogi such as **Little Polish Diner** in Parma, a suburb with a large Polish population; **Olesia's Taverne**, a Ukranian-American restaurant in Richfield; and **Dick & Alice**, another Parma spot that serves up pierogi in a handful of varieties as well as Italian, Hungarian and Slovenian sausages. And if you're visiting Cleveland in June, keep an eye out for the annual Slavic Village Pierogi Dash, a fun run that ends with a pierogi party. That sounds a lot more enjoyable than worrying about whether the Browns will ever be good enough to make the Super Bowl.

OTHER FOODS OF OHIO

Shredded chicken sandwich

Whether you're just passing through Ohio or heading to one of its major urban centers, it's worth venturing off the beaten path to stop for lunch at a roadside drive-in. But instead of a standard burger or hot dog, look out for a regional dish that rarely crosses the state's borders: the shredded chicken sandwich (sometimes known as a hot chicken sandwich).

Originally created to make use of leftover cooked chicken, and frequently served at church potlucks and other community events in the Buckeye State, the shredded chicken sandwich is the result of cooking the title ingredient in a crockpot with cream of chicken soup, spices and seasonings and a thickener such as crackers or potato chips. The creamy, saucy chicken is typically served on a soft bun.

You'll mostly find shredded chicken sandwiches at restaurants and drive-ins in the central and northern parts of the state. One option outside Columbus is **Clay's Cafe**, a small restaurant in Hebron that's also known for its stromboli and ice cream. In Newark, another well-regarded spot is **Mick's Soft Serve**, and in Baltimore, check out **Schaffner's Drive-In**. And if you're heading to Canton to honor the greatest players in the NFL, try **Woody's Root Beer Stand**, which serves a "creamy chicken" sandwich while it's open during the summer. You'll have to judge for yourself whether the dish is worthy of induction to the sandwich Hall of Fame.

JoJos

See Other foods of the Pacific Northwest and Alaska

Although these fried potato wedges are mostly found in the Pacific Northwest, you'll also see them in pockets of Ohio, at spots including **Raisicci's Pizza** in Akron and **Jo Jo's Sports Bar & Grill** in Medina.

Sauerkraut balls

In Greece, it's traditional to smash a pomegranate against the front door on New Year's Eve. In Brazil, it's common to wear red underwear that night. And in Akron, Ohio, and other communities in the northeast part of the state, it's customary on New Year's Day to eat sauerkraut balls – the official dish of Rubber City.

Sauerkraut balls are an appetizer made with fermented cabbage, sausage or ham (or sometimes ground pork or beef), cream cheese and herbs. The mixture is then rolled in breadcrumbs and either baked or deep-fried. They're usually served hot with either cocktail sauce or mustard.

The dish originated at a now-closed German restaurant called Gruber's in Shaker Heights in the late 1950s, and became especially popular in the 1960s at **Waterloo Restaurant** in Akron. Although sauerkraut balls are a holiday specialty in the region, they're eaten year-round at other restaurants and bars like Akron's **Ido Bar & Grill** and **Main Street Saloon**, and you can also find frozen versions in local supermarkets.

If there's any doubt that this dish has captured the imagination of Ohio food lovers, there's a sauerkraut festival in Waynesville at which the appetizer is celebrated each fall. And in Akron, the city's minor league baseball team, the RubberDucks, was even renamed the Sauerkraut Balls for one game in 2023. It's unclear whether fans sang Auld Lang Syne during the seventh-inning stretch.

Buckeyes

Some colleges have easily identifiable mascots – like the Clemson Tiger or Wisconsin's Bucky Badger. But then there's Ohio State's, Brutus Buckeye, a humanoid version of the poisonous seed that comes from the state's official tree. Ohio State students were called buckeyes for decades before the school adopted it as its official symbol in 1950. But around the time Brutus came around, in 1965, local confectioners began making a candy that resembled the buckeye nut, and it soon became one of the state's favorite sweets.

A buckeye is a peanut butter ball that's been dipped in chocolate, leaving a small circle of the peanut butter visible to make it look like the tree nut. While candymakers most often use milk chocolate, other varieties of the buckeye can employ either dark or white chocolate.

Buckeyes are available in candy stores and gift shops all around the region, especially in Columbus, the home of Ohio State, where **Anthony-Thomas Chocolates** operates a dozen locations. Other reputable spots include **Malley's Chocolates**, a large confectioner in the Cleveland area, and **Marsha's Homemade Buckeyes** in Perrysburg, just outside Toledo.

According to local folklore, keeping a buckeye nut in your pocket is supposed to bring good luck. I wouldn't recommend keeping the candy there – unless your idea of good luck is being followed by a hungry Cincinnati Bearcat.

Other Ohio dishes to sample:

- **Ohio Valley-style pizza**, characteristic of Steubenville, a town bordering the Ohio River in the eastern part of the state. This variety of pizza is baked on a sheet pan with a thin layer of melted cheese, with additional mozzarella and other cold toppings placed on top of the pizza after it comes out of the oven. The classic place to try this style is **DiCarlo's Pizza**, which also has branches in Akron and Columbus as well as a few locations outside Ohio.
- **Barberton chicken**, a style of breaded, fried chicken with Serbian roots that's characteristic of the town of Barberton, a suburb of Akron. The chicken is served with a vinegar-based coleslaw, French fries and a side dish of rice cooked with tomatoes and hot peppers that's known as hot sauce or hot rice. There are a handful of restaurants in town where you can enjoy this meal, including **Belgrade Gardens**, the establishment that originated the style in 1933.
- **Johnny Marzetti**, a casserole that contains ground beef, pasta, tomato sauce and mozzarella cheese that's native to Columbus. An apocryphal story says that Johnny was the brother-in-law of an Italian-American restauranteur there named Teresa Marzetti, who was said to have named the dish after him as early as 1896. But a recent local report showed that this story was probably not true. Nonetheless, versions of the dish still appear at old-school restaurants in Columbus such as **Tommy's Diner**. A similar dish is known as American goulash across the upper Midwest, particularly in Wisconsin and Minnesota, and is called American chop suey in Massachusetts and New Hampshire (*see Other foods of New England*).

OTHER FOODS OF THE MIDWEST

Quad City-style pizza

If you're planning to stop for pizza along the Illinois-Iowa border, you might make a few assumptions that you'll soon learn are flat-out wrong. First, the pizza here probably won't taste like any pie you've ever had before. The unique way it's cut may also be unfamiliar. And then, just when you think there aren't any more disorienting surprises, you'll realize that there are actually five Quad Cities – Davenport and Bettendorf, Iowa; and Rock Island, Moline and East Moline, Illinois – not four.

Both the crust and the sauce make Quad City-style pizza unique. The dough is flavored with malt, and sometimes also molasses, that lend it a slight sweetness, while the sauce contains cayenne pepper and chili flakes that provide a contrasting kick. Fennel-flecked sausage is a common topping for this style of pie. But instead of layering it above the cheese, it's buried underneath (one pizza-maker is said to use a pound per pie). And don't expect to get a typical wedge-shaped piece, or even a rectangle from a Midwestern party cut – Quad City pies are sliced, sometimes with special pizza shears, into thin, irregular strips that always include a piece of the crust.

Like the local geography, the history of this dish is murky. But Quad City-style pizza seems to have been created by the Maniscalco family in the mid-1950s, one member of which opened a restaurant in Silvis (near East Moline) that today is called **Frank's Pizza**. Another account says that **Harris Pizza**, which opened in 1960 in Rock Island and calls itself The Original Quad City Style Pizza, invented the style. Harris still operates its premier spot, but also now has locations in Davenport and Bettendorf (staying away from Frank's side of town, in what is believed to be an informal arrangement).

In addition to these competitors, other well-regarded spots for pies of this style include **Quad City Pizza Company** and **Top Hat Pizza** in Moline, and **Saint Giuseppe's Pizza** in East Moline. But if you're on the other side of Illinois, and you get a hankering for Quad City-style pizza, you can also stop by any of the four locations of **Roots Handmade Pizza** in Chicago. That's one for each of the original Quad Cities, before Bettendorf joined the party in the late 1940s. Although there was some discussion about changing the name of the region, Quint City-style pizza just doesn't have the same ring to it.

Coney Island hot dog

The story of the hot dog that's enjoyed widely across the Midwest, but especially in Michigan and Cincinnati, Ohio, has as many twists and turns as the famous Cyclone roller coaster on Coney Island itself.

A Coney Island hot dog is a frankfurter that's nestled in a soft steamed bun and topped with a tomato-based meat sauce along with yellow mustard and chopped white onions. Although Charles Feltman sold sausages on Brooklyn's Coney Island starting in 1871 – and one of his employees, Nathan Handwerker, opened a rival hot dog stand in 1916 that eventually became the area's most famous – neither of these entrepreneurs was responsible for the Coney Island style. While the history is murky, that honor likely goes to one of several Greek and Macedonian immigrants who passed through New York's Ellis Island, probably in the 1910s, who were influenced by the popularity of the hot dogs eaten nearby.

One of these was George Todoroff, a Macedonian immigrant who opened Todoroff's Original Coney Island in Jackson, Michigan, in 1914, serving hot dogs with a meat sauce made with ground beef, onions and spices. Although the original restaurant closed in 2008, you can still buy **Todoroff's** chili online, and several other hot dog stands are still popular in Jackson, some of which use ground beef heart in their sauce – a characteristic of both Jackson- and Flint-style coneys (which are often made with frankfurters produced by the local manufacturer Koegel's).

The Coney Island hot dog exploded in popularity over the next decade after two brothers, the Greek immigrants Bill and Gust Keros, began to sell them at a pair of stands in downtown Detroit. **American Coney Island**, opened in 1917, was followed in 1924 by **Lafayette Coney Island** next door, and both restaurants continue to attract Detroiters who argue over whose meat sauce, slightly wetter than those in other parts of the state, is best. Detroit is also home to dozens of other spots to enjoy a coney, including the popular chain **National Coney Island**, with locations across the metro area, the diner **Duly's Place** in Southwest Detroit and **Apollo Coney Island** in Sterling Heights.

While Michigan is the epicenter of the Coney Island hot dog, the style also took root in other locations across the Midwest including Fort Wayne, Indiana, and Duluth, Minnesota, as well as in pockets of Oklahoma. One place where the coney is especially well-known is Cincinnati, where two brothers from Macedonia, Tom and John Kiradjieff, opened a hot dog stand called **The Empress** in 1922 and began serving their cinnamon-spiced meat sauce on top of frankfurters as well as spaghetti. Today you'll see coneys as well as cheese coneys (with an additional topping of shredded Cheddar) on the menus of the two most famous local chains, **Skyline Chili** and **Gold Star Chili**, as well as at other restaurants around the area.

You'll also find similar meat-topped hot dogs in other parts of the country, but they're often called by different names, including a New York System hot wiener in Rhode Island and a Michigan hot dog in Plattsburgh, New York. But on Coney Island, a meat-topped frankfurter at **Nathan's Famous** is just a chili cheese dog.

City chicken

A bear claw isn't actually made from bears, there aren't any grasshoppers in grasshopper pie – and there's no chicken in the Midwestern dish known as city chicken.

City chicken consists of cubes of meat, usually pork, that are skewered and either fried or pan-fried and then baked. Sometimes the meat is breaded before cooking, and, depending on where you're eating it, it's often served with a brown gravy.

This dish can mostly be found in the cities of Cleveland; Detroit; Erie, Pennsylvania, and Binghamton, New York. It developed among Polish and Ukrainian immigrant communities during the mid-1920s when cooks were looking for an alternative to chicken, which at the time was seen as a luxury item. Sometimes the skewered meat, which made use of scraps of pork, veal or beef, was shaped to make it look like a chicken drumstick.

Grocery stores in these cities still sell skewered meat packaged as city chicken, and you'll also find it a few old-school eateries. In Cleveland, look for city chicken at **Marie's Restaurant**, which serves an Eastern European menu, and at **Red Chimney** in Slavic Village. And at **Fast Eddie's** in Parma, city chicken is offered as a Wednesday blue plate special – which might not actually be served on a blue plate.

Almond boneless chicken

When dining at Chinese restaurants in the Midwest, particularly around Detroit and Columbus, it's important to know your ABCs. In this case, that stands for almond boneless chicken, a regional staple that you'll rarely find anywhere else.

Almond boneless chicken, known in Chinese as war su gai, is a dish made with white-meat chicken that's battered and deep-fried until it's crispy. It's typically served on a bed of iceberg lettuce with a mild brown sauce that's made with chicken broth, cornstarch and soy sauce, along with vegetables that may include water chestnuts, bamboo shoots, mushrooms and celery. The dish is garnished with a sprinkling of almonds, and is usually accompanied by white rice.

The origin of this dish is murky, but it may have originated in the 1920s in Bexley, Ohio, a suburb of Columbus. It later came to Detroit's Chinatown, where Cantonese immigrants who opened restaurants typically shared their recipes with each other. As almond boneless chicken spread across the region, it became a popular comfort-food dish for generations of Detroiters.

A few restaurants around Columbus still serve almond boneless chicken, including **New China Express**, with a quartet of locations north of the city. In Michigan, it continues to be a staple at establishments such as **Lim's Chinese Restaurant** and **Wing Lee Chinese Restaurant**, both in Sterling Heights, **Ten Yen Restaurant** in Livonia and **The Peterboro** in Detroit. The latter restaurant offers a contemporary version, using chicken thighs instead of the typical breast and adding dehydrated shiitake mushrooms as well as yuzu to the sauce. But even with these fancy ingredients, making it taste like the original is as easy as ABC.

Pączki

Even among non-Christians, Mardi Gras, or Fat Tuesday, is widely celebrated as the final day before the pre-Easter period of Lent begins. But that day is also the culmination of a week when the Polish pastries known as pączki reach their annual peak.

Pączki are round, puffy donuts made from an enriched yeasted dough that contains milk and eggs. They're filled with fruit or custard – though they come in dozens of flavors, rose petal and prune are traditional varieties – and are typically topped with icing, glaze or powdered sugar.

These pastries are prominent among communities with large numbers of Polish-Americans, including Chicago, Milwaukee, Detroit, Cleveland, Toledo, Pittsburgh and Buffalo. They're widely available at European bakeries in these cities – especially in the weeks leading up to Lent – as well as in smaller communities like Hamtramck, Michigan, which has a concentration of Polish bakeries such as **New Palace Bakery** (as well as a 5K run the day before Fat Tuesday, "to help you feel better about eating those pączki, or ... scout out your favorite place to purchase them").

On the annual holiday called Pączki Day, which coincides with Fat Tuesday, customers line up for hours outside of these shops to get their hands on the decadent treat. But those in the know get their pastries in time for Fat Thursday, five days earlier. That's when pączki are traditionally eaten in Poland, at the beginning of the week when Christians try to use up all the foods that can't be consumed during Lent.

At **Rudy's Strudel** in Parma, Ohio, outside Cleveland, you can order pączki as early as mid-January, in two dozen sweet and a handful of savory flavors. But the party reaches its climax on Fat Tuesday, when Rudy's prepares 70,000 pączki for the massive crowds who arrive in time for the bakery's 5 a.m. opening – and stay all day for live music and traditional Polish food. Sounds like a good way to celebrate Mardi Gras without having to make a trip to New Orleans.

Kolache

The kolache is a sweet, round pastry that was brought to America by Czech and Slovak immigrants beginning in the 1870s. It's baked with a yeasted dough and is usually filled with preserves made from apricots, cherries, prunes or other fruits (though they can also contain sweetened cheese or poppy seeds). Savory Czech pastries filled with sausage, ham or potatoes that are made from the same dough are sometimes also called kolaches, but these are technically a different pastry called a klobasnik.

Because the Czech community is spread widely across the Midwest (as well as in pockets of Texas, Oklahoma, Nebraska and South Dakota), you'll find kolaches in European-style bakeries in numerous states. A few of the larger Midwestern cities where you'll be able to track them down most easily, with a suggested location in each, are Cedar Rapids, Iowa (**Sykora Bakery**); Chicago (**Kolatek's Bakery & Deli**); Green Bay, Wisconsin (**Olde World Pastries Plus**); and Minneapolis (**Taste of Scandinavia Bakery & Cafe**, with three locations in the metro area).

You'll also see kolaches in small towns in the upper Midwest that honor their Czech heritage at annual events. During the Czech and Kolache Festival in Kewaunee, Wisconsin, as many as 12,000 kolaches are sold during the weekend.

Snickers pie

If you're invited to a potluck dinner or a church social in the Midwest, particularly in Minnesota or Iowa, there's a good chance you'll encounter a Snickers salad. This dish consists of Snickers bars – the candy containing nougat, caramel and peanuts that's all enrobed in milk chocolate – along with Granny Smith apples that are both chopped up and mixed with Cool Whip and vanilla pudding. Because it's called a salad, it's sometimes served alongside savory dishes, although its sugar content suggests that it's more suitable as a dessert.

During your travels you're unlikely to run across a Snickers salad on restaurant menus. But what you'll often see is Snickers pie, a dish that features the candy bar in a filling made with peanut butter and whipped cream, poured into a graham-cracker or cookie crust and topped with caramel sauce.

A few places you might encounter this treat include **Breitbach's Country Dining** in Sherrill, Iowa; **Uncle Mike's Bake Shoppe**, with three locations in the Green Bay, Wisconsin, area; **Sweetwater Tavern & Grille** in Chicago; and **Machine Shed Restaurant**, which has a half-dozen locations in Iowa, Minnesota, Illinois and Wisconsin. But even if the pie you come across happens to include apples, you probably won't find it at the salad bar.

Blue moon ice cream

What's your favorite kind of ice cream? Chocolate chip? Strawberry ripple? Coconut almond fudge? Well, if you're from the upper Midwest, you might answer blue moon, a mysterious, Smurf-colored flavor that's rarely found outside of ice cream parlors and stores in Wisconsin and Michigan.

The taste of blue moon is hard to pin down: Some say it reminds them of marshmallows or cotton candy, many detect notes of berries or citrus, and others suggest that the flavor is reminiscent of Froot Loops. But there seems little doubt that blue food coloring is added to give the ice cream its distinctive color.

Blue moon is usually one of the components of Superman ice cream, a three-flavor combination of red, blue and yellow scoops that's often found in Wisconsin and Michigan. Because the name Superman is not officially licensed from DC Comics, it's sometimes sold under different names, with strawberry or cherry serving as the red flavor and lemon or vanilla as the yellow.

A company called Weber Flavors now owns the secret recipe for blue moon. Although no one knows for sure, a prevailing theory about its history says that it was developed by a chemist named Bill Sidon at Milwaukee's Petran Products in the 1950s. Sidon had come to the U.S. in 1939, fleeing the Nazis in his native Austria before becoming the company's chief flavor chemist.

The only problem with this story is that according to recent research, blue moon may have existed for as long as two decades prior, and might not have originated in the Midwest at all.

As you travel around the upper Midwest, you'll be happy to learn that this flavor isn't as rare as a blue moon. In Wisconsin, you'll find it at places such as **Hansen's Ice Cream Parlor** in Burlington and Wilmot; **Mullen's Dairy Bar** in Watertown and Oconomowoc; and **Chocolate Shoppe Ice Cream**, with seven locations in the Madison area. And in Michigan, try **Michigan Creamery** in Ann Arbor and **Ray's Ice Cream** in Royal Oak. At any of these spots, you can ponder the origin of this perplexing flavor, and try to determine just what magic ingredients it might be made from.

Another Midwest dish to sample:

- **Lutefisk,** a Scandinavian dish of preserved whitefish cured in lye that's typically eaten during the holiday season in Michigan and Wisconsin, frequently alongside lefse. You'll rarely find it on regular restaurant menus, but you can buy it in Norwegian and Swedish markets such as **Ingrebetsen's Scandinavian Gifts & Foods**, as well as at fishmongers such as **Olsen Fish Company**, also in Minneapolis. It's sometimes served at special dinners like the ones at **Norske Nook Restaurant** in Wisconsin, as well as at Lutheran churches in both Minnesota and Wisconsin.

Jambalaya

LOUISIANA

The unique history and culture of Louisiana – and its major city, New Orleans – is the reason that it's more concentrated with regional food specialties than just about anywhere else in the U.S. Its low-lying geography, while making the state prone to natural disasters, also provides an abundance of seafood that features prominently in its cuisine. And the hot, humid climate provides fertile conditions for growing rice, a staple used in many characteristic dishes. Some of Louisiana's regional food is most prevalent at fancy restaurants, especially in the Crescent City. But it's also possible to dine extremely well on a budget, with plentiful options for snacks and sandwiches that will still allow you to eat like a local.

The first settlers in Louisiana, joining the indigenous people already living there, came from France in the late 1600s, and that country retained control of the province until Spain claimed ownership in 1762 following the Treaty of Fontainebleau. Influences from each of those cultures, along with slaves from West Africa and other European and Caribbean immigrants, combined to create what became known as Creole cuisine. Many of the state's iconic dishes first emerged from Creole kitchens, including gumbo, jambalaya, red beans and rice and more.

Creole recipes often feature a pair of French cooking techniques: a sauce made from a roux, a mixture of flour and butter, and the diced vegetable base called mirepoix. But instead of using carrots, Creole dishes make use of green bell peppers, along with onions and celery – a trio of ingredients that became known as the holy trinity. Creole specialties also frequently include tomatoes, which were introduced to Louisiana by Spanish colonists, as well as peppers and other spices that gave these preparations heat as well as seasoning.

But the food of Louisiana has been equally shaped by the French-speaking colonists who came to the state after being evicted from a region of Eastern Canada known as Acadia in the early 1700s. These settlers eventually made their home along the bayou, and over time developed a unique rural cuisine that became known as Cajun. While there's considerable overlap between Cajun and Creole specialties and cooking methods, a few characteristic Cajun dishes include shrimp étouffée, which uses a smothering technique also commonly employed for crawfish; boudin balls, deep-fried fritters made from a pork and rice filling often stuffed into sausage casings; and dirty rice, adapted by the Cajuns from a dish originally created by plantation slaves, using locally available wild game as well as additional spices.

Much of the food found in New Orleans today has evolved from either Cajun or Creole traditions. The Acadians were responsible for introducing the French pastries called beignets to the city, while Creole culture is visible through menu items like grillades and grits, and shrimp Creole. But some of the city's most famous dishes originated at other historic eateries and remain popular among both visitors and locals, including Oysters Rockefeller, invented in 1889 at **Antoine's Restaurant**; the muffuletta, introduced in 1906 at **Central Grocery**; and Bananas Foster, created in 1951 at a restaurant that later became known as **Brennan's**.

The economy and culture of New Orleans took a massive hit in 2005 when Hurricane Katrina destroyed many neighborhoods and killed nearly 1,400 people. But the city rebuilt and today, its dining scene is as vibrant as ever. While Paul Prudhomme and Emeril Lagasse were once its brightest culinary lights, highlighting Cajun and Creole dishes on the world stage, today celebrity chefs such as Isaac Toups and Nina Compton have put their own spin on the city's native cuisine, with the latter incorporating Caribbean influences from her native St. Lucia.

But you don't need to dine at high-end restaurants to eat like royalty in the Big Easy. There are po' boys, sandwiches made from French baguettes with shrimp, oyster or other fillings on practically every corner, and a bowl of gumbo or jambalaya is usually hearty as well as inexpensive. When you need to satisfy your sweet tooth, it won't cost you an arm and a leg to try a praline candy or two, or a piece of Doberge or Chantilly cake. And if you happen to be in New Orleans around Mardi Gras, when a city that celebrates food and music year-round swells with parades and parties, don't miss the opportunity to sample king cake. If you're fortunate enough to have the plastic baby in your slice, that might be all the luck you'll need to ensure you'll come back soon, so you can keep eating everything New Orleans (and Louisiana) has to offer.

LOUISIANA

New Orleans

Po' boy

You could probably dine on nothing but po' boys for a whole week in New Orleans and still have barely scratched the surface of all the possibilities.

A po' boy is a sandwich served on a particular style of French baguette that has a crispy outside and a soft interior. It usually contains either fried seafood such as shrimp, soft-shell crab or catfish, or roast beef or other meats, and is typically dressed with mayonnaise, shredded lettuce, tomato slices and pickles. On a roast beef po' boy, it's common to have debris, a meaty gravy, spooned on top of the filling.

Local legend says that the po' boy was invented at Martin Brothers' Coffee Stand and Restaurant in 1929, when the owners offered free sandwiches, made with long loaves of bread baked by John Gendusa, to striking streetcar workers. When one would walk into the store, one of the brothers would say, "Here comes another poor boy!," a line that's said to give the dish its name. But because similar sandwiches had long been eaten in New Orleans, and the tale didn't spread until many decades later, this story seems unlikely to be true.

You can eat po' boys any hour of the day or night, and with so many standouts to choose among, that's probably a good idea. A few of the most iconic options include **Parkway Bakery & Tavern** in Mid-City, an institution that's been open since 1911 with a wide range of meat and seafood choices (smoked alligator sausage, anyone?); **Domilise's Po-Boy & Bar** in West Riverside, known especially for its roast beef debris, served with or without Swiss cheese (although it'd be hard to beat the roast beef po' boy I devoured at **Parasol's** in Irish Channel); **Johnny's**

Po-Boys, a French Quarter mainstay whose shrimp po' boy has been known to be my first bite in town; **Verti Marte**, a deli counter in the back of a French Quarter convenience store that's open 24 hours; and **Liuzza's by the Track**, a short distance from the more touristed parts of town but well worth the drive, especially for the BBQ shrimp po' boy, one of the best things I ate during my last visit.

If none of these choices appeal, though, you won't be able to walk more than a few blocks in the Big Easy without encountering another po' boy shop. And since these are some of the least expensive eating options in town, they're perfect for any meal of the day – and because this is New Orleans, the meals you'll want to consume between all of your other meals.

Oyster loaf

A sandwich that likely pre-dates the po' boy but remains a signature dish of New Orleans is the oyster loaf. This typically consists of a hollowed-out baguette stuffed with breaded and fried oysters, that's often dressed with the same combination of toppings that you'll find in a standard po' boy (although pickles are sometimes excluded).

The sandwich is also called a peacemaker, for the practice, described in an 1893 article, of a man coming home after a night of carousing carrying a conciliatory oyster loaf for his lady. Decades later, a San Francisco newspaper described a similar custom, and claimed – almost certainly erroneously – that a local tavern had invented the sandwich. (Today, a peacemaker sometimes refers to a sandwich with a mixture of fried shrimp and oysters, or even shrimp and roast beef, to help you make peace with yourself when you can't decide what to order.)

The classic place to go for an oyster loaf is **Casamento's**, an East Riverside stalwart open since 1919 that uses buttered, lightly fried bread rather than a baguette and also serves fried shrimp, trout and catfish loaves.

These days you'll only occasionally see oyster sandwiches referred to as loaves, with **Mandina's Restaurant** in Mid-City being one prominent exception. But there are tons of bivalve-centric spots where you can get an outstanding oyster po' boy, including **Felix's Restaurant & Oyster Bar** and **Acme Oyster House**, both in the French Quarter (and other locations). And if you decide to take an extra sandwich back to your hotel, you can think of it as carrying on a century-old tradition.

Oysters Bienville

The 18th-century governor of French Louisiana named Jean-Baptiste Le Moyne de Bienville is today remembered as the founder of New Orleans. But he certainly had no idea that a street in the French Quarter would one day carry his surname, and that his name would also be used for a baked oyster dish that's one of New Orleans's classic seafood appetizers.

Oysters Bienville consists of oysters on the half-shell, topped with a mixture of shrimp, mushrooms, green onions and herbs that are all cooked in a white-wine sauce. The oysters are then baked until golden-brown, and immediately served warm. The dish is believed to have originated in the 1930s at **Arnaud's**, a Creole restaurant in the French Quarter (located on Bienville Street), although the chef may have been inspired by a similar preparation at **Antoine's Restaurant**, a New Orleans institution around since 1840 that today serves its Oysters Bienville with peppers, pimentos and grated Romano cheese.

Both restaurants are iconic, but fancy, places to try Oysters Bienville. But you'll also find it at seafood spots such as **Felix's Restaurant & Oyster Bar** and **Mr. Ed's Oyster Bar & Fish House**, both in the French Quarter (and other locations), and **Briquette** in the Warehouse District, which adds pork belly to the already decadent Bienville topping. Unless Monsieur le Gouverneur were a stickler for tradition, I highly doubt he'd mind.

Oysters Rockefeller

Another baked oyster dish that's even more famous than Oysters Bienville is Oysters Rockefeller. Named for John D. Rockefeller, who at the time of its creation was the wealthiest man in America, it's prepared in the same manner, but the ingredients in the topping usually include butter, spinach, green herbs and breadcrumbs. Some recipes also suggest a sprinkling of diced bacon for some additional, um, richness.

Oysters Rockefeller was created in 1889 by Jules Alciatore, the chef at **Antoine's Restaurant**, who used the locally plentiful bivalves as an alternative to French escargot. Alciatore's recipe was widely imitated in other New Orleans restaurants, but the exact ingredients remained a secret until 1986, when a chemical analysis of a plate of Antoine's Oysters Rockefeller determined that its characteristic green color came from a combination of parsley, celery, green onions and capers.

If you want to try the original dish, go ahead and make a reservation at Antoine's. Or you can visit almost any oyster house or seafood restaurant in the city, which will likely offer their own take on it. A few standouts include **Gallier's Restaurant & Oyster Bar** and **Trenasse**, both in the Central Business District, and **Coterie Restaurant & Oyster Bar** in the French Quarter. Another option is to head to **Galatoire's Restaurant**, a classic French Creole spot on Bourbon Street that's been open since 1905, where the spinach in its Oysters Rockefeller is flavored with herbsaint, an anise-flavored liqueur. If you're feeling like an oil magnate yourself, be sure and order a second plate.

Oysters en brochette

It's said that everything tastes better with bacon. And that's certainly true when it comes to oysters en brochette, another way New Orleans prepares its plentiful supply of local seafood.

To make oysters en brochette, raw oysters are threaded onto a long skewer, alternating with pieces of bacon. The combination is then either breaded and deep-fried, broiled or sautéed. After the skewer is removed, the cooked oysters and bacon are served on triangles of toasted bread with a Meunière sauce consisting of brown butter, parsley and lemon.

Oysters en brochette originated at **Galatoire's Restaurant**, where you can still enjoy it today in its original form. It's a bit of a classic dish, though, so you'll rarely find it outside of old-school restaurants, like **Arnaud's**, where the oysters and bacon are accompanied by a marchand de vin sauce made from red wine, butter and shallots.

Much more common is for menus to feature either char-grilled or char-broiled oysters, which are typically served in a buttery sauce cooked with garlic, herbs and cheese. That preparation is still a great way to get your fill of the local shellfish, though — even if it doesn't involve any bacon.

Muffuletta

Aside from the po' boy (and its close cousin, the oyster loaf), no sandwich better represents New Orleans than the Sicilian-inspired specialty known as a muffuletta.

A muffuletta is a large sesame-seed roll that's sliced in half horizontally and layered with cured ham, salami and mortadella; Provolone (and sometimes also Swiss) cheese; and a marinated olive salad seasoned with Italian spices and herbs. The entire sandwich is usually cut in quarters (a half is usually enough for a healthy appetite), and can be eaten either warm or cold. The name of the sandwich may be a diminutive form of the word muffe, meaning mushroom, for the round bread's resemblance to a mushroom cap.

The muffuletta originated in 1906, when a Sicilian immigrant named Salvatore Lupo opened a delicatessen called **Central**

Grocery across from the French Market, where tens of thousands of his countrymen were known to shop for Italian products. Lupo created the sandwich to combine the meats and cheeses that he was typically selling individually, and developed a recipe for a tangy olive salad that became popular among his clientele.

Although the store was damaged during Hurricane Ida in 2021, Central Grocery remains the iconic place to buy a muffuletta, which you can either order online for nationwide shipping, or pick up at a few local shops, including next door at **Sidney's Wine Cellar** and at **Moisant Market** in the New Orleans airport. But there are plenty of other worthy options all around the Big Easy.

A few of the best places to enjoy a muffuletta include **Cochon Butcher** in the Warehouse District, where all of the meats are cured in house; **Welty's Deli** in the Central Business District, which offers both a classic muffuletta and a customizable version; **Napoleon House** in the French Quarter, where the sandwich is served in a historic French Quarter building that was once intended to provide refuge to the exiled Napoleon Bonaparte (although he died before making it to New Orleans); and **Verti Marte**, a 24-hour deli counter inside a convenience store, also in the French Quarter. And a quick tip: if you buy a whole sandwich just before you leave town, eat half and wrap the rest of it up tightly, you'll be able to bring a taste of New Orleans back home with you for lunch the next day.

Red beans and rice

Got a case of the Mondays? In New Orleans, the surest way to chase away the beginning-of-the-week blues is with a heaping bowl of red beans and rice.

Red beans and rice is a Creole dish consisting of kidney beans (or other red beans), rice, the trinity of onions, celery and green bell peppers, herbs such as thyme and bay leaves, Andouille sausage or other meats and the ham bone that was customarily left over from Sunday dinner. Red beans and rice was traditionally cooked on Mondays because it was laundry day, so it was convenient to put a pot of beans on the stove and let it simmer for a few hours while attending to the wash. The stew is sometimes served with fried pork chops or fried chicken, but it can also be eaten as a simple, yet flavorful, main dish.

It's likely that red beans and rice came to New Orleans with French-speaking refugees who were fleeing Haiti during that country's revolution in the late 18th and early 19th centuries. It was a favorite dish of famous jazz trumpeter Louis Armstrong, who was known to sign his letters "red beans and ricely yours."

The tradition of red beans and rice is so ingrained in the Crescent City that restaurants will sometimes offer it as a Monday special, although some keep it on their menus for the entire week. A few of the best places to try the dish include **Mandina's Restaurant** in Mid-City, where it's a special every Monday, served with either Italian sausage, a grilled pork chop or veal cutlet; as well as three spots in Tremé: **Willie Mae's Scotch House**, which is famous for its fried chicken (probably the best I've ever eaten) and offers red beans and rice as a daily side dish; **Li'l Dizzy's Cafe**, where the Monday special includes either sausage or fried chicken; and **Dooky Chase's Restaurant**, which ironically, is closed on the traditional day for eating red beans and rice but serves it during its Tuesday, Wednesday and Thursday lunch buffet. Perhaps on Mondays the owners are home doing laundry while gearing up for the long week to come.

Eggs Sardou

The French dramatist Victorien Sardou is best-known for writing the play that inspired Puccini's opera Tosca, as well as for another, in 1882, that popularized the fedora, which was worn by the actress Sarah Bernhardt and soon became a sought-after fashion accessory for women. In New Orleans, though, he's best remembered for an egg dish created in his honor by the chef at **Antoine's Restaurant**, Jules Alciatore, upon Sardou's visit to the city in 1892.

Eggs Sardou consists of poached eggs that are nestled inside hollowed-out artichokes, which are placed atop a bed of creamed spinach and covered in Hollandaise sauce. At Antoine's, where it's offered during weekend jazz brunch, the dish is garnished with tasso ham and black truffle shavings and is served with asparagus spears.

You can also find this decadent dish at several other upscale restaurants around the French Quarter, including **Brennan's**, which serves it with a Choron sauce made from tomatoes, butter and egg yolks; **Arnaud's**, which features it on its Sunday jazz brunch menu; and **Galatoire's Restaurant**, where you can order it for either lunch or dinner. That restaurant has a strict dress code, with jackets required for men in the evening – but everyone can pay tribute to the writer who inspired eggs Sardou by doffing a wide-brimmed hat before sitting down to eat.

Beignet

It's best not to wear a black shirt when you're digging into an order of beignets, New Orleans's favorite breakfast pastry. These rectangular fritters are typically covered with a liberal dusting of powdered sugar, which invariably will leave the evidence of what you've eaten all over your clothing.

A beignet is a French creation that was introduced to New Orleans by 18th-century colonists, including the Acadians who had been deported from Nova Scotia back to France and, after arriving in Louisiana, were responsible for developing the city's Cajun culture. The airy pastries are best when consumed hot, and are typically served alongside a steaming cup of café au lait.

The iconic place to go for beignets is **Café du Monde**, which was established in 1862 in New Orleans's French Market. They're the only food item on the menu, served in orders of three, and are often accompanied by dark roasted coffee with chicory, with or without milk. Another traditional (and in my view, better) option is **Cafe Beignet**, with four locations in the French Quarter and the Central Business District, which sprinkles a generous helping of powdered sugar atop the namesake pastry. Or head uptown to **Morning Call**, a coffee stand in Navarre that's been open since 1870 and serves beignets that some declare are the city's best.

Because beignets are such a blank culinary canvas, chefs around the city have started enhancing them with a variety of flavors. You'll find one well-regarded savory option at **La Petite Grocery** in Uptown, where the award-winning blue crab beignets are available at brunch, lunch and dinner. Another good choice is **The Vintage** in Irish Channel, where you can choose between classic beignets, dusted with either powdered or cinnamon sugar, or fancy ones, that may include flavors like s'mores or strawberry. And at **Ruby Slipper Cafe**, with a half-dozen locations around town, you can enjoy seasonal specials, like the beignets I ordered during my last trip that were stuffed with blueberry compote and topped with lemon curd and whipped cream. It's a good thing there wasn't any powdered sugar on them, or else everyone I encountered the rest of the day would have known precisely what I had eaten for breakfast.

Bananas Foster

By the middle of the 20th century, New Orleans was a major hub for importing bananas into the U.S. from Central and South America. And in 1951, when Owen Brennan, owner of Vieux Carre restaurant, was planning to host a dinner honoring his friend Richard Foster, the chairman of the New Orleans Crime Commission, he asked his sister Ella and his chef, Paul Blangé, to create a new dessert that promoted the city's role in the banana trade.

Ella recalled that her mother would caramelize bananas for breakfast, cutting them in half and sautéing them with butter and brown sugar. Using that as a starting point, she and the chef decided to gussy up the dish by flavoring it with cinnamon, rum and banana liqueur, plating it over a scoop of vanilla ice cream, and setting it on fire at the table, where the alcohol would dramatically burn off. They named the dessert for the evening's honoree, and it went on to be featured at the family's French Quarter flagship, **Brennan's**, when the restaurant moved to its current location in 1956.

Today, Brennan's is said to make use of 35,000 pounds of the fruit each year for its Bananas Foster, which is still flambéed tableside. Similar to most other establishments that serve it, the restaurant requires a minimum of two orders per table.

In addition to Brennan's, you'll also find Bananas Foster at Creole restaurants in the French Quarter like **The Court of Two Sisters**, **Palace Café** and **Arnaud's**. And keep your eyes open around town for dishes like French toast, crepes and bread pudding that sometimes make use of similar flavors. Just like Brennan's signature dessert, these preparations are great ways to showcase bananas. But if you see flames shooting out of your food, it's probably a good idea to call 911.

Praline

What's the right way to pronounce the word praline? If you're in New Orleans, it's "prah-lean," not "pray-lean." But no matter how you say it, this sweet, nutty confection would be a great souvenir of your trip to the Crescent City.

Pralines are a candy that's made with sugar, milk, butter and pecans, cooked together until they achieve a soft, creamy consistency. Spoonfuls of the mixture are typically dropped onto wax paper and harden slightly once they cool. You can buy pralines of all shapes and sizes, and they're sold in a variety of flavors, with coffee, coconut and chocolate being among the most popular ones.

Originally a creation of the French, pralines were introduced in New Orleans in 1727 by Ursuline nuns who helped women prepare for marriage by making the candy. While European pralines were often prepared with almonds, the ones made in America used the nuts from the native Louisiana pecan trees. In the mid- to late 19th century, women called pralinières – some of whom were minorities or came from poverty, giving them a rare economic opportunity – would sell the confection on the streets of the French Quarter. This helped increase the candy's popularity among residents and tourists alike, a trend that continued with the formation of several praline companies in the 1930s and '40s that are still in business today.

There are countless places to pick up a bag of pralines around the French Quarter and other parts of the city, and many vendors sell them online as well. A few standouts include **Bernard's Pralines**, which you'll find in Central City and at many local grocery stores; **Leah's Pralines** in the French Quarter; **Aunt Sally's Pralines**, with shops in the French Market and the Warehouse District; and **Loretta's Authentic Pralines**, named for the first Black woman to own a praline company in the city, now with stores in the French Market and Faubourg Marigny. Both of these locations also dish up the company's much-loved praline beignets – and when you order a plate of these, you can practice pronouncing two delectable New Orleans words at once.

King cake

The weeks between Epiphany on January 6 and Fat Tuesday, celebrated on a varying date between mid-February and early March, is Carnival season in New Orleans. And it's the only time of year when local bakeries show off their king cakes, the colorful, ring-shaped dessert that's a symbol of Mardi Gras.

King cakes are typically made with a brioche pastry that's enriched with cinnamon, and are often filled with cream cheese, fruit or other flavors. On top, they're iced with sweet frosting and decorated with green, gold and purple sugar, representing faith, power and justice, respectively. The circular cake is said to resemble a king's crown, and whoever bakes it is responsible for hiding a tiny plastic baby Jesus inside. (Commercial king cakes usually place the baby on top of the cake or package it separately, fearing a potential choking hazard.) The baby symbolizes good luck, and if you find it in your slice, you get to be king for the day – but you're also on the hook for buying king cake the following year or throwing the next Carnival party.

Although similar sweet pastries had long been eaten in Spanish-speaking countries to celebrate Epiphany (a custom that continues among Mexican-Americans in Phoenix and other parts of the U.S.), the tradition of eating king cakes as part of Carnival celebrations in New Orleans likely began with French settlers in 1870. Bakers at that time would typically hide a bean, a coin or a nut inside the cake. But in the 1950s, a bakery called McKenzie's popularized the use of porcelain, and later plastic, baby figurines, amplifying the trinket's religious significance.

Countless bakeries in New Orleans sell whole king cakes during Carnival season (one estimate says the city goes through around 750,000 each year), and you'll also be able to find slices at cafés and on restaurant dessert menus around town. A convenient one-stop shop is **King Cake Hub**, which has a French Quarter pop-up as well as a larger shop uptown, both selling king cakes from numerous establishments.

If you decide to head straight for the source, a few of the most famous options are **Haydel's Bake Shop** in Irish Channel (with a larger bakery outside of downtown); **Dong Phuong Bakery**, an award-winning Vietnamese pastry shop in New Orleans East; **Hi-Do Bakery** in Terrytown; **Manny Randazzo King Cakes** in Metairie; and **Gambino's Bakery**, also in Metairie. Although most places stop making king cakes after Mardi Gras, Gambino's sells (and ships) them year-round. So if you were the one lucky enough to find the king cake baby, you can pay off your debt and keep the Carnival celebration going for as long as you want.

Doberge cake

When celebrating your birthday in New Orleans, it's customary to pin a dollar bill to your lapel – and if you're lucky, passersby will add their own cash to yours while offering a festive greeting. Another great way to commemorate your natal day is with a Doberge cake, a New Orleans original that's as spectacular to look at as it is tasty to eat.

A Doberge cake (pronounced "doh-bash") consists of five to eight thin layers of sponge cake, with each separated by custard or pudding. The entire cake is covered with buttercream frosting and fondant, or sometimes glaze. It's common for a doberge cake to be made with two flavors side-by-side, with chocolate and lemon, or chocolate and caramel, being among the most popular options.

A New Orleans baker named Beulah Ledner created the first Doberge cake in 1933, modeling it after a multilayered Hungarian dessert known as the Dobos torte and selling cakes out of her home during the Depression. In 1946, Ledner, who was by then known as the Doberge Queen of New Orleans, sold her business and cake recipe to **Gambino's Bakery**. Decades later, Ledner opened another bakery in the suburb of Metairie that was eventually purchased by **Maurice's French Pastries** after she retired.

Both Gambino's and Maurice's are still well-regarded places to get Doberge cake, but other bakers have also taken up Ledner's mantle, such as **Haydel's Bake Shop** in Irish Channel. Another popular choice is **Debbie Does Doberge**, which offers whole cakes as well as "Dobite" petit fours that come in flavors such as chocolate, lemon, red velvet and cookies 'n' cream. You can order either option for pickup at **Bakery Bar** in the Lower

Garden District or at **Debbie on the Levee** in Kenner, and Doberge cakes can also be shipped nationwide via Goldbelly. And if you've spent enough time walking around collecting birthday cash, you might be able to afford the most expensive selection on their menu.

Chantilly cake

Another dessert with a surprising connection to the Crescent City is Chantilly cake, a confection made with vanilla-flavored pastry, a fluffy white frosting and fresh berries. The cake was created by Chaya Conrad, inspired by a recipe from her grandmother, while she was a baker at a branch of **Whole Foods Market** in West Riverside that opened in 2002. It became so popular that Whole Foods started selling it in stores across the South and Southwest, and eventually nationwide.

Chantilly cream is another term for whipped cream, which may or may not be sweetened. The frosting in this cake isn't made from just heavy cream, though – there's also mascarpone and cream cheese. Fresh berries, including strawberries, blueberries and blackberries, are mixed into the frosting to separate the layers, and are also used for decoration on top of the cake.

While the original Whole Foods version used a yellow sponge cake as its base, once Conrad left the grocery store she adapted her recipe to employ a white almond-flavored cake. (Don't confuse the Louisiana version of Chantilly cake with the variety eaten in Hawaii, a light chocolate chiffon cake with a butterscotch-like icing.)

When you're in New Orleans, the best place to try Chantilly cake is **Bywater Bakery** in the neighborhood of the same name, which Conrad and her husband opened in 2017. There you can choose among three different varieties: classic berry, lemon-flavored and dark chocolate with strawberries.

You'll also find a version of Chantilly cake – here, called Berry Gentilly – throughout Southern Louisiana at **Rouses Markets**, whose bakery operations Conrad led starting in 2009. And if you want to continue to trace her cake-making career back in time, you can always stop by the nearest Whole Foods, whether that's in New Orleans or wherever you happen to be.

Other New Orleans dishes and drinks to sample:

- **Oyster and artichoke soup**, a combination of ingredients that was popularized at a now-defunct restaurant called LeRuth's in Gretna, which opened in 1966. Other restaurants around New Orleans soon copied the idea, some adding cream for additional richness. Today you can still buy LeRuth's artichoke soup base at local markets (just add your own oysters), or you can sample the dish at a few classic restaurants around town, including **Mandina's Restaurant** in Mid-City.
- Crawfish, a hard-shelled crustacean, the vast majority of which are produced and consumed in Louisiana, and that are often eaten communally at boils during the spring harvest season. A crawfish boil is seasoned with Cajun (or sometimes Vietnamese) spices and generally includes vegetables such as potatoes and corn as well as sausage and other meats. A few popular places to enjoy crawfish boils in a restaurant setting are **Deanie's Seafood**, with four locations around New Orleans, and **Bevi Seafood Co.** in Mid-City. While the mudbug is in season, you can also enjoy dishes such as fried crawfish, crawfish bisque and crawfish pie at eateries around town.
- Remoulade, a pinkish mayonnaise-based condiment that often accompanies seafood served as an appetizer or in sandwiches. Other ingredients in the sauce typically include Creole mustard, cayenne pepper and either ketchup or paprika, which provides the red tint. A common dish in New Orleans is shrimp remoulade, with the seafood served cold on a bed of iceberg lettuce, and the remoulade either on top or on the side. One place to try it is **Felix's Restaurant & Oyster Bar** in the French Quarter (and other locations).

- **Yaka mein**, sometimes spelled as one word or as yet-ca-main, a noodle soup with beef or other meats, seasoned with Creole spices and garnished with a hard-boiled egg and sliced green onions. A hybrid of Asian and Black culinary traditions, yaka mein is thought to have been introduced by Chinese immigrants who came to work on Louisiana's sugar plantations and railroads during the 19th century. The dish is sometimes called Old Sober for its use as a hangover cure. Today you're most likely to find it sold by vendors at street festivals or at corner grocery stores, such as **Eat-Well Food Mart** and **John & Mary Food Store**, both in Mid-City.
- **Pain perdu**, meaning lost bread, New Orleans-style French toast that's typically eaten for breakfast. It's made by soaking French bread in an eggy custard that's sometimes spiked with alcohol. After it's pan-fried, the bread is topped with powdered sugar, sweet syrup or fresh fruit. You can try this dish at **Ruby Slipper Cafe**, which makes a Bananas Foster-flavored version at its half-dozen cafés around town.
- **Bread pudding**, a related dish made with stale bread that's also soaked in custard and usually eaten as a dessert. After being baked, it's served in warm squares, sprinkled with powdered sugar, and topped either with a sauce made with spirits or caramel or with whipped cream. At **Brennan's** in the French Quarter, the bread pudding is laced with rum-soaked raisins, and the dish is served with a whiskey sauce and accompanied by buttermilk ice cream.
- **Tarte à la bouillie**, meaning burnt milk tart, a traditional Cajun dessert made with a sweet dough crust and a custard filling. It's often garnished with fresh fruit such as strawberries and may be dusted with powdered sugar. One place you can try it is **Tableau** in the French Quarter, where it's served with a rum caramel sauce.

- **Snowball** (also spelled sno-ball), made with finely crushed ice and flavored syrup, and topped or stuffed with ice cream or condensed milk. Snowballs have been eaten as a sweet treat during stifling hot summer days in New Orleans ever since 1939, when Ernest Hansen established **Hansen's Sno-Biz** in West Riverside after inventing a motorized machine for shaving ice. In addition to Hansen's, you'll also find snowballs at other stands and shops throughout the city, in flavors that may include grape, coconut and wedding cake, along with New Orleans-themed ones like Bananas Foster, praline and king cake.

- **Sazerac, hurricane and Ramos gin fizz**, a trio of cocktails invented in New Orleans that are part of the city's rich drinking culture. A Sazerac, first concocted in the late 1800s, is a mixture of rye whiskey, absinthe and Peychaud's bitters, garnished with both a sugar cube and a lemon twist. The iconic place to imbibe one is **The Sazerac Bar** in the Roosevelt Hotel, just outside the French Quarter. For something a little sweeter, try a hurricane, made with light and dark rums, orange, lime and passionfruit juices and grenadine. They're available everywhere, but to get a good one, visit **Pat O'Brien's** right off Bourbon Street, where the drink became popular among sailors in the 1940s. Or try a frothy gin fizz, invented in 1888 by bartender Henry C. Ramos, who devised a drink with gin, cream and egg white with dashes of lemon and lime juice that was traditionally mixed for 12 minutes by teams of servers called shaker boys. For this drink, head to **Henry's Gin Bar**, named for Ramos and located a block away from the Central Business District location where he invented the cocktail. Another great, if pricey, option for other classic New Orleans tipples is the rotating **Carousel Bar** at the Hotel Monteleone, where you can sample drinks like the Pimm's Cup or Vieux Carre, each with its own bit of Crescent City history.

OTHER FOODS OF LOUISIANA

Gumbo

Gumbo isn't just the official state food of Louisiana, it's also one of its favorite conversation topics. You could spend hours debating the right combination of ingredients, which thickener to use, how dark the roux should be – and who makes the state's best version.

Gumbo is a thick soup that's prepared with meat and shellfish, along with the vegetable trinity of onions, celery and green bell peppers, and one or more thickeners. It's typical to start your gumbo with a roux, made by cooking flour and butter together until the paste reaches a desired color and flavor. This can range from a light blond to a dark brown, a version that adds a deep, earthy note to the stew. Gumbo usually includes a second thickening agent, either filé powder, made from dried sassafras leaves, or okra, which can be either fresh or dried. After it simmers for hours, the stew is usually served over white rice, which is cooked separately and helps make it possible for a pot of gumbo to feed a crowd.

This dish is a product of the many cultures that have shaped both Creole and Cajun cuisine, with influences from France, Spain and West Africa, as well as Native tribes in Louisiana. The word gumbo likely derives from the word for okra in the language spoken by the enslaved people who came to Louisiana from West Africa beginning in 1719. Over the course of the next century, the dish incorporated French cooking techniques and Spanish spices, and was documented in its familiar form in cookbooks during the late 19th century.

Eventually, two styles of gumbo emerged – Creole, which was once more closely associated with New Orleans, and Cajun, historically more prevalent along the bayou in the southern part of the state. Creole and Cajun gumbos are less distinct than they once were, but the former typically contains shellfish such as shrimp, crab and oysters, and also incorporates tomatoes, while the latter is prepared with chicken or duck and Andouille sausage, and is sometimes topped with parsley and green onions. A third and often meatless variety, gumbo z'herbes, made with a variety of stewed greens, is sometimes eaten during Lent.

One of the most iconic versions of gumbo in the state can be found at **Dooky Chase's Restaurant**, the legendary Tremé spot where Black Americans gathered during the civil rights movement in the 1960s and that continues to draw diners from all backgrounds for its weekday lunch buffet and weekend dinner menu. Other favorite options in the French Quarter include **Mr. B's Bistro**, which offers both Creole and Cajun styles, and **Gumbo Shop**, where you can sample either variety as well as gumbo z'herbes.

Outside the Crescent City, a few well-regarded options include **Chef Ron's Gumbo Stop** in Metairie, which dishes up nine different kinds of gumbo, further blurring the lines between Creole and Cajun varieties; **Rice and Roux**, with two locations in Baton Rouge where you can also sample both styles; and **Bon Creole** in New Iberia, a restaurant that, despite its name, offers both seafood-centric and meat-heavy gumbos. The town it's located in hosts the World Championship Gumbo Cookoff each fall, which is a great place to dig your spoon into several bowls of gumbo and continue the argument about how the dish should rightfully be cooked.

Jambalaya

If you've already eaten jambalaya in New Orleans, you might think you'd be able to move onto the next item on your gastronomical wishlist. But if there were tomatoes mixed in with your rice, you're actually missing a whole other style of this one-pot dish.

Jambalaya, which comes from a Provençal word meaning mishmash, consists of rice that's mixed with chicken, sausage, the trinity of green bell peppers, onions and celery and sometimes seafood. The New Orleans, or Creole, style, which is known as red jambalaya, is where you'll also find tomatoes, while the Cajun style that's typically eaten in other parts of Louisiana is called brown jambalaya, for the cooked bits of meat that give the dish a more earthy flavor.

The lineage of either type of jambalaya, which was first documented in Louisiana cookbooks in the late 19th century, isn't entirely clear. But culinary historians believe that red jambalaya is either a derivation of West African jollof rice, or that it may have evolved from Spanish paella, with the settlers substituting tomatoes for the saffron that wasn't available in the New World. Brown jambalaya, on the other hand, may have come from the Acadians who made their home in the Louisiana bayou, where the dish would have included a variety of game meats as well as local Gulf Coast seafood.

If you'd like to try both styles of jambalaya, you'll need to get out of New Orleans and head to other parts of the Pelican State. But while you're still in the city, it's worth trying some classic Creole jambalaya preparations like the ones at **Gumbo Shop** and **Coop's Place** in the French Quarter, and **Jacques-Imo's**, uptown in Leonidas. Then hit the road and stop at well-regarded spots such as **Pot & Paddle Jambalaya Kitchen**, with seven locations throughout the state; **The Jambalaya Stop** in Addis; and **The Jambalaya Shoppe**, with a handful of branches around Baton Rouge and nearby communities.

Or you can head to the town of Gonzales, the self-proclaimed jambalaya capital of the world, which holds an annual festival that celebrates the dish every spring. With dozens of cooks vying for the title of World Jambalaya Cooking Champion, you'll undoubtedly get to taste both Cajun and Creole styles, and be able to cross this food off your culinary bucket list entirely.

Grillades and grits

The first word in this Creole dish may be evocative of an outdoor cookout. However, it actually refers to thin cutlets of beef, pork or veal that are pan-fried. The meat is typically accompanied by a brown gravy, made from a roux and the trinity of onions, celery and green bell peppers, as well as tomatoes, and is served on a bed of corn grits.

Grillades and grits is a New Orleans creation, where it was first documented in a 1901 cookbook. But you'll find it at Creole restaurants throughout Southern Louisiana, as well as in the Big Easy, as either a brunch or a dinner dish.

A few recommended spots outside the Crescent City where you can try it include **Cafe Sydnie Mae** in Breaux Bridge, which prepares grillades and grits with beef tenderloin; **Louisiana Lagniappe Restaurant** in Baton Rouge, where it's also made with beef and is offered as either an appetizer or main course; and **Dab's Bistro** in Metairie, which uses medallions of pork tenderloin. And in New Orleans, you'll find this dish at **Gris-Gris** in the Lower Garden District, where it's prepared with chicken gizzards; and at **Cafe Degas** in Fairgrounds, which serves veal grillades in a red Creole gravy on its weekend brunch menu. And with any luck, your meal will be over in plenty of time for you to get hungry before your friend's backyard barbecue later in the day.

Shrimp Creole

New Orleans is the birthplace of jazz, and joyful sounds spill out of bars and clubs every night of the week on thoroughfares like Bourbon Street in the French Quarter and Frenchmen Street in Faubourg Marigny. If you're a fan of this genre, you know that one of its hallmarks is frequent improvisation, which allows a featured musician to play an extended solo, sometimes with the backing or his or her band. And similarly, experienced chefs know that improvising on the initial structure of a dish is the best way to make it their own. One such culinary canvas is shrimp Creole, which has a basic framework that highlights seafood and tomatoes but allows endless possibilities for subtle variation.

Shrimp Creole is prepared by combining fresh tomatoes, the vegetable trinity of onions, celery and green bell peppers, and herbs and spices such as cayenne pepper, bay leaves, thyme and oregano. After the sauce simmers to develop its flavors, the shrimp are added, and it takes just a few minutes until they're done.

Similar to gumbo, shrimp Creole is served over white rice, which is cooked separately, but unlike that dish it typically doesn't include a roux or other thickening agent. Chefs sometimes add other proteins or vegetables to the stew, depending on what's available in their kitchens, and can vary the level of heat to the diners' taste with additional cayenne or hot sauce.

The dish is a staple of Creole cuisine, whose development during the 18th and 19th centuries drew influences from elements of French, Spanish and West African cultures. Although Creole food was historically more prevalent in New Orleans than in the surrounding countryside, the spread of Creole culture across the state, as well as the soft lines between many Cajun and Creole dishes, means that you'll find shrimp Creole both in the Big Easy and in other parts of the state, even in restaurants that describe themselves as primarily Cajun.

A few spots to check out if you want to try shrimp Creole include **Boudreau & Thibodeau's Cajun Cookin'** in Houma; **Marilynn's Place** in Shreveport; and **Bellue's Fine Cajun Cuisine** in Baton Rouge, where the dish is only offered on Thursdays. And in New Orleans, you can head to **Coop's Place** and **The Gumbo Stop** in the French Quarter, and to **Mandina's Restaurant** in Mid-City, where shrimp Creole is a special of the day on Saturdays, Sundays and Mondays. Be sure to sample a few different versions so you can begin to appreciate the ways in which each chef, like a good jazz musician, adjusts the ingredients and the seasoning to make the shrimp Creole you'll experience a little bit different every time.

Shrimp étouffée

Shrimping is a historically important industry in Louisiana, with its inland marshes and shallow bays especially conducive to the seasonal catch that supports many local fishermen. And one characteristic method of cooking shrimp, especially in the Cajun areas of the state that were settled by Acadians in the 18th century, is étouffée, a French word meaning smothered.

To prepare an étouffée, a technique that can also be used for other seafood or meats, the first step is to create a roux, made with flour and butter and cooked anywhere from a few minutes to a half-hour, depending on what color and flavor you want to achieve. Next, the classic trinity of vegetables is added to the pan (as well as tomatoes, in a Creole version of the dish), followed by the shrimp, which is slowly simmered in stock until they're tender. After reducing the sauce, the dish is typically served over white rice.

In New Orleans, it's less common to find étouffée made with shrimp than with crawfish, with the freshest available during the spring harvest season. But shrimp étouffée is served year-round at a few spots that feature Cajun cuisine, including **The Original**

French Market Restaurant, and **Vacherie**, both in the French Quarter. In other parts of the state, you'll find well-regarded versions of shrimp étouffée at **Bellue's Fine Cajun Cuisine** in Baton Rouge, where it's only offered as a Wednesday lunch special; **Bayou Delight** in Houma, a good place to try a variety of Cajun specialties; and **Lagneaux's** in Lafayette, where it's served on the all-you-can-eat seafood buffet. But if you decide to pile a few other dishes on the same plate, just make sure your shrimp étouffée doesn't leave them smothered.

Dirty rice

While you're visiting Louisiana, it's worthwhile to pay tribute to the devastation caused by Hurricane Katrina in 2005, particularly among the Black population. (A tour of the Lower Ninth Ward in New Orleans that I took a few years later stays with me to this day.) And it's worth considering, too, how one of the state's most iconic foods has been shaped by another shameful chapter in Black history.

Dirty rice is a dish that was created by people who were enslaved on Louisiana plantations during the late 1700s and early 1800s. It consists of rice that was boiled with the less desirable cuts of beef, pork and chicken that were given to the slaves, including organs such as gizzards, hearts and livers. As the meat cooked down, it created a brown gravy, which likely gave the dish its name.

Because it was inexpensive to prepare, dirty rice continued to be eaten by Black Americans after the abolition of slavery, and its affordability also led it to be adapted by rural Cajuns, who incorporated wild game and additional spices into the dish. Today, dirty rice is sometimes known as Cajun rice or rice dressing, and it's usually prepared with the typical trinity of vegetables as well as Andouille sausage and ground beef, pork or turkey.

Although dirty rice is rustic soul food, you'll sometimes find it in New Orleans at upscale restaurants, such as **Saint John** in the French Quarter and **Toups Meatery** in City Park. But you'll have to get out of town to find versions that hew closer to the dish's roots, such as the ones at **Cou-yon's Cajun Bar-B-Q** in Port Allen, where it's called Cajun rice dressing, and **LJK Roun 2** in Baton Rouge, which offers dirty rice as a side to plates of pork chops, chicken or seafood.

A distinct, yet related, dish is rice and gravy, a Cajun working-class specialty that's also prepared using cheaper cuts of meat, usually beef or pork but sometimes turkey or chicken. The meat is browned and then slowly braised with vegetables and spices until it produces a rich gravy that's served over rice. Andouille sausage or tasso ham, a cured meat, is sometimes added into the stew for extra flavor.

Rice and gravy is often found at plate lunch houses in Southern Louisiana, especially in Lafayette, where it's served along with a meat entrée and sides for a fixed price. (It's similar to the meat and three concept that's prevalent throughout the South as well as in Nashville.) A couple of highly regarded spots in that city where you can try this dish include **Laura's Two**, where the daily specials may include stuffed turkey wings and fried catfish, and **The Cajun Table**, which serves sausage-flavored rice and gravy on Saturdays along with country-style pork ribs and sides of corn and fried okra. Sitting down for a homestyle plate lunch is a great reminder that Louisiana's culinary richness comes not just from eating in high-end restaurants, but also from visiting spots frequented by laborers, farmers and fishermen.

Boudin ball

When you take ground pork, mix it with cooked rice, vegetables and spices, and stuff into a sausage casing, you've prepared the Cajun specialty known as boudin. And when the filling is rolled into rounds, breaded and deep-fried – sometimes with an extra layer of molten cheese inside – you've created boudin balls. It's the perfect snack to enjoy between meals while you're on a bayou road trip.

Numerous types of sausages in French-speaking cultures are called boudin, but the ones found in Louisiana are boudin blanc, white sausages made without the blood that's common in other varieties. There's no universal recipe for boudin, however: Cajun versions can include seafood like crawfish or crab, and every butcher has their own seasoning blend that makes their boudin (and their boudin balls) unique.

Look for boudin balls at meat shops and restaurants as you travel across Southern Louisiana, at places such as **Billy's Boudin and Cracklins**, a butcher that sells three varieties of boudin balls including one made with pepper jack cheese, in Lafayette, Scott, Krotz Springs and Opelousas; **Chicken on the Bayou & Boudin Shop**, which offers boudin balls with either pork or crawfish fillings, in Breaux Bridge; and **Chef Ron's Gumbo Stop**, which makes theirs with pork, in Metairie. For more suggestions, you can follow either the Southwest Louisiana Boudin Trail, promoted by the city of Lake Charles, or the Cajun Boudin Trail, which highlights purveyors of this delicacy around Lafayette.

New Orleans is no stranger to boudin balls, either, and there are numerous places where you can sample them in town. A couple of options include **Cochon Restaurant** in the Warehouse District, which serves fried boudin and, at the butcher next door, also includes boudin on its sausage plate; and **NOLA Poboys**, a French Quarter eatery that's open until midnight every day, and 3 a.m. on weekends – making it a perfect place to go when you're craving something fried after a night out on Bourbon Street.

Pistolette

Son of a gun! A pistolette can mean either of two things in Louisiana cooking. In the southern part of the state, Cajun country, it refers to a pastry that's filled with seafood and deep-fried, also known as a stuffed beignet. But in New Orleans, a pistolette can also be a small French baguette that's brimming with seafood, or one that's used for sandwiches.

Why the same word is used for two completely different dishes is unclear. But one theory is that the roll, which is similar to the round Belgian pistolet, may have been introduced by the French in New Orleans, while the fried dough version may have originated with the French-speaking Acadians who settled in Southern Louisiana.

Pistolettes in the bayou are most prevalent around Lake Charles, Lafayette and the surrounding communities. A few spots to check out if you want to try one include **Steamboat Bill's Seafood** in Lake Charles, where the pistolettes are stuffed with either shrimp or crawfish étouffée; **Chicken on the Bayou & Boudin Shop** in Breaux Bridge, outside Lafayette, which serves pistolettes made with crawfish, shrimp, crab or alligator; **Rosie Jo's** in Alexandria, which makes theirs with boudin sausage and covers them with shrimp étouffée; and **Suire's Grocery & Restaurant** in Kaplan, where you can choose among ones made with crawfish, shrimp or crab.

In New Orleans, on the other hand, the pistolettes you'll find are much more likely to be the bread roll version. One that's particularly notable is served at **Liuzza's by the Track**, which stuffs BBQ shrimp into a French bread pistolette. And at **Original Pierre Maspero's** in the French Quarter, you can order a dish called seafood pistolettes, which consists of French rolls filled with a mixture of shrimp and crawfish, combined with a creamy cheese sauce.

You'll also find pistolettes sold at Vietnamese bakeries, such as **Dong Phuong Bakery** in New Orleans East, which uses them to prepare the Vietnamese sandwiches known as banh mi. The pastry shop is so popular that its baked goods sometimes sell out early in the day. But if you haven't pre-ordered, you can always stop by and hope they'll still have the little rolls you're looking for. You may as well take a shot.

Natchitoches meat pie

Take one look at the savory pastry that's a specialty of Northern Louisiana, and for a moment you might be transported to Buenos Aires. That's because the Natchitoches meat pie strongly resembles an empanada.

A Natchitoches meat pie is usually made with ground beef or pork, or sometimes crawfish, cooked with the Cajun trinity of vegetables and seasoned with cayenne pepper (which makes it spicier than the Latin American version). After assembly, the meat pie is deep-fried, and it's eaten warm, sometimes with a dipping sauce.

This dish originated with the Native tribe called Natchitoches (pronounced "nak-uh-tush") and was then adapted by the Spanish colonists in the late 18th century. While the pies were once sold out of home kitchens and from street carts, today you can buy frozen ones in grocery stores throughout the state, especially in its northern half.

If you'd like to try a restaurant version, one option is **Lasyone's Meat Pie Restaurant**, where the turnovers are made with either a mixture of beef and pork, or crawfish. This casual spot, located in the dish's namesake town (which holds an annual meat pie festival in September) also sells its products online and ships them nationwide. Another place worth trying is **Elsie's Plate & Pie** in Baton Rouge, where the Natchitoches meat pies are served with a Bedford sauce that's similar to tartar sauce. In New

Orleans, there are two places in the French Quarter where you can sample the dish: **Original Pierre Maspero's**, where the pies are accompanied by a Cajun ranch sauce, and **The Will & The Way**, a pub where they come with a similar dip made with green tomatoes. After a few orders, and maybe a few drinks, you'll be ready to put on your dancing shoes and try the tango.

Hot chicken

APPALACHIA

The states that I'm grouping in Appalachia – Kentucky, Tennessee and West Virginia – have countless attractions that make them appealing destinations for a rewarding vacation. The region might beckon you with the opportunity to hear country music artists perform at the Grand Olde Opry, watch horse racing at Churchill Downs, hike in the Great Smoky Mountains or whitewater raft in New River Gorge. But don't make the mistake of resorting to eating at subpar restaurants or fast-food chains (ahem, KFC may be based in Kentucky, but it's not local food). Try a taste of the region's distinctive cuisine and your dining experiences will be as memorable as your recreational ones.

In many parts of the country, local food traditions emerged primarily from the ways in which chefs and cooks made use of available natural resources, and took elements from their ethnic heritage to fashion uniquely American dishes. But in Appalachia, the story of local food has as much to do with innovation as it does with either agricultural or industrial development, or immigration. And notably, some of the most unique dishes in the region arose from the creativity of Black and female entrepreneurs.

A few of the most iconic foods in this region include hot chicken, developed by a Black restaurant owner in Nashville after his vengeful lover served him fried chicken that she thought would be too spicy for him to eat; bourbon balls, invented by a woman who founded a candy company that's still in business after more than a century; barbecue spaghetti, a popular side dish made with a sauce built upon Black cooking traditions; and Memphis-style BBQ, where one of the most successful early proprietors was a Black businessman who catered to customers of any color.

Other culinary innovations arose from chefs who found ways to employ common ingredients in newly created food traditions. The hot brown, a fancy turkey melt, came from the chef at Louisville's Brown Hotel, who wanted to cater to hungry late-night dancers; derby pie, a chocolate nut dessert, was invented by a Kentucky couple whose family has fiercely protected their product through the courts; and the steamed hoagie, a Knoxville institution, originated when a local restaurant started using a contraption that warmed its deli sandwiches.

As you explore these dishes, many of which will be most readily available in urban centers, be sure and keep an eye out for opportunities to sample country cooking as well. Burgoo is a regional stew that you'll sometimes find as a side dish at barbecue restaurants; certain parts of Western Kentucky make their BBQ using mutton; and chocolate gravy is a sweet sauce often served over warm biscuits. And though traditional Appalachian dishes are much harder to find, you might get lucky and be able to sample some foods like kilt lettuce or apple stack cake, both of which were historically prevalent in mountainous areas.

Appalachia doesn't have as many ethnic specialties as other regions, but you'll find cultural influences arising in some surprising places. The pepperoni rolls that are the most iconic food in West Virginia were invented by an Italian immigrant who sold his creation to coal miners who needed a portable lunch option. Meanwhile, beer cheese, a favorite snack in the Bluegrass State, likely grew out of a German tradition of combining leftover beer with Cheddar cheese. And jam cake, found in both Kentucky and Tennessee, probably also came from German settlers, who created a familiar spice cake flavored with jam made from local blackberries.

As you travel around these states, you'll find no shortage of tasty and distinctive things to eat. And at the end of the day, be sure and toast your travels with some locally made bourbon or whiskey, or even a medicinal mint julep.

276

KENTUCKY

LOUISVILLE

Hot brown

The hot brown may not have the most appetizing name, but it's a dish that you shouldn't turn your nose away from when you're spending time in Louisville.

A hot brown is an open-faced sandwich consisting of roast turkey with a Mornay sauce made with cream and either Cheddar or Parmesan cheese, topped with sliced bacon and chopped tomatoes and served on toast. It's usually sprinkled with additional cheese before being broiled until the sandwich is, well, browned and melty.

The hot brown was invented at Louisville's Brown Hotel in 1926 by a chef named Fred Schmidt, who wanted to serve something other than ham and eggs to a crowd of late-night diners who were attending a dance at the venue. Schmidt also created a cold brown sandwich, with turkey, hard-boiled egg, lettuce and tomato served with Thousand Island dressing on rye bread, but this dish didn't take off as well as the hot version, which eventually became an iconic specialty of Kentucky.

If you want to try the sandwich in its original incarnation, head to **J. Graham's Cafe**, one of the Brown Hotel's restaurants, where it's always on the menu – or book yourself a stay at the property and order room service. But there are plenty of other places in town to try variations of the sandwich, including **Bristol Bar & Grille** and **Bluegrass Brewing Co.** You'll also find similar flavors in dishes like the hot brown pizza from **Sicilian Pizza & Pasta**, or the hot brown eggs Benedict at **Cheddar Box Too**. And if you're traveling elsewhere in the Bluegrass State, check out the Kentucky tourism board's Hot Brown Hop, which lists restaurants that serve it throughout the state. The sandwich might have a terrible name, but that sounds like a perfect one for the dance that inspired it.

Modjeska

Polish actress Helena Modjeska had such a successful career on stage in America that a park in California, a theater company in Milwaukee and even a World War II-era U.S. cargo ship were all named after her. But her lasting legacy may be the eponymous caramel-covered marshmallow candy that's produced in the Louisville area – but not by the business that initially manufactured it.

In 1883, the actress was performing in Louisville at Macauley's Theatre, starring in the first American production of Henrik Ibsen's play A Doll's House. Anton Busath, a local candymaker, was apparently so enthralled by her acting that he asked if he could name his latest confection for her. She agreed, and sent Busath an autographed portrait that hung in his downtown shop for more than 60 years, until the store burned down in 1947. In order to fulfill his company's Christmas orders that year, Busath asked a fellow Louisville confectioner, Rudy Muth, if he could use his kitchen, and Muth was willing to oblige. Later, when Busath decided not to reopen his business, he gave Muth his modjeska recipe in appreciation for the favor.

Today you can still buy modjeskas at **Muth's Candies** downtown, in either traditional or chocolate-covered varieties. A different version of the candy is sold by **Bauer's Candies** in nearby Lawrenceburg, which renamed its caramel biscuit the modjeska in tribute to Busath after the fire that shuttered his shop. And you can also find them at **Schimpff's Confectionery** in Jeffersonville, Indiana, across the river from Derby City. Or as you might want to start calling Louisville, Modjeskaville.

Benedictine

The first Saturday in May is practically a religious holiday in Louisville: It's Kentucky Derby Day, when thousands of men and women in colorfully decorated hats head to the city's Churchill Downs to watch the first leg of the Triple Crown, the horse racing event that's often called the Run for the Roses.

While a mint julep is the traditional libation during the Kentucky Derby, a popular food is benedictine, a dip or spread that's made with cream cheese, cucumbers, the liquid created by grating onions and cayenne pepper. It's sometimes tinted green with food coloring, or with additional herbs such as parsley and dill. Benedictine is often served on white bread as a crustless tea sandwich or as a canapé, but today you're just as likely to find it as a condiment on a BLT.

You might think that this dish has something to do with monks, like the Benedictine Sisters of St. Walburg Monastery who live in Villa Hills, Kentucky, or that it's somehow related to the French herbal liqueur. But actually, benedictine is simply a food that was invented by a woman named Jennie Carter Benedict, who ran a Louisville restaurant called Benedict's in the early 20th century and was also a cookbook author and caterer.

Look for benedictine spread around town at markets such as **Plehn's Bakery** and **Heitzman Traditional Bakery and Deli**. Or, if you want to try it in sandwich form, a few well-regarded options include **Shady Lane Cafe**, which slathers the benedictine on a sandwich with bacon; **The Café**, which features benedictine on its Queen Anne sandwich with bacon and sliced cucumbers; and **Cottage Cafe** in Middletown, east of Louisville, where yes, you can also request bacon on your sandwich. Be sure to order early if you want to pick up some benedictine in time for the Kentucky Derby – but be careful to lick any remnants off your fingers before you touch your fancy hat.

Mint julep

If you're the sort of person who plans what you'd like to eat and drink far in advance, mark your calendar for the first Saturday in May. That's when it's traditional to watch the Kentucky Derby with a mint julep in hand.

A mint julep is a cocktail made with bourbon, simple syrup, crushed ice and mint. It was traditionally served in a silver or pewter cup, but you'll more often see it in a highball glass with a mint sprig as garnish. A julep, a drink with Arabic origins that had been around for centuries, was especially popular in Virginia during the 1800s, where it employed a variety of liquors including brandy and gin, and was sometimes drunk in the morning for medicinal purposes. One story claims that Kentucky Senator Henry Clay was the first to use bourbon in a mint julep, in a recipe that dates from around 1850. But it wasn't until 1938 that the cocktail became officially associated with the Kentucky Derby.

Each year Churchill Downs sells about 120,000 mint juleps during the weekend of the race, making use of 1,000 pounds of mint and over 10,000 bottles of a pre-mixed Old Forester cocktail. If you want a luxe version, you can buy a $1,000 cocktail made with Woodford Reserve that's served in a silver cup – or a gold cup for $2,500 – with proceeds going to charity.

Most bourbon bars and restaurants all over the state will mix you a mint julep (just ask your bartender), but you'll mainly find them on cocktail menus around Derby time. A few highly regarded spots in Louisville – the home of the Kentucky Derby – include **Lobby Bar & Grill** at the Brown Hotel, **The Silver Dollar** and **Proof on Main**. And if you decide to start celebrating your love of horse racing with a morning libation, you'll hardly be the only one.

OTHER FOODS OF KENTUCKY

Burgoo

If you're a culinary adventurer, it's worthwhile to seek out some country cooking during your visit to Kentucky, and burgoo is a great place to start. Similar to the Midwest's booyah and the South's Brunswick stew, burgoo is a dish made with a variety of meats and vegetables that are slow-cooked in a tomato-based sauce, often in a giant outdoor pot for a communal celebration. Burgoo was historically prepared with game meats such as squirrel or raccoon, but today pork, chicken and beef are typically used, while the vegetables can include potatoes, corn, cabbage and beans, or whatever else happens to be on hand. It's traditionally served with a side of cornbread or corn muffins and can also be found in pockets of Southern Illinois.

No one knows for sure where the name burgoo – or the dish itself – came from, but it probably dates to the 19th century and may be a mispronunciation of barbecue or bird stew. A French chef named Gustave Jaubert is said to have created an early version around 1860 for a military squadron, shortly before he became a cook at Buffalo Trace Distillery, where burgoo was among the dishes for which he became famous. Burgoo was also often served at livestock sales, which may explain its connection with horse racing – as does the coincidence that in 1932, a horse named Burgoo King won the Kentucky Derby.

In Kentucky, you'll find burgoo at a handful of barbecue joints and traditional restaurants around the state, including **Old Hickory Bar-B-Que** in Owensboro (which is also known for its mutton BBQ), **Stella's Kentucky Deli** in Lexington and **Derby Café** and **Mark's Feed Store** in Louisville. Or you can do burgoo while watching horse racing at Lexington's Keeneland Racetrack, where up to 100 gallons of burgoo are served each week during racing season at its **Track Kitchen** restaurant. The racetrack sometimes offers to-go containers that serve eight, which sounds like a much easier way to feed a crowd than hunting down some game and tending to a fire for a day or two.

Beer cheese

Kentuckians certainly like to drink their bourbon, but another popular beverage is what's used to create their favorite snack: beer cheese.

Beer cheese is a spread that's made with Cheddar cheese, flattened beer and spices that may include cayenne pepper, paprika, garlic and mustard. It's usually served cold, with crackers and vegetables, although it can also be eaten warm with pretzels or chips. There isn't a standard recipe for beer cheese, so the type of beer that's used can vary, with IPAs and pilsners being common styles.

It's likely that the dish originated in the 19th century, possibly in Germany, among bartenders who wanted to use up leftover beer so that it wouldn't go to waste. Beer cheese traces its local roots to Winchester, where it was first served in the 1940s at Driftwood Inn, a restaurant that was owned by a man named Johnnie Allman. Although Allman later lost his restaurant in a bet, the beer cheese recipe survived, and today you can find Allman's Beer Cheese in grocery and liquor stores around the region. Another variety, Hall's Snappy Beer Cheese, was created by the couple who bought a successor to Driftwood Inn and renamed it **Hall's on the River**. Queen Elizabeth II was said to be a fan of their brand of beer cheese, which is still widely available across Kentucky as well as at the restaurant.

Beer cheese is also eaten around the Midwest, especially in Ohio and Wisconsin, but even in America's Dairyland, it's not nearly as prevalent as it is in Kentucky. Numerous pubs and breweries throughout the state serve their own versions, so you'll need to try a few to find your favorite. Some highly regarded options include **Monnik Beer Company** and **River City Drafthouse** in Louisville, **The Cellar Bar & Grille** in Lexington and **Woody's Sports Bar & Grill** in Winchester. That city's also where you'll find the Beer Cheese Festival every June, and a Beer Cheese Trail that highlights local restaurants serving the dish. It's a good way to mix things up if you're spending most of your time in Kentucky tasting bourbon.

Bourbon ball

There are dozens of bourbon distilleries in Kentucky, with Buffalo Trace, Maker's Mark and Woodford Reserve being just a few of the most famous names. And at many of these places, you'll have the opportunity to buy more bourbon-infused products than you could ever imagine, including barbecue sauce, maple syrup, coffee and candy. A treat that's a great souvenir of your trip to Kentucky is a package of bourbon balls – a confection consisting of a bourbon-infused, creamy candy center that's covered in dark chocolate and usually topped with a pecan.

The original bourbon ball was invented in 1938 by Ruth Booe, who had co-founded a candy company two decades earlier with Rebecca Gooch, who like Booe was a substitute schoolteacher. Today you can still buy these treats from **Rebecca Ruth Chocolates** in Frankfort, a company that was unusual for its time in being run by women and that's still owned by members of the Booe family.

A second option for a bourbon ball, using liquor from Woodford Reserve, is made by a company that was founded by another Ruth – **Ruth Hunt** – and has locations in Lexington and Mt. Sterling. And you'll also find bourbon balls at Kentucky gift shops such as **A Taste of Kentucky** in Louisville and **Old Kentucky Chocolates** in Lexington – as well as at pretty much every stop on the Kentucky bourbon trail.

Derby pie

The chocolate nut pie that's a staple at Kentucky bakeries is one of the most decadent desserts you'll find anywhere – but it's also one responsible for the most litigation.

In 1954, a couple named Leaudra and Walter Kern, owners of the Melrose Inn in Prospect, invented a pie with a sweet filling containing chocolate and walnuts, poured into a pastry crust. They called it derby pie, picking the name out of a hat from a handful of options. But the Kerns were so enamored of their decision that 14 years later, they registered "Derby-Pie" with the U.S. Patent and Trademark Office. Since then, the Kern family has vigorously protected their trademark by sending cease-and-desist letters to hundreds of restaurants and websites that called their creations by the same name, and filing dozens of lawsuits, even once suing Bon Appetit Magazine for publishing its own derby pie recipe. (After a long legal battle, an appeals court eventually upheld the Kerns' trademark.)

Ironically, many of the derby-like pies that you'll find around town use pecans instead of walnuts, and unlike the Kerns' pie, flavor the filling with bourbon rather than vanilla. A few recommended pies to try include the Mayday Pie at **Missy's** in Lexington, the pecan chocolate chip at Louisville's **Homemade Ice Cream & Pie Kitchen**, and a similar one called Pegasus Pie at **Heitzman Traditional Bakery and Deli**, also in Louisville.

Or, if you want to try the original "Derby-Pie," you'll find it for purchase online through the **Kern's Kitchen** website, at **Kroger** and other local supermarkets, at **Carson's** in Lexington, and in Louisville restaurants including **Bristol Bar & Grille** and **Derby Café** (located in the Kentucky Derby Museum at Churchill Downs). You could also make your own version, of course. But don't try calling it derby pie, or you'll probably be hearing from some Kentucky lawyers.

Another Kentucky dish to sample:

- **Kentucky butter cake**, a dense pound cake made with a vanilla-flavored sauce that's infused into it after it cools, making the cake moist and buttery. The cake became famous after Nell Lewis entered it into the Pillsbury Bake-Off Contest (which it did not win) in 1963, a few years before Jell-O popularized the idea of making poke cakes that were flavored with its signature product. Although Lewis was from Missouri, her original recipe used bourbon in the sauce, which is probably why it's named for Kentucky. This cake is easy to make but hard to track down, though you'll sometimes see it at local restaurants, such as **Porch Kitchen and Bar** in Louisville.

TENNESSEE

MEMPHIS

Memphis-style BBQ

Together with the Carolinas, Texas and Kansas City, Memphis can claim one of the most influential barbecue traditions of the entire country. The meat that's eaten in Elvis Presley's hometown is primarily pork, which cooks slowly while being smoked in an outdoor pit, often over charcoal. The shoulder, used for making pulled, chopped or sliced pork, is usually dry-rubbed with a mixture of paprika, garlic, sugar, salt and pepper. Similarly, ribs can be dry-rubbed, but they can also be basted before, during and after cooking with a thin sauce made with tomatoes and vinegar or molasses. Both pork shoulder and dry ribs are typically served without sauce, while wet ribs often come with extra sauce on the side.

Memphis-style BBQ began to emerge during the 1920s when businessmen including John Mills set up shop near Beale Street, the city's entertainment district. Mills served pork shoulder and wet ribs to a mostly Black clientele, with exceptions being celebrities such as Bing Crosby, who was known to stop by whenever he was in town for a performance. Another local institution, **Leonard's Pit Barbecue**, was founded around the same time and served a similar menu to white patrons, but remained segregated for decades.

It wasn't until the late 1950s that dry ribs entered the scene, at a restaurant called **Charlie Vergos' Rendezvous**, where the owner created a signature rub that included a mixture of oregano and cumin, spices that his father had used for Greek chili in his own restaurant. While Mills's restaurant is long gone, both Leonard's and Rendezvous are still around, with the former east of downtown in Fox Plaza and the latter a more convenient stop if you're club-hopping on Beale Street.

A few other spots worth checking out include **Central BBQ**, with five locations around the city and whose dry ribs are frequently named as among Memphis's best; **Cozy Corner Restaurant**, which has served dry and wet ribs as well as sliced pork and barbecued Cornish hens since 1977; **A&R Bar-B-Que**, offering a variety of traditional meats as well as rib tip and sausage sandwiches; and **Tops Bar-B-Q**, a chain with 16 locations in the city that each has its own charcoal pit where pork shoulder and slabs of ribs are unusual examples of fast food that's slow-cooked.

If you're not interested in a sandwich or a plate of meat with sides like beans and coleslaw, most barbecue joints in Memphis also sell BBQ nachos, chopped pork served atop a plate of tortilla chips, with optional extra toppings. Another related food is barbecue pizza, invented by **Coletta's Italian Restaurant** in the 1950s and said to be one of Elvis's favorite things to eat. Along with ribs and pulled pork, these dishes have become as characteristic of Memphis-style BBQ as burnt ends are of Kansas City.

Barbecue spaghetti

Some barbecue aficionados believe that the requisite side dishes for a rack of ribs are potato salad, baked beans and coleslaw. And then there are those who think that the only appropriate side dish is ... more barbecue. If that's you, then the Memphis specialty called barbecue spaghetti, which became especially popular in Black-owned restaurants, will certainly hit the spot.

Barbecue spaghetti is pasta combined with a sauce that's prepared with a mixture of marinara and barbecue sauce. The noodles are cooked as they normally would be, but the sauce is slowly simmered, sometimes over a pit for many hours, with vegetables such as onions and peppers, spices and pulled smoked pork.

The dish was invented by a former railroad cook named Brady Vincent at a restaurant called Brady and Lil's, which he sold to a couple named Frank and Hazel Vernon in 1980. The Vernons eventually renamed it **The Bar-B-Q Shop**, and the restaurant still serves sides of Bar-B-Q Spaghetti using Vincent's original recipe. Vincent also shared his creation with another Memphis barbecue legend, Jim Neely, who opened Interstate Bar-B-Q in 1979 and still owns two branches of a successor restaurant in Memphis, **Jim Neely's Interstate Bar-B-Q**. (If that name sounds familiar, it may be because Jim's nephew Pat, along with Pat's former wife Gina, were once Food Network TV personalities, and several other Neely family members have also opened barbecue restaurants.)

When you want to try barbecue spaghetti, The Bar-B-Q Shop and Interstate Bar-B-Q aren't your only options. You'll find this dish all over town at spots such as **A&R Bar-B-Que**, **Pollard's Bar-B-Que** and **Leonard's Pit Barbecue**. And in case you want to make pasta your main dish, you could always order a large plate of barbecue spaghetti – with a couple of ribs on the side.

Nashville

Hot chicken

The origin story of Music City's most famous dish is likely apocryphal – but that hasn't stopped it from being recounted in numerous articles as well as on countless podcasts and websites. As the tale gets told, in the 1930s a good-looking man named Thornton Prince loved to enjoy the Nashville nightlife, and was known for having many dalliances with local women. One morning, Prince's lover, who had been left at home the previous night, cooked up a plate of fried chicken with what she thought would be a recipe for revenge – as one website puts it, a "devilish amount of peppers and spices." But instead of recoiling at the cayenne-flavored chicken, Prince loved the heat and asked for another helping. And within a few years, he had developed his own recipe and opened up a restaurant called BBQ Chicken Shack.

From its roots in the Black community, Nashville hot chicken has since spread to cities all across the country, as one of the most trendy dishes of the past decade – and one that's even been adopted by chain restaurants like **KFC** and **Buffalo Wild Wings**. But for an authentic taste of what's become an iconic regional food, you'll have to get yourself to Nashville.

Some 90 years after that initial attempt at vengefulness, **Prince's Hot Chicken** is still owned by members of Thornton Prince's family, with locations downtown as well as in south Nashville. At Prince's, as well as at other hot chicken joints across the city, you can order your bird with either white or dark meat, and at a variety of spice levels ranging from plain – no spice at all – to mild to hot to "XXX hot." (Choose wisely: I ordered mild, and it still left my tongue burning.) The chicken is usually served on white bread, with pickle chips on the side.

Like fried chicken throughout the South, birds prepared in the Nashville style are usually marinated in buttermilk and breaded before being fried – with the cayenne-inflected, lard-based paste being applied right after cooking. But unlike Buffalo-style fried chicken, hot chicken isn't dipped in blue cheese or ranch dressing. If the heat's too much for you to handle, just sip your sweet iced tea and go down a level next time.

Besides Prince's, the other most famous place in town for hot chicken is **Hattie B's**, which has four locations throughout the city (as well as ones in Memphis and Birmingham). Heat options here range from Southern (no heat) to mild to hot to "shut the cluck up!!!" (When I visited, I found the mild level not quite as hot as Prince's, and the chicken not quite as crispy, but your mileage may vary.)

There are plenty of other spots in town to get your hot chicken fix, too, like **Biscuit Love**, a breakfast café that serves a hot boneless thigh atop a buttermilk biscuit; **Pepperfire Hot Chicken**, where the tenders are served on a brioche bun with your preferred amount of heat; and **Slow Burn Hot Chicken** in nearby Hendersonville, which offers a dozen different flavors and heat levels for your meat. But if you've been out philandering, make sure you put your own order in instead of having your significant other do it for you – or you might end up with a mouthful of hot pepper.

Meat and three

A style of lunch restaurant that you'll find as you travel around the South – and especially in Nashville, where it's believed to have originated – is known as the meat and three. Diners select one protein from a list containing a handful of hearty options such as fried chicken, meatloaf and pork chops, and then up to three vegetables from a dozen choices that may include collard greens, creamed corn and squash casserole. The meal is usually served with cornbread, biscuits or dinner rolls, and is accompanied by sweet tea. And if all that doesn't fill you up, you can also order a dessert like peach cobbler or banana pudding.

Some meat and threes resemble cafeterias, with guests pushing trays alongside a steam table where employees ladle out your selections, while others offer menu service. The origin of this type of establishment is murky, but likely dates to the first half of the 20th century, when a Nashville diner called Hap Townes Restaurant dished out plate lunches to factory workers at the nearby May Hosiery Mill. The style of dining spread across the city and the region, and notably, meat and threes were some of the first restaurants to integrate Black and white diners.

Although the legendary Arnold's Country Kitchen, a cafeteria-like restaurant that opened in 1981, recently closed for business, there are still dozens of meat and threes to check out in Nashville. A few recommended options include **Monell's**, an all-you-can-eat joint with a rotation of daily specials and fried chicken served at every meal; **Wendell Smith's**, a diner open since the 1950s; and **Ramzy's Meat & Three**, known for soul food favorites like fried catfish, mac-and-cheese and turnip greens. But even though it's called a meat and three, you can still order your entrée with just one or two sides – or even as a meatless plate with as many as four vegetables.

OTHER FOODS OF TENNESSEE

Steamed hoagie

Eastern Tennessee isn't just known for being the gateway to the Smoky Mountains and the home of Dolly Parton. In Knoxville and nearby towns, a steamed hoagie is a distinctive take on a deli sandwich that's found almost exclusively in this region.

Almost any combination of cold cuts, cheese and condiments can be used to create a steamed hoagie, which is usually made on a white or pumpernickel roll. But what makes it unique is the Fresh-O-Matic device that introduces steam after it's constructed, softening the bread, melting the cheese and marrying the sandwich flavors together. The hoagie is typically served warm, accompanied by pickles or pepperoncini peppers.

The steamed hoagie was first introduced by a Knoxville sandwich shop called **Sam & Andy's** in the 1970s, possibly to make use of bread that was going stale. Since then, dozens of other shops in and around the Marble City have adopted the style. In addition to the spot that invented it, among the most famous places to get a steamed hoagie in town are **Nixon's Deli**, a Knoxville staple since the 1970s, and **Gus's Good Times Deli**, a favorite of University of Tennessee students. Or if you're heading out to Dollywood, keep going a few miles and stop in at **Parton's Deli** in Gatlinburg. The restaurant's owners aren't related to the singer, which probably explains why their weekday hours only run from 9 to 4 – because it would be a fitting tribute to Dolly if they stayed open just one hour later.

Smoked bologna

See Oklahoma

Among the most famous places for a smoked bologna sandwich in Memphis are **Central BBQ**, **Cozy Corner Restaurant** and **A&R Bar-B-Que**. Or head out of town and try **Helen's Bar BQ** in Brownsville or **Roy Boy's Barbecue** in Dyersburg.

Other Tennessee dishes to sample:

- **Kilt lettuce**, also known as killed or wilted lettuce, a traditional salad eaten in the Appalachian Mountains. This dish combines watercress or other lettuce greens with scallions in a warm dressing containing bacon drippings that causes the greens to shrivel up. One place where you can try it is **Clinch Mountain Bakery & Restaurant** in Thorn Hill.
- **Appalachian apple stack cake**, a traditional dessert made with many thin layers of dough that are held together by and covered with a spread made of crushed apples and spices. In the 19th century it was customary for wedding guests to each bring a layer of the cake to the bride's home, where it was put together before being served at the wedding. Today you can still find this specialty at **The Village Bakery** in Knoxville.
- **Vinegar pie**, a type of desperation pie, one made using pantry ingredients during times of hardship when fresh fruits such as lemons were too expensive (or out of season). Its custardy filling is similar to Southern chess pie or buttermilk pie, but with vinegar providing a tangy flavor. You can try this pie at **Clinch Mountain Bakery & Restaurant** in Thorn Hill.

WEST VIRGINIA

Pepperoni roll

A treat you shouldn't pass up while traveling around Appalachia is a Moon Pie. Made in Chattanooga, Tennessee, since 1917, a Moon Pie is a sandwich of two chocolate-covered graham cracker cookies with a marshmallow filling. Although it's now an iconic example of food from the region, it was originally made as a snack for Kentucky coal miners to put in their lunch pails.

But the Moon Pie, and the pasties of Montana and Michigan, aren't the only examples of foods created to nourish laborers working in difficult conditions. In the 1920s, coal mining in Northern West Virginia attracted many immigrants from Italy, especially the region of Calabria, who made up a majority of the state's foreign-born workers. One of these miners, Giuseppe Argiro, was also a cook. He created the first pepperoni roll, a combination of bread dough and a spicy meat stick – two foods that up until then had usually been eaten separately, but melded together when baked, with the spicy oil from the pepperoni soaking into the bread. In 1927, Argiro began to sell his rolls at **Country Club Bakery** in Fairmont, and they quickly became popular among the Italian miners, especially because the rolls didn't need to be refrigerated or warmed before eating, making them ideal for an easy lunch.

Today pepperoni rolls sometimes include cheese as well as toppings such as onions and peppers, and they're often eaten warm. But they remain a staple in pizza parlors, Italian bakeries, taverns and convenience stores around West Virginia, which continues to have a sizable Italian population. In addition to Argiro's original spot, which still uses his recipe (and ships its pepperoni rolls nationwide), recommended options include **Tomaro's Bakery** in Clarksburg, which has been open since 1914 and celebrated its centennial by creating a world-record, seven-foot-long pepperoni roll; **Abruzzino's Italian Bakery** in

Gypsy; **Taste of Heaven Bakery** in Maxwelton; and **Homegrown Pizza** in Morgantown. Grab a Moon Pie at the local minimart and you'll have an entirely handheld meal that you can enjoy on the go – even if you're not heading out to work in the coal mines.

OTHER FOODS OF APPALACHIA

Chocolate gravy

When you imagine a pitcher of gravy, you're probably thinking of a savory, brown sauce that's usually eaten with either turkey or mashed potatoes. But in Appalachia, it's common to make gravy out of a mixture of flour, sugar, butter and chocolate that's thinned out with milk or water and served as a topping to fresh, warm biscuits.

While the dish is called chocolate gravy, it's really more like a sweet chocolate pudding or chocolate sauce (and is sometimes called "soppin' chocolate"). There isn't a standard formula for making chocolate gravy, but cooks will often introduce a savory note with the addition of bacon drippings or crumbles.

It's thought that the dish came to the Appalachian region via Spanish colonists in the late 18th century. Today you'll find it at breakfast cafés such as **Stover's Country Kitchen** in Livingston, **Cumberland Biscuit Company** in McMinnville, **Pat's Cafe** in Lawrenceburg and **Biscuit Love** in Nashville, all in Tennessee; and **Biscuit Belly** in Louisville and **Country Tyme Diner** in Summer Shade, both in Kentucky; as well as at similar restaurants in Arkansas. At any of these places, you can dig into a hearty breakfast – and being able to eat chocolate before noon is just gravy.

Red eye gravy

See Other foods of the South

In Appalachia, you'll find red eye gravy served with either country ham or biscuits at places such as **The Loveless Cafe** in Nashville and **Big Bad Breakfast** in Louisville, Memphis and other locations.

Corn pudding

See Other foods of the South

You'll find corn pudding served as a barbecue side dish throughout the region, at places such as **Back Alley BBQ** in Dickson, Tennessee, and **HoneyFire BBQ** in Nashville. Or try its close cousin, spoonbread, at **Boone Tavern Restaurant** in Berea, Kentucky, a town that also hosts an annual spoonbread festival each fall.

Jam cake

Both Kentucky and Tennessee claim ownership of jam cake, a confection that's made with layers of pastry containing pecans or walnuts and warming spices such as cinnamon, nutmeg and cloves. Each tier is separated with blackberry jam, and the whole cake is covered with a caramel-flavored icing.

This cake probably came to Appalachia via German settlers who arrived there from the Old World (as well as from Pennsylvania) during the mid-19th century and used jam to sweeten their desserts, because sugar wasn't always widely available. Jam cake is often eaten as a holiday treat, but you'll also find it year-round at a handful of European-style bakeries.

At **Heitzman Traditional Bakery and Deli** in Louisville, you can opt for traditional blackberry jam cake, or their other flavor, strawberry. Other places you'll find this specialty include **J Clayborn's Bakery & Cafe** in Lebanon, Tennessee, a long-time local business known for its jam cakes that reopened under new ownership in 2022, and **Spalding's Bakery** in Lexington, Kentucky, where the single- or double-layer jam cakes are a seasonal offering. Make sure you call and order ahead, or else your lack of holiday dessert might leave you in a jam.

REGIONAL PIES OF THE U.S.

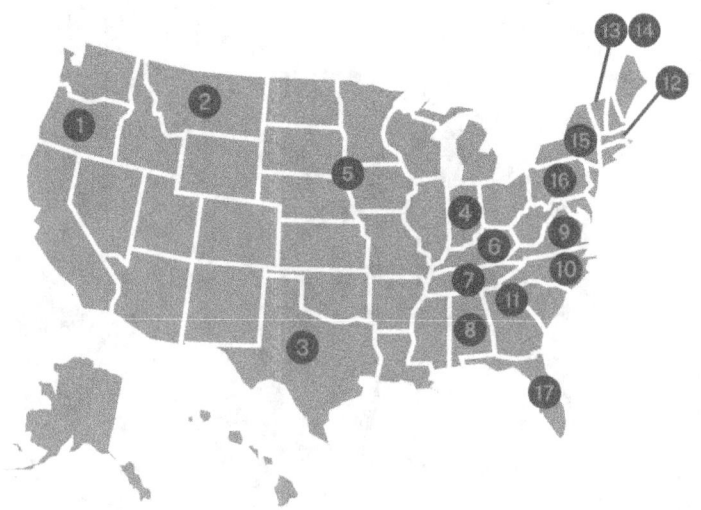

1. Marionberry pie
2. Huckleberry pie
3. Pecan pie
4. Sugar cream pie
5. Snickers pie
6. Derby pie
7. Vinegar pie
8. Mud pie
9. Peanut pie
10. Atlantic Beach pie
11. Chess pie
12. Boston cream pie
13. Maple cream pie
14. Apple pie topped with Cheddar
15. Grape pie
16. Shoofly pie
17. Key lime pie

Deviled eggs

THE SOUTH

It wouldn't be at all surprising if you already had a conception in your mind of what Southern food is – and it's probably not on the healthy side of the spectrum. Iconic eats from the region are stereotypically fried or overly sweet, and chock-full of caloric ingredients like buttermilk, heavy cream and mayonnaise. But as you dig deeper into the characteristic dishes of the South, you'll soon realize that there's much more to the story than sugar and bacon fat.

The tradition of barbecuing meat, especially pork, is central to the culinary identity of this part of the country, and many dishes make use of local vegetables that grow in abundance. The culinary heritage of the region has been influenced, too, by the numerous cultures that have left an indelible stamp on the South. These include the indigenous people who created staple dishes using native crops, the Europeans who settled the area, and the enslaved Blacks who were forcibly brought there. But perhaps most jarring to what you might think about Southern food, some dishes that we strongly associate with the region today were actually invented elsewhere.

Before going any further, you might be wondering which states constitute the South, since there isn't universal agreement on just how the region should be defined. (Even the Southern Food & Beverage Museum in New Orleans takes a sweeping approach, including not just the states you might expect but also Oklahoma, Kentucky and Maryland.) In this chapter, I've included seven states that have many overlapping regional specialties – Arkansas, Mississippi, Alabama, Virginia, North Carolina, South Carolina and Georgia. Although the northern parts of Louisiana and Florida share some traditions with these states, their culinary identities are largely distinct, and so I've broken them out separately. And just like the chapters on the Midwest and other parts of the U.S. that contain several states, I've covered state-specific dishes first (for all but Arkansas, which doesn't have any particularly notable dishes of its own), followed by Southern foods that are found in multiple states or widely across the region.

As you travel around the South, you'll have the opportunity to compare how similar foods are eaten in different parts of the region. One good place to start is with barbecue. While the pit smokers across the South all feature slow-cooked pork shoulder, the condiments that accompany the meat are vastly different, with vinegar-based sauce characteristic of Eastern North Carolina and the Pee Dee region of its southern neighbor, tomato-based sauce predominant in Western North Carolina, and mustard-based sauce a hallmark of the South Carolina Midlands. And in Alabama, both pork shoulder and smoked chicken are eaten with a white mayonnaise-based sauce, especially in its northern cities.

You'll also find numerous dishes in the region that capitalize on its long growing season, with produce such as corn, tomatoes and peaches starring in iconic Southern specialties like hushpuppies, Brunswick stew and cobbler. But these fruits and vegetables are also used as key components of dishes that may be less familiar, like South Carolina's Frogmore stew, Mississippi's Delta tamales and North Carolina's sonker.

Some of the foods that we think of as being Southern, like Hoppin' John and fried okra, came to the region as a consequence of the Atlantic ships that transported hundreds of thousands of enslaved Blacks from West Africa between the early 1700s and early 1800s. These vessels also brought okra, black-eyed peas, peanuts and sesame, crops that were soon widely planted across the South and became used in regionally specific dishes. The Gullah people, many of whom worked in the Lowcountry fields, were also responsible for the invention of several South Carolina rice-based specialties, including Charleston red rice and chicken bog. And as a result of the weekend fish fries that were once a common practice among enslaved people, fried catfish is now a soul food staple across the South.

While indigenous crops like collard greens and squash also feature prominently on Southern tables, numerous foods were created by European settlers, adapting familiar dishes to locally available ingredients. In North Carolina, German immigrants developed livermush, a processed pork product, as well as the chicken pies, spiced cookies and sugar cakes associated with the Moravian religious group. In South Carolina, she-crab soup is an adaptation of the seafood bisque that was a favorite dish among Scottish settlers. And carrot cake and chess pie, two of the region's best-loved desserts, probably originated in England before becoming popular in the Southern U.S.

Some of the region's other favorite foods have a more circuitous past. A close look at their history reveals that popular dishes like banana pudding, pimento cheese and red velvet cake were first widely popular across the country before taking on a Southern identity in more recent decades. Hummingbird cake didn't originate in the South, but in Jamaica. And shrimp and grits was a dish originally eaten by the Gullah people in the coastal Lowcountry before becoming iconic across the entire region in the 1980s and '90s. (Even sweet tea, which some consider the quintessential Southern beverage, perhaps second only to Cheerwine, wasn't commonly consumed in the region until the last 40 years or so.)

As you explore small towns in the countryside as well as big cities with robust food scenes, like Raleigh, Charleston, Atlanta and Birmingham, you'll undoubtedly discover a wide range of eating options, from meat and threes serving homestyle food to upscale restaurants on par with what's offered in Los Angeles or Chicago. But don't miss the opportunity to veer off the well-worn path. That way you can sample some of the region's lesser-known specialties, like Mississippi's slugburger, Richmond's sailor sandwich, the chili-topped burgers and hot dogs of North Carolina, and Alabama's Lane cake.

But the more you eat throughout the region, the more you'll come to understand that your initial perceptions of Southern food might not have been so wildly off-base. You could make an entire meal out of fried chicken and fried green tomatoes (and maybe a fried pie for dessert). Deviled eggs wouldn't be as tasty if there weren't mayonnaise in their filling (especially if the chef used Duke's, a South Carolina brand). Without its heavy cream binder, corn pudding would just be a corn casserole. And unless Southern cooks hadn't made good use of buttermilk, we wouldn't have flaky biscuits, perfect for eating with salty country ham or dipping in red eye gravy.

Even vegetables are sometimes cooked with added sugar in the South, as you'll taste in side dishes like sweet potato casserole and tomato pudding. But even if you don't happen to get a chance to try these delicacies, be sure to finish up your trip around the South by picking up a box of divinity to take home as a souvenir. That way you'll have a lasting reminder of just how sweet Southern food truly can be.

MISSISSIPPI

Slugburger

The delicacy that you'll see on restaurant menus in Northeast Mississippi is called a slugburger, but that's no reason to feel disgusted. Although this burger isn't entirely made of meat, it doesn't contain any actual bugs.

A slug is slang for a nickel, and that's what it would have cost during the 1910s and '20s to get one of these burgers at a roadside drive-in. John Weeks, who owned a chain of hamburger stands with his brothers, decided to add fillers like potato flakes and flour to their meat mixture in order to stretch a limited supply of ground beef and pork. They called their creation a Weeksburger, but as its popularity grew, other restaurant owners adapted the recipe, and the burger became known by its current name.

Today, a slugburger is typically made with a mixture of beef and pork, plus an extender or two, often soybean meal or soy grits. The meat is pressed into thin patties that are deep-fried, giving them a crunchy exterior, and served on a soft bun with mustard, chopped raw onions and pickles.

The epicenter of the slugburger is Corinth, where Weeks first created the dish and where an annual festival celebrating it is held every summer. You can try one in town at **White Trolley Cafe**, a cash-only establishment serving inexpensive breakfast plates, sandwiches and hot dogs; **Borroum's Drug Store and Soda Fountain**, where you can also see artifacts from more than 175 years of the building's pharmaceutical history; and **Slugburger Cafe**, which offers single, double and loaded versions of its namesake specialty. You can order all-beef burgers there, too – just in case you're equally afraid of soy products as you are of insects.

Delta tamale

You won't be singin' the blues once you sample a unique type of tamale that's eaten in the Mississippi Delta, the region that runs alongside the Mississippi River between the state's northern border and Vicksburg. The Latin American version of this food may be more familiar, but Delta tamales, also called Delta hot tamales, are the only ones that were the subject of a 1937 recording by blues singer Robert Johnson, They're Red Hot.

A Delta tamale, like its Mexican cousin, is wrapped in a corn husk, but it's typically a bit smaller, is made with cornmeal rather than masa, and is simmered in a pot rather than being steamed. Delta tamales can be prepared with beef, pork or turkey, and are usually flavored with chili powder, paprika, cumin and cayenne pepper, rather than salsa or mole. They're also sometimes served with sauce or smothered in chili, which isn't typical for Latin American or Southwestern tamales.

Though some believe that the tamale came to Mississippi with soldiers returning from the Mexican-American War, it's more likely that it arrived with migrant workers who worked on local farms in the late 19th century picking cotton alongside Black laborers. Over time, Black cooks adapted and influenced Mexican traditions, and a standard version of the dish eventually emerged.

You can follow the Southern Foodways Alliance's Hot Tamale Trail to find suggestions for street carts and restaurants that serve this local delicacy. A few popular choices include **White Front Cafe Joe's Hot Tamale Place** in Rosedale, **Solly's Hot Tamales** in Vicksburg, **Abe's Bar-B-Q** in Clarksdale and **Doe's Eat Place** and **Scott's Hot Tamales** in Greenville. That's the self-proclaimed Hot Tamale Capital of the World, where you'll find an annual festival dedicated to the dish – featuring artists who undoubtedly will be happy to perform a few verses of the song that celebrates it.

Mud pie

The Mississippi River largely defines the western border of the Magnolia State, with hundreds of miles of riverbank running in close proximity to the cities of Vicksburg and Natchez. The river has been historically important as a conduit for shipping and receiving goods, and it's played a significant role in shaping the state's ecology – and it's also the geological feature responsible for its namesake dessert.

Recipes for mud pie, also known as Mississippi mud pie, generally have only two things in common. First, they contain some kind of chocolate, either in the form of pudding or cake.

Other Mississippi dishes to sample:

- **Mississippi roast**, a recipe created by Robin Chapman of Ripley that went viral in the early 2000s, consisting of beef chuck braised with butter, packets of dry ranch dressing and gravy mixes, and pepperoncini. You're unlikely to find this dish on restaurant menus in Mississippi, but if you have a hankering for some slow-cooked beef, **Quave Brothers Poboys** in D'Iberville serves pot-roast-and-gravy sandwiches as well as plates.
- **Comeback sauce**, also spelled as kumback sauce, a mixture of mayonnaise, ketchup, chili sauce, mustard and spices that's eaten as an accompaniment to fried seafood or French fries, or as a salad dressing. It was likely invented in Jackson, Mississippi, in 1935 at a seafood spot called **Mayflower Cafe** (which still sells bottles of its recipe), and was soon adopted by several other Greek restauranteurs in town, each of which wanted their patrons to come back for more.

And second, there's a crispy chocolate crust and a gooey interior, a combination that's said to resemble the banks of the Mississippi River. (A similar pie is known as black bottom pie, but its provenance is disputed.) Aside from those two components, there are endless variations on how this dessert can be prepared. Ingredients like nuts and marshmallows are common inclusions, and it's often topped with chocolate syrup and either ice cream or whipped cream.

The history of this dish is as murky as the river itself, but it was likely first created in the 1970s, possibly based on an older dish called Mississippi mud cake. It's not featured on very many restaurant menus in Mississippi, but one place where you can try a slice is **Strawberry Cafe**, a Madison eatery named after the produce farms that once dotted the area. If it were located any closer to the Mississippi River, it might have to rename itself Chocolate Cafe.

ALABAMA

Alabama-style BBQ

Fans of barbecue from Memphis, Kansas City, Texas or the Carolinas may scoff. But in Alabama, smoked chicken and pork shoulder are cooked in and served with a white sauce that's a mixture of mayonnaise and vinegar, seasoned with lemon juice, salt and black pepper.

White barbecue sauce was first created in 1925 at **Big Bob Gibson's Bar-B-Q** by Robert Gibson, who used it to keep the chickens he pit-smoked from drying out. Members of Gibson's family still look after two branches of the restaurant that remain open in Decatur, with the chickens being dunked in a vat of white sauce to keep them moist after coming off the pit, and bottles of white sauce left on the table for diners to use at their discretion. (You can also buy bottles of the sauce online and in grocery stores throughout the South.)

Although BBQ spots throughout Alabama feature pork, chicken and ribs served with a variety of vinegar-, tomato-, and even mustard-based sauces, the white sauce has become emblematic of the state's barbecue, especially in its northern cities. A few recommended places where Gibson's innovation has spread include **Miss Myra's Pit Bar B Q** in Birmingham; **Moe's Original BBQ**, with two dozen branches around the state, including in Birmingham, Huntsville and Mobile; and **Saw's BBQ**, with a handful of locations in the Birmingham area as well as Hoover. That last spot offers pulled chicken sandwiches cooked Alabama-style as well as a menu item that should keep Tennessee traditionalists happy – pulled pork with red sauce.

Lane cake

In To Kill a Mockingbird, the classic 1960 novel by Harper Lee, the narrator Scout Finch describes her neighbor Miss Maudie Atkinson's famous Lane cake as "so loaded with shinny it made me tight." And while this boozy sponge cake is relatively hard to find, compared to some better-known Southern confections, it's worth tracking down the prize-winning dessert whenever you find yourself in the Yellowhammer State.

Lane cake is a layered white sponge cake with a frosting that includes raisins, pecans and coconut, along with a healthy portion of bourbon. It was created by a woman from Clayton, Alabama, named Emma Rylander Lane, who won first place for her cake at a county fair in Columbus, Georgia, and shortly afterwards published a recipe for it in her 1898 cookbook, calling it Prize Cake. It's similar to Lady Baltimore cake, a Charleston specialty, and its frosting is reminiscent of German chocolate cake, with the additions of whiskey and raisins.

(Another alcohol-infused dessert that was once commonly eaten across the South is tipsy cake, which consists of sponge cake soaked in sherry, whiskey or brandy, similar to a variety of English trifle. But these days you're only likely to encounter it in a home setting or at a church social.)

Though Alabama declared Lane cake to be its official cake in 2016, there are only a few spots left that will bake one, typically by special request. If you're in Dothan, you can sample Lane cake at **Simply Cakes Bakery** and at **Specialty Bakeshop Desserts by Jolando**, and in Andalusia, you can order one from **Dean's Cake House**. And though Maycomb, Alabama, is a fictional place, if you found a way to pay a visit, you can be sure Miss Maudie would have a Lane cake ready for you, cooling on the windowsill.

Other Alabama dishes to sample:

- **Strawberry pretzel salad**, a layered dessert consisting of a pretzel crust, a filling containing cream cheese and Cool Whip and a topping with fresh or jellied strawberries. The recipe was especially popular during the 1970s at picnics and potluck dinners, and can now be found at Southern restaurants such as **Main Street Cafe** in Madison and **Dallas Mill Deli** in Huntsville.
- **Butternut cake**, a pound cake that includes the flavor of butternut, also known as white walnut, in the batter as well as the frosting. You can taste this confection at **Dean's Cake House** in Andalusia, which makes it as a layer cake with pecans in the icing.

VIRGINIA

Sailor sandwich

The original town grid of Richmond, the capital of Virginia, was laid out by a civil engineer named William Mayo. But the deli that was known for feeding naval trainees during World War II missed the opportunity to pay tribute by including a glob of Hellman's in the dish that's the most notable regional food of its home city. Instead, the sailor sandwich is made with a layer of spicy brown mustard.

A sailor sandwich consists of hot beef pastrami, melted Swiss cheese and knockwurst (a short, stubby German sausage cut in half and grilled) on rye bread, with the aforementioned condiment. It originated at **New York Deli** in 1943, when seamen from the nearby University of Richmond's V-12 Navy College Training Program would frequent the restaurant and order the sandwich, which the deli eventually named for them.

It's worth trying the original version, but you'll also find sailor sandwiches all over Richmond at spots including **Perly's**, a Jewish restaurant downtown that adds chicken liver and pickled cabbage to the standard recipe; **Chiocca's** in the Museum District; **Joe's Inn** in the Fan District; and **Dot's Back Inn** in Bellevue. And if you don't feel like eating pastrami but still want to pay homage to the Navy, Dot's also offers a variety of submarine sandwiches – some of which even include mayo.

Mint julep

See Louisville

Although the mint julep is now closely associated with Kentucky, it was historically important in Virginia, where an Englishman reported in 1803 that they were commonly imbibed in the morning. If you're in Richmond, you'll have to wait until happy hour to try a classic cocktail at **The Jasper**, or a creative version at **Julep's**, where the drink is made with sparkling wine and apple brandy.

Another Virginia dish to sample:

- **Peanut pie**, a dessert with a gooey filling of roasted, salted nuts, made famous by **Virginia Diner** in Wakefield, located near the country's first commercial peanut farm. Another favorite version is baked by **Red Truck Rural Bakery** in Marshall and Warrenton, which includes chocolate cake crumbs, coconut and honey in its recipe and ships its pies nationwide.

NORTH CAROLINA

North Carolina-style BBQ

The Hatfields and the McCoys seem like one big, happy family compared to the advocates of the two different types of North Carolina barbecue, commonly referred to as Eastern and Lexington style. The dispute over which one best represents North Carolina once got so heated that the state legislature had to reject a pair of bills proposing the latter as the official barbecue of the Tar Heel State.

Both Eastern-style BBQ and its counterpart in Western North Carolina, also called Piedmont style, feature pork that's seasoned with a dry rub and slow-smoked in a pit over hickory or oak. But there are key differences in the cuts of meat, the sauce and the slaw and other side dishes that it's typically served with.

In Eastern North Carolina, where barbecue originated in the state, pitmasters make use of the whole hog (as the saying goes, everything but the squeal). During cooking, the pork is mopped with a thin vinegar-based sauce seasoned with red pepper and sugar, that's also used for dipping the chopped meat. And Eastern-style BBQ is typically accompanied by a mayonnaise-based coleslaw that can be added to sandwiches, or served on a BBQ plate along with other sides like hushpuppies, collard greens and Brunswick stew, with sweet iced tea to drink.

Lexington-style BBQ, on the other hand, is primarily prepared with pork shoulder. Western cooks sometimes use a vinegary mop sauce as well, but it includes tomatoes or ketchup that adds a bit of sweetness. The meat can either be chopped or sliced. It's usually served on sandwiches with additional sauce, but can also come on plates with hushpuppies, baked beans and red slaw. That's a variation of coleslaw that either mixes a bit of the Western-style "dip" into the recipe, or is made from scratch with green cabbage, ketchup, vinegar and other spices and seasonings – but in both methods, doesn't include any mayonnaise.

Both Eastern and Western BBQ also feature pork ribs, using each region's distinctive sauce, with the meat either being slow-smoked over a pit or grilled.

The inspiration for the earliest barbecue in the state came from John White, a 16th-century explorer and governor who ventured to the North Carolina coast under the direction of Sir Walter Raleigh and encountered the cooking technique used by Native Croatans, who smoked meat and fish over a wooden structure called a barbacoa. Western-style BBQ was probably influenced by the German settlers who came to North Carolina from Pennsylvania during the 1700s, although it didn't become widely popular until around World War I, when pork shoulder started to be more economical than cooking an entire pig.

Ask a dozen North Carolinians what their favorite barbecue spot is and you'll get 12 different answers. But a few places that frequently appear on best-of-Eastern BBQ lists, all of which have been around for decades, include **Wilber's Barbecue** in Goldsboro, **Kings BBQ** in Kinston, **Parker's Barbecue** in Wilson, **Skylight Inn** in Ayden and **Clyde Cooper's** in Raleigh.

For Piedmont-style 'cue, a great first stop is **Lexington Barbecue**, located in the same city that hosts an annual barbecue festival that was the subject of the lawmakers' dispute about the state's premier barbecue style (a compromise was reached in 2007 declaring it the official food festival of the Piedmont Triad region). Another worthwhile spot in Lexington is **Barbecue Center**, the oldest restaurant in town that still cooks using traditional pits. And in Greensboro, **Stamey's Barbecue** is a long-established favorite, also serving Western BBQ. It's only a short drive from the unofficial dividing line between the state's two different styles – so you can try both and decide whether you prefer whole-hog barbecue or having ketchup mixed into your slaw.

Carolina burger

It would be natural to assume that a Carolina burger is simply a burger smothered in pulled pork. Sounds tasty, but no. A Carolina burger has less in common with North Carolina-style BBQ than it does with a Los Angeles-style burger, with toppings of chili and onions as well as coleslaw and yellow mustard.

The origin story of the Carolina burger has been lost to history, but an iconic place to try one is **Melvin's Hamburgers & Hot Dogs** in Elizabethtown, which has been serving burgers with all four toppings, a style called "all the way," since 1938.

Other popular spots for a Carolina burger include **Duke's Grill** in Monroe (just be aware that "all the way" here doesn't include mustard); **Wayback Burgers** in Raleigh, Durham and other locations across the state; **Al's Burger Shack** in Chapel Hill; **Will's Grill** in Fayetteville; and **Town Hall**, a chain with locations in Raleigh, Durham, Briar Chapel and Holly Springs. The latter option also does offer a burger topped with pulled pork, if that's what you're hungry for. But know that you'll be ordering a Tar Heel burger, not a Carolina burger – which could make a big difference if you're a fan of Duke basketball and eschew all things related to UNC.

Carolina dog

You won't be at all surprised to learn that a Carolina dog has the same toppings as the similarly named burger: chili, onions, coleslaw and mustard. And there's no shortage of old-school hot dog stands across the state where you can try one. In Eastern North Carolina, many of the hot dogs you'll encounter have a deep red color – they're the ones called Bright Leaf hot dogs, made by a local company, Carolina Packers.

A few recommended options where you can go "all the way" and order the characteristic toppings include **The Trolly Stop** in Wrightsville Beach, Southport and Chapel Hill; **Shorty's Famous Hot Dogs** in Wake Forest; **Snoopy's Hot Dogs & More** in Raleigh and Garner; **Zack's Hot Dogs** in Burlington; and **Kermit's Hot Dog House** in Winston-Salem. And at **JJ's Red Hots** in Charlotte, you can choose among the "Char Heel," a traditional Carolina-style dog, or ones that celebrate a version eaten in Chicago, which includes tomatoes, pickle relish, sport peppers and celery salt, and Cincinnati, with toppings of chili, cheese and onions. Just add some coleslaw and mustard to the latter and you can call it "Caronati" style. Although you'd probably confuse the server less if you just ordered a Carolina dog with cheese.

Livermush

Head to the foothills of the Blue Ridge Mountains, west of Charlotte, once you gather enough courage to try livermush. That's North Carolina's version of a processed pork product, similar to Pennsylvania's scrapple and Ohio's goetta, that was likely also introduced by German settlers, probably in the 18th century.

Livermush is prepared with pork liver (by law, at least 30 percent of the product) as well as other scraps from the head of a pig, all bound together with cornmeal and spices including black pepper and sage. It's typically pressed into refrigerated blocks that are sliced and deep-fried. It's often served as a breakfast food, alongside grits or biscuits, or in a sandwich accompanied by yellow mustard.

There are only a handful of manufacturers who produce livermush, including Jenkins Foods in Shelby. But you'll be able to find it at local grocery stores as well as at small-town cafés and restaurants all around the area, including **Ball's Grill & Produce** in Gastonia; **Lincoln Cafe & Catering** in Lincolnton; **Norman's Cafe** in Vale; and **Shelby Cafe** in Shelby. That's the town that loves its livermush so much that it holds an annual event called Mush, Music & Mutts every October during which it holds a beauty pageant and crowns both a Little Miss and Mister LiverMush. Not to be outdone, a competing festival in Marion includes both hog-calling and pig-squealing contests – and as much livermush as you can stomach.

Moravian chicken pie

When pastors in Winston-Salem calculate the budget for renovating their churches, the unit of measurement isn't always dollars, but chicken pies. That's because fundraisers at which these meat-filled pastries are sold have been staples in Moravian congregations for decades.

A Moravian chicken pie consists of a flaky puff-pastry shell that's filled with cooked (often leftover) poultry, mixed with a broth that's been thickened with flour and butter, with a second crust layered on top. Unlike a pot pie, a Moravian chicken pie doesn't include vegetables like peas or carrots. After baking it's typically sliced and smothered in a rich gravy, with vegetables served on the side.

The original Moravians were German immigrants who came to North Carolina beginning in the 1750s, and established a settlement in Salem (now called Old Salem, part of the city of Winston-Salem) in 1766. Today there are about 20,000 Moravians in the Tar Heel State, and church groups continue to make these meat pies for community gatherings, although they're also available frozen in grocery stores for you to bake at home.

The iconic place to sample Moravian chicken pie, The Tavern in Old Salem, closed in 2019, but you can pick one up to take home from either **Salem Kitchen** or **Mrs. Pumpkin's**, both in Winston-Salem. Or if you're lucky enough, perhaps you'll be in town while the Moravians are raising funds for their next construction project.

Moravian spice cookie

More than a million pounds of spiced cookies are baked each year in Winston-Salem, and these Moravian delicacies have become another characteristic food of central North Carolina. This specialty likely derived from a German confection called lebkuchen, a gingerbread-like baked good, which was brought to North Carolina by the early religious settlers in the 18th century.

The most common variety of Moravian cookies is prepared with molasses as well as ginger, cinnamon and cloves, although there are other popular flavors including lemon, chocolate and butterscotch. They're traditionally cut into very thin, wafer-like rounds that bake quickly, making the cookies extremely crisp morsels.

You can get your fill of Moravian spice cookies at a few bakeries in Winston-Salem, including the historic **Winkler Bakery** in Old Salem, which features a wood-fired dome oven that dates to 1800; **Wilkerson Moravian Bakery**, which serves the classic variety as well as other kinds including vanilla, lemon, butter rum and orange brandy; and **Mrs. Hanes' Moravian Cookies** in nearby Clemmons, where you can buy ginger, butterscotch, black walnut and other flavors and also take a tour of the bakery. And even if you can't arrange a trip to North Carolina, you should be able to find Moravian spice cookies in your home supermarket, made by **Dewey's Bakery**, a local business with a handful of branches in Winston-Salem.

Moravian sugar cake

It wouldn't be Easter in North Carolina – or Christmas, for that matter – without a taste of Moravian sugar cake, another food that came to Salem via German kitchens and, in modern times, was made popular by **Dewey's** and other Winston-Salem bakeries.

Moravian sugar cake is prepared with an enriched yeasted dough. But the recipe contains a surprising ingredient that makes it denser and less sweet than a typical sugar cake would be – mashed potatoes. After the mixture is spread into a pan, the baker creates divots with their thumbs, which allows a buttery, cinnamon-brown sugar topping to soak deeply into the cake. (Traditionally, having large thumbs was prized among Moravians, because it meant the baker could create larger wells.) The cake is usually eaten warm, often as part of a holiday celebration.

Your first stop for Moravian sugar cake should be Dewey's (and if you can't visit yourself or have a local relative pick one up for you, they ship their cakes nationwide). But the other Moravian bakeries in town, **Winkler Bakery**, **Wilkerson Moravian Bakery** and **Mrs. Hanes' Moravian Cookies**, also make their own versions. And the only way you're going to decide which is your favorite is to buy one of each.

Sonker

Cobbler, buckle, grunt, slump and pandowdy are just a few of the names for various types of baked fruit desserts that would require a magnifying glass to sort out their differences. But in Western North Carolina, this dish is called sonker, and it's frequently made with blueberries, peaches, apples and even sweet potatoes.

Sonker can be prepared with either a biscuit-like or a cake-like dough. Depending on whose recipe you follow, the pastry either lines the bottom and sides of the baking pan or covers the fruit in clumps, or is a batter that soaks into it. (One theory about the name of the dish is that it derives from the dough being sunk into the filling, although it's more likely that it's based on an imaginative baker's interpretation of the Scottish word for a straw saddle, which a sonker is said to resemble.)

The dish was likely created in the 1800s to serve large groups of farmhands and to make use of late-season fruit, which is typically mixed with sugar or molasses for additional sweetness. That makes a sonker particularly juicy, compared to other types of fruit desserts. It's sometimes served alongside a "dip," a vanilla-scented sauce commonly eaten with sweet potato sonker, and can be topped with ice cream.

Other North Carolina dishes to sample:

- **Tomato pudding**, a casserole of fresh or canned tomatoes that are mixed with cubes of stale bread or biscuits and sweetened with sugar. You'll find it on the menu at **Heritage House Restaurant** in Windsor.
- **Pig pickin' cake**, a citrus-flavored cake with a pineapple frosting, usually prepared with boxed yellow cake mix and canned mandarin oranges, and traditionally eaten after a communal hog roast. If you want to try a slice, you'll find it at **Stubbs & Sons** in Sanford, Carthage and Pittsboro, restaurants better known for their BBQ that, unlike the cake, is actually made from pork.
- **Atlantic Beach pie**, a lemon dessert with a saltine cracker crust and whipped cream topping that was made famous at a Chapel Hill restaurant called Crook's Corner that closed in 2021. I've searched, well, fruitlessly for this pie in Atlantic Beach and other towns on the North Carolina coast, but you can order one during the summer from **Carolina Pie Company** in Mooresville, on the opposite side of the state. And Crook's Corner opened a pop-up shop selling Atlantic Beach pies for Fourth of July weekend in 2022, so keep an eye on their social media in case they do so again. Or console yourself with a slice of lemon meringue pie, another specialty that's a staple on dessert menus across the South.

There are only a handful of places where you can find sonker, but conveniently, they're all located in a few small towns in Surry County that are connected by the Surry Sonker Trail. A few recommended spots include **Southern on Main** in Elkin, which bakes either blueberry or apple sonker to order; **Anchored Bake Shop** in Mount Airy, which uses seasonal fruit; **The Tilted Ladder** in Pilot Mountain, where it's a featured dessert; and **Rockford General Store** in Rockford, where you can get sonker made with berries, peaches, apples or sweet potatoes. Or you can visit Mount Airy in October for the annual Sonker Festival, where you can try a few different varieties of this local specialty in one place. And even if you accidentally call it a cobbler or a buckle, you'll probably still get served a heaping bowlful.

SOUTH CAROLINA

South Carolina-style BBQ

The Palmetto State ranks just 40th on a list of America's largest states by area. But South Carolina packs a lot of barbecue tradition into a small land mass – with four distinct sauces that go with the meat that's smoked in various regions of the state.

In Columbia and surrounding towns in central South Carolina, known as the Midlands, as well as in Charleston and the Lowcountry, pork is typically cooked with and accompanied by a bright yellow mustard-based sauce, often sweetened with brown sugar and made tangy with cider vinegar. That's the sauce that South Carolina barbecue is most famous for. But in the northeast quadrant known as the Pee Dee region, including the city of Florence, the sauce is vinegar-based, and made spicy with lots of red pepper. Upstate, in Greenville and other northwest locales, barbecue is often accompanied by a thicker condiment known as heavy tomato. And in towns on the state's western edge, the sauce is related to the Pee Dee style, but sweetened with the addition of ketchup, which is why it's called light tomato.

The earliest barbecue in South Carolina was the Pee Dee style, which is the only region today that predominantly uses whole-hog cooking. German immigrants to South Carolina in the 1700s and 1800s can take credit for influencing the flavor profile of both the mustardy Midlands and ketchup-based sauces, while the heavy tomato sauce, similar to the sweet, bottled versions found in grocery stores, only became prevalent in the mid-20th century.

No matter where you eat your barbecue in South Carolina, it's likely to consist of chopped pork that's served in sandwiches, or on plates with sliced white bread and typical barbecue sides like coleslaw, mac-and-cheese and baked beans. But a side dish that's distinct to the Palmetto State is hash, a mixture of ground meat and scraps left over from cooking barbecue, along with vegetables, sauce and spices that include sage and red pepper. All of those ingredients are simmered in a large pot for hours, and the result is often served over rice (the dish is commonly known as hash and rice, although the stew is sometimes just eaten with white bread).

It'll take you a few days to hit all the hotspots of South Carolina barbecue. But a few well-regarded places include **Hite's Bar-B-Que** in West Columbia, serving Midlands-style sandwiches and plates, but only on Fridays and Saturdays; **Melvin's BBQ** in Charleston and Mt. Pleasant, famous for its mustard-based sauce; **Dukes Barbecue** in Walterboro, which offers an all-you-can-eat buffet common among South Carolina BBQ joints; **Scott's Bar-B-Que** in Hemingway, for Pee Dee-style whole-hog pork mopped in a vinegar sauce with a kick; and **Smoky Dreams Barbecue** in Greenville, which offers a choice of sauces based on tomatoes, mustard and vinegar at varying heat levels. It's a one-stop shop to help you figure out your preferred South Carolina barbecue sauce, so you can head straight to the part of the state where you'll find your favorite everywhere.

She-crab soup

You might well be inspired to dance the Charleston once you get your first taste of the dish that South Carolina's largest city is best-known for. But your revelry could soon be interrupted once you start wondering what a she-crab is, and whether this rich, creamy soup can also be prepared with he-crabs, if such a thing exists.

A she-crab, as you might have guessed, is simply a female crab, and it's typically used for making soup because the female crab produces the roe called for in traditional recipes that provides an intense, briny flavor. But fishing regulations make it illegal in some states, including South Carolina, to harvest female crabs bearing visible eggs (which are carried in a yellow sponge outside the shell). So chefs who want to adhere to the classic recipe have to use eggs collected from inside female crabs' shells, source the roe elsewhere or use substitute ingredients like uni or egg yolk.

In addition to the roe, she-crab soup consists of lump crabmeat, usually from the Atlantic blue crab, that's cooked in a base of milk or heavy cream, seafood stock, aromatics such as onions and shallots, and mace as well as other seasonings. It's typically served in a cup or bowl with a dash of dry sherry.

It's uncertain when she-crab soup was first created, but it originated in the Lowcountry region along South Carolina's coast, possibly brought by 18th-century Scottish settlers who adapted their recipe for seafood bisque. One theory is that it may have been a winter specialty, because female crabs are easier to catch during that season, when they tend to stay closer to shore than do the males. (Male crabs also tend to be larger than she-crabs, which may have made the latter desirable only when demand for seafood increased and the supply of males was exhausted.) The dish became popular after U.S. President William Taft's visit to Charleston in 1909, when William Deas, the chef working for the city's mayor, added orange crab roe to his usual recipe for crab bisque in order to make it fancier and more colorful for the visiting dignitary.

If you're on the East Coast and want to make your own version of she-crab soup, fish markets will help you distinguish between male and female crabs (one telltale sign is the red tips on female crabs' claws). But if you don't want to go to the trouble, there are numerous places to order she-crab soup in Charleston. A few recommended options include **Charleston Crab House**, where you can make an entire meal out of all their crabby offerings; **Hyman's Seafood**, a city institution that's been in business since 1890; **Poogan's Porch**, a favorite Holy City dining spot; and **The Palmetto Cafe**, whose menu features she-crab soup as well as an appetizer of jumbo crab cakes. But don't be fooled by their large size – that doesn't necessarily mean they're prepared with the males of the species, which, in case you were wondering, aren't really called he-crabs. The actual term for them is Jimmies. And even without having any roe, they probably make a mighty tasty soup.

Frogmore stew

Kermit can rest easy – there aren't any frogs in Frogmore stew. Sometimes called Lowcountry boil or Beaufort boil, this dish was named after a fishing community called Frogmore on South Carolina's St. Helena Island in the 1960s, by a restauranteur named Richard Gay.

Frogmore stew is a one-pot meal that includes shrimp, smoked sausage, new potatoes and corn on the cob, all boiled with onions and seafood seasoning and often cooked outdoors. Beer is often used for some of the liquid, and crab, scallops or fish are sometimes added to the kettle as well.

There are numerous places to eat Frogmore stew in the Lowcountry, especially in Charleston and along the South Carolina coast. A few recommended options include **Bowens Island Restaurant**, an informal establishment named for and located on a small island and renowned for its waterfront views; **Grace & Grit** in Mt. Pleasant, where the dish is reinterpreted as a salad; and **The Crab Shack** in Charleston and Folly Beach, where you can customize your seafood platter to include snow crab, shrimp and oysters. But your Frogmore stew will have to be frogless – there aren't any amphibians on the menu.

Chicken bog

Throughout most of the 18th and 19th centuries, South Carolina plantations grew and exported more rice than anywhere else in North America, until production began to move to other states in the 1880s and the industry eventually dried up entirely. But one local dish that hearkens back to this era is chicken bog, a simple stew made with chicken, rice, smoked sausage, onions and spices. It's traditionally made by boiling a whole chicken, with the bones and other inedible parts removed from the pot before the rice is added to absorb the remaining liquid. No one knows for certain why it's called chicken bog, but one theory is that the meat gets bogged down in the moist, starchy rice.

A dish that's quite similar is perlau (sometimes spelled perloo or pilau), a stew prepared with shrimp and bacon cooked with rice along with tomatoes and other vegetables – although just to confuse matters, it's often made with chicken and smoked sausage as well.

Both of these dishes are most prevalent in the Pee Dee region of South Carolina, in the northeastern part of the state, but you'll also find them in the boggy Lowcountry. A few places where you can try chicken bog are **Missy's Cafe** in Florence, **Pickled Cucumber** in Conway, **Simply Southern Smokehouse** in Myrtle Beach and **Shelter Kitchen & Bar** in Mt. Pleasant. And if you'd like to sample perlau, head to **Tubb's Shrimp and Fish Co.** in Florence, **The Grocery** in Charleston and **Grace & Grit** in Mt. Pleasant. Just don't get bogged down if you can't decide what else you'd like to order.

Charleston red rice

Perhaps no dish better represents the influence of Gullah history on the cuisine of the Palmetto State than Charleston red rice, often simply called red rice. The Gullah are a Black community with roots in West Africa who originally came to the Lowcountry as enslaved people, on ships that arrived at Charleston's port between the early 1700s and 1807. Many of the Gullah worked in rice fields along the coast of South Carolina, cultivating a long-grain crop called Carolina Gold that became the basis of several local food specialties.

Charleston red rice is similar to the Senegalese staple called thieboudienne, which later became known as jollof rice. The dish consists of white rice that's cooked with crushed tomatoes or tomato paste (which colors it red), vegetables including onions, celery and bell peppers, and minced bacon or sausage. It's generally eaten as a side dish, but can sometimes include enough meat to make it an entrée.

You'll find red rice on all sorts of restaurant menus across its namesake city. A few popular choices in Charleston include **Magnolias**, where it's served as part of a main dish with blackened catfish; **Dave's Carry-Out**, where it appears on the Tuesday lunch menu; **82 Queen**, an upscale restaurant downtown where you can order it as a family-style side; and **Bertha's Kitchen**, a soul food spot in north Charleston, where you can also try dishes like okra soup and stewed lima beans, and start to gain a richer understanding of Gullah cuisine.

Another South Carolina dish to sample:

- **Groundnut cake**, which is actually a candy made with molasses, brown sugar, butter and roasted peanuts. In the 1800s and early 1900s, these confections were sold for a penny by women on the streets of Charleston, using the Carolina African variety of peanut, commonly known as a groundnut, that was once prominent in the Lowcountry. Today South Carolina farmers are once again cultivating this species, and the candy is making a comeback, too. You can buy groundnut cakes from **Bert and T's Desserts**, a bakery that sells its wares online for pickup in north Charleston.

Benne wafer

You probably shouldn't leave South Carolina without a taste of a delectable Charleston chew, the benne wafer. Benne is the Bantu word for sesame, and this crop came to the Lowcountry in the 1700s with West African slaves, who planted it extensively across the South and used its high-nutrient seeds and oil to supplement their meager diet.

Benne wafers are thin, crispy cookies made with toasted sesame seeds, butter, sugar and flour that are said to bring good luck to anyone who receives them as a gift. They're widely available in Charleston gift shops, and are made by three local companies: **Olde Colony Bakery**, which claims to have the original recipe for Lowcountry Benne wafers and has baked them since 1940; **Charleston Specialty Foods**, which also offers a wide variety of locally made food products; and **Southern Sisters Bakery**, which creates its cookies with all-natural ingredients and sells them daily at **Charleston City Market** downtown. They're a perfect souvenir of your time in Charleston and a good reminder that enslaved people played a major role in shaping the city's culinary identity.

GEORGIA

Country captain

Country captain owes its popularity to two important figures in 20th-century American history. The first is future U.S. President Franklin D. Roosevelt. When FDR would spend time at his Southern retreat in Warm Springs, Georgia, during the 1920s, he once attended a dinner party hosted by Mamie Bullard, a doyenne of society in the nearby city of Columbus. Bullard served Roosevelt a dish called country captain, prepared by her cook, Arie Mullins, that the dignitary became so enamored with that he eventually introduced it to the second influencer: George S. Patton, who would request it whenever he visited the adjacent Fort Benning. And its acclaim among the military led it to being added to the U.S. Army's roster of meals-ready-to-eat from 2000 to 2004, in Patton's honor.

Country captain is a curried chicken stew made with tomatoes as well as currants and almonds, that's typically served over white rice. It likely originated as an Indian dish that was eaten aboard ships that sailed along Asian spice routes in the 1800s (those who were in charge of those vessels were called country captains).

Although similar recipes appear in a few late-19th century cookbooks, country captain didn't start to become popular in the U.S. until a Swiss chef working in New York City, Alessandro Filippini, included it in his influential 1906 cookbook that highlighted dishes from international cuisines. It was Bullard and Mullins, though, who can take credit for the addition of whole tomatoes to the stew, and they became a standard part of the recipe that was a mid-1900s staple in Southern restaurants and homes, especially in Columbus.

Today country captain is much harder to find, but you'll still encounter it in Columbus at **Mark's City Grill**, which serves fried chicken fingers in a roasted tomato curry over steamed rice. Meanwhile, two restaurants in Savannah use it as inspiration for reinvented dishes. At **The Grey**, an eatery in a restored 1938 Greyhound bus terminal, country captain is served for the table in a sourdough bread bowl. And at **Fleeting**, its flavors are presented as spring rolls that contain chicken, almonds and coconut. But there's no need to be afraid of the dish's new forms. To paraphrase FDR, the only thing you have to fear is that it might be 86'd for the night.

Peach cobbler

License plates in Georgia no longer feature the state's nickname, Peach State, although a graphic of the fruit still appears in the background on most plates. Yet surprisingly, Georgia only produces a tiny percentage of the nation's peaches, growing fewer than either California or South Carolina. (Yet Georgia's farmers are responsible for more than half of the peanuts grown in the U.S., and more pecans than any other state. Perhaps it's time to come up with a new moniker?)

If there's one dish that best represents Georgia, though, it's probably peach cobbler, a dessert that features the fruit covered with biscuits or batter that creates a sweet crust when baked. There's no telling when Georgians first decided to make this dish, but peaches weren't grown commercially in the state until the mid-1800s, when farmers began looking for alternatives to the lucrative cotton crops that were being decimated by the boll weevil. The fruit's notoriety peaked in the 1920s, when Georgia put on a series of festivals to showcase the local crop, featuring an elaborate pageant telling the story of the Georgia peach, parades and even a live camel.

If you're on the road in Georgia during the summer, it's worth stopping at growers like **Lane Southern Orchards** in Fort Valley and **Dickey Farms** in Musella for a taste of their cobbler, as well as other products made with fresh peaches. But you'll also find outstanding versions at bakeries and BBQ spots including **Aunt**

Evelyn's Peach Cobbler in Atlanta, which makes cobblers in squares, rounds and mason jars and ships them nationwide; **The Peach Cobbler Factory** in Atlanta, Savannah, Dalton, Stockbridge and other locations around the Southeast, where you can top your cobbler with ice cream, nuts or caramel; **Goolsby's** in Evans, where peach cobbler is a sweet ending to a meal of ribs or barbecue chicken; and **Mary Mac's Tea Room** in Atlanta, which has been serving up Southern specialties since 1945. But when you're looking to celebrate a Georgia crop that's more beneficial to the state's economy than peaches – but nowhere near as famous – find a café where you can order a peanut butter sandwich and a slice of pecan pie.

Another Georgia dish to sample:

- **Potlikker**, sometimes spelled pot liquor, a broth made from the liquid left over from cooking beans and collard greens, sometimes with added bits of pork or turkey. It's either eaten as a soup, with cornbread crumbled into it for extra body, or used as an ingredient in other dishes. You can sample it at **Mary Mac's Tea Room** in Atlanta.

OTHER FOODS OF THE SOUTH

Shrimp and grits

Like Sonny & Cher, Bonnie & Clyde and Tom & Jerry, shrimp and grits are a classic duo, featured on Southern restaurant menus from Birmingham to Biloxi. But you might not realize that this comforting classic has its roots in the Lowcountry cooking of coastal South Carolina and Georgia, and only began to spread regionally during the past few decades.

Shrimp and grits was traditionally eaten as a breakfast dish, with the succulent shellfish served over hominy, which is coarsely ground, processed corn. Today the grits are usually cooked with milk and either Cheddar or mascarpone cheese to make them a smooth, creamy base for the sautéed shrimp, with the plate often being enhanced with crisp bacon or smoky sausage.

While corn was known to be ground by the Native Muskogee tribe, the addition of shrimp to the dish is properly credited to the Gullah, who came to the Lowcountry as enslaved people from West Africa beginning in the 1700s. But it wasn't until the 1980s that shrimp and grits began to become popular elsewhere in the South. That's when Bill Neal, the chef at Crook's Corner, a now-closed restaurant in Chapel Hill, North Carolina, put the specialty on his menu, and publicity from the New York Times and other publications helped it become his best-selling item. Beginning in the '90s, restaurants in Charleston, New Orleans and other cities began to create elevated versions of shrimp and grits, and the trend became so widespread than a Southern food writer named Nathalie Dupree published an entire cookbook dedicated to the dish in 2006.

Today you'll find credible versions of shrimp and grits just about anywhere you travel throughout the Southern U.S. A few recommended options include **Yo' Mama's** in Birmingham, **Cape Fear Seafood Company** in Raleigh, **Atlanta Breakfast**

Club in Atlanta, **The Public Kitchen & Bar** in Savannah and **Poogan's Porch** in Charleston, where the dish is served with Andouille sausage and tasso ham gravy. That's a pairing that – just like shrimp and grits – deserves a place in the pantheon of famous duos.

Fried catfish

On the Internet, catfishing means to mislead someone by creating a false identity. But there's little chance you'll be fooled when you stop at a catfish house for lunch or dinner. The fish is typically coated in cornmeal and fried to a golden crisp, and you won't mistake its distinctive taste for anything else.

Catfish became a Southern staple in the 1700s and 1800s, when it was typically eaten by enslaved people from West Africa as part of weekend fish fries. The fish was a familiar species from their homeland, and they found a plentiful supply in the South's lakes and rivers. The catfish industry took off in the 1960s when farmers who were struggling with their declining cotton and soybean crops began raising catfish commercially. Today the U.S. produces nearly $400 million of catfish annually, with Mississippi waters responsible for more than half of the yield.

Travel around the South, especially in Mississippi, Arkansas and Alabama, and you'll find numerous catfish houses serving whole fish as well as fillets on plates with French fries, coleslaw and hushpuppies. A few popular choices include **Catfish Corner** in Jayess and **Taylor Grocery** in Taylor, both in Mississippi; **David's Catfish House**, with eight locations in Alabama (and two on the Florida panhandle); **Grampa's Catfish and Seafood** in North Little Rock and **Bubba's Catfish & Seafood** in Hot Springs, both in Arkansas; and **Walden's Restaurant** in Covington, Georgia.

South Carolina has its fair share of fried catfish joints, too, but another dish worth keeping an eye out for there is catfish stew, in which the seafood is cooked in a tomato-based broth seasoned with bacon. You'll find well-regarded versions at **Oak Grove Fish House** in Lexington as well as at **Maryland Fried Chicken, Shrimp & Seafood**, whose name sounds like it's catfishing you into thinking it's from somewhere up north – but is actually in Florence.

Chitlins

Sometimes it's best to try a food before you learn exactly how the sausage got made. And that's certainly the case for chitlins (also known as chitterlings), the intestines of a pig that are a traditional Southern delicacy. After being thoroughly cleaned and then boiled with onions and other aromatics, they're usually battered and deep-fried, and served with accompaniments of apple cider vinegar and hot sauce.

Chitlins were part of the cuisine of enslaved people, who were given the less desirable parts of the pig to eat (the wealthy landowners who dined on the choice cuts were said to be living high on the hog), and continued to be part of Black soul food after emancipation. In the 1960s, theaters and music clubs that were viewed as safe places for Black artists to perform in the segregated South were said to be part of the Chitlin Circuit.

Because this dish is labor-intensive to prepare, it's sometimes saved for holidays and other special occasions. But you'll find chitlins on the menus of soul food restaurants throughout Southern states. A few places to try them include **Big Mama's Soul Food** in Augusta, Georgia; **The Chicken Hut** in Durham, North Carolina, where they're served as a Friday special; **Taylor's Soul Food** in Rock Hill, South Carolina; **Mary's Southern Cooking** in Mobile, Alabama, which offers chitlins on Sundays; and **Nana J's Soulful Kitchen** in Ocean Springs, Mississippi. Or head to the town of Salley, South Carolina, on the Saturday after Thanksgiving for the annual Chitlin Strut, a festival with all the pork intestines you can eat. And hopefully, knowing just where they came from won't have ruined your appetite.

Country ham biscuit

Residents of Raleigh know to avoid the area near **The Honey Baked Ham Company** around Christmas and Easter, when massive congestion caused by shoppers picking up their holiday meals creates a traffic headache known as the ham jam. But those who are able to make it home in time and are lucky enough to have honey ham – or its salty cousin, country ham – left over from dinner can enjoy a regional specialty for breakfast the next morning by combining two classic Southern foods.

Throughout the South, biscuits are typically made with buttermilk, along with flour and butter, and can be flavored with cheese, peppers or other ingredients. They're usually baked in rounds that are sliced in half horizontally, and are best when eaten warm.

To make a country ham biscuit, you'll naturally need country ham, a salt-cured meat that's especially prevalent in Virginia and North Carolina. (At the Isle of Wight County Museum in Smithfield, Virginia, you can check out the world's oldest ham, a 120-year-old specimen, which you can also keep an eye on 24/7 via webcam.) Other ingredients in the sandwich can include fried eggs or pimento cheese, along with condiments such as mustard and fruit preserves.

You'll find excellent versions of country ham biscuits at numerous restaurants and bakeries across the region, including **Old Chickahominy House** in Williamsburg, **The Fancy Biscuit** in Richmond, and **Scratch Biscuit Co.** in Roanoke, all in Virginia; **Biscuitville**, a fast-food chain with dozens of locations across North Carolina; **The Biscuit Company**, which has three branches south of Greensboro; **Stilesboro Biscuits** in Kennesaw, Georgia; and **Rise Southern Biscuits**, with more than 20 locations in Richmond, Raleigh and other cities. Or you can stay away from traffic and make your own version of this sandwich at home. Just be sure to balance the salty meat with some sweetness by adding some jam to your ham.

Red eye gravy

It takes just two ingredients to make a credible red eye gravy – black coffee, and the drippings from a pan-fried slice of country ham, which is a cured and smoked meat product characteristic of Virginia, Kentucky and other states. And some Southerners claim you can make the dish even more simply, with water instead of coffee. No wonder it's sometimes called poor man's gravy.

Compared to country gravy (also known as sawmill gravy), which is thickened with a roux of milk and flour and usually contains bits of sausage, red eye gravy is a thin sauce, normally used as an accompaniment to ham, as a topping for grits or as a dip for biscuits.

There isn't a definitive explanation for its name, but one imaginative theory is that when the drippings and coffee were mixed together, their heterogeneity caused them to resemble a human eye. Another, likely apocryphal, story says that future U.S. President Andrew Jackson once asked his cook to prepare some gravy as red as his eyes, which the general saw were bloodshot from the cook's having spent the previous night drinking.

You'll find red eye gravy on breakfast menus in restaurants all over the South, as well as across Appalachia. A few places to sample it include **Big Ed's** in Raleigh and Garner, North Carolina, where it accompanies a meal of country ham, grits and eggs; **Biscuit Head** in Asheville, North Carolina, and Greenville, South Carolina, where it naturally comes with biscuits; **Jerry's Country Kitchen** in Carrollton, Georgia, where you can get your biscuits with either red eye or sawmill gravy; and **Waysider Restaurant** in Tuscaloosa, where it's dished out with country ham and eggs. Any of these spots would be good places to go for breakfast if you've had to fly cross-country all through the night. A strong cup of coffee and a serving of gravy might be everything you need to recover from the red eye.

Chicken and dumplings

Today we tend to think of chicken and dumplings as an old-fashioned soup with humble beginnings, when (as the story gets told) Southerners made use of inexpensive ingredients during economically lean times to feed a crowd. But the reality is far more complicated.

Chicken and dumplings consists of a poultry-flavored stock that's used to cook small pieces of biscuit-like dough. The liquid the chicken boils in sometimes includes aromatics and vegetables, and the stewed chicken is typically added back into and served with the soup, which can have either a thinner, broth-like or thicker, gravy-like consistency.

Although the ingredients are basically the same everywhere, there are a few different regional styles and names for the dish. In the South, the soup is more often made with rolled dumplings, which are thick, noodle-like strips of pastry similar to pie crust, while the North favors dropped dumplings, using small balls of dough. The dish is sometimes known as chicken and pastry in North Carolina and chicken and noodles in Indiana, while in Appalachia it's referred to as chicken and slicks. And in Pennsylvania Dutch country, a similar soup is called bott boi.

Dumplings are rooted in European cuisine, especially German, and the early versions of them in American cookbooks, in the mid-19th century, often call for suet, or beef fat. Instructions for cooking dumplings in chicken broth didn't appear until 1879, when Marion Cabell Tyree published Housekeeping in Old Virginia. In the ensuing decades, chicken, which were typically raised for their eggs, started to become seen as a luxury food item. That idea helps explain Herbert Hoover's 1928 presidential campaign slogan highlighting "a chicken in every pot," a reminder that if he were elected, Americans would continue to realize the prosperous standard of living that they enjoyed during the Roaring Twenties. (Spoiler alert: Hoover got elected, but the following year didn't go so well for him.)

During the first half of the 20th century, chicken remained more expensive than beef, but the industrialization of the poultry industry in the 1960s helped transform it into a commodity protein. It wasn't until the 1990s that Americans started to eat more chicken than beef, and the former began to be viewed as an inferior type of meat. This may help explain the modern perception of chicken and dumplings as a dish for meager times.

If you'd like to dig into this regional specialty, you'll find it at barbecue and soul food restaurants all over the South, including **Mama Hamil's Southern Cookin' and Bar B Que Buffet** in Madison, Mississippi; **Brown Bag** in Northport, Alabama; **Stone Mill Cafe** in Bentonville, Arkansas, which serves chicken and dumplings on Mondays, Thursdays and Saturdays; **Let's Eat Soul Food** in Durham, North Carolina; **Simply Southern Smokehouse** in Myrtle Beach; and **Mary Mac's Tea Room** in Atlanta. And even though it wasn't historically a frugal dish, when you order a bowl of this hearty soup, you certainly won't feel like you're breaking the bank.

Chicken mull

When you're mulling over which side dish to order with your next plate of barbecue, consider a bowl of chicken mull. This pale-colored stew consists of chicken that's been simmered in a simple broth consisting of milk or cream, butter, salt and pepper. It's thickened with saltine crackers and is usually served with hot sauce and additional crackers on the side.

The mull in chicken mull is probably a variant of muddle, a word for other chicken- or fish-based stews that were historically eaten in Virginia and North Carolina. Like Wisconsin's booyah and Kentucky's burgoo, chicken mull was traditionally cooked in a large outdoor kettle for a community meal. Chicken mull was not only the name of the dish, but also the term for the event at which it was served (although these days, it's sometimes just called chicken stew).

Today chicken mull is difficult to find in restaurants, outside of a small sliver of Northern Georgia and Northern South Carolina, but you'll be able to track it down as a side dish at a few BBQ spots and old-time Southern establishments.

A few places to go if you want to sample chicken mull include **The Inked Pig** in Gainesville and **Butt Hutt BBQ** in Athens, which offers the stew to go by the pint, quart or gallon, both in Georgia; and **Holden's Ranch** in Roebuck and **Midway BBQ** in Buffalo, both in South Carolina. And in North Carolina, the town of Bear Grass hosts an annual chicken mull festival every October. Once you try a bowl you'll probably be wondering why the dish seems to be disappearing from restaurant menus. It's a good question, so you may as well order a second helping and mull it over.

Brunswick stew

A Southern staple with a questionable history is responsible for a long-simmering, yet good-natured, feud between Virginia and Georgia. Call it the Battle of Brunswick: Two locales with the same name both take credit for originating Brunswick stew, a slow-cooked mélange of shredded chicken or pork, tomatoes, lima beans, corn and other vegetables, seasoned with spices including cayenne pepper and Worcestershire sauce.

The earliest record of Brunswick stew comes from Virginia, where a cook named Jimmy Matthews is said to have created the dish for a hunting party in Brunswick County in 1828, preparing it with squirrel, which was a common game meat in early recipes. But Brunswick, Georgia, across the river from St. Simons Island, argued in the 1940s that the original version of the stew was cooked there, and even erected a monument with the pot purported to be used for the first batch in 1898. (Georgia's claim is likely to be spurious, based on research that uncovered references to the stew long before that date, and referring to it as a Virginia dish. But that didn't stop a local county commission from passing a resolution in 1988 that declared Georgia as Brunswick stew's official birthplace. Not to be outdone, the Virginia General Assembly adopted a competing proclamation the same year.)

The dish has also been said to be a favorite of both U.S. President Franklin D. Roosevelt and Queen Victoria, although there's no record of them ever eating it together, and these accounts are also of dubious historical worth.

What is true is that there are minor regional differences in the components of Brunswick stew that you'll find in Virginia and Georgia, as well as in North Carolina. Virginia's version is more often made with chicken, and sometimes uses potatoes as a thickener, while North Carolina tends to use pork, and Georgia often has less emphasis on tomatoes. But there are no hard and fast rules, as every cook makes their version a little differently.

Wherever you travel in the Southeast, you're likely to find Brunswick stew on the menus of barbecue restaurants, either as a side or a main dish. A few recommended options in the two states that claim its creation include **Pierce's Pitt Bar-B-Que** in Williamsburg, which serves it during the fall and winter seasons, and **Pungo Boys BBQ** in Virginia Beach, both in Virginia; and **Southern Soul Barbeque** in St. Simons Island and **Cue Barbecue** in Alpharetta, both in Georgia. And in the buffer region of North Carolina, you can try the well-regarded versions at **Parker's Barbecue** in Wilson and **Stubbs & Sons**, with locations in Sanford, Carthage and Pittsboro. Or if you really want to stir the pot, order some stew at **BBQ House** in Oak Island, North Carolina – in that state's Brunswick County – and tell everyone that's where the dish was actually invented.

Meat and three

See Nashville

Meat and threes, casual lunch restaurants with a wide range of proteins and vegetables, are widespread around the South, especially in its major cities. Some of the most famous ones are **Busy Bee Cafe** in Atlanta, opened in 1947 by a Black cook named Lucy Jackson and frequented by Martin Luther King Jr. and other civil rights leaders during the 1960s; **Big Mike's Soul Food** in Myrtle Beach, known for gigantic portions of hearty Southern food; **Niki's West** in Birmingham, which offers as many as 10 entrée choices every day, including barbecue pork and Greek chicken; and **Bully's Soul Food Restaurant** in Jackson, Mississippi, where the daily specials like liver-and-onions and turkey wings are served with your choice of any two vegetables. But if you want the true meat and three experience, just order an extra dish of fried okra or mashed potatoes.

Deviled eggs

Despite a well-known reality TV family's hilarious effort to rebrand them as "yellow pocket angel eggs," there's nothing Satanic about deviled eggs. Instead, the term comes from the original recipe's use of spicy ingredients such as mustard and cayenne pepper. The same adjective is often applied to other flavorful dishes like deviled crab, deviled ham and even fra diavolo (Brother Devil) tomato sauce – but not devil's food cake, which is probably called that because of its sinful richness, or possibly because it was originally reddish in color.

Deviled eggs are ones that have been hard-boiled and cut in half, with the yolks removed. The whites are then stuffed with a filling made from the yolks, mayonnaise, chopped pickles and seasonings, and are often garnished with a sprinkle of paprika or a morsel of bacon. They're typically served as a cold appetizer or side dish, and a plate may include just a few or as many as a dozen halves.

This delicacy originated as far back as ancient Rome, but the earliest American recipe was published in Montgomery, Alabama, in 1877, and the first one suggesting mayonnaise as a binder came in 1896, in a cookbook written by Fannie Farmer. Over the subsequent decades, deviled eggs became a staple in

Southern homes and at church gatherings (where they were sometimes called stuffed eggs or dressed eggs to avoid an association with Lucifer), and special trays for carrying them eventually became commonplace.

A recent survey found that nearly two-thirds of Americans were planning to eat deviled eggs on Easter, a holiday when many find themselves with a surplus of eggs. But you can enjoy this dish year-round at spots like **Firebirds Wood Fired Grill** in Montgomery, which serves deviled eggs with hot honey-glazed pork belly and goat cheese; **The Pantry** in Little Rock, which offers an elevated version with a truffled filling and Parmesan crisps; **Hayes Barton Cafe and Dessertery** in Raleigh, where they're a popular lunch side dish; **Fall Line Kitchen & Bar** in Richmond, which serves BLT deviled eggs with peppercorn aioli; and **There on Fifth** in Atlanta, which highlights the dish's diabolical nature with a touch of sriracha in the filling. Grab your (pitch)fork and enjoy every bite without worrying that by ordering them, you've made a deal with the Devil.

Pimento cheese

Every April, golf fans line up at the Masters Tournament in Augusta, Georgia, for $1.50 pimento cheese sandwiches. Columbia, South Carolina, stakes a claim to have invented the pimento cheeseburger in the 1960s. And food lovers throughout the Carolinas have their own secret recipes for what's been called the caviar of the South. So you may be shocked to learn that one place this dish is particularly popular is the Philippines, and that it may not actually have Southern origins at all.

Pimento cheese is a smooth or chunky spread made with either processed cheese, Cheddar cheese or cream cheese, mixed with chopped pimentos – a type of red pepper – and other vegetables, mayonnaise, spices and seasonings. It's commonly served with crackers, chips or crudites as an appetizer, or on bread as a sandwich, but creative chefs often make use of it as an ingredient in dishes such as grits, mac-and-cheese and fried sausage balls.

The original versions of pimento cheese date from around the turn of the 20th century, featuring processed cream cheese made in New York and peppers that had been imported from Spain. An early recipe, published in 1908 in Good Housekeeping magazine, suggested making sandwiches using the spread, with a recipe that combined cream cheese, pimentos, mustard and chives. In the 1920s and '30s, pimento cheese became immensely popular throughout the country, with several companies based in New York and Wisconsin manufacturing their own versions, some relying on a burgeoning industry of Georgia-grown pimentos.

But none of that history explains why pimento cheese became so widespread across the South, especially over the past few decades. One theory is that it's a result of marketing efforts by Duke's Mayonnaise, a South Carolina-based product that got its start in 1917 when Eugenia Duke and her daughter began selling pimento cheese sandwiches at the Army canteen near Greenville.

In the Philippines, where it's also commonly eaten, the spread is called cheese pimiento (these days, Americans generally spell the pepper without the second i) and remains a legacy of the military troops who were stationed there during the first half of the 20th century. The dish continues to be a popular snack in that country, more than 75 years after the U.S. granted its independence in 1946.

If you don't have a ticket for the Masters (and don't want to pay the price of more than 100 pimento cheese sandwiches for its special Taste of the Masters concessions package, which you can purchase online), you'll find options for consuming pimento cheese in various forms in nearly any Southern city you visit. A few appealing options include **Seed Kitchen & Bar** in Marietta, Georgia, where you can try pimento cheese crostini served with country ham, apples and arugula; **Poole's** in Raleigh, where the spread is dished out with fried saltine crackers; **Urban Cookhouse** in Birmingham, which serves a pimento cheese BLT; **Callie's Hot Little Biscuit** in Charleston, where you can order biscuit sandwiches or bowls of grits that feature the spread, which you can also buy in containers online; and **No Name Deli** in Columbia, whose menu features both pimento sandwiches and cheeseburgers. That city also offers a pimento cheese passport as an incentive to explore the dozens of restaurants that serve versions of it. By the time you've finished stamping yours, you'll be convinced that the spread was invented down South after all.

Hoppin' John

If it's New Year's Day and you want to guarantee that the upcoming year will be a prosperous one, be sure to eat a bowl of Hoppin' John. That's a dish made with rice and peas, which represent coins, that's typically accompanied by a plate of collard greens, whose color is symbolic of American money, as well as cornbread, which stands for gold.

In many places across the South, Hoppin' John is traditionally prepared with black-eyed peas, along with rice, onions and either chopped bacon or pork. But in the South Carolina and Georgia Lowcountry, it was typically made with Sea Island red peas, also called cowpeas or field peas. These legumes were brought to the state along with the enslaved people from West Africa and were grown on rice plantations, becoming an important part of their diet. Production began to dry up in the late 19th century, and this crop has only recently begun to be grown again in South Carolina, perhaps explaining why black-eyed peas are more typically used in modern versions of the dish.

Hoppin' John was probably eaten by the Gullah people in the colonies as early as the 1700s but wasn't documented in American cookbooks until the 1840s. Its name may come from a mispronunciation of the Haitian Creole word for black-eyed peas, pois pigeons, although more colorful tales about its origin suggest that a man with a limp sold it on the streets of Charleston, or that children would hop around in anticipation while it was being cooked.

Hoppin' John can be found on restaurant menus in both South Carolina and Georgia, at places including **Poogan's Porch**, where it accompanies fried chicken, and **Dave's Carry-Out**, which serves it as part of Thursday lunch service, both in Charleston; **Tubb's Shrimp and Fish Co.** in Florence; **Southern Soul Barbeque** in St. Simons Island; and **Maepole** in Atlanta and Athens. But if you can't get to any of those spots on New Year's Day, you might want to lock in your good fortune by cooking your own recipe. Just be sure to accompany the dish with as many foods that remind you of wealth as you possibly can.

Fried green tomatoes

The actresses Kathy Bates and Jessica Tandy are the major reason that fried green tomatoes are thought of today as a Southern dish. Until the 1991 release of their movie by the same name, this preparation was considered one of the best ways to make use of unripened tomatoes, with interest in the dish peaking during the 1940s and '50s, mostly in the Midwest. But after the film made two cafés – one real and one fictional – famous, fried green tomatoes became immensely popular at those establishments, as well as at other restaurants throughout the South.

Fried green tomatoes are slices of unripened tomato that are soaked in buttermilk, dredged in cornmeal and fried in oil or bacon fat until they're crispy and golden. They're best when eaten hot and are sometimes served with a buttermilk dressing or dipping sauce. They're also used as a component of dishes like fried green tomato BLTs and may accompany other Southern classics like fried okra, grits and pimento cheese.

If you want to try this dish while retracing the steps of Hollywood royalty, the first place to go is **The Whistle Stop Cafe** in Juliette, Georgia, a restaurant initially created as a film stage in a location that was once nearly deserted, but is today a major tourist attraction. Another spot that saw a boom after the release of the movie is **Irondale Cafe** in Irondale, Alabama, which Fannie Flagg used as inspiration for the original Whistle Stop restaurant in her 1987 novel on which the film was based. Irondale Cafe now serves 600 to 800 slices of fried green tomatoes daily, except on Saturdays, when they stay closed every week other than during the annual Whistle Stop Festival.

Other recommended places to try fried green tomatoes are, naturally, **Fried Green Tomatoes**, a chain with five locations in Georgia; **Sweet Potatoes** in Winston-Salem, North Carolina; **Magnolias** in Charleston; and **Crescent City Grill** in Hattiesburg, Mississippi. Or make the dish yourself at home while watching the film. Just be sure to have a stack of napkins at the ready, both to wipe your hands and dab your tears.

Chow chow

While you're chowing down on barbecue and all of the other tasty Southern food, be sure and keep an eye out for a condiment called chow chow. There are several regional variations of this specialty, including an Amish version in Pennsylvania. But in the South, chow chow is typically prepared with green tomatoes, peppers and cabbage that are all pickled in vinegar, along with other vegetables and seasonings that can make it either spicy, sweet or tangy. The condiment is usually served cold and can be eaten by itself, or used as an accompaniment to meat, seafood and vegetable dishes.

There are numerous speculative theories about the origin of chow chow (one clue is that chou is the French word for cabbage), but what we do know is that making this condiment was a traditional way of preserving vegetables for later use at the end of the summer growing season.

If you'd like to sample chow chow, you'll find it in jars at specialty food stores including **The Relish Barn** in Rose Hill, Virginia, and **Stripling's General Store** in Tifton, Georgia. But you'll also see it on restaurant menus including at **Full Moon Bar-B-Que**, with a dozen locations in Alabama and Mississippi; **Maepole** in Atlanta and Athens, Georgia, where you can use it to accent a healthy grain bowl; and **South on Main** in Little Rock, which serves it as an accompaniment to fried chicken as well as a smoked bologna sandwich. They're undoubtedly plates that you'll want to eat with relish.

Seven-layer salad

You've probably purchased seven-layer bars – a confection made with butter, graham cracker crumbs, sweetened condensed milk, butterscotch and chocolate chips, coconut flakes and chopped nuts – at a community bake sale, and you may have even made these magic cookie bars (a term introduced with the recipe printed on cans of Eagle Brand milk) yourself. But have you ever encountered a seven-layer salad? It's a dish that first became popular at Southern picnics and church gatherings in the 1950s, and is usually served in a glass trifle bowl to highlight the colorful foods that are layered inside.

A seven-layer salad was originally known as a seven-layer pea salad, and generally includes green peas along with iceberg lettuce, sliced tomatoes, onions and cucumbers, shredded Cheddar cheese and chopped bacon. The ingredients (and their number) are often varied to include other meats and vegetables, though. The salad is typically topped with a creamy mayonnaise- or sour cream-based dressing, such as ranch, that probably negates any nutritional value the salad might claim to have.

If you'd like to try this dish, you'll find classic versions at **Pennington Market and Grill** in Butler, Alabama; **Mrs. Lacy's Magnolia House** in Sanford, North Carolina; and **Mayberry's** in Seneca, South Carolina. But at **Our Place** in Gardendale,

Alabama, the menu item called a seven-layer salad is turned on its head. It's constructed with the tomatoes, onions, cheese and bacon that are characteristic of the original recipe – but the restaurant then adds layers of pickles, a chicken breast and a cheeseburger, and hilariously, serves it with crackers. I suppose there's no reason you couldn't take the ingredients for magic cookie bars, swap the chocolate chips for sweet peas, and call that a seven-layer salad, too.

Sweet potato casserole

Alabama and North Carolina have such a love affair with sweet potatoes that both states – along with Louisiana – have declared it to be their official vegetable. And while sweet potatoes are often made into fries or turned into soup, another preparation where they play a starring role in both of these places is sweet potato casserole.

This dish, often featured on holiday tables, consists of sweet potatoes that are mashed, topped with brown sugar and pecans, and baked until brown. There's no record of when the casserole originated, but enslaved people throughout the region began eating the plentiful vegetable beginning in the late 17th century as a substitute for the yams they were familiar with in West Africa.

If you can't wait until Thanksgiving to enjoy this specialty, you'll find sweet potato casserole as a side dish at steakhouses and BBQ restaurants throughout the South. A few options in the states where it's the official vegetable include **Steak 48** in Charlotte, **The Pit Authentic Barbecue** in Raleigh, **Briquette's Steakhouse** in Mobile and **Bricktop's** in Birmingham. And once you finish your main course, if you don't think you've had your fill of this ingredient, just order a slice of sweet potato pie for dessert.

Corn pudding

Why stick to corn on the cob when you can turn a familiar vegetable into a decadent casserole? Corn pudding is a Southern (and Appalachian) specialty in which fresh corn is mixed with eggs and heavy cream as well as spices and other ingredients, and baked until it's fluffy and golden. The dish has endless variations – it can be made either sweet or savory, and with a custardy or a cake-like texture – and is often eaten as a Thanksgiving side dish.

This delicacy originated with early American settlers, who adapted the savory puddings that they were familiar with in Europe with the abundant corn that was a Native staple. It was typically made in the summer using fresh corn, but during other seasons, it was prepared with green corn, a term for dried ears that had not yet matured. It's quite similar to spoonbread, a looser version of cornbread that's especially prevalent in Virginia and Kentucky.

You'll easily be able to find corn pudding at Southern restaurants and BBQ spots, especially across Virginia, Georgia and the Carolinas, as well as in Tennessee. A few well-regarded places to try it include **Liberty Station** in Bedford, Virginia, located in a restored 19th-century railroad terminal; **Q Barbeque** in Midlothian and Glen Allen, also in Virginia; **Sweet Potatoes Kitchen** in Savannah; **Lewis Barbecue** in Greenville and Charleston, South Carolina, which prepares its corn pudding using Hatch green chiles; and **City Barbeque**, with more than a dozen locations throughout Georgia and North Carolina (as well as across the Midwest).

How about a corny joke to end this section? Don't be hesitant to order this dish whenever you see it on the menu. Who knows, you might find it a-maize-ing.

Cornbread dressing

At Thanksgiving dinner, do you eat stuffing or dressing? If you're from the South, it's probably the latter, and a favorite way to accompany a holiday turkey in this region is with a platter of cornbread dressing. (A New York Times study found that Google users in Arkansas and Mississippi were five times more likely to search for the dish during the week before Thanksgiving, relative to population size, as were residents of other states.)

This casserole is prepared with crumbled cornbread that's mixed with eggs, butter, vegetables such as onions and celery, herbs that may include parsley and sage, and sometimes bacon or sausage, nuts or other ingredients. It's then baked until golden-brown and is usually served in squares. Even when cornbread dressing is cooked inside a turkey (a practice discouraged by the U.S. Department of Agriculture), it's still known in the South as dressing, not stuffing.

While cornbread dressing usually appears at festive meals, its origin comes from the enslaved people of West Africa. During the 18th and 19th centuries, they subsisted on a meager dish called kush that was made from cornmeal as well as meat or vegetable scraps, and was said to remind them of a food eaten in West Africa that resembled couscous. A similar mixture, called Confederate cush, was often eaten by Southern troops during the Civil War.

If you'd like to sample cornbread dressing, a few places you can find it include **Bully's Soul Food Restaurant** in Jackson, Mississippi; **J.W. Beverette's Soul Food** in Montgomery, Alabama; **Annie Laura's Kitchen** in Riverdale, Georgia; and **The Daily Dish**, with two locations in Hot Springs, Arkansas, that offer it by the pound for holiday dinners at home. And if you're from the North and decide to call it stuffing, no one needs to be the wiser.

Hoecakes

*See Rhode Island (**Johnnycakes**)*

While these fried cornmeal pancakes are usually known as Johnnycakes in the North, in the South, they're called hoecakes because they were cooked on an iron pan called a hoe (and not, as commonly thought, on the blade of a field hoe). You'll find them at **Mt. Vernon Inn Restaurant** in Mt. Vernon, Virginia, and **Hillbilly Hide-A-Way Restaurant** in Walnut Cove, North Carolina.

A similar dish, hot water cornbread, is prepared by adding flour to the cornmeal batter and frying it in oil. One place you can try this dish is **E&N** in Madison, Alabama.

Hushpuppy

Slip on some comfortable footwear and head out to your favorite BBQ joint or seafood spot for a taste of the deep-fried cornmeal fritter that's called a hushpuppy.

Hushpuppies are prepared with a batter consisting of cornmeal that's mixed with milk or buttermilk, flour and eggs, and are fried in oil until the outside is golden-brown and crispy. These versatile morsels, which are either round or oblong, can be flavored with green onions, jalapeño peppers or other seasonings, and are usually served warm. They're served with barbecued meats or fried seafood, along with coleslaw and other sides, either plain or accompanied by honey butter or a creamy dipping sauce.

There are countless tales about where the name hushpuppy came from, most of them probably untrue. One favorite is that cooks frying the dish gave morsels of the dough to their dogs to quiet them while they were getting dinner ready. It's more likely, though, that the term hushpuppy was used in American vernacular before this food became popular, meaning something to eat that would stop one's stomach from growling.

In South Carolina, fried cornmeal batter was originally known as red horse bread, because it was typically eaten with a type of fish by that name. These fritters were a specialty of a Black cook named Romeo Govan, who hosted fish fries in the late 19th century on the bank of the Edisto River. Although they were also known by other names, including wampus in Florida, the term hushpuppy was being used in Georgia by the 1920s, and eventually caught on across the region. Just after World War II, a North Carolina entrepreneur named Walter M. Thompson Jr. introduced a packaged mix for making hushpuppies, called Thompson's Fireside Hushpuppy Mixture, that helped male them popular nationwide.

Today, hushpuppies are ubiquitous on Southern restaurant menus. A few well-regarded places to enjoy them are **Barbeque Exchange** in Gordonsville, Virginia; **Sho Nuff Seafood** in Durham, North Carolina; **Hudson's Seafood House on the Docks** in Hilton Head Island; **Southern Soul Barbeque** in St. Simons Island; and **Bubba's Catfish & Seafood** in Hot Springs, Arkansas.

And what about those casual shoes? The Hush Puppies company was founded in 1958, with a product that aimed to provide relief to sore feet, otherwise known as barking dogs. And the early buyers didn't keep quiet about them – within five years, one in ten adult Americans owned a pair. You'd have to think they wouldn't have sold nearly as well if they had been called red horse shoes.

Chocolate gravy

See Other foods of Appalachia

In Arkansas, you can enjoy biscuits with chocolate gravy, a sweet sauce akin to pudding, at **Chery's Diner** in Cabot, **Miss Anna's** on **Towson** in Fort Smith, **Stick's Deli & Diner** in Morrilton and **Bucket List Cafe** in Center Ridge. In Northern Alabama, try the dish at **Puck's Restaurant** in Crossville or **Libby's Catfish & Diner** in Decatur. And in Northern Mississippi, you'll find it at **Joe's Diner** in Corinth.

Red velvet cake

A crimson-colored layer cake with a fluffy cream cheese frosting is seen today as a quintessential Southern dessert. But the history of red velvet cake includes a stop at the Waldorf-Astoria Hotel in New York City, some innovative marketing by a food extract company, and the adoption of the dish into the canon of Black soul food. And red velvet has become a popular flavor in products as diverse as lattes and lipstick.

The earliest recipe for red velvet cake, from 1911, was a mash-up of two baking innovations. During Victorian times, a fancy cake with a soft crumb was known as a velvet cake. And around the turn of the century, bakers began making devil's food cake, a dark-brown cake with a rich chocolate flavor. Instead of using chocolate, though, the red velvet cake was prepared with cocoa, which at the time was typically unprocessed. And the acidity of the buttermilk that was mixed in caused the cocoa to take on a reddish hue.

By the 1930s, red velvet cake had begun to become popular across the country as a Christmas cake. But around the same time, the cake was featured on the menu at the Waldorf, where a man named John Adams sampled it. Adams had founded a company that made vanilla extract and other flavorings, and decided to use the popularity of red velvet cake as an opportunity to sell red food coloring for home bakers to use in the batter. The recipe the Adams Extract Company promoted also included an ermine frosting made with boiled milk (cream cheese frosting wasn't invented until the late 1940s) along with their vanilla extract. During World War II, with rationing for butter in effect, some bakers started using beets as a substitute to provide additional moisture, which had the additional benefit of deepening the cake's red color.

In recent decades, red velvet cake has joined the roster of red foods, symbolizing bloodshed, that have traditionally been part of Juneteenth celebrations in the Black community, which commemorate the end of slavery in 1865. This may partially explain the cake's popularity throughout the South, although the 1989 film Steel Magnolias, which included a red velvet cake in the shape of an armadillo, may also be a contributing factor.

You won't have any trouble tracking down red velvet cake at Southern bakeries, no matter where you find yourself in the region. A few recommended options include **Midtown Cafe and Dessertery** in Winston-Salem, North Carolina, which frosts its red velvet cake with a vanilla-flavored cream cheese icing; **The Velvet Bar** in Atlanta, where you can choose from an entire menu of red velvet cakes, cupcakes and cake jars; **Kaminsky's Dessert Cafe**, with locations in Charleston and Columbia, South Carolina; **Sugar & Salt** in Richmond; and **The Pound Cakery** in Hattiesburg, Mississippi, which makes three flavors of red velvet cake, including one with Oreos. And once you've run out of red velvet products to try, you could always move onto an equally trendy flavor – pumpkin spice.

Hummingbird cake

Another dessert with a Southern pedigree actually has its roots substantially further south – in the Caribbean island of Jamaica.

This fruity spice cake is baked with ripe mashed bananas, crushed pineapple, pecans and vegetable oil (instead of the typical butter), and is usually frosted with cream cheese icing. It was invented in Jamaica in the 1960s, as part of an effort by the country's tourism board to showcase its local produce. The confection was called doctor bird cake, named for the island's national bird, the red-billed streamertail.

The dessert made its way to the U.S. in the late 1960s and was known under a few different names, including A Cake That Lasts (because its moist texture made it less likely to spoil) and Bird of Paradise Cake. But it didn't become a Southern favorite until a woman from Greensboro, North Carolina, L. H. Wiggins, submitted a version of it to Southern Living magazine in 1978, featuring canned pineapple. The magazine called it hummingbird cake, and it eventually became its most popular recipe.

If you'd like to celebrate these colorful birds with a slice of tropically flavored cake as sweet as the nectar they drink, you'll find it at bakeries and restaurants throughout the South. A few recommended spots include the aptly named **Hummingbird Dessert Boutique** in Norfolk; **Bull City Bake Shop** in Durham, North Carolina; **JThomas Kitchen** in Savannah; **Sugar Bakeshop** in Charleston; and **Chappy's Deli**, with five locations in Alabama. Or book yourself a flight to Montego Bay, so you can bake your own version using fresh fruits from the island where it originated. That will certainly please the local tourism board.

Carrot cake

During the health-food craze of the 1970s, some Americans believed that a confection made with Bugs Bunny's favorite vegetable was more nutritious than other desserts – despite the thick layer of frosting that was commonly slathered on top. And this idea may have contributed to carrot cake's enduring popularity across the South.

In addition to shredded or grated carrots, this cake is typically prepared with pineapple or raisins for extra sweetness as well as walnuts or pecans for crunch, with warm spices such as cinnamon, nutmeg and ginger also mixed into the batter. The cake is usually iced with cream cheese frosting. Although you'll find it at bakeries all across the region, carrot cake – like sweet potato pie, another dessert made with a sweet vegetable – is sometimes considered a soul food specialty.

The roots of carrot cake can be found in 18th-century England, where sweet puddings with carrots as a primary ingredient were commonly eaten. Carrot cake was also said to have been served by George Washington during parties at his Mt. Vernon home – so an appropriate place to fork into a slice is **The Mt. Vernon Inn Restaurant** in Mt. Vernon, Virginia. Other highly regarded bakeries where you can try it include **Side Street Bakery** in Southport, North Carolina; **Unforgettable Bakery + Cafe** in Savannah; **JJ's Treats** in Huntsville; and **Continental Bakery** in Birmingham. Just don't fool yourself into thinking that what you're eating is less indulgent than any other piece of cake.

Chess pie

The recipe for chess pie is so simple that you don't need to be a grandmaster in the kitchen to bake one. This sweet, custard-like dessert consists of little more than butter, sugar, eggs and a thickener of cornmeal or flour. Flavorings such as chocolate, coconut or lemon are sometimes added into the mixture, which can also include an acidic liquid like vinegar or buttermilk for extra tang. (Buttermilk pie is similar to chess pie, but the latter doesn't have to include buttermilk, and the former doesn't use cornmeal.) The filling is baked in a pastry shell, and the pie can be served either warm or chilled.

(A variation of chess pie, called Jefferson Davis pie and named for the Confederacy president, contains raisins, dates and pecans in the filling. But this pie, not surprisingly, has largely been forgotten around the South.)

Although we know that chess pie originated in England, its name remains a mystery. One theory is that chess is a shortened form of cheese, because this pie was similar to a British cheesecake. Another is that the name is a derivation of chest, on account of the pie being made with pantry ingredients and being able to be stored in a cupboard rather than a refrigerator.

When you're ready to make your move on a chess pie, you'll find great options at bakeries and restaurants throughout the South. A few recommended spots include **Woodruff's Cafe and Pie Shop** in Monroe, Virginia, which offers both chocolate and lemon chess pies; **Carolina Pie Company** in Mooresville, North Carolina, where you can order those two flavors as well as coconut; **Husk Restaurant**, with locations in Charleston and Savannah, which has featured a chocolate chess pie with duck fat caramel and bourbon whipped cream on its dessert menu; **The Pie Hole** in Roswell, Georgia, where you can also procure either chocolate or lemon chess pies; and **Sugaree's Bakery** in New Albany, Mississippi, which offers a classic buttery chess pie. Wherever you go for yours, it's a good idea to become friendly with whoever's serving you. That way, when you're ready for the bill, you can ask for it like this: "Could I please have the check, mate?"

Banana pudding

Perhaps no Southern dessert is more iconic than banana pudding. But as it's typically prepared today, there's nothing particularly Southern about it. Bananas don't typically grow in the region, vanilla custard or pudding can come from anywhere, and Nabisco's Nilla wafers are available in any decent-sized grocery store. So why, then, is banana pudding, which is essentially just alternating layers of those three ingredients (with some whipped cream or meringue on top), served at nearly every bakery and barbecue spot in the region?

One clue – that turns out to be a red herring – comes from the burgeoning shipping industry of the late 19th century. That's the period when the U.S. began importing millions of bunches of bananas from Latin America and the Caribbean annually, mostly through New Orleans and other Southern ports. But with the maturing of America's railway network, the fruit was easily transported outside the region. So bananas weren't any more available in the South than they were in other parts of the country.

By the end of the 1800s, bananas were beginning to be used in numerous dishes all across the nation, including as the key component of its namesake pudding. The earliest recipe for banana pudding was published in 1888 in the Massachusetts-based magazine Good Housekeeping, which called for sliced bananas to be layered with sponge cake and custard, and topped with whipped cream.

Over the next quarter-century, periodicals across the U.S. featured various methods for preparing this dessert, with some being baked, but most of them relying on refrigeration, the most common way of making it today. By 1921, when a banana pudding recipe featuring vanilla wafers appeared in a Bloomington, Illinois, publication, cookies had replaced cake as the pastry component of the dish. Two decades later, Nabisco started printing instructions for its version of banana pudding on boxes of its cookies, where you can still find it currently. And the company's coast-to-coast distribution certainly helped increase the popularity of banana pudding nationwide.

It wasn't until the 1960s, though, that banana pudding had become firmly associated with the South. That's when Jell-O marketed its new banana cream-flavored pudding, released in 1964, as being particularly useful for Southern Banana Pudding. One theory as to why banana pudding became particularly popular in the South, compared to other regions, is that it was a no-bake dessert that could quickly be produced during hot summer days. Its sugar content may have made it a favorite dish among a population with a reputation for having a sweet tooth. And it would have been easy and inexpensive to prepare for a crowd, making it suitable for community gatherings and dinner parties during which hostesses could show off their culinary skills as well as their Southern hospitality.

Other Southern dishes to sample:

- **Calabash-style seafood**, lightly battered and deep-fried shrimp and other sea creatures that's a specialty on the North Carolina and South Carolina coasts, often eaten alongside hushpuppies. One of the original Calabash, North Carolina, restaurants that began serving this style of fried seafood in 1940, **Beck's Restaurant**, is still in business, as is an establishment owned by members of the same family that opened a decade later, **Ella's of Calabash**. You'll also find this seafood preparation at all-you-can-eat spots in Myrtle Beach, South Carolina, including **Captain Benjamin's Calabash Seafood Buffet** and **Crabby George's Calabash Seafood Buffet**.
- **Cheese straws**, a flaky pastry made with Cheddar cheese in the dough as well spices such as rosemary or cayenne pepper, and shaped into long rounds or strips before baking. They're typically eaten as an appetizer or a snack to accompany cocktails. Recipes for cheese straws were first documented in cookbooks in the late 19th century and were historically a way that Southern cooks preserved cheese from spoiling in the summer heat. You'll find this delicacy at grocery stores throughout the region, as well as at specialty bakers including **Ritchie Hill Bakery** in Concord, North Carolina; **Dee Dee's Gourmet** in Charlotte; and **Mississippi Cheese Straw Factory** in Yazoo City, Mississippi.
- **Ambrosia**, a fruit salad composed of canned or fresh pineapple and mandarin oranges, marshmallows, coconut and other fruits and nuts, mixed in a creamy dressing made from whipped cream, sour cream or mayonnaise. You'll find it at Southern restaurants that feature retro dishes, including **Supperland** in Charlotte and **The Mod Olive** in Suffolk, Virginia.

- **Watergate salad**, a related dessert salad made with pistachio pudding, canned pineapple, marshmallows, pecans and whipped topping. Although this type of sweet salad was commonly eaten in the 1950s and '60s, the dish was probably created in the 1970s, around the time of the Watergate scandal, when Jell-O first introduced instant pistachio pudding mix. It may have been named for a cake with similar flavors and pistachio icing that around the same time became known as Watergate cake. If you want to give the salad a try, you can order it at **The Avenue Home Cooking Café** in Cedartown, Georgia, and at **Dukes Barbecue** in Charleston. But you won't find it at the Watergate Hotel in Washington, D.C.

- **Lady Baltimore cake**, a white layer cake made with egg whites, with a fluffy frosting that incorporates dried fruits and nuts. It was likely created at the Women's Exchange tearoom in Charleston by Florrie and Nina Ottolengui, and was a favorite of writer Owen Wister, who used it as inspiration for his 1906 novel Lady Baltimore, which made the cake famous. The Ottolenguis were said to bake and ship a cake for Wister every year in gratitude. This specialty was once widely available in Charleston, including most recently at **Sugar Bakeshop**, but today it's only available by special request. You'll also find it at **Dean's Cake House** in Andalusia, Alabama.

Regardless of your own reasons for trying this dish, you'll find it readily available at BBQ restaurants and bakeries all around the region. A few places where you can search for your own favorite version include **Pass the Pudding**, a banana pudding-themed dessert shop in Myrtle Beach; **Baker Dude Select** in Atlanta; **Mockingbird** in Charlottesville; and **Miss Myra's Pit Bar B Q** in Birmingham. And if you find yourself in Raleigh, be sure to try the spectacular banana pudding layer cake at **Hayes Barton Cafe and Dessertery**. Even though their confection could have been made anywhere, it'll take just one bite for you to be certain that what you're eating is truly a Southern specialty.

Divinity

Once you eat enough of this white, nougat-like candy that's popular in the South, you should feel free to declare yourself (taking Gilbert and Sullivan's The Pirates of Penzance out of context) "a doctor of divinity ... located in this vicinity."

Divinity is created by boiling corn syrup and sugar to a hard-ball stage and then combining the liquid with well-beaten egg whites. Sometimes chocolate, coconut or other flavors are added to the mixture, which is also often enhanced with pecans or dried cherries. It's typically dropped by the spoonful onto trays and left to harden into irregular clusters.

A variation of divinity uses the same cooking method, but with brown sugar replacing white. This results in a darker candy that's called sea foam.

Divinity is frequently enjoyed in the South during the holiday season, when it's much easier to prepare than during the hot, humid summers that prevent the candy from setting properly. But like a few other regional specialties, it didn't originate there. The earliest recipes for divinity come from the early 20th century, just a few years after the Corn Products Refining Company of New York and Chicago introduced Karo light and dark corn syrups as sugar substitutes in 1902. The corporation helped popularize divinity by promoting a recipe for it in an early version of its cookbook featuring the brand. It's not known who named the candy, but an oft-retold story is that someone once tasted it and declared it to be divine, and the label stuck.

If you'd like to sample this ethereal sweet, you'll find it at candymakers and bakeries all around the South (many of which also sell their wares online). A few recommended spots include **Savannah's Candy Kitchen** in Savannah and Charleston (as well as Nashville), which tops each piece of its divinity with a pecan half; **Priester's Pecans** in Fort Deposit, Alabama, where you can buy either pecan or no-nut divinity; and in Mississippi, **Sugar Magnolia Takery** in Flowood, which sells divinity and other Southern candies by the pound, and **Nandy's Candy** in Jackson, where you can order divinity as well as, during the Easter season, a chocolate-covered divinity egg dipped in caramel. Or save the candy for later and head to **Sugaree's Bakery** in New Albany, also in Mississippi, which makes a coconut cake with divinity icing. That should get you the last few credits you need to earn your doctorate in divinity.

Boiled peanuts

While you've probably shelled peanuts at a baseball game or eaten them as a bar snack, you might not have enjoyed them as Southerners sometimes do – dropped into a fizzy bottle of Coke (or, historically, RC Cola). And unless you've road-tripped through the region, you may not have tried boiled peanuts, a snack consisting of green, or freshly harvested, nuts that are boiled in their shells in salt water, sometimes with Cajun spices or other seasonings. Instead of the dry, crunchy morsel that you're likely familiar with, boiling the peanuts makes them soggy and soft, but keeps them salty and flavorful.

Peanuts first came to America aboard slave ships, although the crop wasn't native to Africa, either, having first been cultivated by the Portuguese in Brazil. But the legume was similar to the indigenous African nut called the groundnut, and it was a natural evolution for Black laborers to begin boiling peanuts to eat during the short harvest season. Although some accounts claim that Confederate soldiers were the ones who invented the snack, it's more likely that they ate plenty of "goober peas" during the Civil War, just not boiled ones.

In the early 20th century, boiled peanuts became a fashionable dish to serve at Southern weddings, especially in small towns along the Carolina coast. And by the 1920s, more farmers had begun growing peanuts as an alternative to cotton crops that were being decimated by the boll weevil, and the practice of boiling peanuts spread widely across the region.

Today, they may be an acquired taste, compared to their crunchier cousins, but you'll still find plenty of places to sample boiled peanuts at farm stands (some of which are marked with P-Nut signs), in Virginia, Georgia and other peanut-growing regions. A few spots worth stopping at include **Whitley's Peanut Factory** in Glen Allen, Gloucester and Williamsburg, Virginia; **Hardy Farms**, which has several locations in central Georgia; **Fred's Famous Peanuts** in Helen, Georgia; **Fred's Pit Stop Peanuts** in Summerville, South Carolina; and **Alabama Peanut Company** in Birmingham. And at **Wreck of the Richard and Charlene**, a restaurant in Mt. Pleasant, South Carolina, you can order boiled peanuts as a side dish. No one would probably bat an eye if you asked for a Coke to plop them into.

REGIONAL SAUSAGES OF THE U.S.

1. Maxwell Street Polish
2. Italian sausage
3. Beer brat
4. Cudighi
5. Goetta
6. Polish Boy
7. Boudin ball
8. Livermush
9. Scrapple
10. Pork roll
11. Half-smoke

Lobster roll

NEW ENGLAND

When the English settlers known as the Pilgrims landed at Plymouth Rock in 1620, the first places they colonized were the six states that constitute present-day New England: Massachusetts, Vermont, New Hampshire, Maine, Connecticut and Rhode Island. And it's there that you'll find many of the oldest regional foods in the country, especially those based upon its abundant seafood and native crops.

But the specialties of this area have also been shaped by the triangle trade that left New England with a surplus of molasses, by the traditions instilled and adapted by waves of immigrants from Europe and elsewhere, and by the inventiveness of chefs and entrepreneurs who created new dishes that remain popular choices for intrepid travelers. Although there are fewer truly iconic foods here than in other parts of the country, you'll still have countless opportunities to sample the wide range of flavors that make New England unique.

The Puritans, of course, were not the first people to make their home in the region, with as many as 100,000 Natives living there at the beginning of the 17th century. It was from these tribes, including the Wampanoag, the Narragansett and others, that the Pilgrims learned to grow beans and corn, which was critical for their subsistence given the lack of wheat or barley in the New World. And these vegetables feature prominently in certain dishes that are still eaten today, including Boston baked beans and Johnnycakes, a Rhode Island specialty. Meanwhile, the seafood that the Natives introduced to the Europeans, including the hard-shell clam known as the quahog, remains a foundational piece of the region's cuisine, visible in dishes such as New England-style clam chowder as well as stuffies, a baked version of the bivalve that's eaten as an appetizer in coastal areas of Massachusetts and Rhode Island.

Another product that's core to several lasting regional dishes is molasses, which is used as a key ingredient in Boston baked beans as well as anadama bread, New England brown bread and the dessert known as Indian pudding. As part of an exchange during the 18th century known as the triangle trade, West Africa sent enslaved people to the West Indies, where they worked on sugar plantations to produce molasses. That product was imported to New England and converted into rum, which was then exported to the European colonies. While refined sugar was an indulgence mainly enjoyed by the wealthy, molasses became the most widely available sweetener, with few alternatives aside from maple sugar, which was traditionally used (especially by abolitionists opposed to the rum trade) to make the Vermont specialty known as maple cream pie.

By the mid-19th century, New England had started to diversify, with waves of immigrants who came to work in its textile mills, primarily from Ireland and French-speaking areas of Canada. By the early 1900s, laborers from Italy and workers from China had also begun to migrate, with the latter finding the region more hospitable than other places where anti-immigrant sentiment often ran high. And all of these cultures have contributed to the fabric of its cuisine, which you'll see in dishes as wide-ranging as New England boiled dinner, an American version of corned-beef-and-cabbage; tourtière, a French-Canadian meat pie; apizza, New Haven-style pizza; and the chow mein sandwich, a Chinese-American hybrid.

The latter dish also illustrates the innovation that characterizes many long-lasting regional dishes, as businessmen and women created new markets for their ideas. Another good example is the steamed cheeseburger, a Connecticut specialty that serves up a unique take on a burger by using a tall metal cabinet as a cooking device. Also notable is the fluffernutter, made with a marshmallow crème product invented by a pair of siblings who were eventually put out of business by a competitor with some clever marketing techniques. A third example is the Toll House cookie, created by a Massachusetts baker who decided to experiment with putting chocolate chunks in her batter, to great success. And while we may think of clam rolls and lobster rolls as obvious ways to make use of the copious local seafood, both sandwiches were created by restauranteurs as new concepts that eventually became popular among their customers.

If you could only choose one destination in this part of the country, Boston might have the greatest number of high-end restaurants, with celebrity chefs including Todd English, Barbara Lynch, Ken Oringer and Jamie Bissonnette setting the standard for fine dining (despite recent accusations that Lynch consistently mistreated her employees). But Rhode Island, which has the highest concentration of regional specialties in New England, and perhaps the entire U.S., should be at the top of your list. In a state that's the country's smallest by area, and with a population of just over a million, you'll find dishes as singular as the New York System wiener, a unique take on a hot dog; clam cakes, a savory seafood fritter; and coffee milk, a drink that's often thickened with ice cream to become a shake known as a cabinet.

But every state in New England has its share of local delicacies (aside from New Hampshire, which doesn't really have any of its own). Sometimes they're based upon iconic ingredients, like the Vermont maple syrup that's used to make sugar on snow, or the Maine blueberries that flavor candies called needhams and feature in cobbler-like desserts known as slumps. But sometimes the dishes are created by accident, as was the case with the Parker House roll, invented by an angry pastry cook at a Boston hotel, or circumstance, which is why roast beef sandwiches are a popular dish on the North Shore of Massachusetts. And when local resources are combined with marketing ingenuity, sometimes what you get is the cider donut, perhaps the most quintessentially New England food of all.

The Pilgrims would scarcely have imagined any of these dishes having a place at the first Thanksgiving table. But the development of the region's cuisine over the ensuing four centuries gives countless reasons for adventurous eaters to be grateful.

MASSACHUSETTS

BOSTON

Boston baked beans

Baked beans are so essential to the culinary identity of Boston that the city is sometimes called Beantown, and the annual hockey tournament played by four local colleges is known as the Beanpot.

Boston baked beans is a dish consisting of navy beans that are slow-cooked in an oven (or traditionally, a brick hearth) with molasses, salt pork, onions and dry mustard, until they thicken into a rich stew that's sometimes served with frankfurters. It's believed that it originated in the 17th century with the Pilgrims at Plymouth Colony, who baked beans in earthenware pots and may have learned the technique from indigenous people. (The Natives probably used maple syrup as a sweetener, a version of the dish that's still how baked beans are prepared today in Vermont, with bacon instead of salt pork. In Maine, another state that knows beans about beans, native varieties are employed, such as the yellow-eye beans that have thicker skins and break down less than do the navy beans in the Boston version of the dish.) Because the Puritan settlers didn't work on the Sabbath, it was typical for them to cook their beans overnight on Saturday and eat them warm the next morning.

By the early 20th century, beans were a local staple during harsh New England winters, and molasses was widely available in Boston, which imported it from the West Indies as part of the triangle trade, primarily for its use in making rum. But a sticky situation developed in 1919, when a storage tank in the North End exploded, killing 21 people and causing a river of molasses to flow through the city at an estimated 35 miles per hour. For decades, neighborhood residents claimed they could still smell molasses on warm days.

There's another version of Boston baked beans that isn't a vegetable – it's also a candy that was invented in Chicago. In the 1930s, the Ferrara Pan Candy Company created a confection of sugar-coated peanuts that both resembled and were named for the East Coast dish. The boxed candy was designed to resist melting during hot summer weather and can still be purchased today, especially in the Midwest.

If you'd like to sample the local version of Boston baked beans, you'll find the dish at **Bostonia Public House** and **Union Oyster House** in the Financial District; **Boston Burger Company**, with locations in the Fenway, Cambridge and Somerville that offer a side of baked beans with your hamburger; and **The Bittersweet Shoppe on Newbury** in Back Bay, where you can get your Boston baked beans atop a hot dog. And once you've picked a favorite spot, don't be afraid to tell everyone you know about it. You may as well spill the beans.

Parker House roll

The buttery, pillowy-soft bread known as the Parker House roll is the namesake of the Boston hotel of the same name, now called the Omni Parker House. This food was created by accident during the 1870s when a pastry cook named Ward is said to have angrily thrown a batch of yeasted rolls into the oven before they were ready to be baked. They emerged with a distinctive shell on top that left them light and puffy on the inside, with a crisp exterior – unlike any other bread that existed at the time.

Within a few years, these fluffy dinner rolls became extremely popular at the Parker House, so much so that they inspired French composer Jacques Offenbach to write a little ditty about them. Recipes for similar rolls began appearing in several late-19th-century cookbooks, and the hotel started to package and ship its creation to lodging and dining establishments nationwide. The exact recipe stayed secret, though, until 1933, when U.S. President Franklin Roosevelt requested that the rolls be prepared for a White House dinner.

Today, Parker House rolls are typically brushed with butter after baking, enriching their flavor and leaving them with a golden-brown shine. You can compare two local versions at **Puritan & Company** in Cambridge and **Black Lamb** in the South End, which enhances its rolls with Cheddar cheese and scallions, and serves them with either maple butter or pimento cheese. Or make a reservation at the Omni in downtown Boston and dine at its flagship eatery, **Parker's Restaurant**, to try the original recipe. Just be on the lookout in case the hotel still employs a disgruntled baker.

Boston cream pie

"Is it cake?" asks a popular Netflix series in which bakers are tasked with recreating everyday objects in pastry form. And sometimes it's very hard to tell. But when it comes to the misleadingly named Boston cream pie, the answer is undoubtedly yes.

Boston cream pie consists of two layers of rum-glazed yellow sponge cake that are separated by vanilla custard or pastry cream, with the top and outside frosted with chocolate and garnished with almonds. It was invented at Boston's Parker House by Mossburg Sanzian, an Armenian-French pastry chef, for the hotel's opening in 1856, when the dish was called chocolate cream pie. That's because at the time, there was little distinction between a cake and a pie, and this confection was probably baked in a pie tin. Muddling the story even further, Boston cream pie was based on a colonial recipe called pudding-cake pie, so it was natural for it to be called a pie rather than a cake.

The popularity of Boston cream pie can also be attributed to its innovation in being one of the first confections to use chocolate as a pastry topping. Although Boston was home to the country's first chocolate mill, by the mid-19th century most diners would have typically consumed it only in the form of drinking chocolate.

The most historic place to try Boston cream pie is **Parker's Restaurant** downtown, located in the Omni Parker House Hotel (which also sells the pastry online for nationwide shipping). But you'll also find Boston cream pie – which was declared the official dessert of Massachusetts in 1996 – at countless bakeries around the city. A few recommended choices include **Flour Bakery + Cafe**, which provides its own take on the dessert at nine branches all over town, with a coffee-flavored sponge cake that's covered in vanilla cream and frosted with chocolate ganache; **Greenhills Irish Bakery** in Dorchester, where the dish goes by chocolate cream pie; and **Bova's** in the North End, a 24-hour bakery that casts convention aside and calls its version a Boston cream cake.

But if you want to avoid the whole cake versus pie debate entirely, just have your Boston cream in donut form. A Boston cream donut is a yeasted pastry filled with vanilla-flavored cream and frosted with chocolate icing. And it's just as heralded as its namesake dessert, having been declared the state's official donut in 2003.

A couple of great places to try one are **Blackbird Doughnuts**, with six locations around the Boston metropolitan area, and **Lyndell's Bakery** in Somerville – which, despite its location outside the city limits, also makes Boston cream pie. Which, as you now know, is actually a cake.

OTHER FOODS OF MASSACHUSETTS

Roast beef sandwich

Some people people prefer eating a roast beef sandwich with mustard. Others wouldn't go without a layer of horseradish. But on the North Shore of Massachusetts, in towns such as Beverly, Peabody and Revere, the standard toppings are James River barbecue sauce, mayonnaise and white American cheese – a combo known as a three-way.

Roast beef sandwiches in this part of New England are constructed with a mountain of thinly sliced beef that's cooked medium-rare, and piled onto either a toasted plain roll (for junior size), a sesame-seed hamburger bun (for regular size) or an onion roll (for super size). They come with lettuce and tomato, as well as the customer's choice of condiments, and are typically served with French fries or onion rings and a stack of napkins.

North Shore restaurants have been competing over roast beef sandwiches ever since 1951, when **Kelly's Roast Beef**, then a hot dog stand in Revere Beach, found itself with three extra roast beefs on its hands after a couple cancelled their wedding. The next day, Kelly's began thinly slicing the meat and served it on grilled rolls. The sandwich was so popular that the business soon made it its signature food item, and other area restaurants started imitating the dish. Even **Arby's**, the fast-food chain, was inspired by Kelly's to create its own version of the roast beef sandwich in 1964.

Kelly's now operates four locations in Massachusetts (as well as branches at Logan Airport and in New Hampshire and Florida), and prides itself on having invented this regional dish, which you can also order online. But there are numerous other options for you to try in towns all along the North Shore. A few popular choices include **Peter's Super Beef** in Revere, **Nick's Famous Roast Beef** in Beverly, **Billy's Famous Roast Beef** in Wakefield and **Jamie's Roast Beef** in Peabody, which offers the standard toppings as well as condiments that include Cajun aioli, ancho-chile honey and "fancy sauce" – so you can feel free to buck tradition and customize your roast beef sandwich however you like.

Pizza bagel

See New York City

While New York is famous for both its pizza and its bagels, entrepreneurs in Ohio, California and Massachusetts have all claimed to have invented the pizza bagel in the 1970s. At **Katz Bagel Bakery** in Chelsea, Massachusetts, you can still sample a highly regarded pizza bagel that was at least one of the first versions – bagel dough (without a hole) that's topped with tomato sauce and melted mozzarella cheese.

Toll House cookie

For a couple of years in the late 1930s, Bay Staters were chomping on chocolate chip cookies without having any idea they were doing so. That's because of the innovation of Ruth Graves Wakefield, a baker at the Toll House Inn in Whitman, Massachusetts, a hotel that she owned with her husband on the toll road between Boston and New Bedford.

In 1938, Wakefield was working on creating a new type of cookie for the inn's family-style restaurant, when she chopped up a Nestlé semi-sweet chocolate bar and added it to her batter for a batch of Butter Drop Do cookies. Unlike baker's chocolate, which would have melted into the dough, the chocolate chunks retained their shape, and Wakefield realized that she had created something special. She published the recipe the same year in a cookbook called Toll House Tried and True Recipes, calling them Toll House Chocolate Crunch Cookies, and also sold the recipe to Nestlé in exchange for a lifetime supply of chocolate.

The next year, Nestlé began publicizing the recipe for the cookies on the packaging for its chocolate bars. But it wasn't until another year went by, when chocolate chips were still thought of as just a type of candy, that the corporation started selling its signature product as pre-cut, teardrop-shaped morsels that were easier for bakers to use when making cookies.

By the early 1940s, the Toll House cookie's popularity exploded, in part because of the care packages that were sent to Massachusetts soldiers overseas, who shared the cookies with their colleagues from other states. And in addition to its traditional name, people started referring to the confection generically as chocolate chip cookies.

Although Nestlé attempted to trademark the name of the Toll House cookie, a federal judge decided in 1983 that it couldn't – which means that you should feel free to call it that if you like, regardless of whether you're using the morsels made by Nestlé or by one of its competitors.

When you're hungry for a Toll House cookie in Massachusetts, you'll have no trouble finding a bakery that satisfies your craving. A few standouts include **The Boston Chipyard** in Faneuil Hall, which bakes seven kinds of chocolate chip cookies including traditional, macadamia and oatmeal raisin; **Clear Flour Bread** in Brookline, whose baked goods include a well-regarded chocolate chunk cookie; **Cookie Time Bakery** in Arlington, where you can choose between chocolate chip cookies without nuts or with M&Ms; and **The Cookie Monstah** in Danvers, Beverly, Burlington, Swampscott and Needham, which makes chocolate chunk cookies as well as versions that cater to gluten-sensitive eaters as well as vegans.

You can also pay pilgrimage to the Toll House Inn by visiting the sign and plaque that marks its location on Route 18 in Whitman, flanked today by a Wendy's and a Walgreens. Sadly, the hotel burned down on New Year's Eve in 1984. But Wakefield, who had passed away seven years earlier, can rest in peace knowing that its cause was a grease fire in the kitchen, not a batch of overdone cookies.

Another Massachusetts dish to sample:

- **Scrod** (sometimes spelled schrod), a term for a fillet of small whitefish such as cod or haddock that's topped with breadcrumbs, baked or broiled and served with a lemon wedge. The Parker House Hotel claimed to have invented the word scrod as a placeholder for the unknown species of the catch of the day, but that story is likely to be as equally false as the belief of some New Englanders, who say that scrod is an acronym for "select catch received on the day." More likely, the term comes from the Anglo-Cornish scraw, which describes a way of cutting fish open and drying them, or the Dutch scrod, meaning small, cut-up pieces. You can sample scrod at numerous Massachusetts seafood restaurants, including **Boston Tavern** in Middleborough.

VERMONT

Maple cream pie

Vermont is responsible for more than twice as much maple syrup production as anywhere else in the country, and food artisans throughout the Green Mountain State have found countless uses for the sweet nectar. You can eat it poured over flapjacks (pancakes) at the local diner, in frozen form as a creemee (a rich, soft-serve ice cream), as a luscious maple-leaf shaped candy – or in a signature state dessert, maple cream pie.

Maple cream pie, also called maple custard pie, is made with a filling that's traditionally sweetened with maple sugar, which is manufactured from the sap of the maple tree (after the water needed to make syrup boils away, the sugar is what's left). In the 18th century, prominent New England abolitionists including Benjamin Rush argued for the use of maple sugar instead of cane sugar, which was being produced by enslaved people in the West Indies and exported to the U.S. That's why this pie is sometimes seen as a symbol of New England individuality and freedom.

Another Vermont dish to sample:

- **Apple pie topped with Cheddar**, a controversial combination that's sometimes eaten in Vermont, using cheese from the local Cabot Creamery. One place where you can try this pairing for yourself is **Vermont Apple Pie Bakery** in Proctorsville.

Modern versions of maple cream pie are prepared with maple syrup that's combined with egg yolks, milk or heavy cream, brown sugar and vanilla. The mixture is then poured into a pastry crust and baked. The dessert is often topped with almonds and is sometimes served with whipped cream to offset the sweetness of the filling.

If you'd like to sample the official state flavor of Vermont in pie form, you'll find highly regarded versions at **The Creamery Restaurant** in Danville, **Poorhouse Pies** in Underhill and **Wayside Restaurant, Bakery and Creamery** in Montpelier. And if you want your pie a la mode, just take your slice to go and pick up a pint of **Ben & Jerry's**, which offers tours at its factory in nearby Waterbury. You'll have to console yourself with a contrasting flavor, though – the delicious-sounding Maple Tree Hugger, with maple ice cream and brown sugar brownie chunks, is now just a footnote in company history.

Sugar on snow

At certain times of the year, some Vermonters believe that all you need for a party is a freezer full of snow, some freshly baked donuts and a jar full of sour pickles.

That's because maple sugaring season, which lasts from late February through early April, is also the time when locals (and visitors) can enjoy sugar on snow, a treat that's the result of pouring hot maple syrup over a bowl of powder. The sugar hardens into a taffy-like candy, which can be eaten with a fork or used as a dip for donuts, with the pickles serving as a palate cleanser that helps cut the sweetness of the maple.

Some maple sugaring houses stay open all year, but they're at their peak during early spring, offering tours and demonstrations to the public when temperatures rise above freezing during the day. The warmer air causes the flowing of sap, which is collected from the trees by the bucketful for processing into syrup.

You'll find sugar shacks where you can sample sugar on snow all over Vermont (as well as in upstate New York), with a few standouts including **Palmer's Sugar House** and **Shelburne Sugarworks**, both in Shelburne, and **Morse Farm Maple Sugarworks** in Montpelier. And after a few tastes, you might just come to realize that there's no better accompaniment to a maple-dipped donut than a zesty, crunchy pickle.

MAINE

Lobster roll

Don't let your cousin from Connecticut try and persuade you otherwise. A true New England lobster roll comes from Downeast Maine, and if you're going to have the crustacean in sandwich form, the best way to eat it is chilled and lightly coated with mayonnaise.

The Nutmeg State's claim to the lobster roll isn't exactly unfounded, though – a long-closed restaurant called Perry's in Milford created the first one in 1929 at a customer's request, placing chunks of warm lobster meat, dripping with melted butter, inside a steamed hot dog roll. That kind of lobster roll is still prevalent in the state and can also be found on Long Island and in pockets of New England. But what Connecticut calls a lobster salad roll, with the cold seafood mixed with mayonnaise and served on a buttery, toasted split-top bun, with potato chips on the side, is now the predominant style in Maine. And it's considered by many to be the state's most iconic dish, especially when eaten on a warm summer day with a view of the rocky coast, or in sight of a lighthouse.

The Maine lobster roll started to become popular in the 1970s – sometimes even served with a side of drawn butter – but it didn't achieve signature status until the dish was featured on the menu at Pearl Oyster Bar in New York City, which opened in 1997 as an homage to New England seafood. By the end of the following decade, the Maine lobster roll was being promoted on national television and featured on the cover of Gourmet magazine. Even **McDonald's** created a seasonal version for its New England restaurants, the McLobster (a previous attempt at a nationwide rollout had fizzled out in the early 1990s).

You'll encounter plenty of variations on the lobster roll throughout Maine, including some that mix chopped celery into the meat for a crunchy component, add a leaf of lettuce (frowned upon by many lobster lovers, as it quickly makes the sandwich soggy), are seasoned with lemon or tarragon, or employ round hamburger rolls or crustier bread. But lobster-roll purists will find numerous places to indulge their vision of the perfect sandwich, too.

A few spots that frequently appear on best-lobster-roll lists include **The Lobster Shack at Two Lights** in Cape Elizabeth, **Boothbay Lobster Wharf** in Boothbay Harbor, **Thurston's Lobster Pound** in Bernard on Mount Desert Island, **The Clam Shack** in Kennebunk and **Red's Eats** in Wiscasset – which straddles both sides of the lobster roll divide by offering a choice of butter or mayonnaise next to the sandwich. But because their lobster roll is served cold, I think it's clear which kind the restaurant thinks is best, despite what your cousin from Connecticut might suggest.

Italian sandwich

It's possible to get a great Italian sub in cities like Chicago and Philadelphia. But the version you'll find in Portland just might be the most controversial – not only because the city claims to have invented the Italian sandwich, but also because the ingredients you'll typically find on it have only a trace of Italian ancestry.

The Italian sandwich was created in 1900 by a baker named Giovanni Amato, who began making sandwiches with fresh loaves of bread for dock workers on Portland's waterfront, many of whom had also emigrated from Italy to New England. Two years later, as his reputation grew, Amato and his wife opened a storefront called **Amato's** on Portland's India Street, which was a hub of the local Italian community.

That's one place where you can still go today to order what Amato's calls the Original Real Italian, which consists of boiled ham, American cheese, vegetables that include tomatoes, onions and green peppers, sour pickles and Greek olives. The ingredients are all sprinkled with salt, pepper and a blend of vegetable and olive oil (presumably Italian), and are piled onto a long, pillowy roll split in the middle, similar to an extended hot dog bun. The sandwich is typically wrapped in waxed paper and eaten at room temperature after the meat and cheese have a chance to soften.

Amato's also operates dozens of locations throughout Vacationland and the rest of New England, but that's not the only place where you'll find a credible Maine-style Italian sandwich. You can also try highly regarded versions at **DiPietros Market** in South Portland and at **George's Sandwich Shop** in Biddeford. And even if the ingredients aren't exactly what you're accustomed to seeing on an Italian sub – there's no prosciutto, no Provolone, no lettuce and no mayo or mustard – just think of it, as Amato apparently did, as a great American sandwich that's simply named for the baker's homeland.

Whoopie pie

Which state is the true home of the Whoopie pie is a hotly disputed question, with the strongest evidence pointing to Pennsylvania as its originator. But Maine has staked a serious claim, leaning into the debate by naming it the official state "treat" (because it couldn't possibly supplant blueberry pie), once creating the world's largest, a 1,000-pound behemoth constructed in South Portland, and even renaming the minor league Portland Sea Dogs for one night as the Maine Whoopie Pies, with special uniforms featuring a "fierce Whoopie Pie character" and "creamy white lettering."

Despite the name of the confection, a Whoopie pie isn't really a pie at all. Rather, it consists of two rounded, cake-like cookies that sandwich a creamy middle. Although the classic version is made with chocolate cookies and white cream (or Marshmallow Fluff), they're often customized with other flavors for both the pastry and the filling. Whoopie pies tend to be the size of a hamburger, and are often cut in half before serving.

It's not known who created the first Whoopie pies in Pennsylvania, where Amish women included them in the meals they prepared for farmers working in the fields. (The name is said to come from the word they exclaimed when discovering one in their lunchbox.) But **Labadie's Bakery** in Lewiston has sold them with the same recipe since 1925, avoiding controversy about their genesis by calling the popular product Maine's first Whoopie pie.

Around the state, at convenience stores and supermarkets, you'll often see packaged versions of Whoopie pies, wrapped in plastic. But you can also get them fresh from other bakeries besides Labadie's, including **Wicked Whoopies** in Freeport, which created the record-breaking Whoopie pie in 2011, and **Cape Whoopies** in South Portland, where you can choose among a dizzying lineup of flavors, including classic chocolate cake with vanilla cream, apple-spiced cake with caramel cream and coconut cake with lime cream.

Another Maine dish to sample:

- **Blueberry slump**, a variation of a cobbler that's cooked on the stovetop in a skillet, using sweet biscuits as the topping. A similar fruit dessert is known in North Carolina as sonker, but in New England, it goes by several other names, including grunt, because of the sound the berries emit while steaming in a pot with a lid; pandowdy, which is usually made with apples, and has a pie crust rolled on top of the fruit; and buckle, similar to a coffee cake, with a streusel topping that collapses during baking. You can sample blueberry slump at **A1 Diner** in Gardiner and blueberry buckle at **Two Fat Cats Bakery** in Portland, which is also known for its pies that make excellent use of wild Maine blueberries.

Another way to celebrate Vacationland's favorite treat is at the annual Maine Whoopie Pie Festival in Dover-Foxcroft, which features a three-kilometer running race that organizers recommend you complete before digging in. But Pennsylvania gets the final word with its own festival, located in the heart of the state's Dutch country. It features over 400 varieties of the confection, a treasure hunt and a slingshot competition that lets you aim a Whoopie pie at a target – with the winner, presumably, shouting a predictable exclamation.

Needham

Mainers aren't shy about creating new foods using the state's natural resources. There's ice cream flavored with chunks of lobster, for one, and numerous baked goods, barbecue sauces and beers that all make excellent use of blueberries. So it shouldn't be surprising that one of the state's signature sweets features another local ingredient – potatoes, which Maine once produced more of than anywhere else in the country.

A needham is a rectangular candy made with dark chocolate that enrobes a filling consisting of shredded coconut, sugar and mashed potatoes. It tastes similar to a Mounds bar, with the potatoes adding to the candy's creamy texture, and similar to North Carolina's Moravian sugar cake, making the treat denser and less sweet than it otherwise would be. The confection was created in the 1870s by a candy manufacturer named John Seavey, and was named for George Needham, a popular Irish-born evangelist who, before he arrived in the U.S., reportedly was once almost eaten by cannibals.

The company that purchased Seavey's Sweets, Lou-Rod Candy, continued to produce needhams until it went out of business in the early 2010s. But fortunately, several other Maine candymakers have picked up the slack. **Robin's Confections** in Biddeford offers two versions of the candy, one made with mashed potatoes and another with sweet potatoes. Another option is to get your chocolates from **Maine Needham**

Company, which sells its candy locally in Saco as well as online, and distributes to **Reny's Department Stores** statewide as well as to grocery stores in Southern Maine. That candymaker produces a few different kinds of needhams, including original, maple, espresso – and of course, blueberry. No word yet on whether a lobster-flavored needham is in development.

CONNECTICUT

New Haven-style pizza

The Southern Connecticut town of New Haven is famous as the home of Yale University. But it's perhaps even more renowned for a unique style of pizza, named apizza (pronounced "ah-beets") by the immigrants who arrived there from Southern Italy in the early 1900s.

Similar to the Neapolitan pies that were characteristic of their home city, apizza has a thin, chewy crust. But instead of baking their pizzas in a wood-fired oven, as was typical in Naples, some of the first New Haven pizzerias, including Frank Pepe Pizzeria Napoletana (or **Pepe's** for short), which opened in 1925, and **Sally's Apizza**, started by Frank Pepe's nephew a decade later, used a coal-fired stove. At the time, this fuel was inexpensive and plentiful, and it cooked the pizzas at extremely high temperatures, up to 1000 degrees Fahrenheit, leaving them crispy and charred in spots, with a subtle smoky flavor.

There are two distinctive kinds of New Haven-style pizza, one of which is tomato pie, sometimes called plain pizza. This is apizza that's topped only with a tangy sauce made from fresh tomatoes, along with a dusting of Pecorino Romano cheese, and is similar to the style of tomato pie that's cooked in Trenton, New Jersey (which typically adds mozzarella as an additional topping). The other is a white clam pie, which replaces the sauce with olive oil, garlic and chopped littleneck clams, harvested locally from the nearby Long Island Sound. Other high-quality toppings, including fresh mozzarella – which doesn't come standard on apizza – are also common, but New Haven-style pizzas tend not to be overloaded with them, and the pies are usually served whole rather than by the slice.

Your first two stops when sampling pizza in this part of the state should be Pepe's and Sally's. The former is credited with inventing the white clam pie and has more than a dozen branches across New England as well as in New York, Maryland, Virginia and Florida. And the latter, which opened in 1938, has been patronized by celebrities including Frank Sinatra and Kamala Harris, and is famous for its version of the tomato pie, which you can also get at several other locations in Connecticut.

A third legendary spot worth visiting is **Modern Apizza**, which opened in New Haven in 1934 and differs from its competitors in using an open-flame brick oven, and constructing its pizzas flush with toppings, including generous portions of fresh mozzarella. And **Bar**, a New Haven-style pizza joint and nightclub of more recent vintage, is also highly regarded locally, especially for its pie covered in mashed potatoes and bacon, which it cooks in a gas-powered oven. Visit all four of these spots and you might decide you want to enroll at Yale just so you can major in apizza.

Steamed cheeseburger

Champions of Connecticut will tell you that the hamburger was invented in the Constitution State. While that's not entirely true, Louis' Lunch in New Haven does get credit from the Library of Congress for the first hamburger sandwich in the U.S., when in 1900, the restaurant served a customer ground steak trimmings on toast.

The Nutmeg State can't take credit for the first cheeseburger, either, as that's generally attributed to Lionel Sternberger, a cook at a Pasadena, California, sandwich shop called The Rite Spot, who created one in 1924. But what Connecticut is famous for, especially in the central part of the state that's a burger mecca, is an innovation called the steamed cheeseburger. This way of cooking hamburgers was invented by Jack Fitzgerald at Jack's Lunch in Middletown in the late 1920s or 1930s, during an era when it was believed that steamed food was easier to digest than fried (but a half-century before Eastern Tennessee's invention of the steamed hoagie).

A steamed cheeseburger uses a cooking method that doesn't rely on a frypan, or a grill, to prepare the sandwich. Instead, the two main ingredients are placed in separate compartments of a tall metal cabinet, with simmering water producing steam that cooks the meat and melts the cheese, while the grease drips away. Although a steamed burger lacks the characteristic grill marks or charred exterior that many find appealing, it does result in a juicy, tender patty that's slathered with a ladleful of gooey cheese. Like any burger, it's typically accompanied by lettuce, tomatoes and standard condiments such as mustard and ketchup.

Jack's Lunch remained open until the 1960s, but by then, another Middletown restaurant that's still in business today, **O'Rourke's Diner**, had started selling its own version of the steamed cheeseburger. And in 1959, **Ted's Restaurant** had begun dishing out similar sandwiches in Meriden, a location it continues to operate, in addition to a food truck that it calls the Steam Machine. Other notable places to try this style of burger include **K Lamay's Steamed Cheeseburgers**, also in Meriden, and **American Steamed Cheeseburgers** in Wallingford. You'll have to decide for yourself whether Connecticut's invention deserves a place in the pantheon of burger history, or whether its big metal boxes would be better put to use as filing cabinets.

RHODE ISLAND

Red strips

What's a pizza without a thick layer of bubbling, melty cheese? In the Ocean State, it's a local delicacy known as red strips, party pizza or bakery pizza. And you'll typically find it at grocery stores or bakeries rather than at pizza parlors.

Red strips are prepared by smothering a thick, doughy crust with fresh tomato sauce, sometimes with additional vegetables or a sprinkle of Parmesan cheese on top. It's baked in large trays and cut into rectangles, and is usually served at room temperature. An alternate style is called white strips, which eschews the tomato sauce in favor of olive oil, grated cheese and fresh herbs.

A good place for your first taste of red strips is **D. Palmieri's Bakery** in Johnston, which was founded in Providence's Federal Hill neighborhood in 1905, around the time when Italian-Americans in that city as well as Philadelphia began creating what was called tomato pie (different from the tomato pies cooked in New Haven and Trenton) as an inexpensive, filling snack. Another good option is **DePetrillo's Pizza & Bakery**, with locations in Warwick, Coventry, Smithfield and North Providence that serve both red and white strips, as well as traditional-style pizza. Or visit **LaSalle Bakery** in Providence, which also offers red and white strips at its two locations – as well as pastries, cakes and other confections that'll make you realize you probably don't need any high-calorie cheese on your pizza.

New York System wiener

The New York System might sound like it refers to either the Manhattan subway or to the city's byzantine alternate-side-of-the-street parking rules. But in Rhode Island, it's a term that denotes a specific style of hot dog, named in the early 1900s by Greek immigrants to associate the dish with the frankfurters that were becoming popular in Brooklyn's Coney Island. (That's the same reason Midwestern dogs are often called coneys.)

A New York System wiener, sometimes called a hot wiener, is a small, thin sausage made from pork and veal. In the classic preparation, called "all the way," it's served on a steamed bun and topped with a meat sauce that's spiced with cumin and chili powder, along with chopped onions, yellow mustard and celery salt. Diners often order a few at a time, and it's common to see a cook constructing them by lining up the buns on his or her arm, with the free hand quickly adding the wiener and condiments one after another.

At traditional New York System spots, the wieners are often accompanied by coffee milk, the state's official beverage, a mixture of milk and sweetened coffee syrup. (Blend in some ice cream and it becomes a coffee milkshake, or what Rhode Islanders call a cabinet. In the rest of New England, similar drinks are known as frappes.)

The oldest existing purveyor of Rhode Island's regional hot dog is Original New York System in Providence, now called **Baba's Original New York System**, which was founded in 1927. Another longstanding establishment in Providence is **Olneyville New York System**, a restaurant that Anthony Stavrianakos opened with his son in 1946, a time when he and other Greek immigrants began launching similar hot dog stands all over the city. (Stavrianakos's descendants now run locations in both Providence and Cranston.) Other popular options include **Wein-O-Rama** in Cranston, which has been in business since 1962, and **Sam's New York System** in Warwick and North Providence, which dates to 1968. After trying a few of these places, you might decide that there's no better way to prepare a hot dog, in Rhode Island or anywhere else, than with the New York System.

Clam cake

There are plenty of ways to enjoy the Ocean State's native quahogs, large clams that are often stuffed, turned into chowder or fried in strips. But perhaps the best way to eat the state's official shellfish (which is also the name for the fictional location of the animated sitcom Family Guy) is in a specialty that's found all along the Rhode Island coast, a dish the locals call clam cakes.

These fritters are prepared by battering and frying chopped pieces of the mollusk, which results in irregularly shaped, golden-brown balls that are akin to a savory donut hole or hushpuppy. They're best when served hot and crispy, straight out of the fryer, and are typically eaten by hand from a paper bag or a cardboard container, either plain or dipped into hot sauce, tartar sauce or vinegar.

While local Native tribes certainly ate (and named) quahogs, it's believed that the first clam cakes were cooked by Carrie Cooper in 1920 at her eponymous restaurant in Narragansett, **Aunt Carrie's**, where she swapped vegetables for seafood one day while making corn fritters.

The beachside spot remains a popular place to order clam cakes, but you'll also find them at coastal clam shacks all around the state. Some recommended options include **Iggy's Doughboys and Chowder House** in Narragansett and Warwick, which ships its clam cakes nationwide; **Flo's Clam Shack**, which was founded in 1936 and stays open only from March through October, in Middletown and Portsmouth; and **Crow's Nest Fish House & Oyster Bar** in Warwick, which serves its clam cakes by the half-dozen or dozen. It's also a good place to try local clams raw, in chowder, with pasta and in just about any other preparation you can think of.

Clams casino

The inventor of clams casino really hit the jackpot with the recipe, which combines shucked, chopped clams with seasoned breadcrumbs, butter, red or green bell peppers and diced bacon. It's usually prepared by putting the filling back into the clamshell before it's baked or broiled, and then garnished with parsley. The dish is typically made with littleneck or cherrystone clams, which are both native to Rhode Island, and is served as an appetizer, with the mollusks sometimes presented on a bed of rock salt.

The oft-repeated origin story of clams casino is that it was invented in 1917 by Julius Keller, an employee at the Narragansett Pier Casino (which was a hotel, not a gambling establishment) for a guest who had requested a special dish for a luncheon at her table. But the preparation might have been invented two decades earlier, or it might not be a Rhode Island creation after all. That's because the guest – a Newport resident who Keller, in his memoir, recalled creating the recipe for – died in 1895, and clams casino actually appeared on menus at restaurants in New York City as early as 1900.

Despite the dish's checkered history, it's undisputed that clams casino features prominently at seafood spots and old-school Italian restaurants all around Rhode Island. A few highly regarded options include **Iggy's Boardwalk** in Warwick, a fancier version of its beachside clam shacks; **Matunuck Oyster Bar** in Wakefield; and **Andino's Italian Restaurant** in Providence. And if you're feeling lucky after dinner, head to either Lincoln or Tiverton, the locations of Rhode Island's two major casinos, and see if you can win enough clams to pay for your next meal.

Johnnycakes

Every spring, Rhode Islanders celebrate their state's heritage with a tradition known as May Breakfast. Churches or community organizations host events that feature traditional breakfast foods as well as clam cakes and apple pie – and sometimes, a local specialty called johnnycakes.

Johnnycakes, which you'll also see spelled as jonnycakes (and which are known in the South as hoecakes), are thin pancakes made from stone-ground white cornmeal, much of it produced by a local business called **Kenyon's Grist Mill**. The cornmeal is mixed with either milk or water (which results in a thicker cake that's sometimes sweetened with sugar), and the batter is cooked in a griddle until the cakes are golden-brown and crispy. They're usually eaten for breakfast with butter, syrup or honey, but they can also be topped with gravy for a savory side dish.

The word johnnycakes probably derives from jonakin, a Native term for corn, and European settlers likely learned the dish in the 1600s from the Narragansett tribe, who cultivated a local variety of the vegetable called white cap flint corn.

You'll find johnnycakes at a handful of traditional diners around the state, including **The Common's Lunch** in Little Compton, **Jigger's Diner** in East Greenwich and **Mae's Place** in North Kingstown. Or visit Kenyon's in Usquepaugh during its autumn tour weekend, when you can check out the mill and get another chance for your first taste of johnnycakes – assuming, that is, that you weren't able to make it to town for breakfast in May.

Other Rhode Island dishes to sample:

- **Grilled pizza**, a style invented at **Al Forno** in Providence in 1980. The restaurant used its wood-fired grill to produce a thin-crust flatbread that it topped with tomato sauce and mozzarella cheese and garnished with scallions.
- **Calamari**, squid rings that are battered and fried with hot cherry peppers and garnished with parsley, in the version of the dish that was declared Rhode Island's official appetizer in 2014 and is often served at local Italian restaurants. One spot that's well-regarded for its calamari is **Marchetti's** in Cranston.
- **Doughboys**, squares of deep-fried pizza dough that are sprinkled with powdered sugar and eaten hot. You'll find them at **Iggy's Doughboys & Chowder House** in Warwick and Narragansett, as well as at pizza shops including **Demo's Pizza Factory** in Warwick and **Townies Feel Good Food** in East Providence, which offers a complimentary doughboy with each order.

OTHER FOODS OF NEW ENGLAND

Pilgrim sandwich

The Friday after Thanksgiving is traditionally a day for getting a jump on your holiday shopping, watching football on TV and, of course, grazing all day on leftovers. But if you'd like to enjoy the flavors of the holiday year-round, New England has just the sandwich for you.

A Pilgrim sandwich, sometimes called a Puritan or a gobbler, is made with the Thanksgiving foods you might expect – roast turkey, herb stuffing and cranberry sauce, all piled between two or more slices of bread, or on a bulkie, a New England variety of sandwich bun with a petaled design on its top. But while those ingredients are typical, they're just a starting point, as the sandwich can sometimes include gravy, Cheddar cheese or vegetables such as lettuce, celery or even mashed potatoes.

You might think that New Englanders have been making good use of leftovers ever since the day after the first Thanksgiving, the harvest celebration held by the pilgrims of Plymouth Colony in 1621. But the Pilgrim sandwich likely became a staple of Massachusetts cuisine only in the 1950s, when recipes for it were published by both the Boston Globe and a magazine called Poultry Tribune. The dish soon spread widely across the region, and started to become especially popular in the early 2000s.

Today you can find a giant, iconic example of this sandwich at **Mike's City Diner** in Boston, whose version Guy Fieri featured in 2007, and the Food Network called one of the best Thanksgiving dishes in the country a few years later. But there are other great options in Massachusetts, too, notably in a pair of towns that are contextually relevant for the specialty, **Lambert's Farm Market** in Sandwich and **Stracco's Subs & More** in Plymouth. Or head out of state to **J's Deli** in Woonsocket, Rhode Island, or **Jon's Roast Beef & Deli** in

Laconia, New Hampshire, and see if the sandwiches they construct can beat the one you made for yourself last Black Friday.

Italian sausage

See Chicago

The Italian neighborhoods of New England are dotted with butchers and delis where you can buy fresh sausage and get a great grinder. Highly regarded places to find a juicy sausage sandwich, loaded with peppers and onions, include **La Rosa's Marketplace** in Hartford and **Pauly Penta's Gourmet Italian Deli** in North Providence, and in Massachusetts, **Dom's Sausage** in Malden and Boston's **Fenway Park**, where sausage vendors line Lansdowne Street on Red Sox game days.

Clam roll

By the middle of the 20th century, the Howard Johnson's chain that had started as a Quincy, Massachusetts, soda fountain had hundreds of orange-roofed locations nationwide. And many of these restaurants featured clam strips, which were pieces carved from the mollusk that were marketed as being "tender-sweet" and were more appealing to Americans than the plump bellies that included the gastrointestinal tract. In 1964, a Howard Johnson's diner could get a fried clam sandwich with French fries and coleslaw for just over a dollar.

While Howard Johnson's was responsible for popularizing the dish beyond New England, the clam had become a regional specialty decades earlier. On July 3, 1916, an Essex, Massachusetts, restaurant owner named Lawrence Woodman, known as Chubby, decided to try cooking freshly dug steamer clams in the oil he typically used for making potato chips, at the suggestion of a local fisherman. After experimenting with different batters, Woodman served the first fried clams the following day at the town's Fourth of July parade, and they proved to be a huge hit.

More than 100 years later, **Woodman's** eponymous restaurant in Essex still sources clams from the nearby Ipswich flats on the Massachusetts North Shore, and serves up both clam strips and whole-bellied clams. You can get the fried bivalves either as dinner plates with French fries and onion rings, in family-style boxes by the half-pint, pint or quart, or in a split-top hot dog bun accompanied by tartar sauce and a squeeze of lemon – the clam roll that's become ubiquitous along the New England coast.

Some highly touted places to enjoy a clam roll include **The Clam Box of Ipswich** (not to be confused with similarly named establishments in Quincy and Brookfield, Massachusetts); **Jim's Clam Shack** in Falmouth, on Cape Cod; **Monahan's Clam Shack** in Narragansett, Rhode Island; and **Bob's Clam Hut** in Kittery, Maine. But you won't find one at Howard Johnson's – the last remaining restaurant in the chain, in Lake George, New York, closed in 2022.

Stuffies

As a one-time resident of New England, it sometimes seemed to me as though locals were speaking their own language. A bubbler is a water fountain, jimmies are sprinkles, a packie is a liquor store – and stuffies are stuffed giant clams.

But not any clam can be a stuffie, of course. The bivalve that's commonly used is the quahog, a hard-shell mollusk native to Rhode Island and also found off the coast of Cape Cod and along the Eastern seaboard. They're filled with a mixture of the minced clam, breadcrumbs, spices and sometimes finely chopped meat such as bacon or the Portuguese sausages called chouriço and linguiça, before being baked and presented on the half-shell. Stuffies are usually sold by the piece and are eaten as an appetizer with accompaniments of lemon and Tabasco sauce.

The inventor of stuffies is lost to the annals of history. But the Narragansett were known to use quahogs for both food and trading, and probably introduced them to 17th-century European settlers along the New England coast.

That's where you're most likely to encounter stuffies today, at Rhode Island seafood spots including **Aunt Carrie's** in Narragansett, **Anthony's Seafood** in Middletown, **Ocean Mist** in South Kingstown and **Red Bridge Tavern** in East Providence. And in Southeastern Massachusetts, you can satisfy your craving at **Quahog Republic** in Falmouth, Wareham and New Bedford, as well as **Marshland Restaurants and Bakeries** in Sandwich and Plymouth. Just know that if you ask a local how to get to one of these places, and they tell you to go through the rotary, they're not talking about an old-timey phone – they just mean a traffic circle.

New England-style clam chowder

The fictional afterlife depicted on the TV comedy The Good Place doesn't hide its disdain for clam chowder, with actress Kristen Bell's character calling the fountain of it that flows in the town square "hot ocean milk with dead animal croutons." But that's a minority opinion in New England, where clam chowder is the region's favorite soup.

New England-style clam chowder features the briny bivalve in a thick broth made with milk or cream, potatoes, onions, salt pork and herbs that may include thyme and parsley. It's usually served by the cup or bowl, accompanied by packets of oyster crackers, which are added to the soup as a garnish.

A variation of this dish that's prevalent in Rhode Island is called clear chowder, which doesn't include any dairy and makes use of the local quahogs, known colloquially as chowder clams. And you'll sometimes also find Rhode Island chowder with a hint of tomato, a modification attributed to Portuguese fishermen, and considered a precursor to Manhattan-style chowder. That version is so blasphemous in New England that a Maine politician once threatened to criminalize it.

Chowder was probably introduced to the region by the early European settlers of the 17th century. The term chowder comes from the French word chaudiere, the communal pot used in coastal fishing villages to share the day's catch. Although fish stews that included milk were a common dish in New England, the addition of clams came later. In 1832, Lydia Maria Child published a cookbook called The American Frugal Housewife, with the first recipe for a chowder containing clams. Within a few years, **Union Oyster House** in Boston was featuring the dish on its menu, and Herman Melville wrote extensively about it in his 1851 novel Moby Dick.

New England-style clam chowder is sometimes called Boston chowder, and that's a great place to find excellent versions of it, including the one still served at Union Oyster House in the Financial District. Also worth trying are the soups at **Neptune Oyster** in the North End, **Boston Chowda Co** in Faneuil Hall and North Andover, and **Legal Sea Foods**, with more than a dozen locations throughout the Boston metropolitan area as well as in Cranston, Rhode Island. And in Portland, Maine, another chowder hotspot, it's worth visiting **Gilbert's Chowder House** as well as **Eventide Oyster Co.** (which also has a Boston location in the Fenway).

But if you agree with The Good Place's take on a cream-based soup, then Rhode Island's clear chowder might be just what you're looking for. You'll find well-regarded versions of it at **Matunuck Oyster Bar** in Wakefield, **Dune Brothers Seafood** in Providence and **Captain's Catch Seafood** in Warwick. And that way, you can avoid having to ingest what Bell's character also calls "a savory latte with bugs in it."

Chow mein sandwich

In Southern New England, it's not uncommon for Chinese restaurants to place a basket of rolls on the table when you sit down. And the reason for this atypical practice also explains why towns in the vicinity of Fall River, Massachusetts, are home to one of the most unusual dishes you'll find in the region – the chow mein sandwich.

In the early 20th century, Fall River's textile mills employed thousands of workers from England, Ireland and Canada. And at the same time, an influx of Chinese had settled in the area, which because of the Chinese Exclusion Act of 1882 could be more welcoming than the West Coast, where anti-immigrant fervor sometimes ran high. Many of these transplants, including Frederick Wong, who had come to the U.S. from Canton, worked in family-owned businesses or opened establishments of their own. And while Wong was working at a cook at his uncle's Hong Kong Restaurant during the 1920s, he came up with the idea for the chow mein sandwich, a union between a traditional Cantonese dish and a typical American food that he thought would make the flavors more appealing to the factory workers. (That's the same impulse behind the rolls on the table, and mirrors the histories of the St. Paul sandwich, a St. Louis specialty, as well as Springfield-style cashew chicken.)

A chow mein sandwich consists of a brown gravy that's ladled over a hamburger bun and topped with thin, crispy noodles. Diners can order it either unstrained, with the sauce incorporating vegetables such as celery, bean sprouts and onions, or strained, without the vegetables – along with proteins that include a choice of beef, chicken, pork or shrimp.

(A related dish is the chop suey sandwich, consisting of bean sprouts and bits of meat in a light-colored gravy that's served on a bun, which you'll find at a couple of restaurants in Salem, Massachusetts – **Kiki's Chinese Food** and **Meilee Express**.)

The crunchy noodles are the hallmark of the chow mein sandwich, and in 1938, Wong opened the Oriental Chow Mein Company in Fall River, selling packaged noodles along with gravy mix to local restaurants, and eventually further afield. Up until recent decades, you could also order a chow mein sandwich at Nathan's Famous in Coney Island, and the dish was a staple in Fall River schools, where it was traditionally accompanied by French fries and orange soda.

Today, however, the specialty can only be found in a handful of restaurants on the Massachusetts-Rhode Island border. A few places where you can try one include **Mee Sum Restaurant** and **China Express** in Fall River, Massachusetts, and in Rhode Island, **China Gourmet** in Portsmouth and **Asian Gourmet** in Tiverton. Just don't be surprised if you place an order to go and you find some extra bread in your takeout bag.

American chop suey

You might have forgotten all about chop suey, the conglomeration of stir-fried meat and vegetables, seasoned with soy sauce and usually served over rice, that for decades was a staple of Chinese cuisine in the U.S. But a casserole that's dubbed American goulash or slumgullion in other parts of the country (or Johnny Marzetti in Columbus, Ohio) is, curiously, known in New England as American chop suey.

American chop suey has little in common with its Chinese counterpart, aside from the idea of mixing ingredients. (The latter likely originated in the province of Guangdong before immigrants brought it to the U.S., anglicizing the Cantonese term tsap seui, meaning various scraps.) The American dish is frequently modified to suit individual tastes. But it generally consists of elbow macaroni or other noodles that are mixed with a thick tomato sauce made with ground beef, sautéed onions and seasonings. The pasta is then topped with cheese and baked.

A recipe for an Americanized chop suey first appeared in a U.S. army cooking manual in 1916, with a sauce made from beef stock and barbecue sauce. By the middle of the century, the dish had been transformed by Italian-Americans, who employed familiar flavors and ingredients. But, retaining some connection to the original dish, they initially used rice as the starch before replacing it with pasta, and substituting the soy sauce for Worcestershire sauce.

If you'd like to try this comfort-food classic, you'll find it at traditional American restaurants and diners in New England, including **Maria's Place** in Salem, **John Brewer's Tavern** in Malden and **Red's Kitchen + Tavern** in Peabody, all in Massachusetts, and **Pine Street Eatery** in Nashua and **Red Arrow Diner** in Manchester, Nashua, Concord and Londonderry, New Hampshire. And while the dish certainly won't remind you of chop suey, it'll at least give you a better appreciation for the vagaries of culinary etymology.

Tourtière

During the darkest days of winter, a celebratory dish eaten in New England towns with a significant population of French-Canadian immigrants is a double-crusted meat pie called tourtière. This dish consists of a mixture of ground pork (and sometimes beef or game meats) and potatoes that's spiced with cinnamon and cloves and baked in a flaky dough.

In these communities, where hundreds of thousands of French-speaking Canadians, mostly from Quebec, settled between 1840 and 1930, tourtière is traditionally part of a holiday dinner called le réveillon that begins after midnight mass on Christmas Eve. Tourtière was named for the shallow dish used for making these and other pies, which are called tourtes in French.

Today you can find this dish at bakeries, pie shops and restaurants all over New England, where tourtière is sometimes just called French meat pie. Some recommended spots include

Flaky Crust Pies in Norton, **Hartley's Original Pork Pies** in Fall River and **Landry's Meat Pies** in New Bedford, all in Massachusetts; **The Post Restaurant**, with two locations in Concord, New Hampshire; **Dakin Farm** in Ferrisburgh, Vermont; and **Hillman's Bakery** in Fairfield, Maine. Pick up a slice (or a whole pie) and you'll have reason to celebrate without having to wait for the holidays to come back around.

New England boiled dinner

The dish known as New England boiled dinner couldn't sound more prosaic. But call it by one of its other names – Jigg's Dinner, a term used in Newfoundland (and Chicago), or even corned beef-and-cabbage – and you might find that you suddenly have an appetite for it.

New England boiled dinner is a one-pot meal consisting of corned beef that's cooked with seasonings along with cabbage and root vegetables such as potatoes, carrots, turnips and rutabagas, until all the components are tender. It's typically served with condiments such as horseradish or mustard.

This specialty was likely created by Irish immigrants to New England during the 19th century, using inexpensive corned beef and winter vegetables to make a meal similar to a dish they would have eaten at home. Today it's often served on St. Patrick's Day, with the leftovers traditionally employed the following day in a dish called red flannel hash. Menus sometimes specify that the corned beef itself is red, to distinguish it from the dull, gray-colored meat prevalent locally that doesn't include the nitrates that are typically used as a preservative.

Although New England boiled dinner is no longer as common as it once was, you'll still see it at a handful of Irish-themed restaurants and pubs in the region, where it sometimes appears only as a weekly special. A few places to try in Massachusetts include **The Irish Cottage Pub** in Methuen; **The Emerald Rose** in Billerica, where it's featured on Wednesdays; and **Portside Diner** in Danvers, where it's served on Thursdays. And in Epping, New Hampshire, you'll find New England boiled dinner at **Holy Grail Restaurant and Pub** – a fitting name for one of the few places you can easily track down this sometimes-elusive dish.

New England brown bread

You've probably eaten canned soup and canned vegetables, and if you drink alcohol, you've certainly popped open a can of beer. But have you ever consumed a can of brown bread? That's the loaf named for either New England or Boston, which is traditionally eaten with hot dogs and baked beans for Saturday-night supper.

New England brown bread gets its dark color from a mixture of flours such as whole wheat and rye, and also contains cornmeal and molasses, as well as, sometimes, raisins or other dried fruits. Instead of being baked, the batter is poured into a can (so that the bread holds its shape), and steamed over a kettle of boiling water. The moist, cake-like loaf is typically sliced horizontally and eaten warm.

This style of steamed bread developed during the mid-19th century, during the Victorian era when sweetening breads with molasses was a common practice. But it became especially popular in New England after B&M, a canning company in Portland, Maine, began packaging bread in 1928 as a companion to its popular brand of baked beans.

If you want to try New England brown bread, you'll still find B&M's product in local grocery stores, but you can also purchase a variety made by R.E. Kimball & Company at **Calef's Country Store** in Barrington, New Hampshire. And in Massachusetts, **Nason's Stone House Farm** in Boxford sells it fresh, with or without raisins, and **Hi Rise Bread Company** in Cambridge makes a version with dried blueberries. Because not many places still prepare this style of bread, either bakery's motto might very well be "Yes, We Can."

Anadama bread

Cornmeal and molasses, two New England staples, feature prominently in anadama bread, a food that's said to have gotten its name from an oft-repeated legend that sounds too preposterous to be true – and probably isn't.

Unusually for a baked good with those two main ingredients (along with flour), anadama bread is leavened with yeast. The resulting loaf has the texture and color of cornbread with a hint of nutty sweetness, and can be eaten by itself or used for sandwiches.

This bread likely dates to the mid-19th century, and is believed to have been invented in the coastal Cape Ann region of Massachusetts. As the story goes, a fisherman in either Rockport or Gloucester was getting tired of the cornmeal and molasses porridge that his wife constantly prepared for him, and so one day he threw it into the oven with some flour and yeast, saying, "Anna, damn her!" Another version of the tale that's more appreciative of Anna's cooking talents claims that the bread was named for the inscription that a fisherman put on his wife's tombstone: "Anna was a lovely bride, but Anna, damn 'er, up and died."

Although these origin stories are surely apocryphal, what we do know is that the term anadama bread was first used in print in 1915, and that the specialty was baked in Rockport at Blacksmith Shop Restaurant beginning in the 1920s. Two decades later, the family that owned the business began producing the bread commercially, and Anadama Bread Company distributed its loaves all throughout New England until the early 1970s.

Today you'll find anadama bread at artisan bakeries all around the region, as well as in local grocery stores. In New Hampshire, head to **Woodman's Artisan Bakery** in Nashua, which bakes anadama bread on Wednesdays; **Vintage Bakery** in Glen, where it's available on Thursdays and Saturdays; and **Abigail's Bakery** in Weare, which also sells its bread online. In Maine, you'll find it at **Dot's Bakery** in Round Pound. And in Massachusetts, visit **When Pigs Fly Bread** in Somerville, which also distributes locally, and **Red Skiff Restaurant** in Rockport on the North Shore, where anadama bread was allegedly created. After one slice, you'll certainly want to praise Anna, not damn her.

Fluffernutter

A childhood favorite of many New Englanders is a salty and sweet sandwich known as a fluffernutter. This gooey concoction consists of equal layers of marshmallow crème (usually the iconic brand called Marshmallow Fluff, made from sugar, corn syrup, egg whites and vanilla flavoring) and peanut butter, spread between two slices of white bread.

While this specialty wasn't named a fluffernutter until decades later, the first recipe for a similar sandwich was published in 1918 by Emma Curtis. She and her brother Amory, descendants of Paul Revere who lived in Melrose, Massachusetts, had invented a product five years earlier called Snowflake Marshmallow Creme. Feeling patriotic during World War I, she named her peanut-butter-and-crème fusion a Liberty Sandwich.

A competing marshmallow spread was also in the works, though, a creation of Archibald Query, who lived in nearby Somerville and sold it door-to-door. But after struggling to make a profit due to the wartime sugar shortages, Query ended up selling his business to H. Allen Durkee and Fred L. Mower, two war veterans who rebranded the product as Tout Sweet Marshmallow Fluff (and later dropped the first half of the name).

Over the next half-century, the Durkee-Mower company popularized the spread with some innovative marketing, including a weekly radio show called The Flufferettes that lasted for two decades, with live music as well as recipes featuring the product. And in 1960, they launched an advertising campaign that promoted Marshmallow Fluff as part of a sandwich they named the fluffernutter. Two years later, what remained of the Curtis marshmallow crème business shut down.

Durkee-Mower continues to produce Marshmallow Fluff today (which you can easily find in grocery stores nationwide), but it found itself in a sticky situation in 2006 when a Massachusetts state senator introduced legislation to limit how often fluffernutters could be served in public schools. But a second bill was proposed by a colleague close to Durkee-Mower's district that aimed to make the fluffernutter the official sandwich of the Bay State. Neither passed into law, but that wasn't the last time the fluffernutter made the news – in 2021, Merriam-Webster added the word to its dictionary.

When you're ready for a bite of nostalgia, you'll find fluffernutters on the kids' menu at several New England restaurants, including **Prospect Beach House** in West Haven, Connecticut; **The Beacon Bar and Grill** in Trenton, Maine; and **Wrap City Sandwich Co.** in Londonderry, New Hampshire. But in Massachusetts, the combination of peanut butter and marshmallow isn't limited to the children's (or the sandwich) side of the menu. At **Fauci's Pizza** in Lynn, you can indulge your craving with a fluffernutter calzone, while **SPoT!** in Norwood offers the combo as a bagel topping, and **Toscanini's** in Cambridge sometimes serves up a fluffernutter-flavored ice cream. Or head to Somerville for the annual What the Fluff? festival, featuring marshmallow-themed merchandise and games, and all the fluffernutters you could possibly eat.

Indian pudding

The name of this traditional dessert is as old-fashioned as the food itself. But some antiquated habits are hard to break, and as far as I know, no one's yet come up with a better term for it.

Indian pudding is a baked custard consisting of cornmeal, molasses, milk and warm spices such as ginger and cinnamon. It's typically served warm and topped with either whipped cream or vanilla ice cream.

The dessert was a 17th-century adaptation by European settlers of a British dish called hasty pudding. But in colonial America, the key ingredients needed to prepare it, sugar and wheat flour, were scarce, and there were ready alternatives in the molasses that was used to produce rum as well as cornmeal, which the colonists called Indian meal. Their brick ovens provided the warmth needed to gently cook the pudding, which is considered the first American dessert and is sometimes still found on Thanksgiving tables.

The dish fell out of favor in the early 20th century, though, when commercially packaged puddings started to become available in popular flavors such as chocolate, which General Foods first introduced in 1934. But today you can still find this delicacy at restaurants that specialize in historic dishes, as well as at a few New England stalwarts. In Massachusetts, you can sample it at **Longfellow's Wayside Inn** in Sudbury, **Concord's Colonial Inn** in Concord and **Plentiful Café** at Plimoth Plantation in Plymouth. And you'll also find it on the menus of **Aunt Carrie's** in Narragansett, Rhode Island, and **Maine Diner** in Wells, Maine.

But while all of these spots still call the dessert Indian pudding, I think it's time to retire that label. Let's call it colonial custard or anadama pudding – and leave the archaic name for this dish to kheer, the creamy rice pudding offered at restaurants that serve the cuisines of India.

Cider donut

The perfect New England fall day includes driving a winding country road to see the autumn colors (an activity that New Englanders call leaf-peeping), and then stopping at a cider mill to pick some apples and enjoy a warm drink and a snack – especially the regional treat called a cider donut.

Cider donuts are fried cake-like rings (or donut holes) prepared with apple cider and buttermilk in the batter, which makes them slightly sweet and tangy. They're often sprinkled with cinnamon sugar, and are commonly eaten warm directly out of paper bags.

You might think that the tradition of cider donuts in New England developed organically. But it was actually a marketing concept invented by the Doughnut Corporation of America (DCA), which introduced the sweet cider donut as its new flavor in 1951, and proclaimed that its "natural fall appeal" would help boost sales at the stores that sold the company's product lines. (The DCA also came up with the idea for National Donut Month, which eventually evolved into National Donut Day on the first Friday of June each year.)

Today there are hundreds of spots throughout New England that fry up cider donuts, all of them cataloged on a map by a Boston-area resident named Alex Schwartz. A few standouts include **Cape Cod Donuts** in Sandwich and **Bolton Orchards** in Bolton, both in Massachusetts; **Congdon's Doughnuts** in Wells, Maine; **Meadow Ledge Farm** in Loudon and **Chichester Country Store** in Chichester, both in New Hampshire; and **Hackett's Orchard** in South Hero and **Burtt's Apple Orchard** in Cabot, both in Vermont.

But don't go looking for cider donuts at the Dunkin' chain that's ubiquitous all over New England. While its fall menu included this specialty until recently, in 2022 Dunkin' chose to take the spotlight away from New England and feature another flavor with natural fall appeal. You might say that the modern version of the cider donut is a pastry made with pumpkin.

Penuche

File this one under "don't believe everything you read on the Internet." An old-fashioned confection that you'll find in candy stores all over New England is alleged to be named after a hockey player named Mark Penuche, a member of the 1924 Boston Bruins who apparently loved maple syrup. But there's no evidence of any player by that name, and while maple flavor is sometimes added to penuche, that's not what makes it distinctive.

Penuche is a tan-colored candy made with brown sugar, milk and butter that's similar to fudge, but doesn't have any chocolate. Vanilla or nuts are sometimes added to the mixture, which is typically cut into squares but can also be used as a cake frosting.

A few recommended options for buying penuche include **Winfrey's Fudge & Chocolates** in Rowley, Massachusetts; **Harbor Candy Shop** in Ogunquit, Maine; **Granite State Candy Shoppe** in Concord, New Hampshire; and **Chapel Sweets** on Block Island in New Shoreham, Rhode Island.

Another New England dish to sample:

- **Poutine**, a Canadian dish of French fries and cheese curds, topped with brown gravy, that's become common in Northern New England because of its large population of French-Canadian immigrants. You can sample it at **Chez Vachon** in Manchester, New Hampshire, and **Duckfat** in Portland, Maine.

So where did penuche come from, if it wasn't named for a hockey player? It's similar to a caramel-like Scottish confection called tablet, and the word likely derives from panocha, which means raw sugar in Spanish. But the Internet claims that the candy originated in Portugal and was popular among New England whaling families. That's certainly possible, but without any documentation, it's just as likely to have been inspired by an imaginary NHL athlete.

Salt water taffy

See New Jersey

In New England, Cape Cod is the place to go for salt water taffy, and you'll find dozens of flavors, including maple walnut, molasses peppermint and fluffernutter, at **Cape Cod Salt Water Taffy** in South Yarmouth, Massachusetts.

REGIONAL HOT DOGS OF THE U.S.

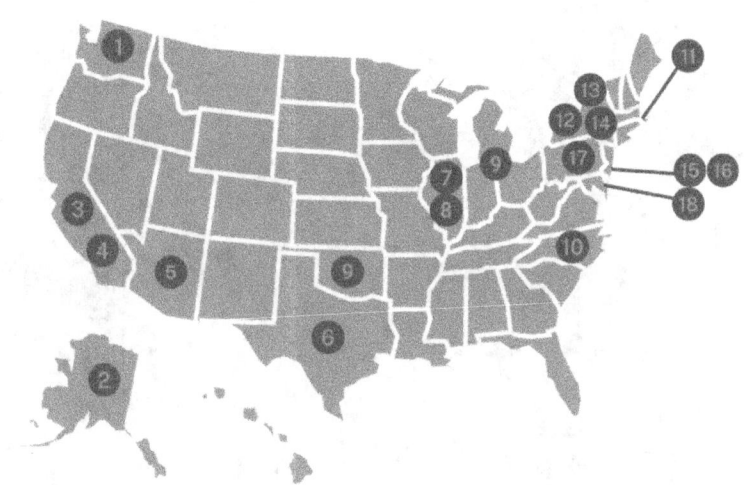

① Seattle-style hot dog

② Alaska-style hot dog

③ L.A.-style hot dog

④ Dodger Dog

⑤ Sonoran dog

⑥ Corn dog

⑦ Chicago-style hot dog

⑧ Francheezie

⑨ Coney Island hot dog

⑩ Carolina dog

⑪ New York System wiener

⑫ White hot

⑬ Michigan hot dog

⑭ Bagel dog & street dog

⑮ Ripper & Italian hot dog

⑯ Jersey breakfast dog

⑰ Texas Tommy

⑱ Bologna dog

Buffalo wings

NEW YORK

Between the late 1800s and first half of the 20th century, nearly 12 million foreigners, mostly from Europe, entered the U.S. through Ellis Island, with the Statue of Liberty proclaiming New York as the gateway to freedom and opportunity in the New World. And it's largely because of this immigration pattern that New York State is home to some of the most iconic regional food in the country.

The five boroughs that comprise New York City are where you'll find the majority of the Empire State's most famous eats. But other dishes worth seeking out are located on nearby Long Island, and along the 300-mile-long stretch of highway from Buffalo to Albany, with one specialty that's hugely popular across the country, and others that are virtually unknown outside the region.

Manhattan-born playwright and composer Lin-Manuel Miranda wasn't talking about its cuisine when, in the musical Hamilton, he called New York the greatest city in the world. But he might just as well have been. In the city that never sleeps, there's a meal for every budget, from the high-end tasting menus offered at dozens of Michelin-starred restaurants including **Le Bernadin**, **Per Se** and **Masa** to the hot dogs sold at food carts on every corner. Manhattan boasts fewer old-school diners than it once did, but the ones that still exist will make your jaw drop at the hundreds of items they serve, catering to whatever your stomach may happen to desire at all hours of the day and night.

Despite their seemingly endless menus, these kitchens produce few of the Big Apple's astounding array of regional foods, representing countries around the world. Some of the best include New York-style pizza, best enjoyed by the slice; chicken shawarma, part of the city's robust street food scene; the chopped cheese sandwich, cooked up at neighborhood bodegas; and the Puerto Rican lasagna known as pastelón. And that doesn't even include the cornucopia of ethnic specialties that don't belong to New York specifically, but offer you the opportunity during your visit to taste the flavors of Asia, Africa, the Caribbean and more.

A majority of the foods that are iconic to New York City trace their ancestry to one particular group of settlers. By the early 1900s, three million Jewish refugees, mostly from Eastern Europe, had joined the city's population, many living in overcrowded tenements in Manhattan's Lower East Side. And that neighborhood remains one of the best places to get a chewy New York-style bagel or a bialy, a pair of breads that originated in Poland, as well as pastrami, a smoked meat first served in a butcher owned by a Lithuanian immigrant.

While the black and white cookie only became an icon of Jewish-American cuisine long after it was invented, Jewish store owners can take credit for a few of the city's other signature dishes, including New York-style cheesecake and the egg cream – but probably not the Reuben, which was more likely invented in Omaha than Manhattan. And they're less responsible, too, for spreading the popularity of hot dogs in New York than other immigrant groups, which is why the Coney Island style is more famous in the Midwest than in the Brooklyn neighborhood that gives the coney its name.

You might also be surprised to learn that a handful of familiar plates were first created at some of New York City's fanciest hotels, where European-trained chefs put their own spin on common ingredients, resulting in dishes as wide-ranging as the Waldorf salad, vichyssoise and steak Diane. Others can trace their lineage to a single restaurant that had a role in numerous dining innovations, **Delmonico's**, where eggs Benedict, lobster Newberg and Manhattan-style clam chowder all likely got their start, along with the eponymous steak for which the establishment is most famous.

While New York City grabs most of the state's culinary spotlight, don't sleep on the corridor of upstate New York that includes Buffalo, Rochester and Utica, each with its own share of regional specialties. Buffalo is most famous for its namesake wings, as well as for sponge candy, a honeycomb-like confection served all over town. Rochester is known for a college students' delight called the garbage plate. And both cities feature delicacies that reflect the German heritage of some of its residents – the former's beef on weck, and the latter's white hots. Meanwhile, Utica is where you'll find a pair of Italian-influenced dishes, chicken riggies and Utica greens. And Binghamton, Plattsburgh and Syracuse all have their own signature dishes worth exploring.

Start getting hungry and put yourself in a New York state of mind. Whether you have plenty of time to explore the huge diversity of its culinary scene, or you're just passing through in a New York minute, you won't soon run out of specialties to try.

NEW YORK

NEW YORK CITY

New York-style pizza

There are literally thousands of pizza places in the five boroughs that comprise New York City, so you've never going to be able to eat at all of them. But no other food better encapsulates the Big Apple's history as a landing spot for immigrants seeking opportunity, or exposes a slice of its impossibly rich dining scene for just a few dollars.

New York-style pizza is characterized by wide, triangular slices of a large pie made with a thin, chewy crust that has a crisp edge. Traditionally, it's topped with an uncooked tomato sauce and low-moisture mozzarella cheese, although pepperoni, sausage or other meats, as well as mushrooms, peppers or other vegetables are sometimes added before cooking. Most pizza places offer dried Parmesan cheese, chili flakes or other condiments so that each diner can customize their piece of the pie. The oversized slices are often served with their edges hanging over a paper plate, and it's common for New Yorkers to walk briskly down the street while folding their pizza in half vertically so it can be eaten with one hand.

Some pizza aficionados believe that the softness and mineral content of NYC tap water is what makes its pies superior to those cooked elsewhere. Restauranteurs have even been known to transport it across the country to make New York-style pizza in other places.

The first pizzeria in the U.S. was **Lombardi's** in Manhattan's Little Italy, which began selling pies for a nickel in 1905. Gennaro

Lombardi had emigrated to New York City from Naples eight years prior. Along with an employee named Antonio Totonno Pero, Lombardi began adapting the wood-fired Neapolitan-style pizza of his homeland with the coal-powered ovens that were available, along with New World ingredients, particularly mozzarella made from cows, not buffalo. Within a few decades, Lombardi's was thriving, and Totonno had left to open his own shop in Brooklyn, **Totonno's**. But several fellow immigrants quickly joined the scene as competitors, including **John's** in Greenwich Village, founded by Giovanni Sasso in 1929, and **Patsy's** in East Harlem, opened by Pasquale Lanceri in 1933. Both expatriates also made their pies in a coal-fired oven, and christened their restaurants with their own Americanized nicknames.

The earliest New York pizzas were usually sold whole, but slice shops began to open around the city in the 1940s after the invention of the gas-powered pizza oven that allowed pies to be cooked at lower temperatures, making slices suitable for reheating. A few restaurants that are still notable for their outstanding slices opened in the 1960s and 1970s, including **Joe & Pat's** on Staten Island, **Di Fara** in Brooklyn and **Joe's Pizza** in Greenwich Village. And by the latter part of the century, there was practically a pizza shop on every corner, with many selling their slices for a dollar or less.

Today you can't go wrong by ordering from any of the historic pizza joints around the city, or the restaurants of more recent vintage that continue to compete over who makes the most iconic pie in town. A few additional recommendations include **Mama's Too!** on the Upper West Side; **Lucali** in Carroll Gardens and **Ops** in Bushwick, both in Brooklyn; **Roberta's**, with locations in Brooklyn and Manhattan; and **Juliana's Pizza** in Brooklyn Heights. And while some of these spots offer sit-down dining, you'll do just as well to order a slice to go from the neighborhood shop. Be sure to eat it while walking quickly down the street, keeping your eyes open for the next pizza place to try.

417

New York-style bagel

A puffy New York-style bagel is nothing like the flat, doughy rolls you'll typically find in mainstream supermarkets. The inside is chewy and dense, while the outside has a crispy crust, sporting a rich brown color that may be covered with sesame or poppy seeds, dried onions or garlic or an egg wash. And while cinnamon raisin is an acceptable variety, traditional bakers wouldn't even think about flavoring one with blueberries, as connoisseurs of New York bagels consider that, well, unholy.

Many Big Apple bakers believe that the reason their bagels are superior to those found in other cities is the mineral content and softness of New York City water, which is said to strengthen the gluten in the yeasted dough. But others say it's because of the cooking technique, which includes boiling the rings in water that's been enriched with barley malt, and then baking the dough in the oven.

Recipes for the first New York City bagels arrived with the Jewish immigrants who came from Poland as well as other areas of Eastern Europe in the late 1800s. By the early 20th century, the Lower East Side was dotted with hundreds of small privately owned bagel bakeries, with craftsmen often working long hours for little pay. Conditions began to improve with the establishment of Bagel Bakers Local 338, a labor union that helped set standards for handmade bagel production. It remained a significant force in the industry until the 1960s, when automation made the bagel widely available in supermarkets and in communities across the country.

While some prefer spreading New York-style bagels with butter or whitefish salad, they're best when eaten with a schmear of cream cheese and the type of smoked salmon called Nova lox, along with slices of red onions and tomatoes as well as capers. And there's rarely any reason to toast a bagel – they're far superior when eaten warm within a few hours after baking.

New Yorkers, naturally, have strong opinions about where to find the best bagels in the city. But a few standouts include **Absolute Bagels** on the Upper West Side (my favorite bagel stop when I'm in town); **Russ & Daughters** on the Lower East Side, notable for the quality and variety of its salmon offerings; **Tompkins Square Bagels** in the East Village, which bucks tradition with flavors like French toast and pumpkin; **Ess-a-Bagel** in Midtown, which features dozens of kinds of cream cheese and other spreads; and **Hot Bagels** in Brooklyn's Williamsburg neighborhood. And several of these bakeries will ship their products nationwide, so you don't have to subject yourself to the bread-with-a-hole that your local grocery store pretends is actually a bagel.

Pizza bagel

The pizza bagel wasn't invented in New York, but it was only a matter of time before two of the city's most famous foods swiped right and met their better half.

A pizza bagel is simply a sliced bagel that's covered with tomato sauce, mozzarella cheese and other toppings characteristically found on a pizza. It first became popular in the 1970s, when restauranteurs in the suburbs of Los Angeles, Boston and Cleveland all created similar mashups. (It's unclear which came first, but Richard Katz of **Katz Bagel Bakery** in Chelsea, Massachusetts, and Bruce Treitman, who worked at **Western Bagel** in Woodland Hills, California, have had a long-running feud over the issue.)

The dish developed nationwide appeal after Bob Mosher and Stanley Garczynski, a pair of recreational tennis partners in Fort Myers, Florida, created the brand called Bagel Bites in 1985. These miniature frozen pizza bagels could be cooked in a toaster oven or microwave, and were a cultural touchstone for kids of all ages in the late 1980s and 1990s.

When you can't decide between a slice of pizza and a bagel, a few spots to get a pizza bagel include **Tompkins Square Bagels** in the East Village, which layers marinara sauce, mozzarella and basil on the bagel of your choice; **Black Seed Bagels**, with 10 locations in Manhattan and Brooklyn that offer open-face cheese or pepperoni pizza bagels; and **Utopia Bagels** in Queens, where you can order a pair of pizza bagel wheels (the two halves of a giant bagel) that weigh 10 pounds and serve dozens of people. It's a great choice for a party or for your next speed dating event – and if you're lucky, you'll find a match as equally suitable for you as a pizza and a bagel are for each other.

Bialy

In the bakeries of New York City, the bialy practically hides in obscurity, especially when compared to its far more illustrious cousin the bagel. But it's equally worthy of attention as one of the city's signature breads.

Like a bagel, a bialy is a round, yeasted roll with a chewy interior, but that's where the similarities end. Instead of a hole in the middle, a bialy has a depression that's usually filled with chopped sweet onions and poppy seeds. It's much flatter than a traditional bagel (although some bakeries do sell flattened bagels, which blurs the distinction). The dough is immediately baked, rather than being boiled and then baked. And a bialy is typically eaten plain or with butter, instead of with cream cheese and lox.

The bialy came to New York City with Jewish immigrants from a town called Bialystock, Poland, in the late 1800s, where the bread was originally called Bialystoker Kuchen, a Yiddish phrase meaning little bread from Bialystock. It became popular in the Jewish community on the Lower East Side, but never achieved the mass appeal of the bagel, and today can rarely be found outside of New York City.

The oldest bialy bakery still in operation is **Kossar's Bagels & Bialys**, which opened in 1936 and now has locations on the Lower East Side and Upper East Side. Other great places to try a bialy include **Best Bagel & Coffee** in midtown Manhattan; **Hot Bialys & Bagels** in Queens; the misleadingly named **Brooklyn Bagel & Coffee Company**, with stores in both Manhattan and Queens (but not Brooklyn); and **Liberty Bagels**, which also has multiple locations in Manhattan and Queens. Sometimes the bialy appears on menus as a flavor of bagel, but don't be fooled – it's a completely different food. And even if it's not as famous as its hole-y cousin, it still deserves a spot in your breakfast rotation.

Pastrami

The smoked meat known as pastrami became famous in the signature sandwich served at New York City's kosher Jewish delicatessens. But its roots are actually Romanian, and it has ancestry that goes all the way back to ancient Turkey.

Pastrami is typically prepared with beef, usually fatty cuts like brisket or round, that's brined and seasoned with herbs and spices such as black pepper, mustard seed and coriander. It's then smoked, steamed and sliced, and served warm in overstuffed sandwiches on rye bread with spicy brown mustard, with dill pickles on the side. Some restaurants use a similar cooking method to make pastrami with turkey, pork or even salmon.

The introduction of pastrami to New York City is credited to Sussman Volk, a Lithuanian immigrant who began serving it in his butcher shop on Delancey Street in 1887. Volk got the recipe from a Romanian friend, who, like many of his countrymen, cooked a dish called basturma or pastirma – sometimes made with goose – that used salt and spices as a way of preserving meat. And this technique originally came from the Ottoman Turks, who employed it for drying lean cuts of beef, goat and mutton.

It's believed that the word pastirma evolved into pastrami because of the latter's lexical similarity to salami, another cured meat sold at local butchers. And as pastrami started to grow in popularity, Volk opened what's considered to be the first New York Jewish deli, with many competitors soon following on his heels.

One of these is perhaps the most famous place to eat a pastrami on rye, **Katz's Delicatessen**, which opened in 1888 on the Lower East Side and may be even more well-known as the setting for an iconic scene in the movie When Harry Met Sally. But there are dozens of other worthy spots to get your pastrami fix around the city, too. A few standouts include **2nd Avenue Deli**, an old-school kosher restaurant on Manhattan's Upper East Side; **Sarge's Delicatessen and Diner** in Midtown, featuring sandwiches piled high with thinly sliced pastrami; and **Frankel's Delicatessen and Appetizing** in the Greenpoint section of Brooklyn, a breakfast and lunch joint that serves hand-carved meat on either rye bread or a challah roll. And if you want to be reminded of where pastrami came from, just order a second sandwich – one containing both turkey and romaine(ian) lettuce.

Reuben

It's often recounted that New York City's other classic sandwich, the Reuben, originated when Arnold Reuben, the owner of Reuben's Restaurant and Deli in the theater district, created a special menu item for an actress named Annette Seelos in 1914.

Sounds like your conventional food origin story, right? Unfortunately, there are a few problems with it. While Reuben made his sandwich on rye bread with Swiss cheese, coleslaw and Russian dressing – key ingredients in our conception of the Reuben today – the meats he used were ham and turkey, not corned beef. And missing in the historical account is any mention of the actress's sandwich being grilled, another important quality of a modern Reuben.

Those discrepancies are why some people believe that the Reuben was actually invented in Omaha, Nebraska. A grocery store owner there named Reuben Kulakofsky, sometimes called Reuben Kay, was said to have requested a special dish at the Blackstone Hotel where he played his weekly poker game in the late 1920s. The European-trained chef, Bernard Schimmel, whose father owned the hotel, went all-in with a sandwich of corned beef, Swiss cheese, sauerkraut and Russian dressing on rye bread, which he grilled and served with a sliced kosher dill pickle, a rose radish and potato chips. It was such a winning hand that the Blackstone soon put the Reuben on its lunch menu. In 1956, a local who worked at one of the elder Schimmel's other hotels submitted the sandwich in a national contest, and its victory helped cement the Reuben's popularity in Omaha.

But few people today associate the sandwich as strongly with Nebraska as they do with New York City. Because a Reuben isn't kosher (since it mixes meat and dairy), it's ironic that some of the best spots for it are also restaurants where you can enjoy classic Jewish specialties like knishes and matzo ball soup. A few options include **Court Street Grocers**, with locations in the Carroll Gardens section of Brooklyn and in Manhattan's Washington Square; **Katz's Delicatessen** on the Lower East Side; **Stage Door Delicatessen** in lower Manhattan; and **S&P Lunch** near Madison Square.

Not surprisingly, New Yorkers tend to have strong opinions about this dish. So if you want to eat a sandwich that mirrors the actress's, with ham and turkey instead of corned beef, just know that you probably shouldn't call it a Reuben.

Chopped cheese

For some New Yorkers, a morning ritual is heading to the corner bodega for a cup of coffee and a bacon, egg and cheese on a soft roll, a sandwich that's fried on the grill behind the counter and wrapped up in a neat foil package. But for others, the neighborhood deli is the place to get your lunch on the go, and a favorite order is the chopped cheese sandwich.

A chopped cheese, sometimes known as chop cheese, is a sandwich made with ground beef that's broken up on the grill with a metal spatula as it cooks. The meat is combined with onions (and sometimes peppers) as well as melted American cheese, and is served on a hero roll with lettuce, tomatoes and condiments such as mayonnaise and ketchup.

The chopped cheese originated at an East Harlem bodega called **Blue Sky Deli**, also known as Hajji's, in the 1990s. There are several stories about its invention. Some say the sandwich was created by a cook named Carlos Soto, who ran out of hamburger buns one day and chopped up the cheeseburger he was grilling to make it fit on the rolls he had in stock. Others claim it was an adaptation of a Yemeni specialty of chopped meat and vegetables called dagha yamneeya that was developed by the workers at Hajji's, many of whom came from that country.

For many years the chopped cheese was not well-known outside Harlem and the Bronx, where it was an inexpensive and sometimes messy specialty. But in the past decade, the sandwich has been featured in an episode of the late Anthony Bourdain's show Parts Unknown, in numerous articles and food blogs, as well as in several rap videos, including one by Harlem artist Cam'ron. It's also been the subject of countless conversations about cultural appropriation, as white restauranteurs in Manhattan as well as in cities across the U.S. have put fancy versions of the sandwich on their menus, with prices to match.

You'll find excellent versions of the chopped cheese sandwich in every borough of New York City, but a good place to start is **Hajji's**, which is open 24 hours. Other great options include **Yankee Twin Eatery** in the Bronx; **Fillmore Delicatessen** and **1773 Deli & Convenience Store** on the Upper East Side and

Fancy NY Grill and Deli in the East Village, all in Manhattan; **Astoria Deli** in Queens; **L Stop Gourmet Deli** in Brooklyn; and **The Sandwich Shop** in Staten Island. Most of these places have an astounding number of items on their menus, but the chopped cheese is a reliably tasty choice in any neighborhood.

Delmonico steak

Delmonico's in lower Manhattan has numerous claims to fame in American culinary history. It's the place where diners first had the option to order individual meals off a menu, and the earliest spot where women were allowed to eat unaccompanied by men, in 1868. Its long-time chef, Charles Ranhofer, was purported to have had a hand in the invention of baked Alaska (as well as eggs Benedict and lobster Newberg, both discussed later in this chapter), and his successor to have created the wedge salad. And Delmonico's is also known for a thick cut of steak that's become synonymous with high-quality beef.

A Delmonico steak isn't a specific part of the cow, though. Although there's only scant evidence about which cut the original steak actually was, today it usually refers to either boneless top loin or ribeye, and is sometimes sold at butcher shops and grocery stores labeled with the restaurant's name.

Shortly after Delmonico's opened in 1837, its namesake steak became one of the signature menu items. From accounts left by several chefs who worked at Delmonico's, it's believed to have been a thick sirloin that was seasoned with salt and pepper and broiled, and accompanied by either Bordelaise sauce, gravy or compound butter. The meat was often served alongside Delmonico potatoes, the restaurant's house spuds, a dish consisting of shredded potatoes that were combined with milk, heavy cream and nutmeg, topped with Parmesan cheese and baked.

Now that the flagship restaurant has reopened after the pandemic, you can once again order a steak called Delmonico at Delmonico's. But when you choose the boneless ribeye at **DK Restaurant NYC** in midtown Manhattan, you'll also essentially be eating one, because its menu alludes to the steak's origin at its sister restaurant. Or visit **Barnea Bistro**, also in Midtown, and select the filet de boeuf or cote de boeuf, and your dish will be prepared with a 28-day dry-aged Delmonico. And at **Reserve Cut** in the Financial District, you have the option of a 16-ounce Delmonico for your umami olive-fed wagyu, a Kosher variety of beef that's butchered from Tajima cattle. While you eat, you can thank Delmonico's not only for the cut of your steak, but for the innovations that allow you to order exactly what you want off the menu – and if you're a woman, that give you the ability to dine, should you so desire, without a man to keep you company.

Steak Diane

By the middle of the 20th century, diners at several of New York City's most exclusive restaurants could order a luxurious dish with a theatrical preparation – steak Diane, beef cooked in a brandy-infused sauce that floor captains flambéed tableside.

It's unknown who invented steak Diane, although it's thought that it was created in Europe in the 1930s, and that the name comes from Diana, the Roman goddess of the hunt. The dish is similar to a French preparation called steak au poivre, in which thinly pounded tenderloin or strip steak is coated with peppercorns and accompanied by a rich sauce made with butter and cognac. Ingredients often vary, but the sauce that's served with steak Diane generally includes shallots, Dijon mustard, Worcestershire sauce and cognac or sherry, and the beef is customarily garnished with chives or parsley.

One theory about the provenance of steak Diane is that it was introduced at New York City's Drake Hotel by Beniamino Schiavon, a European-trained chef known as Nino of the Drake, in the late 1940s or early 1950s. But other high-end dining spots, including the Sherry-Netherland Hotel, the Colony Restaurant and the 21 Club, were known to have their own versions of the dish around the same time.

Few restaurants prepare steak Diane today, as the dish tends to be seen as a vestige of mid-century extravagance. But you can still order it at **Henry's End** in Brooklyn and **Carbone** in Greenwich Village, as well as at **Allora Ristorante**, which has a pair of locations in midtown Manhattan. The latter spot still ignites the sauce tableside, a showy display that, provided it doesn't light your hair on fire, will remind you that flamboyant derives from the French word for flame.

Lobster Newberg

Anyone who's watched (or read) the Stephen King tale The Shining probably picked up on the significance of the word REDRUM, an anagram for murder. And a similar transposition of letters is purported to be a significant milestone in the history of a decadent dish known as lobster Newberg.

Lobster Newberg consists of chunks of the crustacean that are cooked in a cream sauce containing egg yolks, clarified butter and sherry or Madeira wine that's spiced with cayenne pepper. The dish is usually served warm on toast points, with other seafood such as shrimp commonly substituted for the lobster.

Newberg may not have been the original name of this preparation, though, and that's where the anagram comes in. As the story goes, a sea captain in the fruit trade named Ben Wenberg (see where this is going?) is said to have given the idea for the dish to the owner of **Delmonico's**, Charles Delmonico, in 1876. Soon after, the establishment's chef, Charles Ranhofer, added it to the menu as Lobster a la Wenberg, nodding to the sea captain. But either because of an argument between Delmonico and Wenberg, or the latter's desire to remain anonymous, the dish's name was eventually changed to Lobster a la Newberg, and then shortened to lobster Newberg (sometimes spelled as Newburg).

Unfortunately, there's little historical evidence to support this entertaining account. Lobster Newberg wasn't documented in recipes until the late 1880s, and only appeared in Ranhofer's cookbook in 1894, the year after the sauce was featured in a shrimp dish presented at the Columbian Exposition in Chicago.

Delmonico's is now reopened after a long pandemic shutdown, so it's once again a good place to sample this elegant preparation. A couple of other spots that offer it include **DK Restaurant NYC**, an offshoot of the steakhouse where it was first served, and **The Grill**, both located in midtown Manhattan. And on City Island in the Bronx, you can try the dish at **Sea Shore Restaurant**, which provides a choice of lobster, shrimp or a mix of seafood, all accompanied by Newberg sauce. If you decide to stick with the original preparation but feel like playing word games with your waiter, just ask for an order of bolster Wenberg.

Manhattan-style clam chowder

The tomato-based version of clam chowder that originated in New York in the late 19th century is nothing if not controversial. New England travel writer Eleanor Early once suggested that Manhattan-style clam chowder and its New England cousin should never be spoken about in the same breath, because, she wrote, "tomatoes and clams have no more affinity than ice cream and horseradish." And cookbook writer James Beard described the dish as "a vegetable soup that accidentally had some clams dumped into it."

Recipes for Manhattan-style clam chowder call for tomatoes and tomato paste, instead of the cream that's a hallmark of the New England variety. This style of chowder tends to have a thinner broth than the New England version, and incorporates more vegetables, including carrots and celery. The soup also contains seasonings such as thyme and oregano that complement the tomato.

Although New England clam chowder dates back to at least the 1830s, the Manhattan version didn't get its geographic designation until a century later, in a 1934 cookbook. The idea for using tomatoes in a seafood soup probably came from Portuguese and Italian fishermen, who were both known to feature the ingredient in traditional dishes. (The same influence is also why you'll find a hint of tomato in some chowders served in Rhode Island.)

Manhattan-style chowder was first codified, without its current name, in the late 1800s in a pair of cookbooks written by chefs who had worked at **Delmonico's**, Alessandro Filippini and Charles Ranhofer, as well as in another from 1893, where the soup was called Coney Island-style chowder. It's likely that this dish, like so many others, was invented at Delmonico's, and its popularity led it to be widely imitated at other restaurants.

This style of chowder remains far less prevalent than the New England version, perhaps for good reason. But if you want to sample it during your trip to New York City, you'll find it at a handful of seafood spots around town, including **Grand Central Oyster Bar** in midtown Manhattan, **Lobster Place** in the Meatpacking District and **Randazzo's Clam Bar** in Brooklyn. And who knows, you might decide you prefer a chowder made with tomatoes over one with more traditional ingredients. But then again, you might be the sort of person who goes to an ice cream parlor and asks for the special horseradish flavor.

Vichyssoise

The velvety soup known as vichyssoise might sound like something that can be eaten any time of year in the fanciest bistros of Paris. But it was actually conceived in New York City as a summertime dish.

Vichyssoise is an adaptation of the French soup called potage Parmentier, or leek and potato soup. Its inventor, Louis Felix Diat, was the head chef at the Ritz-Carlton Hotel in New York. In

1917, he decided to recreate his mother's practice of adding milk to the soup she would typically make him for breakfast in France, to cool it down on warm days. Her recipe included leeks, potatoes and onions that were cooked with butter and chicken broth. After puréeing and straining his version of the soup, Diat mixed in heavy cream to thicken it, and garnished it with chopped chives.

Diat named the dish after Vichy, the spa near his hometown that was located in a region of the country that he recalled having excellent cuisine. The soup immediately became popular among the Ritz-Carlton's celebrity clientele, and a few years after its creation Diat decided to keep it on the hotel's menu year-round.

Though vichyssoise has gradually fallen out of favor, you can still find it at a few restaurants around town, including **La Lanterna di Vittorio** and **Gene's**, a pair of Italian restaurants in Greenwich Village; **William Poll**, a lunch takeout spot on the Upper East Side; and **La Grenouille** in midtown Manhattan, which alters the standard recipe by making the soup with asparagus. Its menu also includes several classic French dishes, but you can impress your dining companions with the knowledge that vichyssoise isn't one of them.

Waldorf salad

Until it closed for long-term renovations in 2017, the Waldorf-Astoria was one of New York City's fanciest hotels, and had a dining scene to match, with sumptuous feasts of lobster and Beluga caviar being offered in its three main restaurants and through room service, a concept it invented. But a humbler dish, the hotel's namesake salad, is the Waldorf's primary culinary legacy.

The first version of the salad was concocted for a charity ball at the hotel in 1896 by Oscar Tschirky, its long-time maître d' who was known as Oscar of the Waldorf and published a cookbook with many of his creations. In its original incarnation, the

Waldorf salad was prepared only with sliced apples and chopped celery that were mixed into a mayonnaise dressing and presented on a bed of lettuce. But by the time the dish appeared in a few early 20th-century cookbooks, it almost always included the walnuts that are now a key ingredient. More recently, some chefs have bulked up the salad by adding green grapes, blue cheese or sliced chicken, while others have lightened it by making the dressing with yogurt.

Adventurous drinkers can also sample a cocktail version of the Waldorf salad, an adaptation of the drink once served at the Waldorf-Astoria's bar, at **Double Chicken Please** in lower Manhattan. But if you're looking for a more conventional presentation of the dish, you can order Waldorf salad at restaurants and cafés all around New York City. A few spots include **Andrews NYC Diner** in midtown Manhattan, which adds chicken and raisins to the classic recipe; **Certé**, a takeout joint near the Museum of Modern Art that folds in dried apricots; and **Le Crocodile**, a French restaurant in Brooklyn where the Waldorf is made with Stilton cheese. Unfortunately, it's still uncertain whether you'll ever again be able to eat the dish in the place where it was invented. There's no word on when the Waldorf-Astoria will reopen any of its restaurants, or whether hotel guests will still have the option of ordering a room-service Waldorf salad, gussied-up like it used to be with celeriac and truffles, and undoubtedly a price to match.

Eggs Benedict

As is the case for many dishes named after wealthy restaurant patrons, there are competing theories as to which Benedict was responsible for the now-classic combination of poached eggs and Hollandaise sauce, accompanied by Canadian bacon and served on an English muffin.

Was it Mrs. LeGrand Benedict, who frequently dined at **Delmonico's**, and in the 1860s, requested something new for lunch from its chef, Charles Ranhofer? Was it Commodore E.C.

Benedict, who in a 1967 letter an acquaintance wrote to the New York Times's dining critic, was credited as its long-ago creator? Or was it Lemuel Benedict, who claimed to the New Yorker in 1942 that a half-century earlier, he had dined at the Waldorf-Astoria Hotel and had asked for poached eggs with Hollandaise sauce, bacon and buttered toast to help relieve his hangover?

The truth remains elusive, but the strongest evidence points to either Delmonico's, whose chef published the recipe for "eggs a la Benedick" in his 1894 cookbook, or the Waldorf, whose maître d', Oscar Tschirky, had previously worked at Delmonico's and may have adapted the hung-over diner's request into the form of the dish that's typically served today. It's unlikely that the Commodore's account has much merit, especially because the sauce he was said to employ included chopped ham and hot hard-boiled eggs, instead of the creamy version that's typically prepared only with egg yolks, melted butter and lemon juice.

Eggs Benedict is usually served at diners and cafés as a hearty brunch dish, and is often adapted by substituting other meats or vegetables for the classic ingredients. Unfortunately, you won't be able to judge the competing historical claims for yourself, as the restaurants at the Waldorf-Astoria remain closed, and Delmonico's is no longer serving its signature breakfast item.

A few spots where you will find eggs Benedict in New York City, though, include **Russ & Daughters Cafe** in the Lower East Side, where the poached eggs are served with smoked salmon on challah; **Bubby's** in Tribeca, where the Benny comes with a choice of Canadian bacon, smoked salmon or avocado and tomato; and **Mansion Diner** on the Upper East Side, which serves up a classic version on an English muffin with Canadian bacon. And as you eat your meal, consider how lucky we are that the inspiration for this dish wasn't the British actor known for playing Doctor Strange. Instead of eggs Benedict, we might be brunching on a menu item called eggs Cumberbatch. On second thought, maybe eggs Benedict would have been its name after all.

New York-style cheesecake

The creamy, dense cake that's a signature dessert of the Big Apple can be prepared with just a few ingredients, including sour cream, eggs, sugar and vanilla. But it wouldn't be complete without a product invented in New York but marketed as being from somewhere else – Philadelphia cream cheese.

Long before the cheesecake ever came to New York City, similar confections had been eaten across Europe, using cheeses such as ricotta in Italy, Neufchâtel in France, and feta and mizithra in Greece. But in 1872, when a Chester, New York, dairy farmer named William A. Lawrence was attempting to recreate the French cheese in America, he stumbled upon a process that would, decades later, result in the widespread availability of cream cheese. It was sold under the Philadelphia label, which Kraft Foods eventually purchased in 1928, because contemporary shoppers were more inclined to associate creaminess with the dairy farms of Pennsylvania than with New York.

One year later, a Manhattan deli owner named Arnold Reuben (the same man who may have played a key role in the history of the sandwich that shares his surname) started experimenting with using the product in a batter that he baked in a crumb crust. The sweet cake's creamy texture was far superior to the grainy cheese pies that were common at the time, and the dish became popular at his restaurant, which was a favorite of politicians like Mayor Fiorello La Guardia as well as local celebrities.

The cheesecake gained an even stronger foothold in New York City cuisine when a competing deli, Lindy's, lured a cook away from Reuben's and started serving its own version of the dessert in the 1930s. Lindy's cheesecake was made with a graham-cracker crust and was often topped with gelled strawberries, and became so iconic that it was mentioned in the musical Guys and Dolls. And in 1948, when new frozen-food technology inspired an entrepreneur named Charles W. Lubin to name a cheesecake after his daughter, Sara Lee, the New York-born dessert became widely available in grocery store freezers across the country.

Both Reuben's and Lindy's are relics of New York City history, but the cheesecake lives on at bakeries and restaurants all over town. (And if you live far away and need a frozen one that isn't Sara Lee, many NYC stores sell them online.) The most iconic place to try a slice is **Junior's**, with locations in Brooklyn and Manhattan that offer the traditional plain variety as well as flavors such as cherry crumb, chocolate swirl and lemon coconut. Other top options in Manhattan include **Sarge's Delicatessen & Diner** in Murray Hill, **Veniero's** in the East Village, **Eileen's Special Cheesecake** in Nolita and **Ferrara Bakery & Cafe** in Little Italy. And for diners who want to say fuhgeddaboudit to Philadelphia cream cheese, the latter spot also offers a lighter, Italian-style cheesecake made with ricotta.

Black and white cookie

"If people would only look to the cookie, all our problems would be solved," says Jerry Seinfeld in a 1994 episode of his namesake TV show. The comedian posits that the round, cake-like confection – half frosted with vanilla icing and half with chocolate – is a metaphor for racial harmony. But for most New Yorkers, it's nothing more than a local delicacy sold in corner bodegas and fancy bakeries alike.

The black and white cookie was likely invented at Glaser's Bake Shop in Manhattan, a store opened by a Bavarian couple, John and Justine Glaser, in 1902. But around the same time, a Utica shop named Hemstrought's Bakery had started selling a pastry it called the half-moon, possibly in an effort to use up leftover cake batter at the end of the day. Unlike the black and white, which is traditionally made with a light-colored, citrus-infused cake that's sometimes iced with fondant, the half-moon consisted of a domed chocolate cake (although vanilla could also be used), frosted with equal amounts of vanilla buttercream and chocolate fudge.

That confection remains popular in upstate New York as well as in Boston, and the distinction between the two desserts is sometimes hazy. But by the middle of the 20th century, the black and white cookie had become a fixture of Jewish-American culture in New York City. It was also a staple at a handful of Italian bakeries, where a layer of apricot jam was often added under the fondant.

Today you'll find these treats in shops all over Manhattan, including **Russ & Daughters** and **Moishe's Kosher Bakery** on the Lower East Side, **Zabar's** on the Upper West Side, **Empire Cake** in Chelsea, **Pasticceria Rocco** in Greenwich Village and **William Greenberg Desserts**, with a pair of locations on opposite sides of Central Park.

Regardless of whether you get your cookie from one of these places, or from the neighborhood deli, you'll have to make one more important decision: whether to bite into the chocolate side or the vanilla side first, or to eat them together. Perhaps we should look to the cookie for an answer. True, the black and white might not do anything for race relations. But as Seinfeld points out, nothing mixes better than vanilla and chocolate.

Egg cream

To channel Linda Richman, Mike Myers's character from the Saturday Night Live sketch Coffee Talk, chickpeas are neither a chick nor a pea, jelly beans are neither made of jelly nor are they a bean – and an egg cream contains neither eggs nor cream. Let's discuss.

Other New York City dishes to sample:

- **Hot dogs, soft pretzels and more** from the roving vendors that you'll find on every corner of the city, especially in Manhattan. New York City has a more vibrant street-food scene than perhaps any place else in the country, and you could tour the world by eating nothing but ethnic specialties during an entire visit. A few favorite bites include souvlaki, chunks of lamb piled in a warm pita with tzatziki sauce; chicken shawarma, topped with a creamy white or spicy red sauce and served in a platter with yellow rice and salad (**The Halal Guys**, a cart in midtown Manhattan, is its most famous purveyor); knishes, dough stuffed with a mixture of mashed potatoes and onions and often dipped in spicy brown mustard; falafel, fried chickpea fritters best eaten hot with pickled vegetables; and much, much more (with vendors who come and go and change locations frequently). And although it's a brick-and-mortar restaurant, not a mobile stand, don't miss trying an all-beef hot dog from **Gray's Papaya**, accompanied by a drink made with its namesake ingredient or other fruits.
- **Bagel dog**, a hot dog wrapped in a doughy bagel-like breading that's topped with sesame or poppy seeds and then baked. It's typically sold in supermarket frozen-food sections, but can also be found at some bagel bakeries in New York City (as well as in Chicago and Cincinnati). One place where you can try one is **BO's Bagels** in Harlem.

- **Chicken Divan**, a casserole made with chicken that's cooked with broccoli in a Mornay sauce, a bechamel with the addition of grated or shredded cheese. The dish was invented at New York City's Divan Parisien Restaurant at the Chatham Hotel in the early 20th century. It's rarely found today outside of home kitchens, but you can still order it at **Cooper Town**, a diner in Gramercy Park.
- **Pastelón**, a casserole of plantains, ground beef, vegetables and spices that's sometimes described as Puerto Rican lasagna. The dish is said to have been invented in New York City when Puerto Ricans adapted a specialty of the Italians who lived nearby using familiar ingredients, and later brought it to their home island. One place you'll find it, as an occasional special and on the catering menu, is **The Freakin Rican** in the Astoria neighborhood of Queens.
- **Potatoes O'Brien**, a side dish consisting of pan-fried potatoes cooked with red and green bell peppers, onions and sometimes bacon. It's believed to have been invented in the early 1900s at a Manhattan restaurant called Jack's, an all-night establishment frequented by politicians and celebrities, although its provenance may also be a Boston restaurant called Jerome's. You can try this long-forgotten dish at **The Grill**, which offers hashbrown O'Brien as an accompaniment to prime rib.

An egg cream is an old-fashioned, frothy drink served in a tall glass that's made with just three ingredients – milk, seltzer (carbonated water) and a flavored syrup, usually chocolate or vanilla. It's believed to have been invented in the early 1900s by a candy-store owner named Louis Auster. Within a few decades, he was selling 3,000 egg creams every day at his Brooklyn shop, and refused to give up his recipe to competitors – but that didn't stop them from copying the successful idea. When other soda fountains in the Jewish communities in his neighborhood as well as the Lower East Side started selling the drink, many used a syrup called Fox's U-Bet (named after a Texas expression for quality) that was created by a Brooklynite named Herman Fox. Today's egg cream connoisseurs believe that this syrup is mandatory to make an egg cream properly – along with pouring the seltzer from a siphon, not a bottle. Some food historians speculate that egg whites may have been used in the drink's early days to make it frothy, and that the name comes from the idea that the drink was a downtown version of a fancy soda fountain drink made with cream. But it's more likely that the egg cream was actually an Anglicized version of the Yiddish phrase echt keem, meaning pure sweetness.

When you're thirsty for a nostalgic beverage, you'll find egg creams on menus all over the city, but especially in the neighborhoods where the drink first became popular. A few of the best options include **Russ & Daughters**, which makes a traditional egg cream, and **Shopsin's** (where you can try an orange-flavored version, in addition to the standard varieties), both on the Lower East Side; **Ray's Candy Store** in Ukrainian Village, where the drink is offered in a colorful array of flavors including cherry and mango; **Square Diner** in Tribeca, housed in a renovated train car; **Brooklyn Farmacy & Soda Fountain**, located in that borough's Cobble Hill; and **Juliana's Pizza** in Brooklyn Heights – where the egg cream is actually made with cream. But you'll have to look to a different restaurant if you have a hankering for some eggs. Maybe you can order some for breakfast along with a bowl of Grape-Nuts, which, as Linda Richman reminds us, contains neither grapes nor nuts.

Buffalo

Buffalo wings

Eating in Buffalo without ordering wings would be like taking a trip to Paris and skipping the Eiffel Tower. And while you can sample this New York-born specialty anywhere, and you'll find its spicy sauce on pizza, fried cauliflower and just about anything that needs a little extra kick, devouring a plate of wings in the Nickel City will deepen your appreciation for what makes locals tick – aside from coping with winter blizzards and hoping the Bills will finally win the Super Bowl.

Buffalo wings are parts of the chicken – usually the flap or drumette, although boneless "wings," made from chunks of the breast, are also popular – that are deep-fried without breading, and then coated in a mixture of a vinegar-based hot sauce (often Frank's RedHot) and melted butter. The wings can come in a wide range of flavors, textures and spiciness levels, but any heat will be offset by the blue cheese dressing that's usually served on the side, along with carrot and celery sticks.

The oft-repeated legend is that Buffalo wings were invented at a local tavern called **Anchor Bar** in 1964, when owner Teressa Bellissimo decided to create a snack for her son, Dominic, and his college friends, and chose Frank's as the base for her coating because it shared a name with her husband. But historians say that the story is more complicated. Chicken wings had long been eaten in Buffalo, despite being a less desirable part of the bird that was more often used in stocks and sauces. And at a restaurant called Wings & Things, opened in the 1960s by John Young, another key player in the local spread of wings, diners could enjoy deep-fried breaded chicken in a sweet, tomato-based condiment that he called Mambo (sometimes referred to as Mumbo) sauce. (A similar sauce is a staple condiment in Washington, D.C.)

Leaving aside the question of whose chicken wings came first, the dish gained popularity in Buffalo throughout the 1970s, and started to achieve nationwide recognition after several chain restaurants began serving it during the following decade. Today you can eat Buffalo wings just about anywhere, unless there's a repeat of the 2021 nationwide chicken wing shortage, which caused prices to skyrocket and many diners to opt for the boneless versions that cost fewer Buffalo nickels.

A few of the top places to order Buffalo wings in the Nickel City include Anchor Bar, which now has a half-dozen locations in upstate New York (including the original in Buffalo, called **Frank & Teressa's Anchor Bar**) as well as branches in Texas, Georgia, Illinois and Maryland; **Duff's Famous Wings** in Amherst; **Wingnutz** in North Buffalo and Amherst; and also in Buffalo, **Nine-Eleven Tavern** and **Roaming Bison Tavern**. The latter just might be the most appropriate place to order wings in town, as there's a buffalo right in its name. It'll be a great spot to visit in 2032, when the city will celebrate its bison-tennial.

Beef on weck

Until 1998, the chain called **Buffalo Wild Wings** that helped popularize the city's most famous food had an extra W in its name. The business was known as BW3 – with the last letter standing for weck, the roll that's as integral to Buffalo's signature sandwich as hot sauce and blue cheese are to its chicken.

Weck is short for kummelweck, a type of soft German roll that's sprinkled with caraway seeds and pretzel salt, and rarely baked outside of the Buffalo area. To make a beef on weck, the bread is sliced in half and piled high with rare, thinly carved roast beef, with the top of the roll dipped in jus and spread with horseradish. The sandwich is often served with a dill pickle on the side as well as French fries.

Beef on weck likely originated in 1901 when a man named John Gohn opened a boarding house and tavern for visitors coming to the city for the Pan American Exposition. Gohn employed a German baker, William Wahr, who was familiar with the kummelweck roll, and suggested that its saltiness would help Gohn sell more beer to the thirsty travelers. The roast beef sandwich soon became popular at other restaurants, including **Schwabl's** in the nearby town of West Seneca, which opened in 1837 and has been serving the beef on weck continually since at least 1901. (Some say that Wahr worked for this restaurant, and that it was actually the originator of the beef on weck, although there isn't clear documentary evidence for that claim.)

Numerous historic pubs and restaurants around Buffalo feature the beef on weck, including **Charlie the Butcher's**, which operates a handful of locations in town and outlying suburbs, and also serves the sandwich at Buffalo Bisons minor league baseball games at **Sahlen Field**; **Union Pub**, a downtown tavern dating back to 1864; **Eddie Brady's**, a restaurant of more recent vintage with an old-time atmosphere; **Bar-Bill Tavern** in East Aurora and Clarence, which also offers a beef on weck pizza; and **Glen Park Tavern**, which opened in 1887 along a stagecoach route in Williamsville. But you won't find a beef on weck at the local branch of Buffalo Wild Wings – the chain erased the sandwich from its menu along with the superfluous W.

Pączki

See Other foods of the Midwest

With more than 10 percent of the city's population having Polish ancestry, it's not surprising that pączki are a popular Buffalo treat in the week before Lent begins. One place you can get these donuts is **Mazurek's Bakery**, which fills them with black raspberry jam and sells them not only on Fat Tuesday but also on Fridays and Saturdays throughout the year.

Sponge candy

The delicate honeycomb confection that locals call sponge candy is popular year-round, but you'll want to bring a cooler if you're buying some during the summer.

The bubbles that give the candy its name are the result of a chemical reaction between baking soda and vinegar, which leaves tiny air pockets inside the golden-brown toffee center that's made from a mixture of brown sugar, corn syrup and water. The candy is typically coated in milk or dark chocolate, sometimes enriched with orange or other flavors. But that layer doesn't protect the delicate inside from melting during hot or humid weather, which is why sponge candy, similar to Southern divinity, is best enjoyed during the cooler months.

Another Buffalo dish to sample:

- **Pizza logs**, egg roll wrappers filled with mozzarella cheese and pizza toppings, and served with a side of marinara sauce. They're commonly eaten as a snack in the Buffalo area (as well as in Pittsburgh), and you can find well-regarded versions at **Bar-Bill Tavern** in East Aurora and Clarence, as well as at **Sal's** in Depew.

It's not known who introduced sponge candy to Buffalo, though it's also eaten in other parts of U.S. and in other countries under a variety of names, including sea foam (a slightly different version), fairy food candy and hokey pokey. One of the earliest purveyors in Buffalo was Joseph Fowler, who sold chocolates at the Pan American Exposition in 1901 after having lived in England and Canada. More than a century after he opened a candy store with his brother Claude, **Fowler's** now produces over 35,000 pounds of sponge candy annually, and sells it at five locations in the Buffalo area as well as online.

You'll also find sponge candy at confectioners all over town, several of which have multiple branches. A few standouts include **Watson's Chocolates**, which has been in business for more than 75 years and has been frequently declared to have the city's best sponge candy; **Parkside Candy** in Buffalo, Tonawanda and Williamsville; **Alethea's Chocolates** in Williamsville; **Platter's Chocolate Factory** in North Tonawanda, which sells the traditional flavors as well as a variety with peanut butter; and **Mike's Homemade Candies** in Cheektowaga, which also makes a raspberry version. And if it's cool enough for sponge candy but you don't want to venture outdoors, rest assured that many of these spots will also sell their sweets online.

ROCHESTER

Garbage plate

A city that's the headquarters of the Eastman Kodak photography company has a signature food that's one of the least photogenic dishes imaginable – the local specialty known as the garbage plate.

A garbage plate is a hodgepodge of meats such as hamburger patties, hot dogs and sausages, side dishes like home fries, macaroni salad and baked beans and condiments including meat sauce, mustard, onions, ketchup and hot sauce. All of the components are mixed together by the eater before digging in, except for the bread and butter that's typically served on the side and is used to sop up any remnants while cleaning the plate.

This dish originated at a restaurant called Nick Tahou Hots, which opened in 1918 and was famous for its combination plates of hots (red or white sausages) and potatoes. When some college students came in one night during the 1980s and asked for a plate "with all the garbage on it," the owner concocted a mishmash he called the garbage plate, a term he eventually trademarked in 1992.

At restaurants around town, the dish has a variety of ingredients and is known by an assortment of other names, including sloppy plate, junkyard dog plate and dumpster plate. But if you just ask for a plate, everyone will know exactly what you mean.

The garbage plate doesn't sound that appetizing, but if you want to indulge, a few of the most popular places to get one include **Bill Gray's**, where you can choose among cheeseburgers, hots and ground steak on top of a pair of side dishes; **Tom Wahl's**, which offers "55 Junker" plates in honor of the year the chain was founded; **Fairport Hots**, where you can select up to four meats and two sides; and **The Red Fern**, which offers a vegan version called the Compost Plate. And if you attend a Red Wings minor league baseball game at **Innovative Field** on Thursdays, you can pick up a "trash can" from the concession stand and watch the team play as the Rochester Plates. It's a good bet their uniforms will be far more picture-worthy than the food you'll be eating while watching the game.

White hot

Red hot dogs used to contain the best-quality meats available, with its paler sibling comprised of the cheaper cuts and various fillers. But today, the red version is a common hot dog, and Rochester shines its white-hot spotlight on a big-shot combination of fancy meats like pork, veal and beef.

The white hot originated in Rochester's German community, where it was known as a white and porky. Beginning in 1925, the hot dog was commercially produced by a local butcher named Zweigle's. The meats it uses are uncured and unsmoked, which preserves their white color, and they're mixed with a variety of herbs and spices including mustard and paprika. Locals typically grill them over charcoal, and eat them on buns, topped with mustard and chopped onions.

Zweigle's sells its white hots at area sports stadiums and arenas, but you can also enjoy them around town at places such as **Dogtown**, **Empire Hots**, **Webster Hots**, **Henrietta Hots** and **Vasko's on Park**. Or pick up a pack at a grocery store in Western New York and prepare them at home – but be sure to wait to start cooking until your grill gets white hot.

UTICA

Chicken riggies

New York-based food podcaster Dan Pashman, host of The Sporkful, has invented three new pasta shapes in recent years – cascatelli, a ruffled semicircle named after the Italian word for waterfalls; quattrotini, a short tube with four narrow channels at each corner; and vesuvio, whose spirals resemble a volcano. But in upstate New York's Oneida County, there's no room for innovation around its local specialty. The dish called chicken riggies is prepared with a much more traditional shape, rigatoni.

Chicken riggies is a mixture of poultry and pasta that's combined with a spicy marinara sauce and topped with grated cheese. While the sauce in the original version of the dish was made with wine, along with onions and hot and sweet cherry peppers, many versions today use cream instead.

There are competing claims as to who invented chicken riggies, but it was likely first served in the 1970s at a restaurant called the Clinton House. The dish became popular locally after Chesterfield's in Utica put it on its menu in 1989. That restaurant no longer exists, but a new incarnation in town called **Chesterfield's Tavolo** still serves what it labels the original recipe for chicken riggies.

Other good options in the area include **Teddy's Restaurant** in Rome, which won the local competition called Riggiefest three years in a row, and a pair of well-regarded Italian restaurants, **Ventura's** in Utica and **Georgio's Village Cafe** in New Hartford. Both of these places also serve pasta they call hats, which sounds like a fun new shape if you're tired of plain old rigatoni.

Utica greens

The humble greens of the Mohawk Valley weren't always featured as one of the region's signature foods. Many of the Italian immigrants who came to work in the area's textile mills and railroad in the late 1800s and early 1900s planted a variety of endive called escarole in their backyards. Although it was frequently cooked in home kitchens with garlic and olive oil, it wasn't until the 1980s that the vegetable took center stage in a much heartier dish.

To make Utica greens, which is typically eaten as an appetizer, the escarole is sautéed with Italian ingredients such as prosciutto and hot cherry peppers, sometimes along with chicken broth. It's usually topped with breadcrumbs and grated cheese and then browned. The dish can also be expanded into an entrée by incorporating meats such as sausage and salami, as well as potatoes.

Utica greens started to become popular in 1988 when Joe Morelle put it on the menu at Chesterfield's in Utica, where the dish was called greens Morelle. (It's still known by that name at the restaurant's successor, **Chesterfield's Tavolo**.) At other spots around town, you'll sometimes see it labeled with the name of the chef or the restaurant, or sometimes just by the word greens. But you'll be able to find excellent versions in Utica at **Daniele's**, **Basil Leaf Ristorante** and **Utica Pizza Company**, and in New Hartford at **Georgio's Village Cafe**. And at **Nina's Pizza** in Utica, a house specialty is a pie topped with Utica greens – a main dish in which escarole is allowed to step into the spotlight and get top billing on the menu.

BINGHAMTON

Spiedie

You can't be in a hurry if you want to sample the Binghamton sandwich known as a spiedie, pronounced like the problematic cartoon mouse with the surname Gonzales.

That's because the cubes of chicken or pork (or sometimes beef, lamb or venison) that are grilled over a charcoal pit are marinated for at least 24 hours. The sauce typically contains a mixture of olive oil, vinegar, lemon juice and garlic, as well as herbs including thyme, oregano and basil. After the skewered meat comes off the barbecue, it's served on a soft Italian roll with additional marinade drizzled on top.

The word spiedie comes from the Italian spiedo, meaning cooking spit. The dish originated with Italian-Americans in Broome County in the 1930s, and became popular among local railroad workers and shoemakers after Agostino Iacovelli, who owned a restaurant in Endicott called Augie's, put a lamb spiedie on his menu in 1939.

Today you'll find spiedies at only a few places in the area, including **Lupo's Char-Pit** in Endicott, **Spiedie & Rib Pit** in Binghamton and Vestal and **Brooks' House of Bar-B-Q** in Oneonta. But you can pick up some marinated meats at **Lupo's Original Spiedies**, also in Endicott, or a bottle of the house sauce, which it's produced since 1951 (and also sells online). And if you're lucky enough to be visiting upstate New York during the first weekend of August, mark your calendar for Binghamton's annual Spiedie Fest & Balloon Rally. That's where you can take a leisurely hot air balloon ride while you wait patiently for the skewers to finish marinating.

City chicken

See Other foods of the Midwest

Another dish of skewered meat you'll occasionally see in Binghamton is the fried pork cubes called, misleadingly, city chicken. At **Guiseppe's**, you can order it as an appetizer with or without sauce, or as a sub – which makes it a close relative to the spiedie.

OTHER FOODS OF NEW YORK

Grandma pizza

Imagine a home-cooked pizza made for you by an Italian nonna, and you'll have a pretty good idea of what you'll get when you order the Long Island specialty named for her.

Grandma pizza is a thin-crust pie that's baked in a sheet pan in a regular kitchen oven, and cut into rectangular slices. Mozzarella cheese is usually placed underneath a layer of tomato sauce, with other meat and vegetable toppings above.

This style emerged as a thin-crust alternative to the rectangular Sicilian pies that were featured on the menu of Umberto Corteo's eponymous New Hyde Park restaurant, **Umberto's**, which opened in 1965. One day, Corteo asked his brother Carlo to create a pizza that was inspired by the kind their mother would make for them back in Italy. But the result was something that was only eaten by staff and was sometimes also sold as an off-menu specialty for favorite patrons. It wasn't until the 1980s that the specialty made its first appearance on a restaurant menu, after two of Corteo's employees brought the pie to **King Umberto** in Elmont, where a customer named it grandma pizza. In 1989, another cook at King Umberto, Angelo Giangrande, entered it in a local pizza-making contest, and its popularity helped spread the new style to other Long Island restaurants over the following decades.

Today you can sample grandma pizza at both Umberto's, now with numerous locations across Long Island, and King Umberto. But you'll also find it at **Da Angelo Pizza** in Albertson, owned by Giangrande and his son, as well as at other well-regarded spots including **Lombardo's** in Seaford, **Little Enrico's** in Franklin Square and **Toskana** in Roslyn Heights. There may not be an actual Italian grandmother making your pie, but if you don't happen to have one of your own, a pizza that reminds you of how she'd probably cook it is the next best thing.

Michigan hot dog

It's a bit confusing that the favorite hot dog of Plattsburgh is called a Michigan. Sure, Eula and Garth Otis, the couple who owned the first stand that sold them, Garth Otis' Michigan Hot Dog and Sandwich Shop, in 1927, were originally from that state. But the meaty sauce they invented is only somewhat similar to the one put on coneys in Detroit, Jackson and Flint. It's closer to a Greek-inspired sauce eaten since at least 1917 in small towns like Williamsville, Liverpool and Johnson City, New York, where a dog topped with it – equally confusingly – is known as a Texas Hot.

In the North Country of New York, a Michigan hot dog is an all-beef frankfurter covered with a thick sauce containing ground beef and spices. It's served in a steamed bun and is usually accompanied by chopped onions and mustard (which can be placed either above the hot dog or below, a style called buried).

A few recommended spots for a Michigan in Plattsburgh include **Clare and Carl's Hot Dog Stand**, which opened in 1942 and serves a sauce whose recipe purportedly came from Eula Otis; **McSweeney's Red Hots**, with a pair of locations where the sauce also derives from her version; **Gus's Red Hots**, which sells a Michigan with a milder sauce that's served on a firm hot dog roll; and **Michigans Plus**, where you can order the signature dish as well as a pint of Michigan sauce to go – which, come to think of it, sounds like a great topping for a Detroit-style pizza.

Salt potatoes

Syracuse University's mascot, Otto the Orange, wasn't officially recognized until 1995. For much of the institution's history, the school's teams were cheered on by a character called the Saltine Warrior – who wasn't a giant fighting cracker, but an homage to the region's history as a center of salt production. And that industry is what's responsible for the creation of the city's most famous dish.

Salt potatoes are small white potatoes that are boiled in heavily salted water. During cooking, the salinity causes a crust to form on the skin of the potatoes, while the inside develops a creamy texture. They're typically smothered with melted butter and served as a side dish.

By the 1870s, nearly 90 percent of the country's salt was produced around Central New York's Onondaga Lake by the Irish and German immigrants who worked at the salt blocks. These were giant kettles in which the briny water from local salt springs was boiled, leaving the salt residue behind. Many of the Irish workers subsisted on small bags of potatoes, which they would cook in the salt blocks, creating a new method for preparing their most popular food. In 1883, a tavern called Keefe Brothers on the north side of town, run by the offspring of a salt manufacturer, began serving the dish, and it soon became widespread at similar establishments all over the area.

Today you'll find kits for making this specialty, with the appropriate ratio of potatoes and salt, in local grocery stores under the brand Hinerwadel's, which for more than a century hosted summer clambakes that featured salt potatoes. That tradition ended in 2018, but you can still enjoy the dish at a handful of local restaurants including **Oh My Darling** in Syracuse; **Bull and Bear Roadhouse** in East Syracuse, Fayetteville and Liverpool, where the salt potatoes are loaded with pulled pork, bacon and Cheddar cheese; and **The Clam Bar** in North Syracuse. And though a side of salt potatoes is no longer an appropriate way to pay tribute to the nearby university, you can do just that by ordering a glass of orange juice to drink with your meal.

Sugar on snow

See Vermont

Maple sugaring houses in upstate New York join the Green Mountain State in celebrating sap-flowing season with the taffy-like candy called sugar on snow. One place you can try it, during weekends in March, is **Sprague's Maple Farms** in Portville.

Other New York dishes to sample:

- **Chamby burger**, a hamburger topped with American cheese and sliced ham that's a specialty of **Dave's Bun & Burger** in Westhampton Beach and has been adopted by other burger joints as a Long Island regional specialty.
- **Cornell chicken**, a style of barbecued chicken devised in the 1940s by Robert Baker, a Cornell professor (and inventor of the chicken nugget) who came up with an herbaceous vinegar-based marinade for smaller chickens that would be less likely to burn on the grill than traditional sauces. It's frequently used to baste chickens at local cookouts, but you can also try it at **Glenwood Pines** in Ithaca and **Auburn Poultry** in Auburn, where Cornell barbecue chicken is available for takeout on Wednesdays and Saturdays.
- **Grape pie**, a specialty of Naples in the Finger Lakes region, where numerous shops sell purple-colored pies during the autumn harvest season of the local Concord grapes. One place you can get this delicacy year-round is **Monica's Pies**, a bakery whose proprietor calls herself the Grape Pie Queen.
- **Speculaas**, otherwise known as Dutch windmill cookies, a treat eaten on Sinterklaas, a holiday celebrated in the Hudson Valley by the descendants of Dutch settlers who came to New York in the 17th century. The spiced cookies are shaped using traditional wooden molds and often depict St. Nicholas. Today you can enjoy them at the annual Sinterklaas festival in Rhinebeck, as well as at **Sweet Impressions**, a bakery based in Newark, a town located between Rochester and Syracuse.

Cheesesteak

THE MID-ATLANTIC

In the list of America's 20 most populous cities, the East Coast region that includes Pennsylvania, New Jersey, Delaware, Maryland and Washington, D.C., merits just a single entry: Philadelphia. But, as one of the oldest sections of the U.S., home to significant attractions like the Liberty Bell, the Inner Harbor and the Lincoln Memorial, it retains an outsized importance in the country's history and culture, as well as its cuisine. (Well, except for Delaware, which doesn't have much to recommend it culinarily.) Several dishes that come from the mid-Atlantic, like the Philly cheesesteak and the Maryland crab cake, are among the most iconic examples of regional food. And there are dozens of other specialties worth seeking out as you travel along the Eastern seaboard and to destinations further inland.

The cuisine of the mid-Atlantic has been primarily shaped by the groups of immigrants, mostly from Europe, who settled across the region in the late 1800s and early 1900s. Foremost among these were the Italians, especially from the southern part of that country, who came through New York's Ellis Island and established communities in New Jersey, Pennsylvania and other places.

Both of these states feature specialties developed locally that spotlight iconic Italian ingredients. In Newark, don't miss the Italian hot dog, a sausage stuffed into a pizza crust, or the tomato pie, a thin-crust style of pizza that's characteristic of Trenton. In Philadelphia, the Italian hoagie is a favorite type of that city's signature sandwich, containing layers of salami, prosciutto and Provolone, while a stromboli includes similar ingredients wrapped inside pizza dough. And in Pittsburgh, Italian wedding soup, named for the harmony between its meat and vegetables, is often served in that city's red-sauce restaurants.

But there's more than Italian food in this region, as several other ethnic groups have also left a lasting imprint on mid-Atlantic cuisine. These include the Germans, many of whom made their home in Baltimore and can take credit for the Old Bay spice blend that seasons most of its crab dishes, as well as the Berger cookies that have earned their place as the city's favorite confection. In Pittsburgh, the Polish community is most visible in the pierogi and pączki that are staples for many in Western Pennsylvania. And while the food served in Pennsylvania Dutch country is in many ways indistinct from simple, hearty meals you'll find all across the U.S., there are a few traditional Amish specialties worth seeking out, including scrapple (also a dish with German heritage) and shoofly pie, along with variations of chicken and dumplings and chow chow, both of which are also eaten widely across the South.

A common thread among several disparate dishes in the mid-Atlantic is how their development has been shaped to cater to Jewish customers. In Baltimore, a Jewish vendor invented the coddie, a snack that functioned as a kosher alternative to crab cakes. And in Philadelphia, a popular sushi roll employs cream cheese and smoked salmon, common toppings enjoyed atop a bagel, while the city's famous cheesesteak originally didn't include cheese so it wouldn't mix meat and dairy and run afoul of Jewish dietary restrictions.

In addition to all the dishes already mentioned, Pennsylvania may have more regional food with unusual combinations of ingredients than just about any other state. In Pittsburgh, an eponymous salad is topped with French fries, while in Altoona, the city's namesake pizza is made with processed American cheese and salami. And a hot dog purportedly invented in Pottstown, the Texas Tommy, is wrapped in bacon and stuffed with cheese. (Okay, maybe that one's not so unusual, but it does sound delicious.)

Baltimore is also home to a surprising diversity of unique foods, including the pit beef sandwich, the city's answer to barbecue; snowballs, a version of a snow cone topped with marshmallow crème; and the lemon stick, a minty lemon drink. And along the Eastern Shore, don't miss the chance to try any number of dishes made with crab, or the Smith Island cake, a multi-tiered confection first baked on an island that's only accessible by boat.

But many of these recipes are less well-known than a few other, more familiar, dishes that are strongly identified with individual states or cities. You can scarcely think of Maryland without imagining a soft-shell crab sandwich, or Washington, D.C. without its signature sausage, the half-smoke. And New Jersey is famous nationwide for its processed meat called pork roll (or if you prefer, Taylor ham), as well as the salt water taffy that's popular in Atlantic City and nearby seaside towns.

Whether you're spending time in one of the mid-Atlantic's major cities, vacationing in the countryside, or just passing through along Interstate 95, don't miss the chance to explore all aspects of the region's cuisine. While sampling its characteristic dishes is a good way to get to know what makes these places unique, it's also worth trying some of their most well-regarded restaurants, including **Zahav** and **Laser Wolf**, two of Michael Solomonov's Philadelphia dining venues that feature Israeli cuisine, and **Jaleo** and **The Bazaar by Jose Andres**, part of the celebrity chef's D.C. empire. A visit to either of these cities will offer you not only a taste of some outstanding dishes, but a reminder of the hard-fought history that gives you the freedom to choose whatever you want to eat.

PENNSYLVANIA

PHILADELPHIA

Cheesesteak

Few things are more iconic in the City of Brotherly Love than a cheesesteak – except perhaps for the Rocky statue and the Liberty Bell. But, surprisingly, the original version of the sandwich didn't have one of the key elements that defines it today.

A cheesesteak consists of thinly sliced, griddled beef that's covered with melted cheese and nestled in a soft submarine roll, often one made by the local Amoroso's Bakery. Eaters can choose among American, Provolone and Cheez Whiz, and whether or not to have sautéed onions, so a classic order, spoken with a Philly accent, might be "Whiz wit" or "American wit-out." Other toppings and condiments can include mushrooms, peppers, ketchup and hot sauce. (You can also get a similar sandwich with chicken instead of beef, naturally called a chicken cheesesteak.)

The sandwich was invented in the 1930s by Pat Olivieri, a hot dog vendor in South Philadelphia who decided to cook some beef on his grill and served it in an Italian roll to a passing taxi driver. Other cabbies started visiting the stand to try the steak sandwiches, and they soon became popular enough that Olivieri, along with his brother Harry, opened a business in 1939 called **Pat's King of Steaks**.

But it was only after the brothers were operating additional locations in the 1940s that an employee suggested adding Provolone cheese on top of the beef. (The original stand didn't initially serve cheese on its steaks so that it could cater to Jewish customers who didn't mix meat and dairy.) Cheez Whiz didn't become an option until the 1950s, but it's now the most popular choice for a cheesesteak at Pat's.

A second legendary cheesesteak shop, **Geno's Steaks**, opened across the street in 1966, and the two have maintained a friendly rivalry ever since. But there are other worthy options across the city, including **Jim's Steaks** on South Street (temporarily closed due to a 2022 fire, but there's a location at the Philly airport as well as in Springfield), **Sonny's Famous Steaks** in Old City and **Dalessandro's Steaks** in Roxborough. These sandwiches can be a gut-busting bomb, though, so you might want to wait a while after finishing one before you start emulating Sylvester Stallone's famous climb up the Rocky Steps.

Hoagie

In other parts of the country, Philadelphia's second-favorite sandwich is called a sub, or a grinder, or a hero or even (in Boston) a spuckie. But in Philly, it's known as a hoagie – and there are as many explanations as to why as there are alternative names for it.

A hoagie is a sandwich with a combination of cured meats, cheeses, vegetables and condiments, all served on a long bread roll. A popular variation is the Italian hoagie, made with salami, prosciutto and other meats, as well as Provolone cheese. It's usually topped with shredded lettuce along with sliced tomatoes and onions, and sprinkled with oregano, olive oil and vinegar. But there are countless other types of hoagies, including chicken cutlet, ham-and-cheese and even vegetarian.

One popular theory as to the origin of the word hoagie is that it's a derivation of hoggie, a nickname for the Italian-American laborers who worked at the shipyard called Hog Island in South Philadelphia beginning just after World War I. Although many were known to bring their own lunches, the hoagie is said to have grown in popularity after a jazz musician named Al

DePalma opened a sandwich shop nearby in the late 1930s, claiming that only a hog could finish an entire one.

But that's not a definitive account. Another hypothesis is that the word comes from hokey-pokey men, late-19th-century street vendors who sold loaves of bread that were stuffed with meats and antipasto salad. Others say the sandwich was invented in Chester in 1925 by Catherine DiCostanza of A. DiCostanza grocery store (now called **DiCostanza's** and located in Boothwyn), who crafted a sandwich from all of the ingredients she happened to have on hand – although she apparently didn't call it a hoagie. And still another, even more dubious, conjecture suggests that the sandwich refers to Big Band songwriter Hoagland Howard Carmichael, who was nicknamed Hoagy.

Although the origins of the hoagie remain murky, the sandwich has become a mainstay of Philadelphia cuisine, and you'll find dozens of shops all over town that create outstanding ones. A few popular spots include **Vincenzo's Deli** in South Philadelphia, well-regarded for its Italian hoagies made with capicola and soppressata; **Liberty Kitchen PHL** in Fishtown, with a variety of high-quality sandwich options including roasted turkey and chicken salad; and **Ricci's Hoagies**, another South Philly spot that's been open since the 1920s and offers a wide-ranging menu featuring salads and cold cuts. There's no evidence they had anything to do with the invention of the hoagie, but since nobody really knows who did, feel free to make up your own legend about it.

Stromboli

Despite what some may believe, a stromboli isn't just another word for a calzone. Although it shares some similarities with that ubiquitous pizza-like turnover, this specialty is a Philly original. And while the calzone originated in Naples in the 1700s, the history of this dish is wrapped up in a 20th-century sex scandal that was as tumultuous as the volcanic Sicilian island with which the stromboli shares its name.

The key difference between a calzone and a stromboli is in how the two dishes are constructed and eaten. While the former's dough is folded into a semicircle, and the resulting pocket is intended for a single diner, the latter's crust is rolled into a rectangle and sliced into individual pieces. The ingredients contained within either can include Italian meats, cheeses and vegetables. But you'll never find tomato sauce inside a calzone, only in some strombolis.

Most strombolis today are made with pizza dough, but the original version was actually a sandwich made with bread dough. It was invented in 1950 by Nazzareno Romano, the owner of an eponymous restaurant just outside Philadelphia, **Romano's Pizzeria and Italian Restaurant**. Romano was experimenting with a new type of stuffed pizza, and used a combination of cotechino salami, ham, cheese and peppers as the filling inside a crust that he sealed and baked.

While customers enjoyed his new creation, Romano wasn't sure what to call it. The inspiration came from the gossip headline that Italian-Americans couldn't stop talking about, the off-screen romance between actress Ingrid Bergman and director Roberto Rossellini, both married to others at the time, that resulted in the first of their three children together. And the film they were working on? It featured the volcano as a prominent backdrop, and you guessed it – it was also called Stromboli. The affair led to Bergman's being ostracized in the U.S., and even banned from appearing on Ed Sullivan's variety show to promote her new movie.

Stromboli was a box-office bust, and Bergman and Rossellini's marriage wasn't any more successful – it ended in 1957 after the director eloped with a screenwriter he was working with in India. But the stromboli has become a fixture of Philly cuisine. A few recommended spots to try one include **Vince's Pizzeria** in Philadelphia's Fishtown neighborhood, **La Rosa Pizzeria** in South Philadelphia and **Township Line Pizza** in Drexel Hill. Or you can sample the original version at Romano's (but they'll also ship nationwide if you can't make it to Essington). That is, if you're able to recover your appetite after reading about the salacious scandal that gave the stromboli its name. But please, whatever you do, just don't call it a calzone.

Philadelphia roll

The sushi roll made with smoked salmon and cucumber and named for its third key ingredient, Philadelphia-brand cream cheese, wasn't originally going to have a geographic label. According to its inventor Madame Saito, the first female sushi chef in Philadelphia, it was initially conceived as the Japanese equivalent of cream cheese and lox on a bagel, and was intended to be called the Jewish roll.

Saito, a sushi chef and teacher who's known in Philadelphia as the Queen of Sushi, is believed to have created the roll in the 1980s for a demonstration at Longwood Gardens, placing the rice on the outside of the seaweed called nori to appeal to American diners who weren't as familiar with traditional sushi. The audience told her that she should name the roll after the city (and its famous dairy product), and it soon became popular across the area as other chefs followed her strategy of adapting familiar ingredients into sushi rolls that would tempt Western palates.

(In another version of the origin story, dating from around the same time, then-mayor William J. Green is said to have asked Saito to create a signature sushi roll representing the city for her sushi counter at Reading Terminal Market. She invented a roll with a combination of ingredients that she thought would appeal to her mostly Jewish customers.)

Saito continued to serve the Philadelphia roll at several Japanese fusion restaurants that she operated until recent years, including Tokio HeadHouse in Society Hill, where she still offers private sushi-making classes. But you'll find her creation at nearly every sushi restaurant in town that offers the rolls known as makizushi.

A few recommended spots include **Midori Sushi** and **Koto Sushi**, both in Center City, and **Kasumi Sushi** in South Philly. And while you can certainly find a Philadelphia roll in other cities, the one you order in town will taste a little bit creamier, now that you know that it was invented just down the road.

Snapper soup

July 4, 1776, was a momentous day in Philadelphia history. It was a day when the Continental Congress officially adopted the country's Declaration of Independence from Great Britain. And it was a day when John Adams, one of the document's signers, celebrated with a bowl of a favorite delicacy – turtle soup.

Up until the mid-1800s, this wildly popular dish was prepared with massive green sea turtles who could be as heavy as 300 pounds. It was enjoyed by many wealthy diners during colonial times, and was especially beloved across the river in New Jersey at the Hoboken Turtle Club, a social group that lasted for more than a century whose members included Alexander Hamilton and Aaron Burr (although it's not known whether the two shell-fishly dueled over who should get an extra serving).

Eventually, as the supply of green turtles began to dry up, Philadelphians began using diamondback terrapins for the soup, and later replaced them with calf's heads (employed for making mock turtle soup) and then with the abundant snapper turtles found in nearby waterways. And it's this latter form of the dish that remains a local specialty at historic taverns and seafood restaurants around the area.

Snapper soup is made with turtle meat that's cooked with vegetables and aromatic spices in a thick, dark-brown broth, and usually flavored with dry sherry that's served tableside. One of the classic places to eat it in modern times was Old Original Bookbinder's in Old City, which featured it on its menu as Bookbinder's soup. That restaurant has been replaced by the Olde Bar, where until recently you could still order a bowl of it.

Other Philadelphia dishes to sample:

- **Roast pork sandwich**, a Philadelphia specialty also called porchetta that's less well-known than the cheesesteak or hoagie but deserves equal time in the spotlight. It's made with thinly sliced, slow-roasted pork that's topped with melted Provolone cheese and broccoli rabe, and like its sandwich brethren, is served on a long roll. A classic place to try one is **Tommy DiNic's** in Reading Terminal Market, but other great options include **Cosmi's Deli** in the Italian Market and **John's Roast Pork** in South Philadelphia.
- **Pepper pot**, an Afro-Caribbean stew made with beef tripe and vegetables such as potatoes, collard greens and sweet and hot peppers. The dish was frequently eaten during colonial times and sold on the streets of Philadelphia by vendors called pepper pot women. Today it's rarely found outside of kitchens where chefs are working to reclaim historic Black dishes, but one place you might find it on the menu is **Pepperpot**, a Caribbean restaurant in North Philadelphia.

You'll have better luck finding snapper soup at a handful of other restaurants around town, including **Elwood** in the city's Fishtown neighborhood, and in surrounding communities, **Lehman's Restaurant** in Essington, **Zoto's Diner** in Line Lexington, **Pineville Tavern** in Pineville and **The Buck Hotel** in Feasterville-Trevose. Put on a pair of tortoise-shell glasses as you pick up your spoon, and you might decide that this slow-food dish is an appropriate way to celebrate freedom next Fourth of July. Just perhaps not for the turtles.

- **Soft pretzel,** baked dough formed into a figure-eight shape that's sprinkled with salt and often eaten with spicy mustard. With the city's concentration of residents with German heritage, soft pretzels were sold in Philadelphia as early as the 1820s, but didn't become as prevalent as their mass-produced hard brethren until the 1970s. A few iconic places to pick one up include **Philly Pretzel Factory**, in Center City and other locations; **Center City Pretzel Co.** in the Italian Market, which temporarily closed after a fire in 2022; and **Wawa**, the favorite local convenience-store chain that you'll find all around the city and suburbs.
- **Water ice**, also known as Italian ice, a summertime treat in Philadelphia consisting of various flavors of fruit (or chocolate) that are mixed with sugar and water and then frozen into a slushy dessert. A classic place to sample it is **John's Water Ice** in the Italian Market (with a second location outside the city in Huntingdon Valley).
- **Irish potato candy**, a confection made from a mixture of coconut and cream cheese or buttercream that's rolled in cinnamon to make it resemble a small potato. These marble-sized sweets are traditionally eaten in Philadelphia in the weeks leading up to St. Patrick's Day, and can be found at local candymakers including **Shane Confectionery** in Old City, which claims to be America's oldest candy store.

PITTSBURGH

Pittsburgh-style hamburger

Pittsburgh-born artist Andy Warhol is often falsely credited with the expression that everyone will one day enjoy 15 minutes of fame. The most notorious hamburger in Steel City – the Big Mac, which McDonald's introduced in the Pittsburgh area in 1967 before rolling it out nationwide the following year – has been famous for much longer than that, of course. But fortunately, it's not the only notable hamburger in town. You'd be remiss if you skipped a trip to **Primanti Bros.** for its Pittsburgh-style burgers.

A Pittsburgh-style hamburger is one that, like many of Primanti Bros.'s other sandwiches, includes French fries and coleslaw as toppings, instead of having them served on the side, as they usually are. The restaurant's first branch opened in the Strip District in 1933, and the owners decided to add potatoes to their sandwiches to cater to their repeat customers, truck drivers who were then able to drive with one hand and eat with the other.

Today there are dozens of locations of Primanti Bros. in the Pittsburgh area (along with a few other branches across Pennsylvania, as well as in West Virginia, Maryland and Ohio) where you can get a signature "Pitts-Burger." That's a beef patty with lettuce, tomatoes, French fries and coleslaw, sandwiched between two pieces of white bread.

As long as you're in town, you may as well try a few other Pittsburgh restaurants that are well-regarded for their hamburgers. Some popular spots include **Tessaro's** in Bloomfield, a neighborhood bar where the meat is grilled over hardwood; **Burgatory**, with eight locations around town that offer burgers made from beef, bison, elk and more; and **Stack'd** in Oakland (as well as Wexford) where you can customize your burger with your favorite cheese, sauce and toppings. Fries are only served on the side, though, so if you want to make a true

Pittsburgh-style hamburger, you'll have to pile some onto your sandwich yourself.

Pittsburgh salad

In the city that's home to Mister Rogers, it's always a beautiful day for an extra helping of French fries.

Another Steel City specialty that slips some fries in a dish where you might not normally see them is known as a Pittsburgh salad. Its ingredients typically include lettuce, tomatoes and shredded Cheddar or jack cheese, along with a pile of crispy shoestring potatoes and ranch dressing.

A drive-in called **Jerry's Curb Service** in Beaver claims to have invented the Pittsburgh salad in the early 1960s. As the story goes, a customer ordered a steak sandwich one night but asked to hold the bun and add fries and salad dressing. The owner's wife, Donna Reed (not the actress), decided to try this combination on a bed of lettuce, and the restaurant eventually added the dish to its menu.

Today a Pittsburgh salad more typically comes with chicken rather than steak. In addition to Jerry's, you'll also find one on the menu at **Pamela's Diner**, which has locations in the Strip District, Shadyside and Mt. Lebanon; **The Church Brew Works** in Lawrenceville; and a regional chain called **Eat'n Park**, where the dish is named after the restaurant but is just another version of a Pittsburgh salad. It's not known whether Fred Rogers ever ate one himself, but ordering the city's namesake salad from one of its local businesses seems like just the sort of neighborly thing he'd want you to do.

Pittsburgh rare steak

How do you prefer your beef to be cooked: rare, well-done or somewhere in between? When you order a Pittsburgh rare steak, also known as black-and-blue style, you'll be getting a dish that features both extremes at once. (Please don't confuse it with black-and-gold style, which is a term I just made up that refers to steaks eaten at Pittsburgh Steelers games.)

A Pittsburgh rare steak is one that's charred on the outside but red and juicy in the center. While most black-and-blue steaks are grilled over an open flame, a thick piece of meat can also achieve this state when it's seared in an extremely hot cast-iron pan, as long as it's removed from the heat before the inside begins to cook.

Local legend says that this style of beef originated among steel workers who would cook raw steak on a cooling piece of metal or the plant's blow pipes, which were so hot that they would instantly char the outside of a piece of meat while the inside was still rare. Another story, equally likely to be apocryphal, is that a cook at a diner called the Colony Restaurant once joked about an accidentally burnt steak, calling it Pittsburgh-style, and the name stuck.

While most steakhouses will cook your beef to whichever temperature you desire, if you want to try it Pittsburgh rare, you'll have to ask your server if the cook can accommodate your request. There are numerous branches of chain steakhouses in the city, some of which will cost you a Carnegie-sized fortune to eat at. But a couple of independent restaurants popular for their beef dishes include **Meat & Potatoes**, located downtown, and **North Shore Tavern**, just across one of the city's many bridges that span the Allegheny River. The latter spot is famous for cooking its steaks on hot lava stones, which seems like a good technique for getting your filet to be simultaneously black and blue.

Chipped chopped ham

As the original headquarters of Heinz, Pittsburgh is a place where residents love their ketchup. And ranch dressing is the natural accompaniment for a Pittsburgh salad. But it's a third condiment, barbecue sauce, that features prominently in a favorite local sandwich, the chipped chopped ham.

A chipped chopped ham sandwich, or chipped ham for short, consists of wafer-thin slices of a processed meat loaf that's made with ground ham trimmings and seasonings. The shavings are mixed with barbecue sauce and heated, and piled onto a soft round roll.

The lunchtime staple first became popular at a mostly defunct Midwestern dairy chain called Isaly's, which is best-known for having invented the Klondike bar. One vestige of the company remains in West View, a diner called **I.S.A.L.Y.S.** (a nod to the mnemonic acronym used in mid-century advertising, "I Shall Always Love You Sweetheart"), where you can still order a chipped ham sandwich, with or without cheese.

You can also procure Isaly's chipped chopped ham by the pound, along with containers of barbecue sauce, at **Pennsylvania Macaroni Co.** in the Strip District. And a few other places where you'll find chipped ham around town include **Portman's Farm Market** in Bridgeville, where it's served as an occasional lunch special, and **Frisch's** in Whitehall. And if yinz wanted to put some extra ketchup on top of your sandwich, few locals would consider it the least bit unusual.

Italian wedding soup

A tradition at weddings in Pittsburgh is to showcase an elaborate cookie table filled with homemade treats for guests to enjoy. But a soup that sounds like it would be an appropriate first course isn't likely to appear on the reception's dinner menu. Despite what some may believe, Italian wedding soup, also referred to as Pittsburgh wedding soup, isn't traditionally served to new spouses to celebrate their nuptials.

Instead, Italian wedding soup gets its name from the harmonious union of the meat and green vegetables that are combined in a clear chicken broth. In Italian the soup is called minestra maritata, or married soup, a term that was eventually translated into English as wedding soup. It generally consists of meatballs or sausage, along with spinach, escarole, kale or other greens, and sometimes also contains small-shape pasta, beans and Parmesan cheese.

The dish has roots in Naples and became popular among the Italian immigrants who settled in Pennsylvania in the late 1800s and early 1900s. Today you'll find the soup on menus at classic red-sauce restaurants in many Northeastern cities with large Italian-American populations, but it's especially prevalent in Pittsburgh. A few popular spots for it include **Big Jim's** in Greenfield, **Colangelo's Pizza** in the Strip District, **Cucina Vitale** on the South Side and **Buon Giorno Cafe** downtown. Just know that if you're in town for a wedding, it's probably not a good idea to order dessert after finishing your bowl. That way you can save room for all the cookies you'll likely soon be eating.

Pierogi

See Cleveland

Pierogi, the boiled or pan-fried dumplings with either sweet or savory fillings, are a Pittsburgh staple, and a costumed pierogi mascot race is featured at every home Pirates baseball game. You'll find some of the city's best pierogi at **S&D Polish Deli** in the Strip District, which serves a classic potato-and-Cheddar variety with melted butter and sautéed onions, along with other Polish specialties including haluski (buttery noodles with cabbage) and kielbasa.

Pączki

See Other foods of the Midwest

Pittsburgh's high concentration of Polish-Americans means that pączki, the puffy donuts filled with fruit or custard, are big business in the weeks leading up to Mardi Gras. You'll find some of the city's best at **Party Cake Shop** in Brookline, **Potomac Bakery** in Dormont and **Prantl's Bakery** in Shadyside.

Another Pittsburgh dish to sample:

- **Pizza logs**, egg roll wrappers filled with mozzarella cheese and pizza toppings, and served with a side of marinara sauce. They're commonly eaten as a snack in Pittsburgh (as well as in the Buffalo area), and are sold at sporting events, at Steel City pubs such as **Backdraft Bar & Grill** and at **T-Bone's Marketplace** in Wexford, where they feature on the daily lunch menu.

OTHER FOODS OF PENNSYLVANIA

Altoona-style pizza

Many railroad buffs like to pilgrimage to the city of Altoona in central Pennsylvania, where they can check out Horseshoe Curve, a steep, semicircular section of track built to help trains cross the Allegheny Mountains. And while they're in town, some choose to partake of a controversial style of pizza that briefly made Altoona equally notorious, at least on the Internet.

Altoona-style pizza bucks convention by using yellow American cheese instead of traditional mozzarella or Provolone. The thick, Sicilian-style foccacia crust is covered with tomato sauce and is typically cut into squares, so that each slice contains both of the two primary toppings – a green bell pepper ring and a piece of deli salami.

This style of pizza was first created in the 1960s or '70s at the Altoona Hotel, where the chef (and I use that term loosely) topped the pies with processed Velveeta instead of American cheese. Although that building was destroyed by fire in 2013, Altoona-style slices are still served at several other restaurants in town, including **29th Street Pizza Subs & More**, **Dino's Pizza** and **Zach's Sports and Spirits**, which offers three different dishes – round pizzas, flatbreads and stromboli – that feature the Altoona signature flavor combination.

Another unique Pennsylvania pizza style is prevalent in a former coal mining town outside Scranton called Old Forge, a few hours' drive from Altoona in the northeastern part of the state. The pizza there is baked in a rectangular metal pan, and is served by the tray rather than the pie. There are two primary varieties: a red pizza, made with tomato sauce and a blend of cheeses, and white pizza, a stuffed version without sauce that's often garnished with rosemary. A few popular spots in town where you can sample both include **Anthony's**, **Cafe Rinaldi** and **Arcaro and Genell**.

I haven't yet eaten either of these Pennsylvania pizza styles, but one writer who tried the Altoona version after it went viral in 2020 called it "an absolute abomination," and I'm not sure I would disagree. You may find you prefer the pies in the city near Horseshoe Curve, but when I'm ready to forge new pizza ground, I'll invite my friends Jim and Pam from Dunder Mifflin and head to the Scranton area instead.

Texas Tommy

One way to know when a culinary innovation is a true stroke of genius is when nearly identical dishes crop up in multiple places under different names. That's certainly the case with the Texas

Tommy, a style of hot dog that's remarkably similar to the Los Angeles danger dog, the Chicago francheezie and the Jersey breakfast dog. And what do all of these franks have in common? The hot dog is wrapped in bacon – an inspired idea that works on both coasts and halfway in between.

The Texas Tommy doesn't stop with a strip or two of bacon, though. Like the francheezie, it's split lengthwise and is filled with cheese, either American, Cheddar or Cheez Whiz. The bacon and cheese are secured with toothpicks, and the hot dog is either deep-fried or grilled before being served on a toasted bun. Typical condiments include mustard and ketchup, although in one variation of the Texas Tommy, described in a 1955 article as hitched style, a spoonful of macaroni-and-cheese is purportedly ladled on top. (It's possible that no one who ate this variety actually survived long enough to continue spreading the word about it.)

Despite little evidence supporting the claim, the Texas Tommy is said to have been invented in Pottstown in the 1950s, and recipes for it were frequently reprinted in magazines that catered to mid-century housewives. Why this style of hot dog is called a Texas Tommy remains a mystery, but it doesn't seem to have a direct connection to either the Texas wiener that's popular in New Jersey or the Texas Hots that can be found in New York – or the 1910s San Francisco ballroom dance that shares its name.

Compounding the enigma, the only place in Pottstown where you can enjoy a Texas Tommy today appears to be **HG Palermo's Pizza**. But you will be able to find them at plenty of sandwich shops, hot dog stands and diners throughout Southeastern Pennsylvania. A few popular options include **Bevan's Cold Cuts** in West Chester, **R J's Hot Dog Stand** in Essington and **Center City Hot Dog** and **Little Pete's**, both in Philadelphia. And if you're ready for another bacon-wrapped dog after sampling all of those, just hop a flight to L.A. or Chicago and see if someone there has any idea who Tommy is.

Chicken and dumplings

See Other foods of the South

The Pennsylvania version of chicken and dumplings is sometimes known as bott boi, but don't let that name confuse you into thinking it's actually a pot pie – a pastry crust filled with meat and vegetables in a creamy sauce.

Chicken and dumplings in the Keystone State, similar to its Southern kin, is a soup consisting of thick strips of noodles along with potatoes, celery and carrots, boiled in chicken broth that's often seasoned with saffron. (A similar soup made with pork is called ham pot pie.) You can try this dish at **Katie's Kitchen** in Ronks, which offers it as a Wednesday-night dinner special.

City chicken

See Other foods of the Midwest

The fried pork skewers known as city chicken are less prevalent around Pennsylvania than they once were. While I haven't been able to track this dish down in Steel City itself, you can still sample it at **Pittsburgh Inn** in Erie, where it's served as a Tuesday-evening special with mashed potatoes and the vegetable of the day.

Scrapple

The Pennsylvania Dutch pork product known as scrapple is said to be made from everything but the oink. But it wouldn't surprise me if the squeal also found its way in there somewhere.

Scrapple is a mixture of pig parts such as the head, tongue, heart and liver that are all cooked together with cornmeal, wheat flour and seasonings that may include sage, thyme and black pepper.

It's shaped into a loaf and chilled, and thick slices of it are typically pan-fried in butter or oil until they're golden-brown and crispy. Scrapple is usually eaten as a breakfast meat along with eggs or toast, and can be accompanied by condiments such as jelly, ketchup or maple syrup. Alternate versions of it are sometimes made with fowl such as chicken or turkey.

Scrapple is similar to other regional dishes such as Cincinnati's goetta and North Carolina's livermush that all trace their lineage to Germany, where using meat scraps in sausage was a common practice. Of these dishes, scrapple may be the oldest, dating back to the early German settlers who came to Pennsylvania in the 17th and 18th centuries and sometimes called the food panhaas, meaning pan tenderloin.

The dish has also spread across Delaware, Maryland and other nearby locales, though it's most commonly associated with Pennsylvania. Today you'll find loaves of scrapple in grocery stores and specialty butchers across the Keystone State, but it's also served at diners and cafés that serve breakfast staples. A few popular options include **Dutch Eating Place** in Reading Terminal Market and **Champ's Diner** near Temple University, both in Philadelphia; **Upland Diner** in Chester; and **Gus's Keystone Family Restaurant** in Mount Joy and Ephrata. And while you're visiting Amish country, you'll also find scrapple (for breakfast as well as by the pound) at **Stolzfus Meats** in Intercourse. And at **Groff's Meats** in Elizabethtown, you can buy loaves of scrapple as well as pork legs, kidneys and stomachs – just about any part of the pig except the nose.

Chow chow

See Other foods of the South

In Amish country, the relish known as chow chow that's more closely associated with the South is made from a cornucopia of hardy vegetables that can include cauliflower, carrots and green beans. You can try a version of it as a side dish at **Smokehouse BBQ & Brews** in Bird in Hand, or pick up a jar from **Amish Family Recipes**, which you'll find at **Lancaster Central Market**, a farmers' market in Lancaster that's open to the public on Tuesdays, Fridays and Saturdays.

Shoofly pie

The gooey Amish delicacy known as shoofly pie is said to be so sweet that it attracts insects. But its name may have actually been inspired by the brand of one of its key ingredients, a popular minstrel song – and of all things, a traveling circus animal.

Shoofly pie, also called molasses crumb pie, is essentially a coffee cake that's baked in a flaky pie crust. There are two versions, a wet-bottom one that's more custard-like and is characteristic of the Pennsylvania Dutch, and a dry-bottom one that's more fully set. The latter was likely the original form of the pie, which was typically eaten for breakfast. It was a variation of a dessert created in Philadelphia in 1876 to mark the country's hundredth birthday, centennial cake, which was itself a derivation of a British treacle tart.

The pie is characteristically prepared with just a few ingredients, including flour, brown sugar and molasses. In the late 19th century, a Pennsylvania brand of the latter that was commonly used to make it was called Shoo-fly. But that wasn't the first appearance of that word, which somewhere along the way lost its hyphen. Beginning in the late 1860s, minstrel shows often featured the song "Shoo Fly, Don't Bother Me," and the tune became so popular that it was sung decades later by soldiers in the Spanish-American War during a time when mosquito-borne yellow fever was a persistent threat. And, in a completely different use of the word, a contemporary touring circus act showcased Shoofly the Boxing Mule, who wore boxing gloves on his front hooves and sparred with horses.

If you're venturing to Lancaster County in the central part of the state, you'll find shoofly pie at several Amish-themed restaurants, many of which serve Pennsylvania Dutch specialties at their lunch and dinner buffets. A few good options include **Bird-in-Hand Bakery & Cafe** in Bird in Hand; **Katie's Kitchen** and **Miller's Smorgasbord Restaurant**, both in Ronks; and **Hometown Kitchen** in Quarryville. But wherever you decide to go, you'll want to eat your slice quickly, just in case there's a swarm of hungry flies buzzing around.

Other Pennsylvania dishes to sample:

- **Pepperoni balls**, an Erie delicacy consisting of small spheres of pizza dough that are stuffed with pepperoni slices and cheese, and baked. Popular places to get them include **Stanganelli's Italian Foods** and **Art's Bakery**.
- **Teaberry ice cream**, a bright-pink variety made from a berry with a spicy wintergreen-like flavor. It's distributed by Hershey's at ice cream shops around Pennsylvania, including **The Sweet Shop** in Eagles Mere, and can also be found at artisan creameries such as **Gibby's Ice Cream Store** in Levittown.

Whoopie pie

See Maine

The soft cookies that sandwich a fluffy marshmallow filling are especially popular in Pennsylvania Dutch country, where the treat is said to have originated. Two of the Amish bakeries where you can satisfy a sweet tooth are **Achenbach's Pastries** in Leola and **Kitchen Kettle Village** in Intercourse.

In Western Pennsylvania, particularly around Johnstown, a chocolate whoopie pie is known as a gob. You can buy them online from **Dutch Maid Bakery** or at local grocery stores.

NEW JERSEY

Tomato pie

"Trenton Makes | The World Takes" trumpets a famous sign on the Lower Trenton bridge over the Delaware River between Pennsylvania and New Jersey. Although its slogan refers to the capital city's one-time importance as a center of manufacturing, you'd be forgiven if you thought it was heralding the style of pizza that's famous in Trenton and surrounding towns – tomato pie.

Tomato pie starts with a thin, crispy crust that's prepared in a round metal pan. Unlike the construction of traditional Neapolitan pizzas, mozzarella cheese provides the next layer, and lightly crushed tomatoes are then added on top. Despite sharing a name, it's not quite the same thing as the rectangular tomato pies you'll see in Philadelphia as well as Utica, New York, which are referred to as bakery style and more closely resemble Rhode Island's red strips. (New Jersey tomato pies are actually much more similar to the apizzas found in New Haven, Connecticut, with the addition of mozzarella cheese.) Although all of these pizzas trace their ancestry to the Southern Italian immigrants who arrived in the Northeast in the early 20th century and sometimes broke new culinary ground, the Trenton tomato pie is essentially a thin-crust pizza with tomatoes on top.

The first restaurant to serve tomato pie in this part of New Jersey was **Papa's Tomato Pies** in nearby Robbinsville, which opened in 1912 and is still going strong over 110 years later. This establishment is also famous today for its pizzas that include a layer of spicy brown mustard between the crust and cheese. Just across the street, you'll find a worthy competitor, **De Lorenzo's Tomato Pies**, which opened in 1947 in Trenton and moved to Robbinsville in 2007. (The restaurant also operates a second location just across the state line in Yardley, Pennsylvania.)

But these aren't the only places to get a tomato pie in South Jersey. A few other notable options include **Holy Tomato** in Blackwood, **Palermo's** in Bordentown and **Classico Tomato Pies** in West Windsor. They're all good places to discover that the communities around Trenton make a style of pizza that's worth announcing to the rest of the world – whether or not you have a giant sign on your bridge.

Ripper

In most parts of the country, a good nickname for a hot dog would be Frank. But in North Jersey, you could also call it Jack – because the local term for a deep-fried dog is a ripper.

A ripper is a beef-and-pork frankfurter that's cooked in hot oil, causing its natural casing to split open. It's served on a hot dog bun and is typically accompanied by a side of onion rings or French fries.

The iconic place to try a ripper is **Rutt's Hut** in Clifton, which has served them since 1928 and is also known for its signature mustard-based relish. But Rutt's isn't the only place where you can enjoy a ripped hot dog. Another well-regarded spot is **Lover Dogs** in Passaic, which air-fries its hot dogs and claims that they have 65 percent less fat.

A variation of the ripper that tops a deep-fried hot dog with chili is known, inexplicably, as a Texas wiener. Similar to the meat topping found on Midwestern coneys, the chili typically includes spices such as cinnamon, cumin and cloves.

The Texas wiener is believed to have been invented in the 1920s in Paterson by a Greek restaurant owner whose name is lost to history, and the style of chili dog he created soon spread to nearby communities. A few stands where you can try one include **Hiram's** in Fort Lee, **Johnny & Hanges** in Fair Lawn, **Hot**

Dog House in Carlstadt and **Jolly Nick's** in Dumont. Just don't get too attached to your frankfurter, whatever you decide to nickname it – because it probably won't stay on your plate for very long.

Italian hot dog

North Jersey's other favorite style of hot dog isn't what you'd expect from its name. The Italian sausage sandwiches you'll find in Chicago or Boston feature a grilled sausage topped with sautéed peppers and onions, served on a long submarine roll. But in Newark and nearby towns, the Italian hot dog is more like a cross between a pizza, a sub and a side of fries.

The Italian hot dog is a deep-fried beef frankfurter that's stuffed into a slice of a pizza-like crust that's cut in quarters, with each piece folded in half. The sandwich contains peppers and onions, but what makes it unique is the crispy layer of fried, sliced potatoes that are piled on top, which are often covered with ketchup and sometimes mustard. When you order a double, your sandwich will include two hot dogs that are placed side-by-side.

This dish was created in 1932 at **Jimmy Buff's** in Newark, purportedly by owner James Racioppi's grandmother as a meal for her husband and his friends while they were playing cards in the restaurant's basement. While that location no longer exists, Jimmy Buff's still serves up Italian hot dogs in West Orange and Kenilworth. And in Newark, a popular place for an Italian hot dog is **Dickie Dee's**, which has been in business since 1958. Another good option is **Destination Dogs** in New Brunswick, which offers an Italian dog it calls "Nicky Newarker" as well as a few dozen other styles referencing the flavors of Philadelphia, New Orleans, Vietnam and other places – so you can head there and enjoy a cheesesteak, a po' boy or a banh mi, all in hot dog form.

Sloppy joe

The Garden State version of a sloppy joe isn't anything like the lunchroom staple of ground beef in tomato sauce that you might remember from elementary school. And although it was likely invented in Havana, it's not the same thing as a Cuban sandwich, either. Instead, it's a unique New Jersey creation that you'll only encounter in a handful of delis in the northern part of the state.

A sloppy joe is a triple-decker sandwich of cold cuts served on thinly sliced rye bread, layered with Swiss cheese, coleslaw and Russian dressing. The original version of the dish included beef tongue and ham, but today diners can choose among a variety of deli meats including turkey, pastrami, corned beef and roast beef. The sandwich is often cut into three wedges, with the middle one being a triangle.

The sloppy joe dates to the mid-1930s, when the mayor of Maplewood, Thomas Sweeney, returned from a trip to Cuba, where he had eaten a memorable sandwich at a bar called Sloppy Joe's. He asked friends who were the owners of **Town Hall Deli** in South Orange to recreate it for him, and the sandwich became a fixture on its menu. A second restaurant, **Millburn Deli**, also became known for its sloppy joes after opening in Millburn in 1946, and the creation eventually caught on at other sub shops around the area.

After you compare the classic versions of the sloppy joe at both Town Hall Deli (which also offers a few creative takes on it, and ships its sandwiches online) and Millburn Deli (which now has additional locations in Morristown, Montclair and Westfield), be sure to try the sloppy joes at a few other places. Some well-regarded spots include **Petracco & Sons Deli** in Nutley, **The Gourmet Deli** in Cranford and **Rye Deli & Catering** in Springfield. The last option is a kosher deli, so its joes lack cheese, and there's no ham on the menu. But on a positive note, its sloppy joes aren't anything like what you probably ate in the cafeteria – aside from being an equally messy lunch.

Pork roll

Saturday Night Live comedian Joe Piscopo was referencing the state's seemingly endless turnpike when, in 1981, he famously said that if you want to know where someone's from in New Jersey, just ask them what exit. But another geographic identifier in the Garden State is which term a resident uses for its favorite processed meat product: pork roll or Taylor ham.

In North Jersey, the food is typically called Taylor ham, named after the man who created it in 1856, John Taylor of Trenton, who first marketed it as Taylor's Prepared Ham. But when the Food and Drug Administration ruled a half-century later that the product did not meet its definition of ham, he began selling it as pork roll, and that's what it's typically called in the southern half of the state. In 1910, a court decided that competitors could also sell their processed meat as pork roll, which led some proponents of the original, especially in North Jersey, to continue calling it Taylor ham – and that term is now used generically in this part of the state, regardless of who makes it.

In 2016, when U.S. President Barack Obama gave the commencement address at Rutgers University, he joked that he would use his speech to finally settle the Taylor ham versus pork roll question, but then added, "I know better than to get in the middle of that debate." And a few weeks later, New Jersey Governor Chris Christie, born in Newark, attempted to put an end to the discussion by joking that he was considering passing an executive order declaring Taylor ham as the official name. In a more serious effort, two competing bills introduced the same year in the state legislature, one featuring pork roll and the other Taylor ham, aimed to make this delicacy the official sandwich of New Jersey – but perhaps because of the naming stalemate, neither made it into law.

Although connoisseurs might be able to tell the difference between the two major brands, Taylor's and Case's, as well as their smaller competitors, all pork roll is basically the same – a smoked meat consisting of chopped ham that's cured with salt and spices, and shaped into either a long tube or shrink-wrapped rounds. It's typically sliced and fried, and is most often eaten in breakfast sandwiches along with eggs and cheese.

You'll easily be able to find pork roll at meat markets and deli counters all over the state. A few spots to check out in Southern Jersey include **Loeffler's Gourmet** in Trenton, a butcher where you can buy three- or six-pound tubes of pork roll, as well as **Waller's Deli** in Tabernacle and **Hoagie Haven** in Princeton, both known for their pork roll breakfast sandwiches. And up north, both **Leeside Deli** in Elizabeth and **The Bagel Corner** in Kearny sell similar breakfasts made with Taylor ham. Whether you're a longtime resident or you're just passing through, the latter is just a quick detour off the New Jersey Turnpike at exit 15W.

Salt water taffy

A summer vacation on the Jersey shore wouldn't be complete without a bag of salt water taffy, a treat that's been made in Atlantic City (as well as other seaside areas such as Cape Cod in Massachusetts) since at least the 1880s. But while the ocean air might seem like it adds a distinctive geographic flavor to these light, chewy candies, they're not actually made with salt water.

Salt water taffy consists mainly of sugar and corn starch, along with butter and a wide variety of flavorings such as vanilla, strawberry and molasses. After the mixture is stretched to create tiny air bubbles, it's rolled and cut into small pieces that are individually wrapped in waxed paper and sold by the pound.

Although the candy had been made in the U.S. for decades, often by hand at taffy-pulling parties, it didn't acquire its current name until an 1884 storm washed over the Atlantic City boardwalk. A candymaker named David Bradley is said to have remarked that the damp confection could be sold as salt water taffy, and the label stuck.

The first company to sell a boxed version of salt water taffy in Atlantic City, starting in 1885, was **Fralinger's**, which still operates stores there as well as in Cape May and Ocean City. A competitor, **James's Candy Company**, began selling its version in Atlantic City during the same decade, and eventually refined the manufacturing process, making the candy easier to unwrap and eat.

Either of those businesses would be great places to decide which flavor is your favorite. Meanwhile, at **Shriver's** in Ocean City, which has operated since 1898, you can build an assortment with as many as a dozen kinds, including sour cherry, coconut and sea salt caramel – one that just might fool you into thinking you're tasting the current in every bite.

Other New Jersey dishes to sample:

- **Jersey breakfast dog**, a beef hot dog that's wrapped in bacon and topped with a fried egg and shredded cheese. You can try one at **The Original Hot Dog Factory** in Voorhees Township (as well as in Harrisburg, Pennsylvania; Nashville; Hialeah, Florida; and a handful of locations in Georgia).
- **Disco fries**, a side dish resembling Canadian poutine that consists of thickly cut potatoes topped with brown gravy and mozzarella cheese. It became popular in the 1990s at local diners and got its name because it was a favorite late-night snack of hungry revelers returning from disco clubs. One place to try an order is **Pompton Queen Diner & Restaurant** in Pompton Plains.

MARYLAND

BALTIMORE

Pit beef

Some of the nation's best barbecue is meat that's smoked over hardwood, low and slow. Baltimore turns this technique on its head with a specialty known as pit beef, top round that's cooked quickly over a hot charcoal flame. Once the roast comes off the fire it's charred on the outside and rare within.

Pit beef is typically served as a sandwich, so the meat is thinly sliced and piled onto a round kaiser roll. The usual accompaniments are raw white onions and tiger sauce, a mixture of horseradish and mayonnaise, although some diners prefer to top their beef with a sweet, tomato-based barbecue sauce.

Pit beef emerged as a local specialty in the 1970s, when stands in working-class neighborhoods on the east side of town along Pulaski Highway began serving the dish. A shack called **Chaps Pit Beef** that opened in 1987, located on the grounds of a Southwestern-themed nightclub, helped spread its popularity. But it really took off as a Baltimore icon in the early '90s when local legend Boog Powell, a longtime Orioles first baseman, opened Boog's Corner, a restaurant at the new ballpark at Camden Yards.

Today you can still sample the pit beef at Chaps, which operates three locations in Maryland (as well as a fourth in Rehoboth Beach, Delaware), as well as at Orioles Park, where Powell's original restaurant is now called **Boog's Barbeque**. But there are plenty of other well-regarded spots for this specialty around the metro area, including **Pioneer Pit Beef** in Catonsville, **Jake's Grill** in Cockeysville, **Baker's Pit Beef** in Middle River and **Cruiser's Pit Beef** in Sparrows Point. While the meat these places serve isn't technically barbecue, its smoky tenderness may very well remind you of your favorite Texas or Kansas City brisket.

Coddie

If you found yourself in Baltimore with an extra nickel during the 1950s and '60s, you could have purchased a bottle of Coca-Cola or a candy bar at the corner drugstore. Or you could have used that coin to buy a filling snack unique to Charm City, the coddie.

A coddie, sometimes called a poor man's crab cake, is a breaded, deep-fried patty made with mashed potatoes, eggs, onions, cracker crumbs, seasonings and salted codfish, which gives the dish its name. It's usually served with yellow mustard between two saltine crackers.

The coddie originated around 1910 when a food merchant named Leonard Cohen (not the Canadian songwriter) began selling them at Belair Market. Cohen was trying to find a new dish that would support his struggling stall and stand out from the competition. But his wife Fannie refused to let him serve crab cakes because they weren't kosher, so she came up with a recipe for coddies instead. The Cohens eventually started distributing coddies all over Baltimore, a business that continued until the early 1970s, and the snack they invented became popular at establishments such as candy stores, drugstores and bars.

Although coddies aren't as prevalent as they were a half-century ago, you can still find them at seafood restaurants and markets across town. A few recommended spots include **Dylan's Oyster Cellar** in Hampden, **Barracudas Locust Point Tavern** in Locust Point and **Faidley's Seafood** in Lexington Market. And at **Vikki's Fells Point Deli** in Fells Point, a coddie will still cost you just $1.50 – less than the price of a medium fountain soda, so an even better deal today than it was decades ago.

Snowball

When the Michigan Department of Transportation asked constituents to name the state's snowplows, the winning entries included such pun-filled suggestions as Fast and Flurryous, Sleetwood Mac and Clearopathra. Now, you'd think that a business that makes snowballs, the warm-weather treat that's popular in Baltimore, would lend itself to similar wordplay (Snowball'more, maybe?). But from what I can tell, most of the clever names seem to have been left in the deep freezer. Fortunately, the snowball is appealing all by itself, especially on a sweltering summer afternoon.

A snowball, similar to a snow cone or Hawaiian shave ice, as well as the frozen treat of the same name in New Orleans, is a cup of finely ground ice that's covered with sweet syrup. Two things make the Baltimore snowball distinctive, though. First, although some stands offer hundreds of syrup options, one of the most popular ones is egg custard, made from eggs, vanilla and sugar, with another being Skylite, a blue fruity flavor. And second, the snowball is usually topped with a dollop of marshmallow crème. (Connoisseurs know to ask for an additional glob in the middle of their snowball.)

The snowball originated in the late 1800s when Baltimore became a waypoint for trucks delivering ice to Southern cities. Drivers would scrape off pieces for children who wanted to cool off, and the ice shavings were flavored with homemade syrup as an inexpensive snack. Snowballs continued to be popular during the Great Depression when they were sold at stands for as little as two cents.

There are dozens of spots where you can get this sticky specialty, and residents have been known to start a snowball fight as they debate their favorites. A few options include **Icy Delights** in Brewer's Hill, with a handful of other locations just outside the city; **One Sweet Moment** in Hamilton; and **Snoasis** in Timonium, which gets extra points for its titular wordplay. I'm disappointed that there isn't a stand called Edgar Allen Snowball, though. Seems like an obvious, if chilling, choice.

Berger cookie

In an important chapter in Baltimore history, the successful defense of Fort McHenry in 1814 against an onslaught by the British navy inspired Francis Scott Key to write a poem that eventually became the Star-Spangled Banner, the U.S. national anthem. And just over two centuries later, Baltimoreans faced another attack. In 2021, the grocery-store chain Whole Foods started selling a confection it called Charm City Cookies. This controversial move briefly sparked outrage on the Internet (but sadly, no new songs), as the dessert was a blatant ripoff of a product called Berger cookies that's been a local favorite for almost as long as Old Glory has flown over the city's fort.

Berger cookies are shortbread rounds that are covered with a thick layer of sweet chocolate frosting. Some have likened them to the corner piece of a chocolate birthday cake.

Another Baltimore dish to sample:

- **Bologna dog,** an all-beef kosher hot dog that comes wrapped in a slice of fried bologna and is served in a split-top bun with yellow mustard. A classic place to try one is **Attman's Delicatessen** in Jonestown (also known as Corned Beef Row) and Potomac.

This specialty originated with two brothers, Henry and George Berger, who emigrated to Baltimore from Germany in the 1830s and opened a bakery selling cakes. Unfortunately, the Eureka moment that led to their most famous product has been lost to history. Today the cookies are made by DeBaufre Bakeries, still using the original Berger recipe. (A limited run of strawberry, lemon and rum Berger cookies in 2012 was received by traditionalists about as well as Whole Foods's version.)

You'll easily be able to find Berger cookies in local grocery stores and online, as well as at **Berger's Bakery** in Lexington Market. Or try them in a pie called the BaltoBomb at **Dangerously Delicious HQ & Test Kitchen**, made with Berger cookies and a custard filling. It'll certainly fortify you in case you ever have to defend yourself against an attacking armada, or a corporate behemoth.

Lemon stick

Springtime marks the annual arrival of Baltimore's oldest free public festival, Flower Mart, in the city's Mount Vernon neighborhood. And with this floral exhibition comes the only time of year when residents typically walk around sucking the juice out of lemons with a peppermint candy straw. That's because they're enjoying a sweet-and-sour treat known locally as a lemon stick.

Flower Mart began in 1911, and was operated by the Women's Civic League until the end of the 20th century, but no one knows exactly when the lemon-stick tradition began. In the early 1900s they were consumed on steamboats along the Eastern Shore as a salve for seasickness, and contemporary reports show they were sold at the flower festival as early as 1924.

If you can't make it to Flower Mart, it's a simple task to make your own lemon stick at home, provided you can find some peppermint straws. (**Pat's Porch**, an old-fashioned candy store in Catonsville, is one place you'll find them.) Experts say you should cut off only the top of the fruit, and make a hole big enough to insert the stick.

But if you'd rather eat your lemon stick with a spoon, you can try the ice cream version at **The Charmery**, a Baltimore-based chain with one location in Hampden and others in Towson and Columbia. The city branch is just a short stroll away from Druid Hill Park, so if you want to simulate the whole Flower Mart experience, just walk around while you eat your scoop of lemon stick and see what's blooming.

OTHER FOODS OF MARYLAND

Crab cake

If you wanted to travel in style between Baltimore and Norfolk in the early 1900s, taking an overnight steamship on the Old Bay Line was the way to go. And that service shares its name with the signature spice blend that gives Maryland crab cakes their distinctive flavor.

Old Bay seasoning, a blend of celery salt, paprika, cinnamon, cloves and 14 other spices, was invented in 1939 by a Jewish-German immigrant named Gustav Brunn. Shortly after being arrested by the Nazis during Kristallnacht and escaping the Buchenwald concentration camp, he took his family to America. Along with his furniture, he brought a small spice grinder with him, and started working for McCormick & Company, a Baltimore-based spice company.

But Brunn soon decided to set off on his own and founded the Baltimore Spice Company. The seasoning blend he created and sold eventually became popular among local seafood companies, and despite being mostly used for crab and shrimp, was later certified as a kosher product. In 1990, the Old Bay story came full circle when its rights were purchased by McCormick &

Company, which continues to sell the product in its iconic yellow box.

Maryland crab cakes were probably first made before Old Bay came onto the scene, but their popularity skyrocketed after they were featured in the New York World's Fair cookbook in 1939. Today they're typically prepared with lump back-fin meat from the blue crabs that are abundant in Chesapeake Bay, along with binders such as breadcrumbs and eggs as well as Old Bay and other seasonings. There's wide variation in both their size and how they're cooked, but they're mostly either broiled, sautéed or deep-fried. Crab cakes are often served with a lemon wedge and saltine crackers, but can also be accompanied by tartar or cocktail sauce or other condiments, along with side dishes such as French fries and coleslaw.

You won't have any trouble tracking down an excellent crab cake in Maryland, and many places will also ship the seafood nationwide. Some of the most popular spots include **Faidley's Seafood** and **Koco's Pub**, both in Baltimore; **G&M Restaurant** in Linthicum Heights; **Pappas Restaurant**, with locations in Cockeysville, Parkville and Glen Burnie; **Boatyard Bar & Grill** in Annapolis; and **Angelina's of Maryland**, which sells its award-winning crab cakes at farmers' markets in Towson and Catonsville and also offers them online. They don't reveal their secret recipe – except to say that, unlike the cakes made by some purveyors, theirs are only made with Maryland blue crab – but it's a good bet that they contain a healthy amount of Baltimore's most famous spice.

Soft-shell crab sandwich

Don't get crabby if you can't find Maryland's favorite sandwich during certain months of the year. Soft-shell crabs are only in season from May through September. And because the soft-shell stage only lasts about 12 hours at a time, crabbers have to move quickly to get the delicacy to your plate.

Soft-shell crabs are Atlantic blue crabs that have molted their exoskeletons, a process that occurs a few dozen times during their lifespan. After a few inedible parts are removed, the entire crab is battered and deep-fried, or sometimes sautéed. It's usually served whole on white bread with lettuce and tomato as well as mayonnaise, tartar or cocktail sauce.

You'll find soft-shell crab sandwiches all over Maryland, especially during the height of summer. (Another option that's also available at other times of the year is a crab boil at one of the crab houses you'll find all over the state, serving steamed crabs as well as corn on the cob.) In Baltimore, a few recommended spots include **L.P. Steamers** in Locust Point, **Faidley's Seafood** in Lexington Market and **Dylan's Oyster Cellar** in Hampden. And you can also enjoy soft-shell crabs at **Cantler's Riverside Inn** in Annapolis as well as **Harris Crab House** in Grasonville, a dockside restaurant on the Eastern Shore, just steps away from the waterway where your lunch shed its shell mere hours before.

Eggs Chesapeake

The Chesapeake isn't just the bay that supplies Maryland's Eastern Shore with much of its seafood. It's also shorthand for any dish that contains crabmeat. You'll find Chesapeake soup, salad, pasta and even chicken (topped or stuffed with lump blue crab) on menus at countless restaurants in the Old Line State. And a popular breakfast option is the variation of eggs Benedict called eggs Chesapeake.

Eggs Chesapeake is just one of the many possible versions of eggs Benedict, the classic brunch dish made with poached eggs and Hollandaise sauce, and served on an English muffin. (The dish's murky history is recounted in the New York chapter of this book.) If you wanted to make Eggs Florentine, you'd naturally add spinach. Eggs Mornay replaces the Hollandaise sauce with its cheesy cousin. And to make eggs Chesapeake, you'd substitute a Maryland crab cake for the Canadian bacon that typically accompanies the dish.

You won't have any trouble tracking down eggs Chesapeake if you're in the market for a hearty breakfast or brunch. A few places with well-regarded versions include **Twist** in Baltimore's Fells Point neighborhood; **Iron Rooster**, with locations in Annapolis, Baltimore and Cockeysville; **Eggcellence** in Annapolis; **Captain's Table Restaurant** in Ocean City; and **Hunter's Tavern** in Easton, where the specialty has been featured on its holiday brunch buffet. Sometimes the dish is just called a crabby benny, but if you're in Maryland, you'll know that's really code for an order of eggs Chesapeake.

Smith Island cake

The only way to get to Smith Island in Chesapeake Bay, 10 miles from the coast on the border of Maryland and Virginia, is by ferry. But fortunately for land-lovers, it's no longer the only place where you can find Smith Island cake, a local delicacy that became the official state dessert of Maryland in 2008.

Smith Island cake is a multi-layered confection, similar to New Orleans's Doberge cake, that can be anywhere from eight to 10 layers tall. It's traditionally made from extremely thin tiers of yellow cake that are separated by chocolate icing. But other flavors, including red velvet, lemon, coconut and strawberry cream, are also commonly baked today.

The dessert dates from the 1800s, when women would prepare it for their husbands who were leaving on long expeditions to harvest oysters. They iced the cake with a fudge-like frosting because buttercream wouldn't last as long at sea. And they constructed it in thin layers because a taller cake wouldn't fully bake using the only oven that was available at the time – a metal box that they placed on top of their wood stoves.

The bakery that helped raise the stature of this specialty was **Smith Island Baking Company**, which was founded on the island in 2009 before moving to Crisfield on the mainland a few years later. But you can also find Smith Island cakes at other area bakeries including **Classic Cakes** in Salisbury and **Chesapeake Bay Gourmet** in Jessup.

First on my list, though, is **Smith Island Bakery**. This business opened in 2018 in Ewell, one of the island's three inhabited villages, in an effort to support the local economy and appeal to visiting tourists. Although you can buy its cakes online, a ferry to Smith Island seems like a good way to have a maritime adventure and a tasty dessert all in a single excursion.

Another Maryland dish to sample:

- **Smearcase**, a custard-like cheesecake sprinkled with cinnamon and served in rectangular slabs. You can find it at **Fenwick Bakery** in Parkville.

DISTRICT OF COLUMBIA

WASHINGTON

Half-smoke

The nation's capital doesn't have an especially distinctive culinary identity, despite its concentration of high-end restaurants and ethnic neighborhoods including Chinatown and Little Ethiopia. But one iconic D.C. dish that you won't find in other parts of the country is the half-smoke.

No one knows for sure where this oversized, spicy sausage got its name, but a popular (if somewhat obvious) theory is that it usually consists of half beef and half pork and is lightly smoked. The meat tends to be coarsely ground and is seasoned with red pepper flakes. It's sometimes slit down the middle before grilling for customers who want extra char (another possibility for its moniker), and is typically served on a soft white bun with chopped onions, chili and cheese.

The half-smoke originated as a breakfast sandwich at **Weenie Beenie** in Arlington, Virginia, using sausages from a local butcher called Briggs and Company, who started making them in the 1930s. But the establishment that's responsible for the dish's fame is **Ben's Chili Bowl**, which opened in 1958 in the U Street Corridor. Shortly before he became president in 2009, Barack Obama stopped by for a half-smoke, following a long line of Black celebrities and politicians who have been patrons of the historic restaurant.

Ben's now also has a second location in the city, and sells its sausages at both Reagan National Airport and Nationals Park (as well as online). But there are other worthy places to try a half-smoke in town, including **Meats and Foods** in Bloomingdale; **DCity Smokehouse**, a barbecue restaurant just down the street; and any number of hot dog carts all along the National Mall. When you're looking for lunch after a morning of monument-hopping, these stands are a much better choice than the chain restaurants and food courts that mostly cater to busloads of hungry tourists.

Senate bean soup

Congress may be hopelessly gridlocked, but one thing that both Democrats and Republicans can agree on is that a hearty ham-and-bean soup should always be on the menu at the legislators' dining rooms.

The simple dish that's usually known as Senate bean soup consists of navy beans that are simmered with ham hocks, diced onions and seasonings. Both Idaho Senator Fred Dubois, who championed a version of the dish that included mashed potatoes, and Senator Knute Nelson of Minnesota are said to have passed resolutions in the early 20th century requiring it to remain on the Senate dining room's menu daily. A version of the soup has been served at the restaurant since 1903, except for one day in 1943 when wartime rationing left its cooks with a temporary shortage of navy beans.

If you'd like to try Senate bean soup, your best bet is to schedule a visit with either of your state's senators, and make sure to stop in at either the **Senate Dining Room** (by making a reservation when Congress is in session) or **Dirksen Cafe**, open weekdays for lunch. But if you're unable to get an invitation from your senator, you can also try your local representative, because the lower chamber's dining room serves a similar dish – called, naturally, House bean soup.

Key lime pie

FLORIDA

The Sunshine State has no shortage of white sandy beaches and enormous theme parks, either of which could be the centerpiece of your family's warm-weather vacation. And while Florida's attractions, not its cuisine, were probably what led you to plan a trip in the first place, you shouldn't let what you eat become an afterthought during your stay.

Unfortunately, you may have to work harder than you do in other parts of the U.S. to find truly local food. That's because chain restaurants and overpriced vendors abound, especially in heavily touristed areas. And after a long day of recreation, you might feel more comfortable relying on familiar brands when it's finally time to sit down for a meal. But seeking out dishes that probably aren't available in your hometown is well worth the extra effort that it might take.

If you're in Southern Florida, the easiest way to get out of your comfort zone is to visit one of the countless Cuban eateries that you'll find in Miami, especially around its Little Havana and Westchester neighborhoods. Hundreds of thousands of immigrants have made their home in the Magic City in the decades since the 1959 revolution that brought Fidel Castro to power in Cuba, and the city's cuisine is infused with the flavors of that country, from the croquetas and pastelitos that make for a filling snack, to the Cuban sandwiches and fritas that can serve as a tasty alternative to a food-court sub or a fast-food hamburger. And at many Cuban restaurants, you'll find extensive menus that feature native specialties, including steak dishes like ropa vieja and vaca frita, lechón asado (roasted pork) and camarones al ajillo (shrimp in garlic sauce).

Miami's majority-Latino population also means that the city has a high concentration of restaurants that reflect the cultures of, among others, its Nicaraguan, Honduran, Colombian and Venezuelan residents. While none of the characteristic foods of these Central and South American countries have become quite as prevalent as their Cuban counterparts, when you get the chance, it's worth trying specialties like arroz con pollo, arepas, pupusas, maduros and more.

The Caribbean has also left its stamp on the food of South Florida, with a cuisine you'll sometimes see described as Floribbean. It features the frequent use of seafood such as conch and Key West pink shrimp, and seasonings like curry, ginger and several kinds of peppers, spices often found in the cuisines of Puerto Rico, Haiti and other Caribbean countries. And many dishes highlight tropical fruits like mango, pineapple or coconut that serve as a sweet counterpoint to their piquant heat.

In addition to all of these global flavors, your next best option for eating locally, especially if you're along the Florida coastline, is to sample the state's native seafood. Miami is famous for its stone crabs, which are in season during the cooler months, while a grilled or fried fillet from a freshly caught grouper is a good choice year-round for a sandwich in cities like Tampa and Palm Beach. And while Jacksonville is so far north that its cuisine mostly resembles what you'll find in the South, its "fish camp" restaurants – as well as casual spots along the panhandle – are good places to find a variety of fresh and fried seafood, including shrimp, oysters and scallops, all sourced from nearby waters.

You can hardly travel in Florida without a daily dose of freshly squeezed orange or grapefruit juice, products of one of the state's leading industries that grows around 70 percent of the nation's citrus. But if you'd prefer your fruit in dessert form, a fitting ending to just about any meal eaten in Florida is a slice of Key lime pie, named for the Florida Keys, although probably not invented there.

And as long you're visiting Mickey or Shamu, you may as well try a taste of its one of the state's other iconic creatures: alligator, the tail of which is often served as deep-fried chunks. Gator nuggets may not be any healthier than the chicken ones you'll find at every fast-food drive-through – but at least you'll be trying something you probably don't eat at home.

FLORIDA

MIAMI

Croqueta

The deep-fried cylinders known as croquetas are typically filled with ingredients such as ham, chicken or cheese. But creative chefs in Miami have turned the snack into a meal with the flavors of classic American dishes such as the bacon cheeseburger and mac-and-cheese, as well as local specialties like the traditional Cuban sandwich known as a medianoche.

The most important element of a croqueta might be its sauce, which is typically a creamy bechamel but can also be made from different ingredients that better complement the filling. The two are combined along with seasonings, and the mixture is then breaded and fried to a golden-brown. A croqueta is usually served warm, and can be eaten with a dipping sauce or alone as a handheld snack.

The croqueta was originally consumed in European countries including France and Spain (where it can still be found) before making its way in the 19th century to Cuba, and then eventually to Miami. The dish's popularity has exploded in that city over the past decade, with an annual festival known as Croqueta Palooza as well as the opening of several new restaurants that specialize in the dish.

A few noteworthy spots for a croqueta in Miami include **Dos Croquetas**, known for its creative flavor combinations including Buffalo chicken and mojo pork; **Islas Canarias**, a classic Cuban restaurant and café with a pair of locations on the west side of town; **Breadman Miami**, a bakery with branches in Westchester and Hialeah that in addition to traditional flavors, makes a croqueta layer cake; and **Doce Provisions** in Little Havana and Doral, which serves varieties made with either chorizo or goat cheese.

If you're in the Tampa area, it's worth keeping an eye out for a type of croqueta known as deviled crab. It combines meat from the local blue crab with a sauce known as chilau that's made with tomatoes, onions and peppers. Deviled crab was invented in the 1920s in Tampa's Ybor City neighborhood during a strike at the local cigar factories, and got its name from the dish's peppery sauce. You'll find it at casual cafés all over the Tampa area, including **Pappy's Devil Crabs**. However, you probably won't see this flavor of croqueta served in Miami. Judging by what's on offer on restaurant menus and at the croqueta festival, though, just about any other combination of ingredients seems to be fair game.

Frita Cubana

Miami's biggest rivalry isn't between the local Hurricanes football team and the Florida State Seminoles. It's actually between a king and a magician, both of whom make some of the city's best versions of a Cuban burger called the frita Cubana.

A frita Cubana, often referred to as just a frita, is made with a meat patty that's a mixture of ground beef and pork or chorizo, flavored with paprika and other seasonings. After cooking it's piled with a layer of shoestring potatoes and served on a Cuban roll. Other toppings are optional and can include cheese, raw onions, spicy ketchup, lettuce and tomatoes.

This burger was originally sold in the early 1900s by Havana street vendors called friteros. But once ground beef became hard to come by in Cuba, and many people left the country for the U.S., the dish was re-created during the 1960s by Cubans living in Miami who were missing their homeland.

The first frita shop in Little Havana, Fritas Domino, opened in 1962 and lasted for nearly six decades before shutting down in 2021. But it would be just the first of many similar establishments. After selling fritas in Cuba, and seeing how successful they had become in Miami, a man named Victoriano Benito Gonzalez ran a series of restaurants, including one that he boldly called **El Rey de las Fritas**, meaning the king of the fritas. Gonzalez's brother-in-law, Ortelio Cardenas, came to work at the shop, and is credited with being the first to add cheese to a frita, making it more like an American cheeseburger. But the two men eventually had a falling out, and Cardenas went on to start his own place in 1984, which he called **El Mago de las Fritas** – the magician of the fritas.

Both restaurants have become fixtures in Miami, with the late king's family now operating branches in Little Havana, Hialeah, Sweetwater and Westchester, and the magician's daughter maintaining a single location in West Miami. You'll need to try both to decide which has the upper hand in the friendly frita competition. Other places where you can try this burger include **Old's Havana Cuban Bar & Cocina** in Little Havana and **Riconcito Cubano Criollo** in Westchester – either of which is a great choice if you don't want to have to choose between the king and the magician.

Elena Ruz

The surest way to achieve lasting immortality – at least in a culinary sense – is to have a food item named for you. And while its ingredients are less traditional than other, more popular, local sandwiches, the Elena Ruz is still served at Cuban restaurants in Miami nearly a century after it was first created.

During the late 1920s, Elena Ruz Valdes-Fauli was a frequent patron of a Havana restaurant called El Carmelo, and would often order a late-night snack that wasn't listed on its menu: a turkey sandwich on the sweet Cuban bread called medianoche, with layers of cream cheese and strawberry preserves, served warm. After a few orders, the restaurant decided to make it a regular menu item, offered for a quarter. It literally put Elena's name in lights, with a neon sign advertising the sandwich that's said to have horrified Ruz's mother. A few decades later, when hundreds of thousands of Cubans came to Miami after the 1959 revolution that resulted in Fidel Castro's ascendancy as their homeland's leader, the sandwich went along with them, eventually making its way onto the menus at Cuban restaurants all around the city.

Today you'll find the Elena Ruz listed alongside traditional sandwiches like the Cubano, the medianoche and the pan con bistec (steak sandwich). A few places that serve it include **Pinecrest Bakery**, with more a dozen branches throughout the Miami metro area; **El Rinconcito Latino** and **La Carreta**, which both have a handful of locations all across town; and **Versailles Restaurant Cuban Cuisine** in Little Havana.

Elena Ruz remained a fan of the eponymous sandwich throughout her life, and is said to have eaten them regularly until she died in 2011 at the age of 102. But while not much else is remembered about the woman herself, her name will live on through her favorite dish for generations to come.

Batido

When temperatures soar into the 90s in the Sunshine State, there's no better way to cool off than with a creamy, refreshing smoothie called a batido.

Batidos are prepared by blending just about any tropical fruit, including banana, mango, guanabana and mamey (a sweet Latin American fruit that tastes like pumpkin) with milk, sugar and ice. Other popular flavors of this drink include chocolate and trigo, a version made with puffed wheat cereal.

Batidos have been sold in Miami for decades, and you'll find them all over town at Cuban restaurants, fruit stands and smoothie shops. A few recommended spots include **Puerto Sagua Restaurant** in South Beach, **Robert Is Here** in Homestead and **El Palacio de los Jugos**, a chain with 10 branches all over the metro area – which means that when the Miami heat leaves you thirsty, you'll never be more than a full-court pass away from a cold drink.

Other Miami dishes to sample:

- **Stone crab claws**, part of the crustacean that's found in South Florida waters, typically served chilled with mustard sauce, usually from mid-October until the beginning of May. The most famous place to eat them is **Joe's Stone Crab** in Miami Beach, but you'll also find them at restaurants specializing in shellfish like **Luc's Seafood & Grill** in Davie.
- **Pastelitos**, baked puff-pastry turnovers that are typically either square or triangular, and can be filled with either sweet or savory ingredients. Common varieties include guava-and-cream-cheese and picadillo (ground beef). They're often served at Miami's Cuban bakeries or at ventanitas, walk-up windows attached to Cuban restaurants. A popular place to try a variety of flavors is **Bakery Pastelmania** in Little Havana.

OTHER FOODS OF FLORIDA

Cuban sandwich

An iconic sandwich that contains slightly different ingredients in Key West, Tampa and Miami, with all three places advocating for their version as Florida's best, can be enjoyed at all hours of the day and night. But there's one particular type of Cuban that you might want to eat right as the clock strikes 12.

A Cuban sandwich, also called a Cubano or, especially in Key West, a Cuban mix, is constructed on a soft roll with layers of roasted pork (often marinated in a mojo sauce made from orange and lime juice, garlic and spices), Swiss cheese, ham, pickles and mustard. It's typically pressed on a griddle until the cheese melts and the bread gets crispy, and is then cut into diagonal halves and served warm.

A version of a Cubano that's called a medianoche, the Spanish word for midnight, is built with similar ingredients. But it uses a different bread, also called medianoche, an eggy loaf that's softer and sweeter than a traditional Cuban one.

The birthplace of the Cuban sandwich has long been disputed, but it likely originated in the late 1800s among Cubans who worked in sugar mills or cigar factories in Havana, or in Florida once the latter industry moved to the U.S. Key West was the first place in the Sunshine State to become a center of hand-rolled cigar-making, but by the late 1880s, most manufacturing had shifted to Tampa's Ybor City, where plants were staffed by Cuban, Spanish and Italian workers.

Local legend says that the Cuban sandwich was invented in Tampa as part of a contest to create a suitably filling lunch for the factory laborers. And that conjecture might have been enough for Tampa's City Council to pass a resolution in 2012 – while stopping short of saying that the Cuban was invented in Cigar City – proclaiming it as the city's signature sandwich. It prescribed a list of official ingredients and the precise order they should be added, with three sliced dill pickles as the last layer on the bottom piece of bread, and yellow mustard spread on the top.

Tampa's legislation was a salvo against Miami, with which it was engaged in a friendly rivalry over which city had the best version of the sandwich. In Tampa, the classic version of a Cubano includes a layer of Genoa salami, a sandwich addition that might have first become popular among that city's Italian immigrants. But in Miami, where about one-third of the population has Cuban ancestry, the Cubanos that are on the menu at dozens of cafés and restaurants are mostly prepared without salami. Meanwhile, in Key West, a Cuban mix usually does contain salami, and sometimes also includes layers of mayonnaise, lettuce and tomatoes.

You'll have to decide for yourself which city has your favorite version of the sandwich. A few places with well-regarded Cubanos in Tampa include **Columbia Restaurant**, a Spanish eatery that's been open in Ybor City since 1905; **Sabrosito's Cuban Cuisine** near the airport; and **La Bamba Restaurant** in Westshore. If you're in Key West, some spots worth trying include **Corner Sandwich Shop**, **5 Brothers Grocery and Sandwich Shop** and the cheekily named **The Best Coffee in Town**. And in Miami, head to Calle Ocho in Little Havana to sample the offerings at both **Sanguich** and **Old's Havana Cuban Bar & Cocina**. While the former closes before dinner, the latter is only open until 11 p.m. – so you'll have to look elsewhere if you want to eat a medianoche at its namesake hour.

Other Florida dishes to sample:

- **Minorcan chowder**, a soup native to St. Augustine that's made with a tomato-based broth seasoned with datil pepper, a locally grown variety of chili, along with clams or other seafood. One place you can sample it is **St. Augustine Seafood Company**, where it's prepared with conch.
- **Fish dip**, a spread of smoked fish that's mixed with lemon or lime juice, mayonnaise and seasonings, and popular along the Treasure Coast. One variety, known as smak, is made from mahi mahi and wahoo (and is not, as local legend has it, an acronym for "smoked mackerel amberjack kingfish"). One well-regarded spot for fish dip is **Mrs. Peters Smoke House** in Jensen Beach.

Key lime pie

French producers of sparkling wine insist that a product can't be called Champagne unless it's made with grapes grown in the Champagne region of France. So it would be natural for you to assume that Florida's official state pie was not only invented in Key West, but is typically made with the juice of the limes that grow there. However, you'd almost certainly be wrong on both counts.

Key lime pie is a dessert with a pale-yellow filling consisting of citrus juice, egg yolks and sweetened condensed milk, all of which are mixed together and baked in either a graham-cracker or pie-dough crust. The pie can be served chilled or at room temperature and is usually topped with either whipped cream or meringue.

While most recipes call for the juice of Key limes, which tend to be tarter than common Persian limes, they haven't been grown commercially in the Florida Keys since a 1926 hurricane wiped out the existing crops. Most Key limes today are imported from

Mexico or Central and South America, although some are grown in the U.S. in states with warm climates, including Florida, Texas and California.

A legend you'll sometimes hear in the Keys is that the archipelago's favorite dessert was invented in the late 1800s by a woman named Aunt Sally, who worked as a cook at millionaire William Curry's mansion and is said to have adapted local sponge fishermen's practice of moistening stale Cuban bread with lime juice and condensed milk. But, as you might have guessed, there isn't a shred of documentary evidence to support that claim. It's more likely that the pie originated in 1931 as a local adaptation of a marketing effort by the Borden Company, which published a recipe for Magic Lemon Cream Pie – one in which the citrus juice allows the filling to thicken without baking – in an effort to sell more of its condensed milk. It wasn't promoted as a Florida specialty until decades later, and only became the official state pie in 2006.

But there's no reason to let the pie's commercial origins, or its use of imported citrus, stop you from enjoying a slice or two in the place for which it's named. A few recommended spots in Key West include **Limes and Pies**, where you can order either traditional Key lime pie or a chocolate-dipped piece on a stick; **Kermit's Key West Key Lime Shoppe**, which also sells its pies online; **Old Town Bakery**, often said to have the island's best version; and **Key Lime Pie Bakery**, which offers slices, whole pies and bars, as well as cakes, cookies and candy that are all made with Key lime juice.

Another option, if you're visiting Key West in the summer, is to head to the city's annual Key lime festival, where events include attempts to create the world's largest Key lime pie, and to drop smaller ones from the top of a lighthouse without damaging them. But you might want to bring a skeptical eye (and tongue) to the celebration. While locals may consider the Key lime to be the Champagne of citrus fruits, the ones used to make your pie probably weren't grown nearby.

Acknowledgments

I'm grateful to all of the people who have contributed ideas for this book and championed my work along the way. Molly Avery, John Bankhurst, Jeff Berlin, Aidan Brezonick, Zack Brooks, Derek Brown, Sara Caplan, Caron Celestino, Chris Celestino, Joanie Celestino, Sarah Churnside, Greg Cooper, Jon Creasey, Rosemary Elliot, Michael Howard, Chelsea King, Colin Larsen, Bindi Lassige, Dave Lewis, Kevin Lustig, Paige Meszaros, Sara McLaren, Josh Montroy, Cody Moore, Conor Murphy, Paige Meszaros, Matt Sherman, Cindy Smalletz, Mark Stewart, Luke Suttey and many others all provided suggestions of foods to include or recommended favorite restaurants to try.

I'm also appreciative of everyone who provided advice and encouragement about this project, including Brian Alexander, Harriet Baskas, Eve Blanton Otten, Jay Blanton, Chip Celestino (whose enthusiasm and insightful questions provided a boost of inspiration at a critical time), Seth Churnside, Steve Durst, Bob Grabarek, Lisa Grabarek (who gamely helped me try and track down the elusive Atlantic Beach pie), Mary Anne Grabarek, Cara Griswold and her team at Farestart (especially Ella Goodheart for an uplifting chat), Jamie and Lucas Haines and the staff and regulars at Volition Brewing, Todd Krueger, Tim Lassige, Emily McCann, Patrick McCann, Julie McGinnis, Shannen McGinnis, Luke Morgan, Joe Prince, Ross Reynolds, Lloyd Roark, Stephen Savage, Richard Shuping, Jody Stewart, Christy Uchida, Toshi Uchida and many other friends, family members and acquaintances. I apologize to anyone I've left off this list – your contributions are equally valued.

In particular, I'd like to thank Jared LeClerc for being a sounding board who helped me unlock the structure of this book; Gerad Freeman for insisting that we order the Big Ben and try all of the barbecue in Missouri during an unforgettable road trip; and Doug Rainey for being an enthusiastic companion on many food adventures in Chicago and around the country over the past three decades. All of these friends cheered my (mostly) steady progress and helped motivate me to keep going. And Rob Grabarek wholeheartedly backed my decision to leave the corporate world and pursue this project, provided a willing audience for my latest round of research and bad jokes, gamely stomached my attempts at cooking hotdish and country captain, and celebrated my milestones every step of the way to publication, most memorably with some surprise Key lime pie. I wouldn't have finished this book without his support.

My writing has drawn upon several outstanding print sources including Burnt Toast Makes You Sing Good by Kathleen Flinn (who set an example by leaving her own corporate job for a food writing career long before I did, and suggested the concept for my cover art), America the Cookbook by Gabrielle Langholtz, Regional American Food Culture by Lucy M. Long, Oysters by Cynthia Nims and America Eats! by Pat Willard; the excellent exhibits at the Southern Food & Beverage Museum in New Orleans; helpful websites including Atlas Obscura, Barry Popik, Eater, First We Feast, Food Timeline, Grist, New England Historical Society, Only in Your State, Our State, Serious Eats (especially the fine work of J. Kenji Lopez-Alt and Robert Moss), Southern Foodways, Southern Living, The New Yorker (especially Helen Rosner's take on the Chicago-style hot dog), The New York Times, Seattle Weekly, The Stranger, Taste Atlas, Thrillist, What's Cooking America and the food sections of many local and regional newspapers (some accessible via the Internet Archive); and many other online resources including Bing Chat, Facebook food groups (especially The Rambling Epicure and Culinary Travel by Jonell Galloway), Google Maps, The Sporkful, Wikipedia and Yelp.

Kitanda Coffee & Açaí and Luu's Cafe in Green Lake, Mercurys Coffee in Bellevue and the Seattle Public Library's Green Lake branch all provided a quiet workspace when I needed a change of venue from my Seattle office, while Mount Si inspired me from my desk in North Bend. And Emma and Tyler patiently waited me to finish my morning writing sessions before we could go on our midday strolls.

Finally, I'm indebted to all of my readers for choosing to explore the world of regional food during their travels. Eat like a local!

Index

500 WAYS TO EAT LIKE A LOCAL

Page numbers in bold are primary references

OTHER FOODS MENTIONED

About the Author

Jon Douglas is a food writer based in Seattle, Washington, and publishes at SeattleFoodHound.com, a journalistic take on food news, trends, cooking and local restaurants. He was previously an editor for SmarterTravel, MSN Travel and Bing Travel, and has written for USA Today and Frommers Travel. Jon is a graduate of Dartmouth College and an avid traveler and eater who volunteers at FareStart and Hunger Intervention Program, community organizations dedicated to food security for underserved populations. This is his first book.

Follow Jon on Instagram @eatlikealocalus

www.ingramcontent.com/pod-product-compliance
Lightning Source LLC
Chambersburg PA
CBHW071130130626
46553CB00004B/1323